GROWTH THROUGH TORAH:
Insights and Stories for the Shabbos Table

Other books by this author:

Guard Your Tongue
Love Your Neighbor
Gateway to Happiness
Gateway to Self-knowledge

GROWTH THROUGH TORAH

Insights and stories for the Shabbos Table

(Practical lessons from the weekly portions)

by
Rabbi Zelig Pliskin

SKAAR SHALOM SYNAGOGUE
2 SIMONSTON BOULEVARD
THORNHILL, ONTARIO L3T 4L1

ISBN 1-884219-23-3

Address in U.S.:

BENEI YAKOV PUBLICATIONS
1742 East 7th Street
Brooklyn, New York 11223
(718) 376-5903

Yeshiva Aish Hatorah
Jewish Quarter
Old City
Jerusalem

נדפס בדפוס האחים גרויס
Printed in U.S.A. **GROSS BROS. Printing Co. Inc.**
3125 SUMMIT AVENUE, UNION CITY, NJ 07087
Tel. (201) 865-4606 • (212) 594-7757

מכתב ממורי ורבי

הגאון ר׳ **מרדכי גיפטער** שליט״א

ראש ישיבת טלז

בע״ה

מוצש״ק פ׳ חיי שרה תשמ״ח

יקירי מאוד נעלה הרב מוה״ר זליג פליסקין, שליט״א, שלום וברכה נצח לך ולבא״ל!

זה עתה בא לידי מה ששלחת בח׳ מנחם־אב, דוגמאות מעבודתך בהכנת ספר על פרשיות השבוע.

מובטחני שיהא מקור לרוב תועלת לאלה הרחוקים מלשה״ק, כמו בספריך הקודמים. לך הלאה בעבודתך לזיכוי הרבים. ויראו אורה — זו תורה.

בברכת רב הצלחה בכל אשר תפנה,

באהבה,

מרדכי

In memory of my uncle,

RABBI MOSHE HELFAN, z.t.l.

of Telz Yeshiva. His joy and hospitality
gave much happiness to many others.

And in memory of my aunt,

MRS. MIRIAM HELFAN, o.b.m.

Her love and compassion were a great
inspiration to all who knew her.

I am forever grateful for their
many kindnesses.

TABLE OF CONTENTS

Proper order of doing things/ Gratitude for those helping you donate/ Overcoming envy/ Focus on doing Almighty's will

Happiness dependent on closeness with Almighty/ Acknowledge gifts from Almighty/ Be yourself, use your potential/ When in power admit mistakes/ Embarrassment for doing wrong/ Charity according to means/ Internalize Torah values

Demanding that things be as you wish/ Each day first day of your life/ Protect others from embarrassment/ Publicize your good fortune/ Impressing others with humility

Humility and accomplishments/ Consulting others/ Accepting Almighty's will/ Joy with own mind and not artificial stimulants/ Strong will/ Joy for wisdom of others

Motherhood: highest and noblest occupation/ Making peace between people/ Joy of atonement of suffering/ Find a spiritual guide when suffering/ Faults: your own and others/ Irritation of others price for companionship

Feel pleasure when meeting responsibilities/ Think before speaking/ Focus on own faults/ Arrogance implies lack of awareness of Almighty/ Habit of saying, It appears as if / Causing financial loss

Examples to illustrate points/ Concern about what others think/ Joy when cleaning after guests/ Wronging others/ Growth every day/ Good deeds with energy and enthusiasm

Introspect to gain self-knowledge/ Resentment when someone wrongs you/ Rebuke with sincere concern/ Positive influence one

INTRODUCTION

"We must study the Torah looking upon it as a Book given us by the Almighty that we may learn from it to know what we are and what we should be in our earthly existence. It must be to us *Torah*, that is, a source of instruction and guidance in the Almighty's world, a generator of spiritual life within us. We must ask ourselves, 'What will human beings be who recognize the contents of this Book as the rule of life given to them by the Almighty?'" (Rabbi Samson Raphael Hirsch, *The Nineteen Letters*)

Growth Through Torah is a partial reply to this question. While it can be read as a book by itself, it is meant to be a sequel to *Love Your Neighbor* and *Gateway to Happiness*. The Introduction written for *Love Your Neighbor* applies to this work as well.

This work focuses on practical lessons from the weekly portions that are conducive to our spiritual and emotional growth. I have stressed those ideas that I have found in my counseling experience to be most necessary for a large amount of people to integrate. The reader is supplied with a Torah perspective on topics that are relevant for daily living: self-image, emotions, interpersonal relationships, attitudes conducive to happiness and joy, character traits, and the many benefits of living a Torah lifestyle.

This work is geared for both beginners and scholars, young and old. Educators and speakers will find many practical messages that will enhance their talks. Each idea is concise and appropriate for reading at the Shabbos table.

My suggestion is to read through the entire work from beginning to end for a first reading. Then each week review the lessons of that week's portion. By reviewing these ideas you will integrate them and they will become part of your personality.

In each portion the principles that are derived from the verses and their commentaries are in boldface. Sources have been cited for ideas. Comments following the sources and ideas without sources are from the author.

For those unfamiliar with the Hebrew terms a glossary has been provided at the end of the end of the book. Concise biographical information about the Torah scholars cited can be found in *Love Your Neighbor* and *Gateway to Happiness*.

I wish to express my heartfelt gratitude to Rabbi Noach Weinberg, Rosh Hayeshiva of Yeshiva Aish Hatorah. I have gained very much from him in numerous ways. I am especially grateful for his support of the Aish Hatorah Counseling Center.

My sincere thanks to Rabbi Chaim Dov Altusky for graciously taking the time and effort to read and comment on this work. I also thank Rabbi Noach Orlowick for his encouragement and comments.

I thank Wendy Horowitz-Chopra for her painstaking editorial work. I am grateful to Craig Karpel for his practical suggestions.

For those unfamiliar with the Hebrew terms a glossary has been provided at the end of the book. Concise biographical information about the Torah scholars cited can be found in *Love Your Neighbor* and *Gateway to Happiness*.

BRAISHIS

Awareness of the Creator gives one meaning in life.

בראשית ברא אלקים את השמים ואת הארץ. (בראשית א' א')

"IN THE BEGINNING THE ALMIGHTY CREATED THE HEAVEN AND
THE EARTH." (*Braishis* 1:1)

As soon as you start studying Torah, right from the first verse:
"In the beginning the Almighty created," you become aware that
there is a Creator and Ruler of the universe. This first awareness
already makes a major change in you for the rest of your life. You
realize that there is a reason for everything. The world has meaning
and purpose. (Rabbi Yeruchem Levovitz, *Daas Torah: Braishis,*
p.3)

Without meaning in life even if you accomplish very much, have
health and wealth, fame and fortune, there is a strong feeling that
something is missing. It is. Without meaning there is no real
enjoyment or satisfaction. Yes, a person can have moments of
excitement, joy, and even ecstasy. But they are short-lived. When
the high feelings settle down, there is emptiness. Nothing seems to
really matter. But as soon as you internalize the awareness that
there is a Creator of the universe, you see plan and purpose. There
is an inner glow and a drive for spiritual growth. Those who lack
this realization see only the external actions and behaviors of those
who live with the reality of the Almighty. They are unaware of the
rich inner life of such a person. The true believer in the Creator is a

fortunate person. He is the only one on the planet one should envy. He sees divinity in every flower and tree and in every blade of grass. He sees the design of the Creator in every living creature. He sees something special in every human being. His life, regardless of how it unfolds, is full of purpose and meaning. While he appreciates this world as a gift of the Creator, he looks forward to an eternity of existence. This is the profound message of the first verse of the Torah.

A well-known communal leader recalls that he was a teenager the first time he saw Rabbi Moshe Feinstein. The Rosh Hayeshiva was the guest speaker at a *siyum* in a small synagogue. His *hadran* (lecture upon the completion of a Talmudic tractate) was beyond the young listener's comprehension, but one part of the address made an indelible impression. "People destroy their children by always repeating, *'Es is shver tzu zein a yid* (it is hard to be a Jew).' No, it is not hard to be a Jew. It is beautiful and joyous to be a Jew."

Rabbi Moshe Feinstein's face glowed with pride and happiness when he said those simple words, and the young listener recalls that he too became suffused with pride in his Jewishness. (Rabbi Nosson Scherman in *The Jewish Observer*, Oct., 1986)

Rabbi Dovid Kronglas of Ner Yisroel Yeshiva in Baltimore once confided, "People dream of what they would do if they suddenly acquired a great sum of money. They think about how they would spend it and how it would change their lives. As for me, it would not change a thing; but I would return every cent of the salary I received from the yeshiva over the years." (*The Jewish Observer*, March, 1975)

The person who devotes his life to fulfilling the Torah will find so much meaning in his life that even in his fantasy life he will live exactly the way as he is living in reality.

The Almighty sheds light even at the greatest moment of darkness.

והארץ היתה תהו ובהו. וחשך על פני תהום... ויאמר אלקים יהי אור
ויהי אור. (בראשית א' ב-ג)

"AND THE EARTH WAS DESOLATE AND VOID, AND DARKNESS WAS UPON THE WATERS... AND THE ALMIGHTY SAID, LET THERE BE LIGHT AND THERE WAS LIGHT." (*Braishis* 1:2,3)

The Chofetz Chayim used to say that these verses at the beginning of the Torah serve as a tremendous inspiration in times of darkness. At the beginning of creation the world was completely dark without even the faintest hint of any light. One cannot chase away darkness with sticks and axes. But kindle just one small candle and the darkness is gone. When the entire world is in total darkness, one statement of the Almighty, "Let there be light" is sufficient to light up the world. This idea is taught to young children as soon as they begin studying Torah. Although there are times when the world is encompassed by a spiritual darkness which endangers its very existence, there is always hope. In one instant the Almighty can send forth His word and there will be a great light. (*Chofetz Chayim al Hatorah*)

Whenever you feel despair it is because you tell yourself that things are presently awful and that all is hopeless. At such moments you do not feel it possible that there will be a bright future. If, however, you keep in mind that the Almighty has the power to shine forth a magnificent light, you will overcome your negative attitude of despair. From the bottom of your heart you will call upon our Creator to shed light upon the world. Even before the light appears, you will be full of hope. You realize that the darkness itself is part of the Almighty's plan. Whenever you feel darkness, develop the habit of repeating, "Let there be light." Just by repeating these words over and over you will begin to feel the light of the Almighty penetrating your heart and soul. Even if your personal situation remains as it is, when you experience the

Almighty's light you will have the strength to deal with any situation from a position of spiritual strength.

Keep in mind that the Almighty created the world for you to benefit from.

וירא אלקים את כל אשר עשה והנה טוב מאד. (בראשית א' ל"א)

"AND THE ALMIGHTY SAW ALL THAT HE MADE, AND BEHOLD IT WAS VERY GOOD." (*Braishis* 1:31)

Rabbi Avigdor Miller comments on this verse: "When one does not know what he possesses, he is poor. Imagine that you purchased a vacant lot and erected a house on it; and you dwelt there thirty years. Then, one night, the telephone rings, and you hear a quavering old voice: 'I must inform you that I am the last survivor of a group that buried a chest of gems in the premises where your house now stands. I am about to die, therefore I wish you to know.' Now you are so joyous that you cannot sleep. You are wealthy! But actually for thirty years you were the legal possessor of the unclaimed treasure. What makes you happy today instead of thirty years earlier? The knowledge of what you possess.

"Knowledge of what you possess is the true wealth. If you are unaware of what you have, or are only faintly aware of its true nature, you actually do not possess it. Thus: 'He who gives someone a gift should let him know' (*Baitzah* 16a). When giving someone a watch, do not remove the slip which states that 'this watch has an unbreakable crystal, 17 jewels, is shockproof, waterproof, and antimagnetic.' Let him fully enjoy your gift. Therefore when the Creator gave this world to us, He informed us that all He created was very good."

"The Creator declares: 'My children, be sure to be happy, for I give you that which is very good.'" (*Sing, You Righteous,* p.287; see *ibid.* pp.17-8 and *Gateway to Happiness*, pp.35-6)

This message gives a direction for your way of thinking throughout your life. The quality of your life is dependent on what your stream of consciousness is focused on. Unfortunately, many people go through life thinking mostly about what they are missing and what is wrong. But the Almighty wants us to focus on what He has given us. Each and every day make an effort to spend time appreciating what you have.

The Baal Shem Tov showed his disciples how a person's situation can be exactly the same, but one day he will be full of complaints while on another he will be full of joy. To illustrate this point, he once called in a water-carrier and asked him how things were going. "I'm getting older and I feel so weak," the man replied. "My children constantly study and don't help me out. I have to support my sons-in-law, and find the financial obligations a real burden. My wife is so sickly, and I feel like I'm falling apart."

On another day the Baal Shem Tov asked him again how things were. With a big smile, the water-carrier replied, "I am so grateful to the Almighty for all of His kindness. Even though I am old, I am not only able to support myself, but I am even able to support the Torah study of my sons and sons-in-law who study with such diligence. My wife is wonderful to me; with great sacrifice she cooks and cleans just to make me happy."

You constantly choose how you will view your life situation. Even though nothing external has changed, you can still view your life in very positive ways.

Be aware of your greatness as a spark of the Creator.

וייצר השם אלקים את האדם עפר מן האדמה ויפח באפיו נשמת חיים
ויהי האדם לנפש חיה. (בראשית ב' ז')

The Torah describes the creation of the first man:
"THEN THE ALMIGHTY FORMED MAN FROM THE DUST OF THE GROUND, AND BREATHED INTO HIS NOSTRILS THE BREATH OF LIFE; AND MAN BECAME A LIVING SOUL." (*Braishis* 2:7)

What is man? Every fiber of your body is a creation of the hand of the Almighty. Your spirit, the spark of the Divine, your personality, invisible as Deity itself, weave and work in this microcosm and control your intellect and your body. Learn to deem yourself holy as a creature of the Almighty and consecrate yourself to your mission as a "servant of the Creator." (Rabbi Samson Raphael Hirsch, *The Nineteen Letters*, p.37)

We live in a time when many people suffer from feelings of inferiority. But a person who lives with the reality that he is created in the image of the Creator of the universe will feel so positive about himself that he cannot possibly have inferiority feelings. The more you integrate this concept the more you will show honor and respect to others, for they too are created in the Almighty's image, and the better you will feel about yourself.

The Chazon Ish gave a lot of time and attention to a certain young fellow and would have lengthy Torah discussions with him. Someone asked the Chazon Ish why he spent so much time with him when the fellow was insolent and ill-mannered.

The Chazon Ish replied, "He comes from a very poor family and I have to be especially careful to be soft with him and to react compassionately. At present he feels inferior and insecure, therefore at times he acts insolently. The Torah he studies will raise him up in his own eyes and this will have a positive influence on his entire character. The same Torah which teaches a person that he is but dust and ashes also gives him encouragement and elevates him." (*P'air Hador*, vol.4, pp.22-3)

Rabbi Aharon Kotler, Rosh Hayeshiva of Lakewood, would spend a considerable portion of his ethical lectures explaining how inconsiderate it is to raise one's voice in conversation, on the importance of neat appearance and punctuality - all seemingly trivial matters, but each significant when viewed as a mark of respect towards one's fellow man. (Rabbi Shaul Kagan; *The Jewish Observer*, May, 1973, p.7)

Don't allow guilt to discourage you.

ויחר לקין מאד ויפלו פניו. ויאמר השם אל קין למה חרה לך ולמה נפלו
פניך. הלוא אם תיטיב שאת. (בראשית ד' ה-ז)

Kayin and Hevel both brought offerings to the Almighty. The basic difference was
that Kayin offered inferior quality, while Hevel offered the highest quality. The
Almighty accepted Hevel's offering and not Kayin's:
"AND KAYIN WAS VERY ANGRY, AND HIS FACE FELL. AND THE
ALMIGHTY SAID TO KAYIN, WHY ARE YOU ANGRY? AND WHY ARE
YOU CRESTFALLEN? IF YOU DO WELL, YOU WILL BE RAISED UP."
(*Braishis* 4:5,6,7)

Kayin was eaten up with envy over his brother's success and felt
embarrassment and humiliation that his own offering was rejected.
The Almighty told him that his reaction was inappropriate. When
you can correct your mistakes and omissions it is improper to
waste time suffering over what is past. What is appropriate is to try
to make the necessary corrections in the future. (Sforno)

This is a very important lesson for anyone who has a tendency to
wallow in self-pity and guilt when he makes a mistake. The very
fact that you feel guilty is a sign that you have high ideals and
values and you can feel positive about that.

Rabbi Yeruchem Levovitz offered the following analogy. When
two people are fighting with each other and one throws the other
down, if the intention of the stronger person is just to throw him
down, then as soon as the loser is on the ground he will leave him
alone. The person on the ground can then get up right away, and
the fight is over. But if we see that even after the person is on the
ground the stronger person keeps punching and kicking him, and
does everything to keep him down, we can understand that this is
his intention: to make sure he does not get up.

This, said Rav Yeruchem, is the goal of the evil inclination.
Transgressing alone is a great failing, from a high place down to a
deep pit. But this is not enough for the evil inclination. His
intention is that a person should remain down constantly. When a

person is down he holds onto him with both hands so he should not move again and not even lift up his head.

The main idea of *tshuvah* is that a person should strengthen himself and pick himself up. Once a person is standing again, there are many ways to correct his faults and mistakes. This is what the Almighty meant when He asked Kayin, "Why has your face fallen?" Why do you stay on the ground after you have fallen? Your staying down after the fall is even worse than the fall itself. Raise yourself up and then you will be on the road to improvement. Don't engage in self-pity. Keep growing. (*Daas Torah: Braishis*, pp.26-7)

Rabbi Nochum Perchovitz, the late Rosh Hayeshiva of Mir, used to say, "Everyone makes mistakes. That is normal. The wise man, however, only makes a mistake once." (Heard from Rabbi Heshy Weissman, Rosh Kollel of Meshech Chochmah)

A person who is a perfectionist and an idealist will usually need an authority to give him permission to give up his guilt feelings. There is no greater authority than the Almighty Himself who advises, "Don't overdo regret about the past. Keep your focus on improvement in the present and future."

When you have erred or transgressed, the question to keep in mind is, "What can I do in the present to improve?" and "How can I elevate myself right now?"

A person who was guilty of a severe transgression came to one Rabbi and asked to be taught what he could do for repentance. The Rabbi replied, "What I would tell you to do would be too difficult for you. Go to the Chazon Ish and he will help you out."

But the man complained to his Rabbi, "I don't know him. I feel too embarrassed to repeat my story to him."

The Rabbi replied, "The embarrassment that you will suffer will be a partial atonement. You have no other choice."

The person went to the Chazon Ish, who spoke to him privately. Afterwards the man returned to his Rabbi and said, "How good was your advice to consult the Chazon Ish! The Chazon Ish washed me and cleansed my soul and I now feel like an entirely new person." (*P'air Hador*, vol.4, p.37)

Strengthen your resolve to be in control of your impulses.

ואם לא תיטיב לפתח חטאת רבץ ואליך תשוקתו ואתה תמשל בו.
(בראשית ד' ז')

"THE DESIRE OF THE EVIL INCLINATION IS UPON YOU. AND YOU SHALL RULE OVER IT." (*Braishis* 4:7)

Rashi comments that the evil inclination constantly has a strong desire to cause you to err.

Rabbi Yeruchem Levovitz cited the Midrash that equates the longing of the evil inclination to cause a person to transgress with the longing of the Almighty for the Jewish people as expressed in *Shir Hashirim.* The word "constantly" means that at all times a person has impulses to do things that are harmful and counterproductive to his spiritual welfare. Hence the bombardment of the evil inclination is constant and intense. (*Daas Torah: Braishis*, p.27)

Some people might feel threatened by this. "If I have to fight so many impulses, how can I possibly win?" they could say to themselves. The antidote lies in the last words of our verse, "And you shall rule over it." Rashi explains, "If you but want, you will overcome it." What is needed is your will. Whenever you really want to overcome an impulse you will be successful.

We find willpower in one of two ways: reward and punishment. Imagine that you have a strong compulsion to eat a certain food, and find it extremely difficult to overcome your desire for it. "It is impossible for me not to give in to my urge," you hear yourself saying. But if someone were to offer you a large fortune to control your compulsion for a week, you would probably find that you could control it. Focusing on the reward will enable you to strengthen yourself. Similarly with punishment. If someone were to stand next to you with a loaded machine gun and would pull the trigger as soon as you eat the food you find "impossible" not to eat, you would suddenly lose your appetite for that food. Even if the strong urge did remain, you would most likely gain the strength not to eat it. In both situations you have the will to overcome your impulses. To overcome your negative inclinations increase your will. How? By either thinking of the great gain of following your good inclination or by thinking of the great loss of following your evil inclination. The more you reflect on this, the greater inner awareness you will have.

Moreover, every time you exercise your will and gain in self-discipline, further self-discipline will become easier.

Rabbi Chayim of Tzanz once asked a person how he would react if he were to find a purse with a large amount of money in it.

The man replied without thinking, "There is no question that I would immediately run to return the money to its owner."

"That is a foolish answer," said Rav Chayim.

The second person the Rebbe asked this question to replied, "I am not a fool to lose an opportunity to gain money."

The Rebbe rebuked him, "It is evil to keep what you must return."

The third person to whom the Tzanzer Rav asked this question replied, "How can I possibly know now on what level I will be at that moment? Who knows for sure if I will be able to conquer my evil inclination? Perhaps the evil inclination will overcome me and entice me to act improperly. But I pray that the Almighty will strengthen me and help me overpower my evil inclination and I will be able to return the lost object to its owner."

The Tzanzer Rav praised his reply, "That is the answer a wise person will give." (*Maigdolai Hachasidus: Haadmor Maitzanz*, pp.100-1)

Awareness of olam haboh makes suffering easier to cope with.

נע ונד תהיה בארץ. (בראשית ד' י"ב)

After Kayin killed his brother Hevel, one of the punishments he received was the curse of:

"A FUGITIVE AND A VAGABOUND SHALL YOU BE ON THE EARTH."
(*Braishis* 4:12)

A man from a small town would travel to large cities to purchase merchandise which he later sold in small towns. At times he would have to travel a month or two for his business. After his wife died, he poured out his heart to the Chofetz Chayim. When his wife was alive, even when he was traveling he always felt that he had a home to which he would eventually return. Therefore even when he was away from home for a long time he was always comforted by the knowledge that he would eventually return to his own home. But now that his wife passed away, he felt the curse of Kayin. He no longer had a home to return to.

This, the Chofetz Chayim used to say, is the difference between the person who lives with the awareness of *olam haboh* and the person who is missing this awareness. When a person lacks an appreciation of *olam haboh*, all that he suffers in this world is difficult to cope with. But when a person is aware that he has a future home in *olam haboh*, his entire journey through this world goes smoothly. Regardless of any difficulties that arise in his path, he knows that he will eventually have ultimate comfort and pleasure when he reaches his final, eternal destination. (*Chofetz Chayim al Hatorah*)

Learn to accept criticism to grow spiritually.

וירא השם כי רבה רעת האדם בארץ וכל יצר מחשבת לבו רק רע כל
היום. (בראשית ו' ה')

Before the great flood:
"THE ALMIGHTY SAW THAT MAN DID MUCH EVIL IN THE LAND, AND ALL THE THOUGHTS OF HIS HEART WERE EVIL THE ENTIRE DAY." (*Braishis* 6:5)

Sforno explains that "man did much evil" refers to the past, and "the thoughts of his heart were evil" refers to the future. They would not listen to anyone who would try to correct them and therefore there was no hope that they would do *tshuvah*.

Regardless of how many faults a person has, if he accepts criticism there is hope that he will improve. The ultimate level is to love criticism (number 35 of the 48 ways to acquire Torah listed in *Pirke Avos*, ch.6). A person with this attribute will be grateful to anyone who shows him ways to improve. As Rabbi Noach Weinberg says, "Everyone is grateful to someone who tells him that in his carelessness he dropped his wallet with a large sum of money in it. That should be our attitude towards constructive criticism." Even if someone does not appreciate criticism, but he is nevertheless willing to improve himself when he is corrected, he will eventually become a better person. But there is no hope for someone who refuses to listen to those who try to correct him.

What is your present attitude towards criticism? Are you willing to ask five people who know you to give you criticism? If you are sincerely interested in becoming a better person, you will develop a positive attitude towards criticism and will grow in many ways.

One must overcome worrying about the future in order to appreciate what he has.

Rashi (*Braishis* 6:6) cites as an analogy a concept that is crucial for living a happy life. When a child is born, parents are happy. Why aren't they sad that eventually the child will die? The answer is that one must live in the present. At a time of joy experience the joy of that moment. Do not allow future sorrows to destroy the positive aspects of the present.

People who worry focus their attention on what can possibly go wrong in the future. There will always be something to worry about. No matter how perfect the present is you will constantly suffer if you think about potential future problems and difficulties. Of course, one must be concerned with the future and plan accordingly. But the only way to enjoy the Almighty's world is to appreciate the gifts He has given you. Someone who rents a house or a car knows that he will eventually have to return it. Nevertheless, he appreciates his present use of it. The same is true for all that we have.

A worrier destroys his life. Learn to live in the present and you will free yourself from much needless misery and suffering.

Seek the approval of the Almighty, not the approval of man.

ונח מצא חן בעיני השם. (בראשית ו' ח')

"AND NOACH FOUND FAVOR (chain) IN THE EYES OF THE ALMIGHTY." (Braishis 6:8)

There is a natural tendency to try to find favor in the eyes of other people. The need for approval from others is a very strong drive. For some people it is their main motivation in all that they do. In the positive sense it will motivate people to accomplish for the good. But the negative aspect of seeking approval is that it can cause you to do things that are improper if you want to find favor in the eyes of evildoers.

How is it possible to prevent the need for approval to cause you to transgress? The answer is: focus on gaining the Almighty's approval. This is what Noach did. He lived in a generation of evildoers. If he would have wanted the approval of his friends and neighbors, he would have needed to compromise his ideals. But his focus was on finding favor in the eyes of the Almighty. Before doing anything, instead of asking yourself, "What will the neighbors think?" ask yourself, "What will the Almighty think?"

NOACH

Seek the company of people from whom you can learn positive qualities.

אלה תולדת נח נח איש צדיק תמים היה בדרתיו. (בראשית ו' ט')

"THESE ARE THE GENERATIONS OF NOACH. NOACH WAS A COMPLETELY RIGHTEOUS MAN IN HIS GENERATION." (*Braishis* 6:9)

Rashi cites two Talmudic opinions (*Sanhedrin* 108a) regarding the words "in his generation." Some see this as praise of Noach. Even in an evil generation he was righteous. If he were in a righteous generation, he would be even more righteous. Others see this as a negative statement. Only in his own generation was he considered righteous, but if he were living in Avraham's generation, he would not have been considered anything special.

The Chasam Sofer commented on this that both opinions are correct and there is not really an argument. If Noach would have stayed the way he was in his own generation, then in Avraham's generation he would not have been special. But the reality would be that if Noach were in Avraham's generation, he would have been influenced positively by Avraham, and Noach would have been much greater than he actually was. (*Toras Moshe*)

This is a fundamental lesson on the importance of being in the presence of elevated people. We are all influenced by our surroundings. When you are close to people who act in an elevated manner, you are automatically influenced in positive ways.

Rabbi Yisroel Salanter was asked once if had studied under Rabbi Zundel of Salant, who was known to be his teacher. Rav Yisroel replied, "I did not study under him. I saw him."

Just taking a careful look at his actions and habits were already an entire series of lessons in elevated behavior. (*Tnuas Hamussar*, vol.1, p.111)

You yourself become elevated when you help others improve.

את האלקים התהלך נח. (בראשית ו' ט')

"NOACH WALKED WITH THE ALMIGHTY." (*Braishis* 6:9)

Sforno explains that Noach walked in the Almighty's ways, which means to do good to others. How? The people acted corruptly and Noach tried to teach them how to improve their actions.

There are different levels in helping others. We find in the Rambam (*Hilchos Matnos Aniyim* 10:7-14) that there are eight levels of giving charity. The highest level is to help a person earn a living on his own. Why is this the highest level? Because when you help a person become self-sufficient you are helping him not just once but for the rest of his life. Similarly, when you help someone become a better person you are not just helping him for the moment. Rather you are helping him accomplish more his entire life. Not only will he do many more good deeds, but you will have a positive influence on his children and grandchildren. The more elevated a person is the more he will share his high ideals with his family. Hence you are helping this person's future generations. Strive to do the ultimate in helping people by spreading Torah values.

The Alter of Nevardok, Rabbi Yosef Hurwitz, used to say, "If a person would devote himself to spreading the ideals of Torah with the same devotion and energy he has for his own children, he would accomplish immensely." (*Chayai Hamussar*, vol.2, p.201)

Be very careful not to embarrass others.

שפך דם האדם באדם דמו ישפך כי בצלם אלקים עשה את האדם.
(בראשית ט' ו')

"ONE WHO SPILLS THE BLOOD OF A PERSON IN A PERSON HIS BLOOD SHALL BE SPILLED, FOR IN THE IMAGE OF THE ALMIGHTY HE HAS MADE MAN." (*Braishis* 9:6)

The Alshich explains this verse to include one who embarrasses another person. When a person is embarrassed his blood flow changes and the Sages have equated embarrassing someone with murder. The Torah tells us here why this is such a severe offense. Each person is created in the image of the Almighty and therefore must be shown great respect. An attack on a human being contains an aspect of an attack on the Almighty.

When you embarrass someone you cause him much pain. This suffering can be even greater than that felt from a physical wound. But the harm caused is not merely the present pain. Rather when you humiliate someone you lower his self-esteem. Some people feel worthless when they are humiliated. Even a person who usually has high self-esteem will feel lowered when someone embarrasses him. Humiliating someone causes a person to fail to realize his true greatness. The ramifications of this are awesome. Make every effort possible not to cause anyone embarrassment.

Two of the Rabbis of Aitz Chayim Yeshiva came with a group of thirteen-year-old students to Rabbi Isser Zalman Meltzer's house to test them on their Talmudic studies. The Rosh Hayeshiva asked one of the students for an explanation of a certain *Tosfos*, but the student gave the wrong answer. Rabbi Meltzer said to him, "Perhaps you meant such and such in your explanation?" Rabbi Meltzer went on to give the correct explanation. "No," answered the child, "that is not what I meant." And the student again repeated his wrong interpretation. Rabbi Meltzer once again tried to explain the *Tosfos* to the student, this time in an easier way, and then said to him, "Perhaps this is what you meant?" But the pupil kept arguing and clung stubbornly to his wrong idea. For ten minutes Rabbi Meltzer patiently tried to explain the correct interpretation to the student, but the student kept repeating his mistake.

Rabbi Meltzer then apologized to the class and walked out of the room. In another part of the house Rabbi Meltzer repeated to himself over and over again, "Showing respect to other people applies also to children. Showing respect to other people applies also to children." After repeating this a number of times to himself, he returned to the room and sat down as if the students had just entered the room. He then turned to that child with amazing gentleness and said once again to him, "Please tell me how you now will explain this *Tosfos*." (*Bederech Aitz Hachayim*, vol.1, p.211)

Strive for harmony even with people who are different from you.

את קשתי נתתי בענן והיתה לאות ברית ביני ובין הארץ. (בראשית ט'
י"ג)

After the Great Flood the Almighty said:
"MY RAINBOW I PLACE IN THE CLOUDS, AND IT WILL BE A SIGN OF THE COVENANT BETWEEN ME AND THE EARTH." (*Braishis* 9:13)

The rainbow symbolizes peace and unity. A rainbow is made up of various colors and shades of colors and although they are very different from each other, they come together to make one entire whole. Similarly, people are very different from each other. They come from different national backgrounds, and they have different personalities. But if they will look at themselves as one unit there can be peace and harmony despite the differences between them. This is basic for the existence of the world and for the welfare of individuals. For this reason the rainbow is the symbol of the covenant between the Almighty and the earth. (*Otzer Chayim*, vol.1, p.39)

Whenever you see a rainbow, or a picture of a rainbow, let it be a reminder to work towards harmony with other people even if there are major differences between you. While differences in interests and personality might make it difficult for you to become close friends with a specific person, you can still have a harmonious and peaceful relationship with him.

Make it your highest priority to do positive things.

ויחל נח איש האדמה ויטע כרם. (בראשית ט' כ')

"AND NOACH, MAN OF THE EARTH, PROFANED HIMSELF AND PLANTED A VINEYARD." (*Braishis* 9:20)

Rashi notes that Noach is now called a man of the earth instead of "a righteous man" as previously. What happened? The first thing he planted after the flood was a vineyard, but he should have planted other things first.

Rabbi Yeruchem Levovitz commented that it was definitely proper for Noach to plant a vineyard. Grapes which produce wine are necessary and have positive uses. But the fact that from all the things he had to plant, Noach chose grapes to start with shows us his essence. This lowered his previous level. By what you choose first you illustrate whether your focus is on spirituality or materialism. (*Daas Torah: Braishis*, p.61)

Whenever you have a number of things to choose from, note what you choose first. This is a powerful tool to gain greater self-awareness. Regardless of your present level, strive to build up such a love for doing good that it will be first on your list of things to do.

Feel pleasure when you make an extra effort in doing good.

ויקח שם ויפת את השמלה וישימו על שכם שניהם וילכו אחרנית ויכסו
את ערות אביהם ופניהם אחרנית וערות אביהם לא ראו. (בראשית ט'
כ"ג)

"AND SHEM AND YEFES TOOK THE GARMENT, AND LAID IT UPON
BOTH THEIR SHOULDERS, AND WENT BACKWARD, AND COVERED
THE NAKEDNESS OF THEIR FATHER; AND THEIR FACES WERE
BACKWARD, AND THEY DID NOT SEE THE NAKEDNESS OF THEIR
FATHER." (*Braishis* 9:23)

Rashi cites the Talmudic statement that derives from this verse
(because of the singular form of the word *vayikach* - and he took)
that Shem put more effort into the *mitzvah* and therefore he
received a much greater reward than Yefes. Shem's descendants
merited the garment of *talis* with *tzitzis*.

At times when a person works with others for a worthwhile
project, he might feel resentment if he sees that he is putting in
more effort than someone else. But whenever the work you are
doing is worthwhile, the extra effort you put into it elevates you.
This knowledge should give you even greater pleasure when you
put much time and energy into any spiritual endeavor. It is proper
to try to motivate others to put in their best efforts. But your main
focus should be on how you are gaining by your good deeds.

This is an especially important lesson for young children. When
a parent tells a child to do something, very frequently the child will
exclaim, "But the other children are not doing it." While parents
must make certain not to be showing any favoritism, children need
to gain the awareness that the more they do, the greater they are.
When Shem did more than Yefes, he didn't complain that he was
being taken advantage of. Honoring parents is a privilege. The
more one is privileged, the more fortunate one is.

When working for a cause, be sensitive to individuals.

ויאמרו הבה נבנה לנו עיר ומגדל וראשו בשמים ונעשה לנו שם פן נפוץ
על פני כל הארץ. (בראשית י"א ד')

"AND THEY SAID: COME, LET US BUILD A CITY, AND A TOWER WITH ITS TOP IN HEAVEN, AND LET US MAKE US A NAME, LEST WE BE SCATTERED ABOUT UPON THE FACE OF THE WHOLE EARTH." (*Braishis* 11:4)

The Midrash (*Pirke D'Reb Eliezer* 24) states that when the people of the generation of the dispersion (*Dor Haflagah*) were in the middle of their project of building the tower, the following occurred: If a human being fell off the tower and was killed, they ignored it and just continued working. But if a brick fell and broke, they sat down and cried.

This Midrash is a poignant lesson in how easy it is to get sidetracked from your main goals. They wished to make a tower for the benefit of mankind. But after awhile the project itself became the goal and the lives of people were considered unimportant. Similarly, a person can work for *Klal Yisroel*, the Jewish people, and become so involved with the bureaucratic details of his work that he is rude to individuals. When you are doing things for the benefit of people, remember your goals. Do not allow your devotion to a cause to make you callous to people. Keep reminding yourself of the need to be sensitive to the needs of each individual.

LECH LECHO

When you suffer focus on how you can use this experience to help others.

ויאמר השם אל אברם לך לך מארצך וממולדתך ומבית אביך אל הארץ
אשר אראך. (בראשית י״ב א׳)

"AND THE ALMIGHTY SAID TO AVRAM, GO FROM YOUR LAND, AND FROM YOUR BIRTHPLACE, AND FROM THE HOUSE OF YOUR FATHER TO THE LAND WHICH I WILL SHOW YOU." (*Braishis* 12:1)

Rabbi Nachum of Tzernoble devoted much time and effort to redeeming Jews who were put into prisons by anti-semitic regimes. He traveled from place to place gathering funds to make the payments necessary to free those imprisoned. Once when he was in Zhitomer, some people fabricated a libel against him and he was put into prison.

A righteous person came to him in prison and said to him, "Our forefather Avraham was outstanding in his kindness to wayfarers. He took in people who were traveling and expended great efforts to make his guests comfortable. He always wanted to know what more he could possibly do to help his guests. The Almighty told him to travel away·from his father's home, his birthplace, and his land. Only now when he personally experiences being a stranger in a foreign place will he know firsthand what it is like. This will give him a greater appreciation of what he can do to help his guests."

"Similarly with you," the righteous visitor told him. "You are completely devoted to freeing prisoners. From Heaven they are giving you a chance to experience what it is like to be held captive by enemies of our people. This will give you a deep appreciation of the necessity of doing all you can to free other people in the future with all possible speed." (*Mimayanos Hanetzach*)

Whenever you personally suffer any kind of pain or sorrow, remember carefully every aspect of your experience. When other people are in similar situations, you will know with greater depth what they are experiencing. This will help you to help them with greater sensitivity and kindness. Moreover, it will make your own suffering easier to cope with. You will view it as a meaningful learning experience that will assist you in becoming more effective in helping others.

When you start an important project make certain to complete it.

ויצאו ללכת ארצה כנען ויבאו ארצה כנען. (בראשית י"ב ה')

The Torah tells us about Avraham and his family:
"THEY WENT TO GO TO THE LAND OF CANAAN AND THEY CAME TO THE LAND OF CANAAN." (*Braishis* 12:5)

When Avraham made up his mind to travel to the land of Canaan, he followed through on his plans and reached his destination. This stands in sharp contrast with Terach, Avraham's father, about whom we read in the portion of *Noach* (11:31) that he started out to go to the land of Canaan, but when he reached Charan in the midst of his journey, he settled there and never made it to Canaan. This, said the Chofetz Chayim, is a lesson that we should learn from Avraham. If you accept upon yourself a goal to accomplish something, don't become sidetracked. (*Chofetz Chayim al Hatorah*)

There are many people who start numerous projects. Yet they never seem to accomplish anything of significance. Their problem is that they become sidetracked. To succeed in any venture you need to complete what you start. Especially when you have a goal that is very important to reach, become obsessed with it. While obsessions can be negative, they can also be very positive. Learn to finish what you start.

It is improper to try to coerce others to act stringently.

בלעדי רק אשר אכלו הנערים וחלק האנשים אשר הלכו אתי ענר אשכל
וממרא הם יקחו חלקם. (בראשית י״ד כ״ד)

After Avraham's victory over the five kings, the king of Sodom was so grateful to Avraham that he offered him much wealth. Avraham refused to take anything for himself but said:
"EXCEPT THAT WHICH THE YOUNG MEN HAVE EATEN, AND THE SHARE OF THE MEN WHO WENT WITH ME, ANER, ESHKOL, AND MAMRE, LET THEM TAKE THEIR SHARE." (Braishis 14:24)

The Chofetz Chayim noted that Avraham was meticulously careful not to take anything for himself. He did not want to derive any benefit from the king of Sodom, not even a string or shoelace. But he allowed the men who went with him to take their share. This teaches us, the saintly Chofetz Chayim said, that each person has a right to be stringent when it comes to himself. But it is not proper to force others to be more stringent than is actually obligatory. (Chofetz Chayim al Hatorah)

It is easy to tell others not to do things. But it is important to differentiate between an obligation and that which is beyond the dictates of the law. The more elevated one acts, the more praiseworthy. But do not place excessively heavy burdens on others. The Chofetz Chayim himself was a completely spiritual person who symbolized the essence of a tzadik. Yet he was the one who taught the above message.

Be aware of the greatness of even people who seem small in stature.

ויוצא אתו החוצה ויאמר הבט נא השמימה וספר הכוכבים אם תוכל
לספר אתם ויאמר לו כה יהיה זרעך. (בראשית ט"ו ה')

"AND [the Almighty] TOOK [Avraham] OUTSIDE AND HE SAID TO HIM,
LOOK UP, PLEASE, AT THE HEAVENS AND COUNT THE STARS, IF
YOU CAN COUNT THEM. AND HE SAID TO HIM, SO, TOO, WILL BE
YOUR DESCENDANTS." (*Braishis* 15:5)

The Baal Shem Tov explained that the descendants of Avraham
are like stars. We see the stars from a great distance and they
appear to be mere tiny specks but in reality in the heaven they are
gigantic. So, too, in this world many people look very small. But in
reality they have greatness. (*Mayanah Shel Torah*)

When you look at another person, realize that he is like a star.
He might seem small to you. He might not appear as having
accomplished very much. Gain an awareness of the great potential
of each person. View each person as an entire world, as an
enormous being in the cosmos. When you see people in this light
you will behave towards them with great respect. When you show
others this respect, they will gain greater respect for themselves.
This can give a person the encouragement he needs to live up to his
potential greatness.

After a Chinuch Atzmai meeting, Rabbi Yaakov Kamenetzky
and Rabbi Moshe Feinstein stood outside a waiting car discussing
who would sit next to the driver and who would sit alone in the
back seat. Rav Yaakov took the front seat. After Rav Moshe
alighted from the car, Rav Yaakov explained to the driver, "We
were clarifying who would be getting off first. That person, we
decided, would sit in the back. If he would sit in the front, the
longer-riding passenger would be in the back leaving you alone at
the wheel, making you look like a chauffeur. But that is not the
case. We appreciate your importance and did not want to
compromise your dignity." (Rabbi Nisson Wolpin; *The Jewish
Observer*, May, 1986, p.16)

Trust in the Almighty frees a person from fear of negative predictions.

ויוצא אתו החוצה וגו' ויאמר לו כה יהיה זרעך. (בראשית ט"ו ה')

"AND [the Almighty] TOOK [Avraham] OUTSIDE... AND HE SAID TO HIM, SO, TOO, WILL BE YOUR DESCENDANTS." (*Braishis* 15:5)

Rashi cites the Talmudic statement (*Nedorim* 32a) that the Almighty told Avraham to discount the effects of astrological influence. Even if there is a sign in the stars that you will not have children, you will rise above this and will merit having children. From here, the Talmud (*Shabbos* 156a) states, "There is no *mazal* for Israelites." This then is one meaning of the latter half of the verse, "So, too, will be your descendants." The Jewish people need not fear any negative predictions in the stars. (*Megaleh Amukos*, cited in *Biurai Hamekubalim Beniglah*)

Some people become nervous if someone predicts a negative future for them through astrology, chirology (palm reading), cards, etc. Trust in the Almighty and awareness of His unlimited power will free a person from any fears of such predictions. Prayer and the merit of good deeds will be able to change a negative destiny to a positive one (see Rashi to *Shabbos, ibid.*).

VAYAIRA

Make an effort to give people good advice.

וירא אליו השם באלני ממרא. (בראשית י"ח א')

"AND THE ALMIGHTY APPEARED TO [Avraham] AT AILONAI MAMRE." (*Braishis* 18:1)

Rashi cites the Midrash that the Almighty appeared to Avraham on the territory of Mamre because Mamre gave Avraham the advice to perform the circumcision. Rabbi Yeruchem Levovitz stated that from here we see the great merit of giving people good advice. Avraham would have listened to the Almighty's command to be circumcised. But others advised Avraham not to circumcise himself. When Mamre heard about the matter, however, he advised Avraham to do it and for this he was greatly rewarded. (*Daas Torah: Braishis*, p.112)

In reference to seeking the advice of others the Mishnah in *Pirke Avos* (2:7) states that when one asks advice from others one gains more understanding. In his commentary on this Mishnah, Rabbi Chayim of Volozhin cites a popular saying, "Ask others for advice. Then do what your own intellect tells you." The question arises: If in the end you will do what you yourself think is appropriate, why do you need to consult others?

The answer, said Rav Chayim of Volozhin, is that each person has a better inside knowledge of himself than any outsider could possibly have. But every person has some knowledge and understanding that you are missing. Therefore, before making any major decisions, consult as many people as you can to take in ideas and information that you might not have known or thought of. After interviewing various people, you are responsible for making your decisions because only you have the inner knowledge of yourself that is necessary to make the final decision. (*Ruach Chayim* 2:7)

It is important to mention a word of caution about giving others advice. My late Rebbe, Rabbi Chayim Mordechai Katz, Rosh Hayeshiva of Telz, would constantly stress the harm you can cause by giving someone bad advice. In *Viduy* (the standard confession that is listed alphabetically) one fault that is listed is *yoatznu ra* - we have given bad advice. This is considered a fundamental transgression. Bad advice can cause much misery and suffering throughout a lifetime. Conversely, giving someone good advice can help him immensely. Whenever you are in a position of giving someone advice, weigh all the consequences very carefully.

There are two extremes in giving advice. Some people go around giving others advice whether they want it or not. They are overly confident and feel that they have all the answers. At the other extreme, there are people who avoid giving others advice no matter what. They are likely to say, "Let other people make their own mistakes. Each person has to live his own life and it is up to him to learn the hard way." Neither extreme is right. The Torah ideal is to give people good advice as an act of kindness whenever it is appropriate (see *Shaarey Tshuvah* 3:54). At the same time, we must be very careful not to violate the Torah's prohibition against giving someone harmful advice (*Vayikra* 19:14; see *Love Your Neighbor*, pp.253-6).

Rabbi Zundel of Salant collected information on all kinds of practical matters such as advice on health and how to relieve pain, how to prepare homemade mirrors, soap, etc. He wanted to be able to do acts of *chesed* by giving those who needed them helpful hints they could use. (*Tnuas Hamussar*, vol.1, p.114)

The Steipler once said that people came to consult him on matters they themselves could certainly decide by themselves if they really wanted to. But since they found it difficult to make the decision, it was an act of *chesed* to help them. (*Peninai Rabainu Hakehilos Yaakov*, p.107)

When you do acts of kindness each detail is important.

וישא עיניו וירא והנה שלשה אנשים נצבים עליו וירא וירץ לקראתם מפתח האהל. (בראשית י"ח ב')

"AND [Avraham] LIFTED UP HIS EYES AND HE SAW AND BEHOLD THREE MEN WERE STANDING NEAR HIM AND HE SAW AND HE RAN TO GREET THEM FROM THE ENTRANCE OF THE TENT." (*Braishis* 18:2)

From verse 2 until verse 8 the Torah tells us in great detail every specific act of Avraham in his hospitality towards the guests who came to him. "He lifted up his eyes," "And he saw," "And he ran to greet them," etc. There are seven verses describing the details of Avraham's kindness.

Rabbi Yeruchem Levovitz commented on this with an analogy. When a person inherits a house, he will usually just say, "I have a house." He will not elaborate on all the details since he received everything at one time. But a person who builds a house for himself will talk about every detail from the beginning until the end. He will describe how he purchased the land for the site of the house, how he bought the material that went into building the house, and so on. Each aspect is very dear to him. The more effort he put into the house, the more he will talk about it.

Similarly, said Rav Yeruchem, the actions and behavior of the righteous are like a building (see *Brochos* 64a). With each action, a righteous person is building a great edifice. For this reason the Torah tells us about each detail of Avraham's *chesed*. Every movement was another stage in the building of a righteous person. (*Daas Torah: Braishis*, pp.115-6)

When you view yourself as building a great person, every detail of what you do is invested with meaning and importance. Every positive action you do is creating a great human being. Keep this in mind when you do an act of kindness for others. Every movement you make is a necessary part of the entire construction. Don't wait for the end to appreciate what you are doing. Rather, feel the joy of growth in even the smallest act of kindness that you do.

Say little and do much.

ואקחה פת לחם וגו' ואל הבקר רץ אברהם ויקח בן בקר רך וטוב וגו'.
(בראשית י"ח ה-ח)

"AND I WILL TAKE BREAD... AND AVRAHAM RAN TO THE HERD, AND FETCHED A TENDER AND GOOD CALF..." (*Braishis* 18:5-8)

The Sages (*Bava Metzia* 87a) derive from here that the righteous say little and do much. Avraham said he would just take bread. But in actuality he served an elaborate feast. The wicked, however, say much and even a little they do not do, as we see from Efron's false assurances to Avraham in the portion of *Chayai Sarah*.

Rabbi Yeruchem Levovitz commented on this that the whole idea of talking about what you plan to do is negative. When you think of doing some good deed, what does your talking in advance add? If you plan on doing some good deed, just go and do it. Why talk about it? Accept upon yourself to actually do good. Talking about the good that you are thinking of doing is superfluous and frequently very counterproductive. (*Daas Torah: Braishis*, p.117)

It is so much easier to talk about the good that you would like to do rather than making the effort to take action. There is a pleasure in talking about the good you will do, but it is a cheap way of getting honor and approval. "See how great I am. I am planning to do all these wonderful things." First of all, you might not actually do them. Even if you do, needlessly talking about them is likely to change your focus from doing good for its own sake to doing good for the sake of approval.

The righteous person keeps his word. Therefore he is careful about making rash promises that he might later have difficulty fulfilling. If he says he will do something, he will, and he does not want to accept an excessive amount of responsibilities that he might not be able to meet. But the wicked are careless with what they say. Even if they say they will do something, it does not mean that they will actually do it. So it is very easy for them to keep on talking about doing. They don't mind breaking their word. The person who is truly righteous is so busy doing good that he doesn't have time to waste talking about what he'd like to do. Action should be your goal. Don't just talk about the good you plan to do, actually do it. (based on *ibid.*)

Rabbi Nosson Scherman wrote, "If one can sum up Rabbi Moshe Feinstein's personal credo as a human being, perhaps it can be best expressed in his response to a question as to what merit he attributed his eminence: 'All my life I have never hurt a human being.' An understatement, because he went out of his way to bring comfort and accommodation to others." (*The Jewish Observer*, Oct. 1986, p.26)

Rabbi Nochum Perchovitz, Rosh Yeshiva of Mir, would frequently do acts of kindness for his students without any fanfare or publicity. One of his students who was greatly helped only found out after many years that it was Rav Nochum who helped him. This student had great difficulty in purchasing an apartment and he spoke about his problem to Rav Nochum a number of times. He did not expect any practical help but wanted emotional support. Rav Nochum spoke to him at length and each time would say, "The Almighty will help."

A short time later the problem was solved and he received the necessary loans to purchase the apartment. Many years later he found out that behind the scenes Rav Nochum took action on his behalf in some unusual ways. He even had his father-in-law Rabbi Chayim Shmuelevitz write a letter to the appropriate person. Even though Rav Nochum did so much for him, he never mentioned a word about it in all their conversations. (*Yetaid Neaman*, 17 Kislev, 5747, p.6)

Consider it an honor to do acts of kindness for another person.

כי על כן עברתם על עבדכם. (בראשית י״ח ה׳)

Avraham pleaded with the three men who passed near his tent to accept his hospitality, and said:

"BECAUSE YOU HAVE PASSED BY YOUR SERVANT." (*Braishis* 18:5)

Rashi comments: "This [to be my guest] I request of you because you have passed by, for my honor."

Rabbi Yeruchem Levovitz cites the Talmudic (*Kidushin* 7a) principle that when someone gives something to a distinguished person, the fact that the person accepts your gift is considered as if you received something from him. Giving to an important person is actually taking. But who is a person that would be considered distinguished? In the eyes of an arrogant person everyone is considered as nothing. He belittles everyone. But a person with humility considers everyone to be important. He honors and respects every human being. Therefore he considers giving to any person as a personal favor to him.

If someone of the stature of the Chofetz Chayim were to come to our home as a guest, added Rav Yeruchem, we too would be full of joy to serve him. It would be very easy for us to do any amount of work to honor him and assist him. We would feel great pleasure and consider it a great merit that he accepted what we gave him. We would feel that he was giving to us when he allowed us to serve him. For our forefather Avraham this was his attitude towards every person. Every individual was considered distinguished and important. Whenever Avraham gave anything to another person, he considered it as taking from that person. Avraham saw three people walking. They seemed ordinary nomads passing by. What was Avraham's reaction? He ran to greet them and bowed down before them. He personally felt more honor in their coming to be his guests than we would feel if the greatest people of our generation were to visit us.

This, said Rav Yeruchem, is what Rashi means by the words, "for my honor." From every action and every movement of Avraham it was noticeable that they were doing him an act of kindness. This is a new way of looking at the acts of kindness you do for others. I am not doing a kindness for another person. Rather, the other person is doing an act of kindness for me. (*Daas Torah: Braishis*, p.119)

Be careful not to become discouraged over failings nor arrogant because of the good you do.

אולי יש חמשים צדיקם בתוך העיר. (בראשית י"ח כ"ד)

Avraham pleaded with the Almighty to save Sodom and said:
"PERHAPS THERE ARE FIFTY RIGHTEOUS PEOPLE IN THE MIDST OF THE CITY." (*Braishis* 18:24)

Rabbi Meir Simcha Hacohen explains that there is absolute good and good that would only be considered good in relationship to evil. Avraham, the pillar of kindness, requested of the Almighty that even if there could only be found fifty people in Sodom who would be considered righteous when compared to the rest of the evil city, their merit should save everyone else. (*Meshech Chochmah*)

This concept is important to remember in two instances. If you are very idealistic and a perfectionist and therefore feel like a failure because you are not on the high level you wish you were, remember that in relation to the majority of the world you are probably righteous. This will prevent you from becoming discouraged. But if you look around and see that other people are on such a low level and that you begin to feel arrogant, focus on where you stand in absolute terms. When you view your present state in relation to the highest Torah ideals you will be able to regain feelings of humility.

Trust in the Almighty and you will always feel hope.

והשם פקד את שרה כאשר אמר וגו'. ותהר ותלד שרה לאברהם בן לזקניו למועד אשר דבר אתו אלקים. (בראשית כ"א א-ב)

"AND THE ALMIGHTY REMEMBERED SARAH AS HE SAID HE WOULD... AND SARAH CONCEIVED AND BORE AVRAHAM A SON IN HIS OLD AGE." (*Braishis* 21:1,2)

We read this section of the Torah on *Rosh Hashanah*. The reason for this is to develop hope and trust in the Almighty. Nothing is impossible for Him. Sarah was already ninety years old and according to all the standard rules of nature it would have been impossible for her to give birth to a child. Nevertheless, since the Almighty willed it she gave birth to Yitzchok. (*Chofetz Chayim al Hatorah*)

Even when a situation seems bleak and the probability for salvation seems unlikely, do not give up hope. The Almighty's law is more powerful than the law of averages. This awareness is so important for our daily lives that at the beginning of each year we repeat this message: never despair!

Once a person came to the Chazon Ish's house with a very heavy heart. When the man came in, the Chazon Ish had just started reciting the blessing of *asher yotzar*. The person was very impatient and before the Chazon Ish finished the blessing, he blurted out his problem. His young child had polio during the epidemic in *Eretz Yisroel* and the doctors were unable to do anything to help. The Chazon Ish indicated to him with his finger that he wanted to complete the blessing. Reciting each word loudly and clearly, the Chazon Ish emphasized the final words: "The healer of all flesh, and He does wonders." In a very gentle tone, the Chazon Ish turned to the man and said, "You hear that the Almighty makes wonders." This is all the Chazon Ish said and in a very short time the child completely recovered. (*P'air Hador*, vol.4, pp.115-6)

Act with speed even when you have to do something that is unpleasant for you.

וישכם אברהם בבקר ויקח לחם וחמת מים ויתן אל הגר שם על שכמה ואת הילד וישלחה. (בראשית כ"א י"ד)

"AND AVRAHAM ROSE UP EARLY IN THE MORNING, AND TOOK BREAD, AND A BOTTLE OF WATER, AND GAVE IT TO HAGAR, PUTTING IT ON HER SHOULDER, AND THE CHILD, AND SENT HER AWAY." (*Braishis* 21:14)

Here the Torah tells us that Avraham woke up early in the morning to fulfill the will of the Almighty even though this was really against his own wishes. He personally would have wanted Hagar and Yishmael to stay. But the Almighty agreed with Sarah that Yishmael would be a negative influence on Yitzchok and therefore had to be sent away. Avraham quickly took action to fulfill the wishes of the Almighty. (*Chofetz Chayim al Hatorah*, verses 10 and 14)

Sending away Yishmael was the exact opposite behavior that would have been consistent with Avraham's attribute of lovingkindness. Even though Avraham needed to act against his natural tendencies, he woke up early to carry out the command of the Almighty. He could have easily procrastinated and pushed off this most painful of actions. But Avraham's main goal in life was to carry out the will of the Almighty. Therefore his focus was not on whether he personally enjoyed what he did, but on doing what was right in the Almighty's eyes. This self-discipline allowed him to do all he could for his guests and wait on them even when he was ill.

Whether you feel like doing something should not be your major criterion. Rather, ask yourself, "What is the proper thing to do right now?" Once something is proper to do, act with an enthusiasm that comes from an inner acceptance of the importance of doing the right thing.

CHAYAI SARAH

See the good in every life situation.

ויהיו חיי שרה מאה שנה ועשרים שנה ושבע שנים שני חיי שרה.
(בראשית כ״ג א׳)

"AND THE LIFE OF SARAH WAS ONE HUNDRED YEARS, AND TWENTY YEARS, AND SEVEN YEARS. THESE WERE THE YEARS OF THE LIFE OF SARAH." (*Braishis* 23:1)

Rashi comments that all the years of Sarah's life were equally good. The question arises how this could be said about Sarah since she seems to have suffered very much in her life. For many years she was childless; she experienced famine and exile; she was taken captive by the Pharaoh of Egypt and later by Avimelech. Rabbi Zushe of Anipoli explained that Sarah mastered the attribute of constantly saying, "This too is for the good." Even those events that others might consider to be bad, she was aware that they were from the Almighty and therefore she was able to evaluate them as being positive.

The quality of one's life is not dependent on external situations. There are people whose lives seem to run quite smoothly. Nevertheless, they tend to evaluate minor frustrations as tragedies and therefore view their lives in negative terms. The Torah ideal is to be aware that the purpose of your life is to perfect your character and every life situation is an opportunity for growth. Sarah mastered this level of consciousness. Therefore at the end of her life, which was constantly devoted to growth, it could be said about her that all her years were good.

This lesson is most important for us to internalize. See the growth possible in every life event. In each difficult situation ask yourself, "How can I become a better person because of what happened?"

In Rabbi Aryeh Levin's younger years, he studied at the Slutsk Yeshiva where Rabbi Isser Zalman Meltzer was the head. The two met again in Jerusalem when Reb Aryeh had grown to manhood and they became neighbors in the holy city. As Rabbi Isser Zalman once sat talking with Reb Aryeh about his period of study in Slutsk, he asked innocently, "And where did you have your lodgings?"

"Oh," replied the young man, "I was quite comfortably situated. I had a bench in the *Shneider Shul* (the Tailor's synagogue) as my regular place to sleep."

"Hmm," mumbled Rav Isser Zalman, not altogether pleased at the answer. "And where did you eat?"

"Oh, I had fine accomodations. Let me see... On Sundays I went to this family; on Tuesdays to that family; and on Thursdays to this other family." And he named three households in the town.

"But what about the other days?"

"Oh, I managed very well..." said Reb Aryeh; and Rabbi Meltzer realized that as a young student Reb Aryeh had gone hungry.

"Please forgive me for my lack of awareness," said Rabbi Meltzer. Reb Aryeh assured him, however, that he had neither suffered nor felt any neglect. He harbored no memories of deprivation.

That night, Mrs. Meltzer came knocking at his door. Please come at once, she requested. Her husband was unable to sleep. Reb Aryeh found his former teacher sitting up, with tears running down his cheeks. "Whatever will I answer on my day of judgment," he pleaded, "when they ask me how it is that I never knew that Reb Aryeh slept on a bench with no proper bed to call his own; that he did not have enough to eat, and he studied Torah in hardship and suffering?" He continued until Reb Aryeh was able to reassure him that he really did not mind what had happened. (*A Tzaddik in Our Time*, pp.21-3)

Get the commitment of specific individuals when you need something to be taken care of.

שמענו אדני נשיא אלקים אתה בתוכנו במבחר קברינו קבר את מתך איש
ממנו את קברו לא יכלה ממך מקבר מתך. (בראשית כ״ג ו׳)

After Sarah died, Avraham asked the Bnai Chais for a burial place for her. They replied:
"HEAR US, MY MASTER, YOU ARE A PRINCE OF THE ALMIGHTY AMONG US. IN THE BEST OF OUR BURIAL PLACES BURY YOUR DEAD NONE OF THE MEN AMONG US WILL DENY YOU HIS BURIAL SITE TO BURY YOUR DEAD." (*Braishis* 23:6)

Even though the Bnai Chais consented to Avraham's burying his wife on their land, he specifically asked for a place on territory belonging to Efron ben Tzochar. The question arises, since the Bnai Chais said to Avraham, "No person among us will prevent you from burying your dead," why did Avraham make a point of asking Efron for his field? Why didn't he just go and bury Sarah?

Avraham knew, explained the Chofetz Chayim, that when a group of people speak as a whole and say that they will do something, each one will refer you to someone else when it comes to putting the lofty words into action. Therefore, Avraham persisted in wanting to speak specifically to one individual in order to ensure that he would personally allow him to buy the piece of land. (*Chofetz Chayim al Hatorah*)

This concept is important to remember when you try to motivate a group of people to commit themselves to some worthy project. It's easy for an entire group to say, "We'll all help," "You can count on us," "As soon as you need our assistance we'll be there." What they really mean could be, "Someone else will do it. Of course, I won't be able to." Whenever you want to make certain that something will really be taken care of, get a commitment from a person who has the courage to say, "I'll do it."

Feel pleasure when you pay off debts.

וידבר אל עפרון באזני עם הארץ לאמר אך אם אתה לו שמעני נתתי כסף
השדה קח ממני ואקברה את מתי שמה. (בראשית כ"ג י"ג)

"AND [Avraham] SPOKE TO EFRON IN THE EARS OF THE PEOPLE OF
THE LAND, SAYING, IF YOU WILL BUT LISTEN TO ME, I WANT TO
GIVE THE MONEY FOR THE LAND, TAKE IT FROM ME AND I WILL
BURY MY DEAD THERE." (*Braishis* 23:13)

Rashi comments on the word *nasati* (which implies that
Avraham already gave the money although he merely said that he
wanted to give it), Avraham said to Efron, "The money is
completely ready for you. I wish that I had already given it to you."

The Torah contrasts Avraham's attitude towards money with
Efron's. Efron had a strong desire for money and was very exacting
to get a high price for his land even though he spoke of his
generosity. Avraham, on the other hand, was eager to pay his debt
before it was actually due. He did not want to keep money that was
not his even for a very short while. Therefore he said, "I wish I had
already given it." (*Ramat Shmuel*)

There are some people who keep procrastinating when it comes
to paying back debts or paying for an item they have bought. They
are basically honest and would never think of cheating anyone. But
they find it extremely difficult to part with their money. Therefore
they keep pushing off returning money that is due to others. Learn
from Avraham to feel pleasure and joy when you pay off a debt.

A young man in Bnai Brak used to type the handwritten
manuscripts of Rabbi Yaakov Yisroel Kanievsky to prepare them
for publication in the *Kehilos Yaakov* series. Late one winter night,
the typist heard a knock on his door, and found the Steipler
standing there. The young man was taken aback - did he make
some serious typing error?

"I came to pay you for today's work," said the Steipler. "You left the papers at my house when I wasn't home, so I came now."

"But I specifically told you when I accepted the job that it was not necessary for you to pay me right away."

"True," said the Steipler, "you wanted to be sure that I wouldn't transgress the prohibition against delaying payment to a worker overnight; but what about the positive commandment I have of paying a worker on the same day?" (*The Jewish Observer*, Nov., 1985)

Learn to understand the true meaning of what others say.

וישמע אברהם אל עפרון וישקל אברהם לעפרן את הכסף אשר דבר באזני
בני חת ארבע מאות שקל כסף עבר לסחר. (בראשית כ"ג ט"ז)

Efron agreed to give the Mearas Hamachpailah as the burial site for Sarah to Avraham, and after several exchanges:

"AND AVRAHAM HEARD EFRON. AND AVRAHAM WEIGHED FOR EFRON THE SILVER WHICH HE SPOKE ABOUT IN THE EARS OF THE BNAI CHAIS, FOUR HUNDRED SHEKELS OF SILVER THAT MERCHANTS USED." (*Braishis* 23:16)

On the words, "And Avraham heard," the Rashbam commented, "A hint is sufficient to the wise man."

Efron spoke as if he were a generous man. He spoke to Avraham with the greatest respect. He ostensibly offered him the burial site free of charge. He mentioned, however, in passing, "The four hundred shekels that one might usually pay for this is nothing between friends. Your friendship is more precious than money. Take it without payment." (see Rashi and Rashbam to verse 15)

But Avraham took the hint. He was perceptive and realized that Efron did not really want to give the land for nothing. It might seem to a naive bystander that Efron only mentioned the sum of money as an aside, that it was just a passing remark of no significance. But Avraham "heard," and with his well-developed intuition understood Efron's real intentions. He responded to Efron's inner wishes and not to his superficial words.

This ability to differentiate between what someone says and what he really means is an attribute that we must develop. For many areas of spiritual growth it is essential.

A few examples: Someone makes a belittling remark about something he just accomplished. The person would really appreciate a kind word. He might be uncertain about the quality of what he did and wants reassurance. This encouragement could be beneficial in motivating him for further accomplishment. If you really "hear" him, you will say those kind words.

You ask someone if he needs your help. "No, I can do it myself. It's not so difficult," he might say. Taking his words at their face value you might just walk away. But if you are perceptive, you will know that he really needs your help. But he is either too shy or too embarrassed to directly ask you. Learn to be perceptive to realize when your help is needed and really welcomed.

A person might be very busy right now. You would like to take up some of his time about a matter that is not really so important to you. When you ask him if you are disturbing him, he replies, "Not too much. I can always stay up late tonight to finish what needs to be done." Perhaps he can really afford to give you the time. On the other hand, he might be fervently wishing you wouldn't impose on him right now. It's very difficult for him to take off any time today. Learn to "hear" with an awareness of what a person is hinting at.

By gaining this sensitivity and perceptiveness, you will be able to reach greater heights in the *mitzvah* of "Loving your fellow man."

The Steipler used to say in the name of the Chazon Ish that when someone came to speak with him about a number of topics, he knew that as a rule the last thing they spoke about was the real reason they had come to consult him. Everything else was just to conceal this. (*Peninai Rabainu Hakehilos Yaakov*, p.119)

Accomplish something each and every day.

ואברהם זקן בא בימים. (בראשית כ"ד א')

"AND AVRAHAM WAS OLD, HE CAME WITH HIS DAYS." (*Braishis* 24:1)

There is an idea expressed by many scholars that Avraham came with all his days. Not one day in his life was wasted. Each and every day he accomplished something. (*Maayanah Shel Torah*)

Each day is an entirely new and different experience from any other. True, yesterday you might have done a lot, but you still have to make an effort to accomplish something today. At the beginning of each day, ask yourself, "What can I accomplish today?" At the end of each day, ask yourself, "What have I accomplished today?" If you cannot think of an answer to the latter question, make certain to do at least one small thing before you retire for the night. For example, study some Torah, write a *chesed* letter, make a list of goals, etc.

Be very careful to keep to the truth.

ותכל להשקתו ותאמר גם לגמליך אשאב עד אם כלו לשתת. (בראשית
כ"ד י"ט)

"AND SHE FINISHED GIVING HIM TO DRINK. AND SHE SAID, ALSO FOR YOUR CAMELS I WILL DRAW WATER UNTIL THEY FINISH DRINKING." (*Braishis* 24:19)

Note that Rivkah was careful to say that she would draw water for the camels, rather than saying she would give the camels to drink. Rivkah was meticulously careful not to say anything that would be untrue. Therefore she said she would draw water, as if to say, "I don't know for sure if they will drink or not but I will draw water for them. If they want to, they can drink." (Abarbanel)

Rabbi Shmuel Walkin added that we see here how careful we should be to keep away from saying anything untrue. He cites as an example Rabbi Refael of Bershid who was always very careful to refrain from saying anything that was untrue. When it was raining outside and he came into his house and was asked if it was still raining, he would reply: "When I was outside it was raining." He didn't want to say explicitly that it was raining now because perhaps after he came into the house the rain had stopped. (*Ramat Shmuel*)

This might seem to be very minor and inconsequential. But if a person is careful with keeping to the truth in such instances, he will definitely be careful in more important matters. On the other hand, if a person is careless with the truth he can even be tempted to lie in major ways.

TOLDOS

Do not rationalize your faults by blaming others for them.

ויהי יצחק בן ארבעים שנה בקחתו את רבקה בת בתואל הארמי מפדן
ארם אחות לבן הארמי לו לאשה. (בראשית כ"ה כ')

"AND YITZCHOK WAS FORTY YEARS OLD WHEN HE TOOK RIVKAH,
THE DAUGHTER OF BESUAIL THE AROMITE, FROM PADAN AROM,
THE SISTER OF LAVAN THE AROMITE, FOR HIMSELF FOR A WIFE."
(*Braishis* 25:20)

Rashi raises the question that the information in this verse about
Rivkah's background seems superfluous. The Torah has already
stated that Rivkah was the daughter of Besuail, the sister of Lavan,
and was from Padan Arom. The answer, says Rashi, is that this is
to let us know the praise of Rivkah. She was the daughter of an evil
person, the sister of an evil person, and lived in a community of evil
people. Nevertheless, she did not learn from their evil behavior.

Many people try to excuse their faults by blaming others as the
cause of their behavior. "It's not my fault I have this bad trait, I
learned it from my father and mother." "I'm not to blame for this
bad habit since all my brothers and sisters do it also." "Everyone in
my neighborhood does this or does not do that, so how could I be
any different?" They use this as a rationalization for failing to
make an effort to improve.

We see from Rivkah that regardless of the faulty behavior of
those in your surroundings, you have the ability to be more
elevated. Of course, it takes courage and a lot of effort to be
different. The righteous person might be considered a

nonconformist and even rebellious by those in his environment whose standard of values are below his level. But a basic Torah principle is that we are responsible for our own actions. Pointing to others in your environment who are worse than you is not a valid justification for not behaving properly.

If you ever find yourself saying, "It's not my fault I did this. It's because of the way I was raised or because I learned it from so and so," change your focus to, "I'll make a special effort to improve in this area to overcome the tendency to follow in the footsteps of others."

Blaming others for your faults and saying that you cannot do anything to change them will be a guarantee that they will remain with you. Make a list of the negative traits you picked up from your early environment. Develop a plan of action to improve in those areas.

Keep a distance from negative influences.

ויתרצצו הבנים בקרבה. (בראשית כ"ה כ"ב)

The Torah states that when Rivkah was pregnant with Yaakov and Aisav: "AND THE CHILDREN STRUGGLED TOGETHER WITHIN HER." (*Braishis* 25:22)

Rashi cites the Sages who say that when Rivkah passed by the Torah study halls of Shaim and Aiver, Yaakov tried to come out. When she passed by places of idol worship Aisav tried to come out.

The question arises: We can understand why Aisav tried to go to places of idol worship. But what about Yaakov? Before one's birth an angel teaches him Torah, why was Yaakov anxious to leave such a wonderful teacher? From here we see, said Rabbi Chayim Soloveitchik of Brisk, that if one has to be with an evil person like Aisav it is preferable to give up even the opportunity to study with an angel.

We are influenced by our friends. It is crucial to keep a distance from someone who has a negative influence on you even if it means some personal loss.

Use your potentially negative tendencies in positive ways.

ויצא הראשון אדמוני כלו כאדרת שער ויקראו שמו עשו. (בראשית כ"ה כ"ה)

The Torah tells us about the birth of Aisav:
"AND THE FIRST CAME OUT RED, ALL OVER LIKE A HAIRY GARMENT; AND THEY CALLED HIS NAME AISAV." (*Braishis* 25:25)

The Midrash (*Braishis Rabbah* 63) relates that when Shmuel went to appoint David to be the king of Israel, he saw that David was *admoni*, that is, of ruddy complexion. He became very frightened and said, "He too will be a murderer like Aisav." The Almighty told Shmuel that there was no need to be afraid. When Aisav killed it was in cold blood, but David would only take a life to carry out the just decisions of the *Sanhedrin*.

We see from this Midrash that when someone has a basic personality tendency it is a reality of his nature that he will be what he truly is. But a person has free will to choose how this tendency will be manifested. Aisav's tendency towards bloodshed led him down an evil path. David, on the other hand, was a mighty warrior who would utilize his natural tendencies for elevated purposes.

This concept is expressed very clearly by the Vilna Gaon: "A person should not go completely against his nature even if it is bad, for he will not succeed. He should merely train himself to follow the straight path in accordance with his nature. For example, someone who has an inclination to spill blood should train himself to become a ritual slaughterer or a *mohel* (circumciser)." (*Even Shlaimah; The Vilna Gaon Views Life*, ch.1, p.1)

Master your traits to use what is appropriate in every situation.

ויעקב איש תם ישב אהלים. (בראשית כ"ה כ"ז)

"YAAKOV WAS A STRAIGHT PERSON WHO SAT IN TENTS [of study]."
(*Braishis* 25:27)

Rashi defines the word *tam* as a person who is not skilled in deceiving others. As is his heart so are his words.

Yaakov was not called a *tam*, but an *ish tam*. That is, he was a master over the trait of being a *tam*. He was totally honest, a man of great integrity. But in those situations when it was appropriate to use cunning strategy to accomplish something, he was able to do so.

This, said the Rebbe from Lublin, is the way we should be with all traits. A person needs to be the master over all of his traits. Even the most negative traits have situations when they are appropriate. As the Sages say, "Whoever is compassionate when he should be cruel will eventually be cruel when he should be compassionate." If a person fails to apply so-called negative traits in their proper times, he will end up applying them when it is wrong to do so. (*Maayanah Shel Torah*)

Work on internalizing the elevated thoughts that you talk about.

ויאהב יצחק את עשו כי ציד בפיו ורבקה אהבת את יעקב. (בראשית כ"ה כ"ח)

"AND YITZCHOK LOVED AISAV BECAUSE HE WAS A HUNTER IN HIS MOUTH." (*Braishis* 25:28)

Rabbi Eliyahu Eliezer Dessler cited the Ari, *z.l.*, that it is a mistake to think that Aisav was a complete hypocrite and just tried to deceive his father. If Yitzchok made an error there must have been good reason for such an error. The problem with Aisav was that he kept all his spirituality "in his mouth," without swallowing it. Therefore he asked such questions as, "How does one tithe salt?" This was an external matter and not something that would affect his inner being. He spoke spiritual words but did not become a spiritual person.

Therefore, said Rav Dessler, anyone who only speaks ethical and spiritual words without allowing them to penetrate his heart and soul is a colleague of the evil Aisav. (*Michtav Maieliyahua,* vol.1, pp.234-5)

The essence of an elevated person is to be totally integrated: the Torah ideals that one talks about must be part of his very being. There are many different levels along a continuum. Some people are unaware of how far they are from actually feeling what they say. Such a person can say he loves everyone deeply, but a perceptive person can tell that although he believes that he feels that way, in actuality he is very far from it. It is not sufficient to just repeat words like a parrot or a taperecorder. Whenever you learn a new idea, keep reviewing it until little by little it penetrates your soul and your words truly become a part of you.

Speak politely to everyone.

ויאמר עשו אל יעקב הלעיטני נא מן האדם האדם הזה. (בראשית כ"ה ל')

After Avraham died, Yaakov cooked lentil soup as a sign of mourning. Aisav came in from the field:
"AND AISAV SAID TO YAAKOV, PLEASE POUR ME FROM THIS RED THING." (*Braishis* 25:30)

Later in our portion (27:22) Rashi mentions that Yaakov always spoke politely and said *na*, please. Aisav, however, always spoke in a rough manner to his father.

Even though Aisav excelled in honoring his father, he still spoke to him in an insolent and arrogant manner. But we see here that when Aisav had a desire for food he spoke in a respectful manner and used the term *na*, please. This is the manner of people with faulty traits. Even though they constantly talk with *chutzpah*, when it comes to manipulating someone to fulfill their desires they speak softly and humbly. (Rabbi Shmuel Walkin; *Ramat Shmuel, Braishis,* p.125)

There are people who speak politely to their preferred customers in business but fail to speak respectfully to their family and other people. Be aware of how politely and respectfully you speak to someone when you are trying to influence him to help you obtain things you want. Then try to make that manner of speaking habitual.

If at first you do not succeed, keep trying.

ויחפרו עבדי יצחק בנחל וימצאו שם באר מים חיים. (בראשית כ"ו י"ט)

"AND THE SERVANTS OF YITZCHOK DUG IN THE VALLEY AND FOUND THERE A WELL OF FRESH WATER." (*Braishis* 26:19)

The Chofetz Chayim explained that the Torah elaborates on the wells that Yitzchok found to teach us that you should not give up in discouragement when you start something just because you run into difficulties. Do not despair. When Yitzchok dug and did not find water, he kept digging in other places until he finally found what he was seeking. When others quarreled with him and took over his wells, he still did not become discouraged. He continued his digging until he finally found a well with water that he was able to use in peace and he called the area Rechovot.

This, encouraged the Chofetz Chayim, is a practical lesson for all areas of our lives. This applies to spiritual and material matters; to Torah studies and to business. Be persistent when things do not work out at first the way you would wish them to. Especially when beginning to study Torah, do not give up if you find it difficult at first. (*Chofetz Chayim Al Hatorah*)

The reason many people fail to accomplish something is because they give up too soon. If you have the determination to keep trying, eventually you will succeed.

Do not allow the good that you do to conceal your faults.

ויהי עשו בן ארבעים שנה ויקח אשה. (בראשית כ"ו ל"ד)

"AND AISAV WAS FORTY YEARS OLD, AND HE TOOK A WIFE."
(*Braishis* 26:34)

Rashi cites the Midrash that Aisav was compared to a pig. For an animal to be kosher it needs to have split hooves and and to chew its cud. Since a pig does not chew its cud, it is unkosher even though it has split hooves. When a pig lies down, it sticks out its split hooves as if to say, "Look at me and see that I am pure." There are people who steal and deceive others but make an appearance of being kosher. So, too, Aisav used to capture women against their will. But when he was forty years old, he said, "When my father was forty years old he got married. I, too, will get married now."

Rabbi Yeruchem Levovitz used to say that this deception was not unique to Aisav. It is possible for a person to be entirely evil. Nevertheless, as soon as he does one good deed, he shows off to others. He even fools himself into thinking that he is now entirely good. Every person has aspects of this tendency. (*Daas Torah: Braishis*, p.170)

Make every effort to be aware of this tendency in yourself. Look out for your own inconsistencies.

Even if you must speak an untruth be careful to word your statement in the least dishonest way.

ויאמר יעקב אל אביו אנכי עשו בכרך. (בראשית כ"ז י"ט)

Yitzchok wanted to give the blessings of the birthright to Aisav. But Yaakov had already purchased it from Aisav. Following his mother Rivkah's advice Yaakov impersonated his brother and brought good food to his blind father. In answer to Yaakov's questions about his identity, he replied:

"AND YAAKOV SAID TO HIS FATHER, I AM AISAV YOUR FIRSTBORN." (*Braishis* 27:19)

Rashi comments that what Yaakov said was, "I am bringing you the food. Aisav is your firstborn." Yaakov only carried out this deception to fulfill the wishes of his mother, which he understood correctly to be the wishes of the Almighty. Nevertheless, he did everything he could to decrease the falsehood. Instead of saying an outright lie, he was very careful to speak in a manner that could be understood in two ways. This, concludes Rabbi Yeruchem Levovitz, is a practical lesson for us all. (*Daas Torah: Braishis*, p.173)

Honesty, in word, deed, and financial matters, was a hallmark of Rabbi Yaakov Kaminetzky's life. It is well-known that he refrained from eating *gebrochts* (*matzah* that had contact with any liquid) on Pesach, a custom not usually followed in his native Lithuania. One Pesach during his youth, he was visiting a family with standards of *kashrus* that were somewhat lower than his own. When invited to join them for supper, he declined, and not wanting to offend his host, he said that his custom was to refrain from eating *gebrochts*. So as not to be guilty of an untruth, he then and there accepted that restriction upon himself and kept it for the rest of his life. (Rabbi Nisson Wolpin, *The Jewish Observer*, May, 1986)

Be sensitive when you try to show someone that he made a mistake.

ויחרד יצחק חרדה גדלה עד מאד. (בראשית כ"ז ל"ג)

When Yitzchok found out that the son he gave the blessings to was Yaakov and not Aisav:
"YITZCHOK TREMBLED A GREAT TREMBLING, EXTREMELY MUCH." (*Braishis* 27:33)

Rabbi Chayim Shmuelevitz, the late Rosh Hayeshiva of Mir, cited the Sages who stated that Yitzchok experienced greater fear and anxiety at this moment than he did at the *akaidah*. There he was bound and ready to be killed with a sharp blade. From here we see, said Rav Chayim, that the realization that one made a mistake is the greatest of pains. This was not a one time mistake. Rather, Yitzchok realized that all the years he thought Aisav was more deserving than Yaakov he was in error. The anxiety experienced in the awareness of error is a powerfully painful emotion. (Heard from Rabbi Chayim Shmuelevitz)

This is important to keep in mind when you are trying to point out to someone his faults and mistakes. You might think, "It is so obvious that this person is wrong. As soon as I tell it to him he should admit it." But the reality is that admitting a mistake can be extremely painful. For this reason there is a strong tendency for people to deny their mistakes. If you sincerely want to help someone improve, it is crucial to be as tactful as possible. Do all that you can to decrease the amount of pain the person will experience. Refrain from saying outright, "You are wrong. Admit it!" Start out by saying, "It seems to me..." or "I might be mistaken but perhaps..." The more sensitive you are to the feelings of the person you are trying to influence, the more effective you will be.

Be aware of your motivations when thinking about doing something that is questionable.

ויאמר בא אחיך במרמה ויקח ברכתך. (בראשית כ"ז ל"ה)

When Aisav came to his father Yaakov for his blessing, Yaakov said to him: "YOUR BROTHER CAME 'BEMIRMAH' AND TOOK YOUR BLESSING." (*Braishis* 27:35)

Rashi defines the word *bemirmah*, which is usually defined as "with deception," to mean here "with wisdom."

Rabbi Yeruchem Levovitz commented that there are many actions whose labels are dependent on the motivation of the person doing them. If the intention is for the good, then the action is considered good. What in other instances might be deceitful is really wisdom in this case. The same is true for the opposite. If the intention behind the action is bad, the action is considered a falsehood and is labeled deception. Yaakov had only pure intentions and hence his behavior was considered positive. (*Daas Torah: Braishis*, p.174)

This concept illustrates the importance of a person's being honest with himself about his true motivations. At times a person can rationalize his dishonesty but deep down knows that he has negative motivations. When performing any action that is borderline, ask yourself what your real underlying reason is for doing it. Good intentions do not give one license to do something forbidden. (In Yaakov's situation there were factors that rendered his actions proper.) But many things you will have to do in life will be dependent on your inner thoughts. Learn to be honest with yourself and gain awareness of why you are doing what you are doing.

Once two people came to Rabbi Yosef Chayim, author of *Ben Ish Chai* for him to settle a financial dispute between them. The person who denied that he owed any money said that he was willing to make an oath that he was right. But Rav Yosef Chayim, who was very intuitive, perceived that this person was lying and was about to make a false oath. Therefore, he said to this person, "Do you think I will have you make an oath on a regular Torah scroll? I will have you make an oath on the *Shnai Luchos Habris*!" He told his assistant to immerse himself in a *mikvah* and then bring him the *Shnai Luchos Habris*. Upon hearing this the deceitful person became frightened. He thought that Rav Yosef Chayim was going to make him swear on the original Ten Commandments, not realizing that he was referring to the work of the Shaloh by this name. Immediately, the man cried out, "I'll pay what I owe," and he admitted that he originally had lied. (*Oros Maimizrach*, p.89)

Rav Yosef Chayim used a strategy that contained a misleading statement. But his entire purpose was to clarify the truth and in this situation was proper.

VAYAITZAI

Being in a yeshiva has major benefits even if one does not become a great scholar.

ויצא יעקב מבאר שבע וילך חרנה. (בראשית כ"ח י')

"AND YAAKOV WENT AWAY FROM BER SHEVA AND WENT TOWARDS CHARAN." (*Braishis* 28:10)

Commentators ask why the Torah tells us that Yaakov went away from Ber Sheva since we already know that he was there and if he traveled of course he left Ber Sheva (see Rashi). The *Bais Halevi* explains that Yaakov had two goals in mind with every step he took. His mother, Rivkah, realized that his life was in danger because of Aisav's anger and told him to flee from Ber Sheva. Yitzchok, his father, told him to travel to his uncle Lavan to find a wife. Therefore when Yaakov traveled, with every step he took he was both leaving the place where he was to fulfill his mother's command, and going towards the destination of his father's command.

The Steipler, Rabbi Yaakov Yisroel Kanievsky, commented on this that being in a yeshiva has two similar goals. One, to gain Torah knowledge and good character traits. That is, going to a yeshiva for the spiritual benefits one can gain there. Two, to go away from the negative influences that can be found outside a yeshiva environment. Therefore even if someone does not become a great scholar, he still gains much from being in a yeshiva. (*Birchas Peretz, Vayaitzai*)

Very often, if someone studying in a yeshiva does not feel that he is as successful in his Torah studies as he would wish, he might become discouraged. But by focusing on the benefits of the yeshiva to his general spiritual level, his stay in the yeshiva will have a positive effect on him in many ways.

Ultimately, whether a person feels positive about his being in a yeshiva will depend on his expectations of himself. If these expectations are not met, it can lead to lowered feelings and even despair. When I speak to people who feel this way, I frequently share with them a story I heard from Rabbi Shalom Schwadron.

In a certain synagogue in Jerusalem, Reb Shalom heard a person reading page after page of Talmud. From the way the person read the words, one could tell that he was unable to comprehend what he was reading. He stopped and started in the wrong places and could not tell the difference between what was a question and what was an answer.

Rabbi Schwadron approached the man and asked him what he was doing. The man replied, "You are right. I do not understand a word of what I am reading. Then why do I keep coming here to read the Talmud? A loyal patriot wants to know the names of the country's generals. Even though he might not know a thing about war strategy, at least if he knows the names of the generals, he has some feeling for what is going on, albeit a superficial one. Similarly, I want to know the names of the Almighty's generals. I might not understand a word of what anyone is saying. But at least I want to know the names of the famous Talmudic scholars."

I personally have never met anyone studying in a yeshiva who knew less than this person. Yet this man felt very positive about his accomplishment. Anyone studying should at least feel this man's pleasure.

Climb higher on the spiritual ladder each day by growing from life's challenges.

ויחלם והנה סלם מצב ארצה וראשו מגיע השמימה. (בראשית כ"ח י"ב)

"AND [Yaakov] HAD A DREAM AND IN HIS DREAM THERE WAS A LADDER STANDING ON THE GROUND AND ITS TOP REACHED THE HEAVENS." (*Braishis* 28:12)

The Chofetz Chayim cited the idea expressed by many commentators that the ladder Yaakov saw in his dream symbolizes the situation of every person in this world. There are two actions a person performs on a ladder. Either he goes up from the bottom to the top, or else he goes down from the top to the bottom. Each day in a person's life he faces new challenges. If he has the willpower and self-discipline to overcome those challenges, he goes up in his spiritual level. If, however, a person fails to exercise the necessary self-control, he lowers himself. This is our daily task, to climb higher every day. (*Toras Habayis*, ch.10)

There is no standing in one place. When challenges arise, you will either behave in an elevated manner and grow from the experience or you will fail. Learn to appreciate the daily challenges that face you. Every difficulty is a means of elevating yourself. Every time you overcome a negative impulse you grow as a person. When a person climbs a ladder, he feels his progress with each step. So too with your daily victories over your negative impulses. Feel your progress and you will have the motivation to continue climbing.

Whenever you see a ladder, let it serve as a reminder of Yaakov's ladder. When passing near a ladder ask yourself, "Am I presently climbing in my spiritual level or am I going down?" If you ever answer that you are going down, do not despair. Rather, strengthen yourself and start climbing from where you are.

Similarly, Rabbi Yisroel Salanter used to say that a person is like a bird. A bird has the ability to fly very high. But it must continually move its wings. If a bird stops flapping its wings, it will fall. Every person is similar. (cited in *Tnuas Hamussar*, vol.1, p.300)

When you see birds flying, let that serve as a reminder to you to make the necessary movements to raise yourself spiritually.

Yaakov's descendants will be triumphant in the end.

והיה זרעך כעפר הארץ. (בראשית כ"ח י"ד)

The Almighty told Yaakov in his dream:
"AND YOUR DESCENDANTS WILL BE LIKE THE DUST OF THE EARTH." (*Braishis* 28:14)

Everyone in the world tramples on the dust of the earth. But in the end the dust of the earth covers up every one of those people. This will be the history of the descendants of Yaakov, the Jewish people. There will be exile after exile, persecution after persecution. But in the end they will overcome in the days of the final redemption. (*Minchah Blulah*)

Keep checking your behavior to find ways to improve.

וייקץ יעקב משנתו ויאמר אכן יש השם במקום הזה ואנכי לא ידעתי. (בראשית כ"ח ט"ז)

"AND YAAKOV WOKE UP FROM HIS SLEEP, AND HE SAID, THE ALMIGHTY IS IN THIS PLACE AND I DID NOT KNOW IT." (*Braishis* 28:16)

Rashi explains that Yaakov said, "If I were to have realized the sanctity of this place I would not have slept here."

Yaakov was fleeing for his life from Aisav. He was penniless and prayed to the Almighty for just the basic necessities of food to eat and clothing to wear. The Almighty came to him in a dream and gave him a guarantee that He would watch over him and all would be well. When Yaakov awoke, his initial reaction could easily have been one of extreme joy and gratitude for this promise. But what was Yaakov's initial thought? He censured himself for sleeping at a sacred site. (Rabbi Yosef Hurwitz of Nevardok; cited in *Maayanah Shel Torah*)

A person whose main focus is self-improvement and a striving for perfection will always check over his behavior to see what needs correction. Keep asking yourself, "Have I made any mistakes?" When you do find a mistake, feel positive for the opportunity to correct the mistake for the future.

A word of caution. While self-criticism is a prerequisite for character improvement, one must be careful to have a healthy balance. Excessive self-condemnation will be extremely detrimental to one's well-being. You need to master an attitude of joy for doing good and then self-criticism will add to that joy. Every fault that is found and worked on will give you the pleasure of knowing that you are improving.

Rabbi Yosef Salant related in his eulogy on Rabbi Isser Zalman Meltzer that when Rabbi Meltzer was a student in Volozhin yeshiva someone told him that his Rebbe, Rabbi Chayim Soloveitchik of Brisk, had respect for him.

Rav Isser Zalman's response was, "If so, it is a sign that he notices I have great potential. But unfortunately I am not utilizing my potential. I have not reached the level that would be appropriate for me to reach if I would be doing all I can."

"Someone else in his place," Rabbi Yosef Salant added, "might become conceited if he were told that Rabbi Chayim Brisker had praised him. But Rav Isser Zalman utilized this as an opportunity for self-criticism." (*Bederech Aitz Hachayim*, vol.2, p.416)

Be sensitive to the emotional pain of others.

וישא את קלו ויבך. (בראשית כ"ט י"א)

When Yaakov saw his cousin Rochel for the first time:
"HE LIFTED UP HIS VOICE AND CRIED." (*Braishis* 29:11)

Why did Yaakov cry? Rashi cites two reasons. One, that he saw with divine inspiration that he would not be buried next to Rochel. Secondly, he felt pain that he came empty-handed. He said, "Eliezer, the servant of my grandfather, came with many gifts and I do not have anything to give her."

To many people both reasons for Yaakov's crying might seem to be overly sentimental. After death, if you are not buried next to someone, is this so tragic? And if you don't have any gifts to give, is that a reason for a grown man to cry? The answer is that a person with deep sensitivity will feel pain in such situations. Empathize with the pain of another person. Don't belittle someone's emotional suffering. Telling someone who feels deeply about something that might not bother you, "It's nothing" or "It's just a minor matter, why do you get so emotional about it?" will just add to his pain. If Yaakov could cry over such matters, they have significance and we should never look down at anyone for having such feelings. In general, the more sensitive someone is to his own emotional pain, the easier it will be for him to be compassionate towards someone else's suffering.

Do not allow yourself to be misled by an evil person.

ויהי כשמע לבן את שמע יעקב בן אחתו וירץ לקראתו ויחבק לו וינשק לו
ויביאהו אל ביתו ויספר ללבן את כל הדברים האלה. (בראשית כ״ט י״ג)

"AND IT WAS WHEN LAVAN HEARD ABOUT THE COMING OF YAAKOV THE SON OF HIS SISTER, AND HE RAN TO GREET HIM, AND HE HUGGED HIM AND HE KISSED HIM, AND HE BROUGHT HIM TO HIS HOUSE. AND [Yaakov] TOLD LAVAN ALL THAT HAD HAPPENED." (*Braishis* 29:13)

How would you describe Lavan's behavior towards Yaakov from reading this verse? It would appear to be an extremely warm and loving greeting by an uncle who was sincerely happy to see his nephew. But let us take a look at Rashi and see how the Sages in Midrash viewed Lavan's greeting.

"And he ran to greet him": Lavan assumed that Yaakov would be loaded with gifts since when Eliezer, their family's servant, came he brought along ten loaded camels. "And he hugged him": When Lavan didn't see anything, he said to himself that perhaps Yaakov had concealed gold under his garments and therefore he hugged him. "And he kissed him": Lavan said that perhaps Yaakov had diamonds hidden in his mouth and that is why he kissed him. Therefore Yaakov had to explain that he was fleeing for his life and was penniless.

We know how important it is to judge people favorably. But if someone is an evil person we are obligated to judge him unfavorably. Some people might find this rather harsh, but that is the reality: with evil people assume the worst. (Rabbi Yeruchem Levovitz; *Daas Torah: Braishis*, p.192)

We need to master the ability of seeing the good in the bad and the bad in the good. Then we need the wisdom to know when to use each ability. Judging an evil person on the side of merit is not a virtue but a fault. Failure to be on guard to protect yourself from a deceitful person can cause you and others much damage and heartache. There are some people who naively refuse to believe that there are people who do all that they can to cheat them. The way of Torah is to use wisdom to know when to assume negative motivations and when to judge people favorably. Unfortunately, too many people fail to judge others favorably when they really should. But the opposite extreme of believing everyone is considered in *Mishle* (14:15) to be the attribute of the fool.

When you realize the benefit of what you are getting, hard work becomes lighter.
Non-selfish love enables you to have patience.

ויעבד יעקב ברחל שבע שנים ויהיו בעיניו כימים אחדים באהבתו אתה. (בראשית כ"ט כ')

"AND YAAKOV WORKED FOR ROCHEL SEVEN YEARS, AND IT WAS IN HIS EYES AS A FEW DAYS IN HIS LOVE FOR HER." (*Braishis* 29:20)

The question arises: When someone has strong feelings of love for another person and has a deep passion to get married, even a short time seems subjectively to be much longer than it really is.

How could the time have seemed short for Yaakov?

The Malbim gives two answers. His first answer is that Yaakov loved Rochel so much that he thought she was worth working for many more than seven years. Therefore to work only seven years for such a wonderful person was really a bargain.

From this answer of the Malbim we see the principle that the difficulty experienced in any work that we do is totally subjective. It is based on your personal evaluation of the situation. Whenever you feel that you are gaining a lot, the work you do becomes much lighter in your eyes. Keep this in mind and you can lighten your burden by focusing on how you are gaining from what you are doing. This is especially so with the difficulties experienced in Torah studies and other spiritual pursuits.

The Malbim gives a second answer. Yaakov's love for Rochel was not simple passion. When a person feels deep passion, every day he has to wait seems to him like a year. But Yaakov loved her because of her good qualities and this would make her worthy of being the mother of the future Jewish people. Therefore the Torah states "in his love for her." A person whose love is based on his own passion really loves himself and not the object of his love. But when a person loves the good, he truly loves the good thing and not himself. Therefore the time seemed short because it was not selfish love.

Whenever you say that you love someone, be aware if it is a selfish or a non-selfish love. Selfish love is only a temporary state, non-selfish love is long-lasting. We find in our verse one way to test love to see if it is selfish or not. Are you willing to be patient for the sake of the other person? Selfish love is impatient. When there is true love even seven years can seem like just a few days.

The Alshich also addresses the question of the relativity of our experiencing time. As he puts it in his commentary, "When one is deeply in love, a few days feels as if it were a thousand years." The answer, the Alshich said, can be understood from a careful look at the order of the words in this verse.

The Torah states first that Yaakov worked for Rochel seven years. Afterwards the verse concludes that it was in Yaakov's eyes like just a few days because of his love for her. That is, once all the work was finished, Yaakov looked back at the time that he spent working for Rochel. Now that he was with Rochel he had great love for her and his intense positive feelings erased the pain of the waiting of the past.

The idea of the Alshich suggests a tool we can use when we are in a painful emotional situation in the present. Mentally take yourself to some time in the future and view the present from that perspective. This will give you a new outlook on your present situation. Whenever you feel impatient about time passing too slowly because you look forward to the future, imagine yourself already being in the future and looking back at the past.

Do not use sarcasm as a means of correcting others.

ויאמר לבן לא יעשה כן במקומנו לתת הצעירה לפני הבכירה. (בראשית כ"ט כ"ו)

Yaakov complained to Lavan that he deceived him by giving him Leah instead of Rochel:

"AND LAVAN SAID, IT IS NOT DONE IN OUR PLACE TO GIVE THE YOUNGER ONE BEFORE THE OLDER." (*Braishis* 29:26)

With these words Lavan included a subtle insult to Yaakov. He said, "In our place we always insist that the older one marry before the younger one. We are not like you who took away the rights of the firstborn from your older brother Aisav." (*Bais Halevi*)

This is the way a Lavan speaks. He uses sarcasm to attack others. If Lavan was sincerely concerned with censuring Yaakov, he should have spoken directly and to the point. A sarcastic remark just causes pain and is not the method of communication to use when you truly want to correct someone. Rarely does sarcasm motivate anyone to improve. Be aware of when you use sarcasm and eliminate it. When it is proper to correct someone, do it with tact and respect for the other person's feelings.

My late Rebbe, Rabbi Yosef Dov Soloveitchik, Rosh Hayeshiva

of Brisk in Jerusalem, explained. Lavan's reply to Yaakov as follows: Since in our place the oldest gets married first, you should have realized on your own that what I meant was for you to marry Leah and only then Rochel. This is the way of deceitful people. They claim that you are at fault for misunderstanding them. It is not their problem if you do not comprehend accurately.

Beware of people who continually claim that they were misunderstood. Yes, it might be a communication problem. But if it happens frequently, be on the alert for intentional deceit.

Be very careful not to cause friction between a married couple.

וירא השם כי שנואה לאה ויפתח את רחמה ורחל עקרה. (בראשית כ"ט ל"א)

"AND THE ALMIGHTY SAW THAT LEAH WAS HATED AND HE OPENED HER WOMB AND ROCHEL WAS BARREN." (*Braishis* 29:31)

From here, said Rabbi Yeruchem Levovitz, we see how careful we must be not to cause anyone emotional pain. Rochel's being loved by Yaakov caused him to have negative feelings towards Leah. This is not referring to literal hatred, but in comparison with the love and respect he felt towards Rochel it was considered negative feelings. Although Rochel did not do anything directly to cause Leah pain, she was still the cause and for this she suffered. (*Daas Torah: Braishis*, p.184)

Be careful not to make any derogatory comments to a husband about his wife or to a wife about her husband. A negative remark about someone's spouse might seem to you to be of little consequence. But it can easily lead to small amounts of resentment and animosity: touches of hatred. Even if you are mentioning the negative for constructive purposes, be very careful how you word what you say. You might have good intentions but you can cause much suffering.

Conversely, we can learn from here how great is the reward for people who praise a wife to her husband or a husband to his wife.

By increasing the love of one for the other you are helping their entire family. A word of caution: be certain that the praise will be taken by the spouse in a positive way. For example, praising a husband's or wife's generosity or kindheartedness may arouse resentment in a spouse who could view matters as a personal loss to him or herself.

Make an effort to perceive the pain of others.

ותהר לאה ותלד בן ותקרא שמו ראובן כי אמרה כי ראה השם בעניי כי עתה יאהבני אישי. ותהר עוד ותלד בן ותאמר כי שמע השם כי שנואה אנכי ויתן לי גם את זה ותקרא שמו שמעון. (בראשית כ"ט ל"ב ל"ג)

"AND LEAH CONCEIVED AND GAVE BIRTH TO A SON AND SHE CALLED HIS NAME REUVEN, BECAUSE SHE SAID THE ALMIGHTY HAS SEEN MY AFFLICTION, FOR NOW MY HUSBAND WILL LOVE ME. AND SHE CONCEIVED AGAIN AND SHE GAVE BIRTH TO A SON. AND SHE SAID, FOR THE ALMIGHTY HAS HEARD THAT I AM HATED, AND HE GAVE ME ALSO THIS. AND SHE CALLED HIS NAME SHIMON." (*Braishis* 29:32,33)

In these two verses we find two thoughts. One that the Almighty saw affliction and the other that He heard it. (*Daas Torah: Braishis*, p.184)

Since we have a *mitzvah* to emulate the Almighty, we need to learn from here to become more sensitive to the emotional pain of others. People express their pain through words and through variations in their facial expressions and body language. To hear someone's pain, be aware of both the content and the tone of voice of another person. The more perceptive you become, the more you will notice slight nuances in tone of voice that reflect painful feelings. Also, learn to see someone's pain even if he does not express it verbally. Be aware of slight changes in a person's facial expression, skin color, breathing rate, muscle tonus, etc., that serve as an announcement of emotional suffering. The more you are able to notice pain, the more *chesed* you will be able to do.

Rabbi Yisroel of Rizhin said, "A true *Tzadik* needs to have the same quality as quicksilver. As soon as there is a change of temperature the quicksilver immediately reflects it. So too, one needs to be aware immediately of a lack of peace of mind in other people." (*Niflaos Yisroel*, p.39)

Do whatever you can to make shalom bayis (helping couples to have a peaceful relationship).

ותהר עוד ותלד בן ותאמר עתה הפעם ילוה אישי אלי כי ילדתי לו שלשה
בנים על כן קרא שמו לוי. (בראשית כ"ט ל"ד)

"AND [Leah] CONCEIVED AGAIN, AND SHE GAVE BIRTH TO A SON, AND SHE SAID, THIS TIME MY HUSBAND WILL ACCOMPANY ME FOR I HAVE GIVEN BIRTH TO THREE SONS. THEREFORE HE CALLED HIS NAME LEVI." (*Braishis* 29:34)

I heard from Rabbi Chayim Shmuelevitz, the late Rosh Hayeshiva of Mir, that from here we see the importance of making peace between husband and wife. With the birth of Levi, Yaakov now accompanied Leah; there was a close relationship between them. The tribe of Levi was chosen to be the tribe whose members would serve in the Holy Temple. The making of peace between husband and wife sanctified all the descendants of Levi. Whenever the opportunity arises, do what you can to help married couples overcome difficulties between them.

A husband and wife came to the Maggid of Koznitz and said that they had a serious quarrel that was threatening their marriage. Upon questioning them for the source of their difficulties, the Maggid found the following disagreement to be the central factor. The husband complained that Friday nights when he came home after prayers, he was famished and wanted to eat kugel at the start of the meal. But his wife insisted on serving everything else first and when she finally served the kugel he was no longer hungry and it seemed to have no taste. The wife, however, was adamant: "There was a family custom in my father's house that kugel was served at the end of the meal. A custom becomes law. I refuse to deviate from our custom regardless of the consequences."

Thinking of a strategy to satisfy both their wishes, the Kuznitzer Maggid told the wife, "From now on make two kugels each *Shabbos*. Serve one at the beginning of the meal to satisfy your husband, and serve one at the end of the meal to comply with your custom." (*Hamaggid Maikoznitz*)

This pattern is important to remember when trying to settle quarrels. Many people have a tendency to decide who is right and who is wrong. It is preferable to find ways to satisfy the positions of both parties of a dispute and by this means bring about a peaceful settlement. Ask yourself, "What is important to this person and what is important to that person? In what creative ways can both positions be compatible?"

Rabbi Moshe Feinstein was a model of devotion to his family. To a young man who complained that his wife was annoyed if he did not call her during the day, he responded with amazement, "But of course you should call her during the day. I always call my Rebbetzin." (Rabbi Nosson Scherman, *The Jewish Observer*, Oct. 1986, p.27)

When Rabbi Nochum Perchovitz, Rosh Yeshiva of Mir, had money to give to his students, he frequently did so personally and not through a messenger. Once he came to the home of one of the married students of his yeshiva to hand over some money to him. The student was very surprised to see Rabbi Perchovitz and said, "The Rosh Yeshiva could have found me in the yeshiva or could have sent the money with a messenger. Why did the Rebbe personally take the trouble to come to my house?"

"What does it bother you," replied Rav Nochum with a smile, "if your wife will know how important you are?" (*Yetaid Neaman*, 17 Kislev, 5747, p.6)

There is no escaping normal human emotions.

ותרא רחל כי לא ילדה ליעקב ותקנא רחל באחתה. (בראשית ל' א')

Leah had children, while her sister Rochel did not:
"AND ROCHEL SAW THAT SHE WAS NOT BEARING ANY CHILDREN
TO YAAKOV. AND ROCHEL ENVIED HER SISTER." (*Braishis* 30:1)

My father, Rabbi Shmuel Pliskin, *z.t.l.*, used to say, "'And
Rochel envied her sister' is a verse in the Torah." Regardless of
how great one is there is no escaping normal human emotions.
Even though, as Rashi explains, there was a spiritual dimension to
Rochel's being envious of Leah's good deeds, still there was the
trait of envy. We must learn to be sensitive to the potential envy of
another person. Never assume that anyone will be so free of envy
that you can say whatever you want in front of him. Avoid
boasting or praising someone in the presence of a person who
might feel envious. For example, if someone is poor, do not
needlessly tell him about how much money you just made or about
an acquaintance who is financially successful. Whenever you know
that a person is missing something that is important to him, think
twice before mentioning that someone has what he lacks.

This also should lessen the guilt feelings of anyone who feels
envious of another person. Envy is painful in itself. When guilt
feelings are added, it can make the pain very tortuous. While we
need to develop attitudes that will eliminate the destructive trait of
envy (see chapter seventeen of *Gateway to Happiness*), realize that
it is normal to feel envious: "It is a verse in the Torah."

**Be aware of the response you want from another person and
then devise a strategy to elicit that response.**

ותרא רחל כי לא ילדה ליעקב ותקנא רחל באחתה ותאמר אל יעקב הבה
לי בנים ואם אין מתה אנכי. ויחר אף יעקב ברחל. (בראשית ל' א-ב)

"AND ROCHEL SAW THAT SHE WAS NOT BEARING ANY CHILDREN

TO YAAKOV AND ROCHEL ENVIED HER SISTER. AND SHE SAID TO
YAAKOV: GIVE ME CHILDREN. AND IF NOT I AM AS IF DEAD. AND
YAAKOV BECAME ANGRY AT ROCHEL." (*Braishis* 30:1,2)

Rabbi Simcha Bunim of Parshischo offered the following
interpretation of Rochel's words to Yaakov: Since Rochel saw that
because Leah was hated she merited having children, she envied
that hatred. Rochel therefore purposely said things to Yaakov to
arouse his anger. When she too would be hated, she also would
have children. The second verse tells us that she was successful in
her goal, and Yaakov became angry at her. (*Kol Simchah*, cited in
Maayanah Shel Torah)

This is a very important principle in communicating with others:
the meaning of your communication is the results you get. If you
intend to have a peaceful conversation with someone and you
make him angry, you definitely made some mistake. When
someone is irritated with you and insults you, what is the best
technique for ensuring that he will continue insulting you? The
answer, of course, is to raise your voice at him and insult him back.
How unfortunate it is that people who wish someone would
become friendlier and kinder speak in a manner that will bring out
aggressiveness. It is crucial to know what response you want to
elicit from another person. If you are ever in a situation in which
you wish to elicit an angry response, as Rochel did in this instance,
you might find it necessary to talk in a manner that will bring out
that response. But in daily life situations it is very rarely
appropriate. Since in most instances you want others to talk to you
calmly and kindly, make certain to talk to them in a manner that
will elicit such a response.

In spiritual matters have the persistence to continually try.

ותאמר רחל נפתולי אלקים נפתלתי עם אחתי גם יכלתי ותקרא שמו
נפתלי. (בראשית ל' ח')

Bilhah, Rochel's servant, gave birth:

"AND ROCHEL SAID, WITH GREAT WRESTLINGS HAVE I WRESTLED WITH MY SISTER, AND I HAVE PREVAILED, AND SHE CALLED HIS NAME NAFTALI." (*Braishis* 30:8)

Rashi explains that the name Naftali comes from the word meaning being stubborn. Rabbi Yeruchem Levovitz said that from here we learn two things. First, that in spiritual matters it is proper for a person to be stubborn and even obstinate. Rochel saw that the Almighty didn't want to give her children. She did not accept this but fought with all her strength to achieve her wishes. Secondly, we see that in spiritual matters when a person tries to elevate himself and is determined to accomplish this with all his will, he will eventually be successful. When you try to study Torah or engage in other Torah projects, you will usually find obstacles in your path. Do not allow them to stop you. Rather, use the difficulties as a cue to try even harder. When you keep on trying, you will eventually be successful.

Rav Yeruchem adds that when we hear about a great *tzadik* such as the Chofetz Chayim, we usually think that everything came very easily to him. But the truth is that he attained greatness only through perseverance. Our weakness is that we are not persistent enough. Know that if you want to grow at all, you need to be stubborn in your efforts. (*Daas Torah: Braishis*, pp.186-8)

Stubbornness can easily be a negative trait. In interpersonal relationships flexibility is crucial, but in spiritual matters tenacity and persistence are necessary. Unfortunately many people are flexible in spiritual matters and inflexible when it comes to dealing with other people. By using each trait in the right way you will accomplish much while avoiding the potentially negative aspects of that trait.

Learn to read facial expressions in order to improve your understanding of other people.

וירא יעקב את פני לבן והנה איננו עמו כתמול שלשום. (בראשית ל"א ב')

"AND YAAKOV SAW THE FACE OF LAVAN, AND BEHOLD HE WAS NOT WITH HIM AS PREVIOUSLY." (*Braishis* 31:2)

From this verse we see the importance of being able to notice the emotional state of another person from the expressions on his face. Lavan did not say any unkind words to Yaakov. Nothing verbal was communicated that would imply that Lavan felt resentment or animosity towards Yaakov. Nevertheless, Yaakov was sensitive to the look on Lavan's face.

Especially with people you see on a regular basis, take note of how they look when they are pleased with someone. Then take note of how they look when they are displeased with another person. By gaining the sensitivity to detect these differences you will be able to tell when something you said or did offended him or hurt his feelings.

From here we can also see how careful we must be with our own facial expressions when talking to people. This is especially so when the person you are talking to is very sensitive and his feelings are hurt easily. You might be thinking of something unpleasant totally unrelated to the person you are speaking with. But the person might feel that you are upset with him and this could cause him emotional pain. As cited in *Love Your Neighbor*, my Rebbe, Rabbi Chayim Mordechai Katz, used to stress how careful we should be not to cause any suffering to another person even by a grimace. When you master the ability to read facial expressions you will be able to do more *chesed* and will be able to avoid causing others pain.

I once heard from the son of a famous Rosh Yeshiva that his father was always extremely careful to smile and look very happy when he greeted someone. He started making an effort to do this after an incident when he was preoccupied when he greeted a certain person.

"Don't you like me any more? Have I done something wrong?" the man asked him.

"Of course you haven't done anything wrong," replied the Rosh Yeshiva. "What gave you the impression that I have anything against you?"

"You had a frown on your face when I greeted you," the man said.

After reassuring the man that the frown had nothing to do with him, the Rosh Yeshiva resolved from that moment on to always be careful to have a pleased look on his face when talking to others.

A person who threatens others reveals his character.

למה נחבאת לברח ותגנב אתי ולא הגדת לי ואשלחך בשמחה ובשרים בתף ובכנור. ולא נטשתני לנשק לבני ולבנתי עתה הסכלת עשו. יש לאל ידי לעשות עמכם רע ואלקי אביכם אמש אמר אלי לאמר השמר לך מדבר עם יעקב מטוב עד רע. (בראשית ל״א כ״ז-כ״ט)

When Lavan caught up with Yaakov, Lavan said to him:
"WHY DID YOU FLEE AWAY SECRETLY AND ROB ME, AND DID NOT TELL ME THAT I WOULD BE ABLE TO SEND YOU AWAY WITH JOY AND WITH SONGS, WITH MUSICAL INSTRUMENTS? AND YOU DID NOT ALLOW ME TO KISS MY SONS AND DAUGHTERS? YOU HAVE DONE FOOLISHLY. IT IS IN THE POWER OF MY HAND TO DO EVIL WITH YOU. BUT THE G-D OF YOUR FATHER LAST NIGHT SAID TO ME SAYING, WATCH OUT FROM SPEAKING WITH YAAKOV FROM GOOD TO BAD." (*Braishis* 31:27,28,29)

These three verses of Lavan's speech to Yaakov are fascinating. We see Lavan's opening remark giving us a positive picture of the man, until he finally reveals his true colors. "Why didn't you tell me you were planning to leave?" asks Lavan. "I love my daughters and grandchildren so much that I would have wanted to kiss them goodbye before they left. I would have gotten a band and made a farewell party for you. Look what a loving person I am!"

But then Lavan throws in a veiled threat. "You know I could have harmed you." This is the language of power. A truly loving person is forgiving. When you threaten to physically abuse someone for not acting towards you the way you would have wished, you reveal your inner self. A power-hungry person wants control. He doesn't want anyone doing anything independently. Verbally he tells you that he loves you and cares about you. But unselfish love contains no threats. As soon as a person insinuates that he will cause someone else problems for not acting the way he wants him to act, it reveals cruelty which is beneath the surface.

When you claim that you love someone, be aware of your reactions when that person does something against your wishes. You have every right to be assertive and express your wishes. But if you become violent or even threaten violence, it shows that you care about yourself and not the other person.

When you have to use cunning return to total integrity as soon as possible.

וילך וישב לבו למקמו. ויעקב הלך לדרכו. (בראשית ל"ב א־ב)

"AND LAVAN RETURNED TO HIS PLACE. AND YAAKOV WENT ON HIS WAY." (*Braishis* 32:1,2)

Rabbi Moshe Leib of Sassov explained that when Yaakov dwelt with Lavan, at times he had to use cunning strategy to avoid being deceived himself. But as soon as Lavan returned to his place and left him once and for all, "Yaakov went on his way." He once more returned to the trait of complete honesty which was integral to Yaakov's nature.

At times you might find yourself having to resort to cunning because of special circumstances. But there is a great danger that you might continue using this harmful trait even when it is not appropriate. Make certain to return to total honesty as soon as possible.

When the Chazon Ish heard someone say to another person, "Your words are a lie," he corrected him, "That is not the way to speak." Rather say, "Your words are not the truth." Even the word "lie" was something to keep a distance from. (*P'air Hador*, vol.3, p.20)

VAYISHLACH

Once an argument is over don't say anything to arouse it again.

וישלח יעקב מלאכים לפניו אל עשו אחיו. (בראשית ל"ב ד')

"AND YAAKOV SENT MESSENGERS BEFORE HIM TO AISAV HIS BROTHER." (*Braishis* 32:4)

The *Midrash* (*Braishis Rabbah* 75:2) censures Yaakov for sending these messengers. Aisav had already calmed down about Yaakov's taking the blessings from their father Yitzchok and was involved in his own matters. By sending messengers Yaakov started up with Aisav and aroused his anger.

This is a very important principle for two people who were involved in a quarrel. Once the matter is past, don't say anything to the other person that would remind him of the matter. By bringing up the issue when it is not necessary to do so, you will cause a new quarrel that is avoidable. If you were ever in a heated argument with another person and are now getting along peacefully, don't say anything to the effect of, "Remember when you said or did..." Many people spend numerous hours of their lives engaged in quarrels and arguments about matters that no longer make any practical difference. Arguments should be forgotten, not remembered.

Good communication brings closeness between people.

ויצו אתם לאמר כה תאמרון לאדני לעשו כה אמר עבדך יעקב עם לבן
גרתי ואחר עד עתה. (בראשית ל"ב ה')

"AND [Yaakov] COMMANDED [his messengers] SAYING: THIS IS WHAT
YOU SHOULD SAY TO MY MASTER TO AISAV. THIS IS WHAT YOUR
SERVANT YAAKOV SAID: WITH LAVAN I HAVE DWELT AND HAVE
BEEN DELAYED UNTIL NOW." (*Braishis* 32:5)

The *Ohr Hachayim* explains that Yaakov's intention in relating
this to Aisav was to show his brotherly love for him. When two
people love each other, one shares with the other all the things that
happened to him. This includes both the good things and the
misfortunes. Sharing this information is a sign of closeness and for
this reason Yaakov told Aisav about both the good and the bad
that he had experienced.

This is an important principle for someone who wants to become
close to another person. When you open up and share your life
experiences with another person, it helps you develop friendship
and closeness. It is possible to be acquainted with someone for
many years without really knowing him. When you share personal
information with others, you gain an emotional connection. While
one must be careful not to relate information that would constitute
loshon hora or that could cause difficulties, a deep level of
communication is a prerequisite for closeness.

Do good deeds with great enthusiasm.

עם לבן גרתי. (בראשית ל"ב ה')

Yaakov said: "I HAVE LIVED WITH LAVAN." (*Braishis* 32:5)

Rashi comments that the word *garti* in this verse has the
numerical value of 613, the same as the *Taryag Mitzvos* (613
commandments). Yaakov said, "I dwelt with Lavan and kept the
commandments, and I did not learn from his bad deeds."

The simplest meaning of this statement is that even someone on the high level of Yaakov could have been influenced negatively and it was a real accomplishment not to have been.

Rabbi Elchonon Wasserman, however, quotes his Rebbe the Chofetz Chayim that this can be understood to mean that Yaakov was finding fault with himself. When Lavan did something improper, he did it with much enthusiasm and energy. Yaakov said about himself that his zeal in doing good did not reach the same level as Lavan's when he did bad.

The Chofetz Chayim used to say that today we need to learn from the enthusiasm and energy of the spiritual descendants of Lavan. (*Kovetz Maimorim*, p.97)

Whenever you see someone running to do something improper, ask yourself if you run to do good as fast as he. Whenever you see someone having joy in doing things for his personal pleasure, try to experience that joy when you engage in spiritual pursuits.

Personal power over oneself frees one from envying others who have power.

ויהי לי שור וחמור צאן ועבד ושפחה ואשלחה להגיד לאדני למצא חן בעיניך. (בראשית ל"ב ו')

Yaakov sent gifts to Aisav with messengers and he told them to say: "AND I HAVE OXEN AND DONKEYS, SHEEP AND MENSERVANTS AND WOMANSERVANTS, AND I HAVE SENT TO TELL MY MASTER, THAT I MIGHT FIND FAVOR IN YOUR EYES." (*Braishis* 32:6)

Yaakov was not afraid that he would arouse envy in Aisav by telling him that he had wealth. For Aisav the only thing that mattered was having power over other people and as we see he had four hundred men with him. Yaakov's wealth was not envied by Aisav because there was no power with it. (*Haamek Dovor*)

This can give us an insight for overcoming envy. When one has power, one will not envy another person who lacks it. As we find in *Pirke Avos* (4:1) the greatest power is having power over one's own impulses and tendencies. Therefore if you work on mastery of self-discipline, you will have no need to envy anyone else. You will have power over yourself and the feelings of strength this will give you will be so fulfilling that you will be free from feeling envious of others.

Taking care of your welfare is a mitzvah.

ויאמר אם יבוא עשו אל המחנה האחת והכהו והיה המחנה הנשאר
לפליטה. (בראשית ל"ב ט')

Before encountering Aisav, Yaakov divided all that he had into two camps: "AND [Yaakov] SAID: IF AISAV WILL COME TO ONE CAMP AND SMITE IT, THE REMAINING CAMP WILL BE SAVED." (*Braishis* 32:9)

Rashi comments on this that the reason the remaining camp would be saved is because Yaakov said that if necessary I will fight against Aisav. Yaakov prepared himself with three strategies to deal with Aisav: gifts to appease him, prayer, and war.

We see from this, said Rabbi Yeruchem Levovitz, that Yaakov did not rely on his righteousness and he made every human effort possible. This is an important principle: the forefathers kept to natural laws in dealing with life situations. Ultimately the laws of nature are the Almighty's laws because this is the way He set up the world. This is a difficult task: to do everything that is in your own power and still to realize that all that occurs is due to the Almighty's will.

Rabbi Levovitz illustrated this thought by relating something he personally witnessed about the Chofetz Chayim. A grandson of the Chofetz Chayim passed away and there was great mourning and sorrow in the Chofetz Chayim's family; everyone sat and cried. The Chofetz Chayim called someone over and said that food should be served to the entire family. "The funeral will take a long time and the burial will be very late," said the Chofetz Chayim. "Therefore everyone must be sure to eat right now."

This, commented Rav Yeruchem, is the behavior of a great

person like the Chofetz Chayim. He was careful to observe the natural laws of eating. He viewed them as an obligation and a *mitzvah* like every other *mitzvah* in the Torah. There is an obligation to mourn and cry over the death of a loved one, but the order of eating and rules of health must still be kept. The Rambam in *Hilchos Daios* compiled a list of rules for guarding one's health. This is included in his monumental work on Torah law, because taking care of one's health and welfare is a *mitzvah* that we observe in all its numerous details. (*Daas Torah: Braishis*, p.204)

Have the confidence to deal from strength with wrongdoers.

קטנתי מכל החסדים ומכל האמת אשר עשית את עבדך וגו' הצילני נא
מיד אחי מיד עשו. (בראשית ל"ב י"א י"ב)

Before his encounter with Aisav, Yaakov said to the Almighty:
"I AM SMALL FROM ALL THE KINDNESSES AND FROM ALL THE TRUTH WHICH YOU HAVE DONE FOR YOUR SERVANT... SAVE ME FROM THE HAND OF MY BROTHER, FROM THE HAND OF AISAV." (*Braishis* 32:11,12)

Yaakov states here that he is small and unworthy of all the kindnesses that have come his way. On what basis then does Yaakov request to be saved from Aisav? The answer is that Yaakov said, "Look Almighty, I am very small. But in comparison with my brother Aisav I am very worthy. Therefore I can have the courage to ask you to save me." (*Atzai Levonon*)

This balance is very important. We must realize how small we are when it comes to relating to the Almighty Himself. This thought will enable us to remain humble. Yet when it comes to dealing with people who do much wrong, we need the strength and courage to stand up to them. Don't allow the virtue of humility to render you submissive to someone who is unjust or cruel.

Make past enemies into friends.

הצילני נא מיד אחי מיד עשו. (בראשית ל"ב י"ב)

Yaakov prayed to the Almighty:
"SAVE ME FROM THE HAND OF MY BROTHER, FROM THE HAND OF
AISAV." (*Braishis* 32:12)

Yaakov repeated the words "from the hand of" twice. The
reason for this repetition in his prayer is because when a brother
turns into an enemy, he becomes a much more dangerous enemy
than a stranger. (This concept, based on *Mishle* 27:6, is found in
Tosfos to *Taanis* 20a.) (*Megaleh Amukos*; cited in *Biurai
Hamekubalim Beniglah*)

Tosfos (*ibid.*) adds that just as a one-time beloved friend is the
worst enemy, so too when two enemies become friends it is the
strongest of friendships.

When you have difficulties in getting along with someone, don't
think that just because at present you do not like each other it must
last. On the contrary, if you will be able to overcome the animosity
between you, the former negative feelings can be transformed into
extremely positive feelings. On the international scene we have seen
countries who have fought bitter wars against each other finally
make peace and become close allies. This should serve as a lesson
for us in making peace with individuals who have quarreled with us
in the past.

Rabbi Meir Yechiel of Ostrovtzah saved the Jews of his city from
a pogrom during the First World War. The Austro-German army
left the city and the Russian army entered. In other places the Jews
suffered greatly when the Russian soldiers came in. Rav Meir
Yechiel called a meeting of the notables of his city and told them
about his plan to greet the Russian soldiers as liberators. They
would give out food and cigarettes to the soldiers and develop a
friendly relationship with them. This is what they did and the
soldiers acted in a very friendly manner towards the Jewish
population of the city. (*Rebbe Meir Yechiel Maiostrovtzah*, p.44)

Make your happiness in life dependent only on yourself.

ויותר יעקב לבדו. (בראשית ל"ב כ"ה)

"AND YAAKOV REMAINED ALONE." (*Braishis* 32:25)

The *Midrash* (*Braishis Rabbah* 77:1) states that just as the Almighty is alone so too Yaakov was alone (*levado*). We see from this that the Sages understood the word "alone" to be a positive attribute and a form of emulating the Almighty. It is exactly this trait of being "alone" that helped Yaakov to be victorious in his forthcoming battle. This, too, was the great attribute of Yaakov's grandfather Avraham (see *Psochim* 118a); he was willing to be alone for his spiritual ideals.

In this light, said Rabbi Yeruchem Levovitz, we can understand the well-known Mishnah in *Pirke Avos* 4:1. There the Mishnah gives definitions for four key terms. Who is the wise man? The one who learns from everyone. Who is the strong person? The one who conquers his negative impulses. Who is the wealthy person? The one who has joy with what he has. Who is the honorable person? The one who honors others.

This Mishnah reveals a wonderful concept: each person can obtain the most important things in life independently of anyone else. The wise man is the individual who loves wisdom and because of this love wants to learn from everyone, for each person has some wisdom to share. If strength were dependent on being victorious over others, then as soon as someone is stronger than you, you are no longer the strong man. But, says the Mishnah, true strength is having the ability to overcome your negative tendencies and impulses. It is not dependent on anyone else but yourself. Wealth is not dependent on how much money you have or the number of your possessions. If it were, then you could lose your entire wealth overnight. Rather, true wealth is feeling joy for what you do have. This trait is yours regardless of external circumstances. If honor were dependent on how others treat you, what are you supposed to do if others decide not to honor you? Woe to a person whose honor is dependent on the whim of others. True honor is up to you. You are honorable if you honor others regardless of how others treat you. All these important attributes are up to you. You alone decide where you stand as regards: wisdom, strength, wealth, and honor. (*Daas Torah: Braishis*, pp.205-6)

View your possessions as the Almighty's special gift to you.

ויותר יעקב לבדו. (בראשית ל"ב כ"ה)

"AND YAAKOV REMAINED ALONE." (*Braishis* 32:25)

The Sages (*Chulin* 91a) explain that Yaakov remained behind to retrieve some small flasks. From here, say the Sages, we see the principle that for the righteous their possessions are more dear to them than their bodies (since Yaakov placed himself in danger for his possessions). The reason for this, said the Ari, *z.l.*, is that the righteous realize that if the Almighty gave them something, it is important for them to have it. If it were not necessary for their total welfare, the Almighty would not have given it to them. Therefore, they do whatever they can not to lose what they were given. (cited in *Biurai Hamekubalim Beniglah*)

With this understanding, we will gain a greater appreciation for what we have. The more you need something the more you will appreciate it. When you are aware that all that you have is measured out to you by the Almighty for your benefit, you will have a profound sense of gratitude. The positive feelings of ownership will be much greater than what is felt by those lacking this awareness.

Rabbi Yeruchem Levovitz cited the story of a philosopher who wished to be satisfied with the least amount of possessions that were absolutely necessary. After thinking the matter over he gave up everything he owned and kept only a pump to draw water from wells. Once when he was walking on the road he saw a caravan of people. They stopped near a well and drank directly from it without any pumps or cups. The philosopher said to himself, "Now I see that I don't even need a pump." He immediately threw away the pump, his only remaining possession. But from Yaakov we learn otherwise. The spirit of Torah is not to have nothing, but to have a deep appreciation for whatever you do have. (*Daas Torah: Braishis*, p.204)

Realize that negative desires are based on an illusion.

וישאל יעקב ויאמר הגידה נא שמך ויאמר למה זה תשאל לשמי ויברך אתו שם. (בראשית ל"ב ל')

"AND YAAKOV ASKED, AND HE SAID, PLEASE TELL ME YOUR NAME, AND HE REPLIED, WHY DO YOU ASK ME MY NAME? AND HE BLESSED HIM THERE." (*Braishis* 32:30)

Yaakov fought with the spiritual being which was the personification of Aisav, which was also the personification of the evil inclination (the *yetzer hara*). When Yaakov was victorious, he asked the being for his name, but was told, "Why do you ask me my name?" This reply might appear to be a refusal to give a truthful answer. But Rabbi Yehudah Leib Chasman explained that this was actually the name of the evil inclination, "Don't ask!"

The desires of this world draw a person like a magnet. The best way to overcome one's negative impulses is to be aware of how illusory these pleasures actually are. As soon as you take a close look with your intellect at worldly desires you will see how empty and meaningless they are. "Don't ask!" As soon as you start asking questions to clarify the reality of the evil inclination, you will find that there is nothing there. This is analogous to seeing a shadow and thinking that something is actually there. As soon as you light a candle, you realize that what you saw was only an illusion. Use your intellect to see the emptiness of negative desires and you will be free from their pull. (*Ohr Yohail*, vol.2, p.35)

Use strategy to bring about peace even if it might appear as if you are acting out of weakness.

וישתחו ארצה שבע פעמים עד גשתו עד אחיו. וירץ עשו לקראתו
ויחבקהו ויפל על צוארו וישקהו ויבכו. (בראשית ל"ג ג-ד)

Yaakov prepared himself for presents, prayer, and battle before meeting Aisav. When he finally approached Aisav:
"AND HE BOWED DOWN TO THE GROUND SEVEN TIMES UNTIL HE REACHED HIS BROTHER. AND AISAV RAN TO GREET HIM, AND HE HUGGED HIM, AND HE FELL ON HIS NECK, AND HE KISSED HIM, AND THEY CRIED." (*Braishis* 33:3,4)

Rashi comments that when Aisav saw how Yaakov bowed down to him so many times, his feelings of compassion were aroused and he hugged and kissed Yaakov.

Yaakov had great physical strength and was prepared to fight against Aisav, but he still wanted to avoid violence if at all possible. The Sages (*Pirke Avos* 4:1) define the truly strong person as one who has control over his own impulses. There are many people who focus on overcoming other people and gaining power over them. But when it comes to having power over themselves they are weak and even helpless. The desire to fight with others comes from the trait of arrogance and its offshoot, honor-seeking. If a person really wants a true victory, he won't focus on overpowering another person. Rather, he will work on his traits and appear to lower himself before another person. If used wisely, this can bring about peace.

We learn this from Yaakov, said Rabbi Yehudah Leib Chasman. Because of his strength he knew he could defeat Aisav. But even if one wins a battle, there is a loss to oneself and a loss to the other side. Yaakov prepared for a battle, if necessary, but his first strategy was to show respect and honor to Aisav. He called him master, while he called himself a servant. He even bowed down to Aisav many times. With this self-discipline, and it takes great self-discipline to choose to lower oneself for the sake of peace, Yaakov was victorious over Aisav. He made Aisav *his* servant. We see here that Yaakov bowed down to Aisav and called him master, but the real servant was Aisav, who was disarmed by Yaakov's strategy. (*Ohr Yohail*, vol.2, p.37)

There is a big difference between a person who bows down to someone out of weakness and another who bows down out of strength. A person with a low self-image gives in to others because he considers himself as nothing. This is a major fault. One needs to be aware of the inherent greatness in every human being, including oneself.

The root of quarrels is arrogance. Use wisdom and strategy when dealing with difficult people. Be aware of your real goals and don't get sidetracked. To make an enemy into a friend is the ultimate goal and a complete victory. This is a victory in which there are only winners and no losers. But it takes much strength. That is exactly why it is so elevating.

Following this idea will help you get along better with those you have trouble with. So many family quarrels are based on conceit. "How can I belittle myself by showing honor to this person who doesn't deserve it," some people say. And they therefore continue feuds and arguments for years causing hatred and animosity. We must learn from Yaakov to show honor and respect if that is the best way to calm another person. Note that Yaakov had no intention of living near Aisav. If you are dealing with an abusive person who is dangerous to your spiritual, physical, or emotional well-being, keep a far distance. But when you have to interact with him, speak with tact. Keep your focus on your ultimate goals. While such strategy is difficult for many people, it is the behavior of the truly strong person: the one who has mastered control over himself.

Realize that you have what you need.

ויאמר עשו יש לי רב. ויאמר יעקב... יש לי כל. (בראשית ל״ג ט׳-י״א)

"AND AISAV SAID, I HAVE A LOT. AND YAAKOV SAID, I HAVE EVERYTHING." (*Braishis* 33:9,10,11)

The Chofetz Chayim commented that with these two remarks we see the difference in world view between Yaakov and Aisav. Aisav said he had a lot. Even though he had a large amount, he would still want more, for whoever has a hundred wants two hundred. Yaakov, however, said, "I have everything." I am not missing anything at all. Aisav constantly wanted more, while Yaakov felt great satisfaction in what he had. (*Chofetz Chayim al Hatorah*)

Regardless of how much you have, there is always much more that you can want. Having the attitude that you never really have enough will cause you constant frustration. You will always focus on what you are missing and your life will be filled with anxiety and suffering. The attitude to internalize is that of Yaakov, "I have everything that I need." Of course, you have a right to try to acquire more. But if you are unable to, you will feel calm and serene. If you do acquire more, very good. If not, it is a sign that for your best interests you do not really need any more.

When strongly motivated you will be able to have a positive influence on others.

ולא אחר הנער לעשות הדבר כי חפץ בבת יעקב וגו' וימלו כל זכר. (בראשית ל"ד י"ט-כ"ד)

"AND THE LAD DID NOT HESITATE TO TAKE CARE OF THE MATTER BECAUSE HE WANTED THE DAUGHTER OF YAAKOV... AND ALL OF THE MALES WERE CIRCUMCISED." (*Braishis* 34:19-24)

The Torah tells us here the power of one's will. Shchem wanted to marry Dinah, the daughter of Yaakov. His will for this was so strong that the most difficult things became easy. He finished the negotiations with Yaakov's sons very quickly. Without any delay whatsoever, he not only circumcised himself but even convinced the entire city of men to be circumcised in one day. He was successful in influencing others because of the strength of his will. (*Daas Torah: Braishis*, p.213)

Whenever you have a strong will for something, you will have much more power to do it. When you want to have a positive influence on others, the stronger you feel the need to influence them, the more successful you will be.

Rabbi Noach Weinberg, Rosh Hayeshiva of Aish Hatorah, frequently relates the story of a person who owned a nursing home. Most of the residents were not Jewish and were served non-kosher food. The few Jewish residents received kosher food which cost more. When an inspector from the city came to check up on the conditions of the home, an elderly Jewish lady complained to him that although she wanted the same food as everyone else, the owner refused to give it to her. The inspector told the owner of the nursing home that either he give the woman the food she wanted or else the nursing home would be closed because of discrimination.

The owner of the nursing home tried to convince the woman to rescind her complaint. "Kosher food costs more," he told her, "I am actually giving you more expensive food than the others are receiving."

"I don't care," she replied. "I want what everyone else is getting."

"But kosher food is healthier," he argued.

"Look, I'm an elderly person, and couldn't care less if it's healthier. I just want the same as everyone else," she insisted.

The owner then spoke with her at length about the benefits of keeping the *mitzvos* of the Torah. He figured that if she became observant, she would want to keep kosher on her own and he wouldn't have any more problems. He was successful and she began observing Shabbos and all the other commandments, which of course, meant that she herself wanted to eat only kosher food.

"What did you say to her to influence her to become observant?" Rabbi Weinberg asked the nursing home owner.

"I don't know," was the reply. "You see, I just had to influence her to keep *mitzvos*. I couldn't serve a Jewish woman non-kosher food, and if she kept up her complaint, my nursing home would be closed. I just kept talking until she accepted *mitzvah* observance. I just had to do it."

VAYAISHEV

Keep your focus on growth, not serenity.

וישב יעקב. (בראשית ל"ז א')

"AND YAAKOV SAT..." (*Braishis* 37:1)

Rashi cites the Sages who say that Yaakov wanted to live in peace and serenity. But this was not to be, and the troubles of his son Yosef began. The Almighty said, "Is it not sufficient for the righteous that they receive their reward in the world to come? Why do they need to live in serenity in this world?"

The question arises: why is it wrong to want to live in serenity? Yaakov desired serenity not so that he could devote his time to personal pleasures, but rather to be able to engage in spiritual pursuits.

Rabbi Yeruchem Levovitz explained that the purpose of this world is for a person to elevate himself by passing the numerous tests that come to him. The goal is spiritual growth from every life situation. Therefore it was considered improper for Yaakov to place his focus on serenity.

This, said Rav Yeruchem, is an attitude we should all internalize. Every occurrence in this world can make you a better person. When you have this awareness your attitude towards everything that happens to you in life will be very positive. Before, during, and after every incident that occurs reflect on your behavior and reactions. Ask yourself, "What type of person am I after this happened? How did I do on this test? Did I pass it in an elevated manner?" (*Daas Torah: Braishis*, pp.222-3)

Two years before the Steipler passed away, he had medical problems with his foot. When he was asked how he was, he commented, "When Rabbi Yisroel Salanter was asked how he felt, he responded, 'What is the difference if the situation is better or worse? Whatever the Almighty wishes that is what is good.'" (*Peninai Rabainu Hakehilos Yaakov*, p.119)

When angry with someone, talk things over in order to make peace.

וישנאו אתו ולא יכלו דברו לשלם. (בראשית ל"ז ד')

Yosef's brothers were envious of him:
"AND THEY HATED HIM AND THEY WERE NOT ABLE TO SPEAK TO HIM FOR PEACE." (*Braishis* 37:4)

Rabbi Yonoson Eibeshutz commented that it is possible that if the brothers would have spoken the matter over with Yosef they would have been able to make peace. The problem was that they were not talking to each other. This is what frequently happens when people are in the midst of a feud. One does not want to listen to the other. However, when one person tells another that he wronged him, the other person might apologize and accept upon himself not to do it again. (*Tiferes Yonoson*)

If people who are involved in a heated dispute will talk things over with each other calmly, they will often see that they have nothing to argue about. Even if they still disagree in the end, the heavy emotionalism will be greatly diminished. When you hear clearly how the other person views the situation, you will see why he thinks as he does and you yourself will look at it differently.

When you are involved in a dispute with someone else, try to talk things over with him in a calm manner. It is important to repeat over the other person's position. Keep asking, "Is this and this what you mean?" By doing this, much harm will be avoided.

Avoid boasting.

ויחלם יוסף חלום ויגד לאחיו ויוספו עוד שנא אתו. ויאמר אליהם שמעו נא החלום הזה אשר חלמתי. (בראשית ל"ז ה-ו)

"AND YOSEF DREAMT A DREAM AND RELATED IT TO HIS BROTHERS. AND THEY CONTINUED TO HATE HIM. AND HE SAID TO THEM, HEAR THIS DREAM WHICH I HAVE DREAMT." (*Braishis* 37:5,6)

Sforno comments that it was a mistake on Yosef's part to tell his brothers about his dream. What was even worse was his hinting to them about the interpretation of the dream that he would rule over them.

When you boast to others, your intention might be to gain honor and respect from them. But envy is a very powerful emotion which easily leads to hatred. Be careful about boasting to others because the consequences can be very grave. Your boasting might lead to deep feelings of hatred which can arouse harmful thoughts and actions. Refraining from causing others these painful feelings is an act of kindness. Feel pleasure in not boasting because you are gaining in self-discipline and saving someone from suffering. Sharing your successes with a close friend is very different from boasting. Your goal is not to show off but to have someone experience your joy with you. For this you need someone who will sincerely feel positive about your accomplishments, so weigh the matter carefully. Ask yourself, "How will the listeners react? Will they sincerely share my joy, or will they feel the pain of envy?"

Your compassion for others should be strong enough to prevent your feeling joy for their downfall.

ויוספו עוד שנא אתו על חלמתיו ועל דבריו. (בראשית ל"ז ח')

"AND [Yosef's brothers] CONTINUED EVEN MORE TO HATE [Yosef] FOR HIS DREAMS AND FOR HIS WORDS." (*Braishis* 37:8)

The Torah tells us that the hatred was because of Yosef's dreams and his words. "His words" seems to be superfluous since this expression is already included in "his dreams." Rabbi Meir Simcha Hacohen explained this with a statement in *Sifri* (*Korach* 117) that the word *hinaih* denotes joy. Here in Yosef's report of the dream the term *vehinaih* is repeated three times (in verse seven). When Yosef reported his dream, he experienced joy in relating each detail. This joy which Yosef felt because he would rule over them increased their hatred towards him. (*Meshech Chochmah*)

Rabbi Shmuel Walkin commented on this: There are people who feel pleasure when they speak against others. Even if what they say is accurate, it is still very wrong to feel any joy in relating another person's wrongdoings. How is it possible to feel happy about the downfall of others? (*Ramat Shmuel: Braishis*, p.162)

When you are truly compassionate, you will feel the suffering of others. This attribute will prevent your feeling any pleasure at the expense of someone else. Work on increasing your level of compassion and you will find it impossible to speak *loshon hora* against others.

One of Rabbi Noson Tzvi Finkel's students in Slobodka once made a mistake. On *Shabbos* when he came to prayers he rolled up his sleeves to put on *tefilin*, momentarily forgetting that it was *Shabbos*. A student who was standing nearby smiled when he saw this. Later on Rav Noson Tzvi strongly censured that student for taking pleasure in the discomfort and embarrassment of someone else. (*Meoros Hagdolim*, p.247)

Develop compassion for all living creatures.

ויאמר לו לך נא ראה את שלום אחיך ואת שלום הצאן. (בראשית ל"ז
י"ד)

Yaakov sent his son Yosef to check on the welfare of his brothers:
"AND HE SAID TO HIM, GO SEE ABOUT THE WELFARE OF YOUR BROTHERS AND ABOUT THE WELFARE OF THE SHEEP." (*Braishis* 37:14)

Rabbi Noson Tzvi Finkel, Rosh Hayeshiva of Slobodka, commented that Yaakov was concerned about the welfare of his sons. In the same breath he added that Yosef should check on the welfare of the sheep. This is because a righteous person emulates the Almighty who is compassionate and merciful. A person who is truly compassionate will be concerned about the welfare of animals since all of the Almighty's creation is important. (*Ohr Hatzafun, Shmos*)

When I was a young student in Telz Yeshiva I was once walking near my Rebbe, Rabbi Mordechai Gifter. It was late at night and there was a light rainfall. A car was coming down the road and in its path fell a small object. At first I thought it was a leaf but then I noticed that it was a small frog. The Rosh Hayeshiva stood in the road and stopped the car. He bent down to the frog, and said, "Shoo, frog, shoo," making certain it jumped to safety. The driver of the car asked the Rosh Hayeshiva if he wanted a ride. But the Rosh Hayeshiva replied, "No thank you. You almost ran over a frog. It would have been *tzaar baalai chayim* (causing pain to animals)."

When you have a bias be careful about taking action.

ויאמרו איש אל אחיו הנה בעל החלמות הלזה בא. (בראשית ל״ז י״ט)

"AND ONE BROTHER SAID TO ANOTHER, BEHOLD THIS DREAMER IS COMING." (*Braishis* 37:19)

Rashi (*Braishis* 49:5) states that the two brothers here are Shimon and Levi. Rabbi Zalman Sorotzkin noted that Shimon and Levi were the ones who were zealous to save the birthright and future monarchy for Reuven. Reuven himself, however, tried to save Yosef from their hands.

Rabbi Shmuel Walkin commented on this that whenever a person's bias is involved he should not trust himself. It is easy for that bias to blind a person's intellect. Therefore, Reuven, who was the firstborn son and had the most to lose from Yosef's becoming the ruler, avoided doing anything to harm Yosef and even planned to save him. (*Ramat Shmuel, Braishis*, pp.162-3)

When influencing others speak to them from their point of view.

וישמע ראובן ויצלהו מידם ויאמר לא נכנו נפש. ויאמר אלהם ראובן אל
תשפכו דם. (בראשית ל"ז כ"א כ"ב)

"AND REUVEN HEARD AND HE SAVED HIM FROM THEIR HANDS, AND HE SAID, LET US NOT HIT A MORTAL BLOW. AND REUVEN SAID TO THEM, DO NOT SHED BLOOD." (*Braishis* 37:21,22)

Rabainu Bachya states that Reuven wanted to save his brother Yosef. If he were to have said, "Let us not hit him," he would have shown his brothers that his motivation was compassion for Yosef and they would not have listened to him. Therefore, Reuven added the word *nefesh*, "I don't want you to commit murder regardless of who the person is," was his message. Similarly, in verse 22 he said to them, "Do not shed blood." He did not say "his blood." This implied, "I, too, hate him and it is not his blood I am concerned about. Rather, I am concerned that you should not become murderers."

From this observation of Rabainu Bachya we see a very important principle when it comes to influencing someone. The focus of your arguments should be on points that the listener will accept even though your own focus might center on a different aspect of the situation. Reuven's goal was to prevent the shedding of blood. He wanted to save Yosef. But if he would have told them to have mercy on Yosef, they would have disregarded his pleas. He wisely showed them that their behavior was not in their own best interests since they would lower themselves by their actions.

When you want to prevent someone from saying or doing things that will hurt someone else, show the person how he is hurting himself by his words or actions. The questions to keep in your mind are, "What approach can I use in this instance that will be most effective in influencing this person to refrain from this behavior?" "How can I show him that he will harm himself if he hurts this person?"

Where a government ruling would have forced transgression of Torah law, Rabbi Akiva Eger always protested with arguments that would be accepted by the government. He showed that it was in the interest of the government to strengthen religion, to see that the people would follow the Torah. Invariably, he succeeded by using this method in convincing government officials of the ill effects of their rulings and of the necessity to modify or rescind them. (*Jewish Leaders*, p.110)

One of the students in Rabbi Nochum Perchovitz's yeshiva was extremely quiet. He was very shy and lacked confidence. Rav Nochum wanted to speak in learning with him but the student never approached Rav Nochum. What did Rav Nochum do? He found out about a question that this student had asked and then approached him, "I heard a question in your name," Rav Nochum told him. "It is a very good question and I thought about answering it in this manner. What do you think about it?"

This helped for a short while. But then once again the student became silent. Rav Nochum found an original way to motivate him to become more talkative.

"In a short while people will ask about you in reference to *shiduchim*. Certainly one of the questions that they will ask is if you discuss Torah thoughts with me. I think it is worthwhile for you to speak with me from time to time so I will be able to answer that we do speak in learning." (*Yetaid Neaman*, 17 Kislev, 5747, p.6)

Appreciate the minor positive occurrences in your life as messengers from the Almighty.

וישבו לאכל לחם וישאו עיניהם ויראו והנה ארחת ישמעאלים באה מגלעד וגמליהם נשאים נכאת וצרי ולט הולכים להוריד מצרימה. (בראשית ל"ז כ"ה)

"AND THEY SAT DOWN TO EAT BREAD, AND THEY LIFTED UP THEIR EYES AND LOOKED, AND BEHOLD, A COMPANY OF YISHMEAILIM CAME FROM GILAD WITH THEIR CAMELS CARRYING AROMATIC GUM (for censing), BALM, AND LADANUM, GOING TO CARRY IT DOWN TO EGYPT." (*Braishis* 37:25)

Rashi comments on this: Why did the Torah mention what the camels were carrying? To tell us the reward of the righteous. Those caravans usually carried only kerosene and resin (used for fuel) which had an unpleasant odor. But the caravan that carried Yosef to Egypt had pleasant spices.

This seems to be little consolation for Yosef. He was being sold as a slave by his brothers. How would something as minor as pleasant smelling merchandise on the caravan taking him to Egypt make a difference? The answer is that this was a subtle hint from the Almighty to Yosef. It was a message to Yosef that all was not lost. Appreciate the hand of the Almighty that is guiding your life and supplies you with minor pleasures to enhance your life. This is a sign that all the Almighty does is for your ultimate benefit. (Rabbi Mordechai Pragamantsky of Telz; heard from my Rebbe, Rabbi Chayim Stein)

This is an important lesson for anyone undergoing a difficult life situation. Upon facing painful experiences one is apt to become lost in self-pity and despair. It is easy to focus solely on what is going wrong with one's life. But keep your eyes open. Be aware of any positive aspects. Don't ignore anything that you can possibly appreciate. These minor pleasures are messengers from the Almighty. Appreciate them for themselves; and what is more allow them to change your evaluation of your entire situation. Learn to see every situation as a means to help you reach your ultimate potential in this world.

When you need to conceal your behavior it is a sign that something is wrong.

ויאמר יהודה אל אחיו מה בצע כי נהרג את אחינו וכסינו את דמו.
(בראשית ל״ז כ״ו)

"AND YEHUDAH SAID TO HIS BROTHERS, WHAT PROFIT IS THERE IN KILLING OUR BROTHER [Yosef] AND COVERING HIS BLOOD." (*Braishis* 37:26)

The Kotzker Rebbe commented on this verse: When you have to cover up your behavior, that is a sign that you are doing something wrong. (*HaRebbe MaiKotzk*, p.94)

Whenever you are certain that what you are doing is proper, you are willing to let others know about your actions. Even if they will disapprove, your own certainty gives you the necessary confidence to cope with their disapproval. But if you are uncertain about how proper your behavior really is, you will not want others to know what you are doing. Whenever you feel a need to hide your actions, ask yourself, "Is what I am doing really the right thing to do?"

Realize that you can never tell how events will actually turn out in the end.

ויוסף הורד מצרימה. (בראשית ל״ט א׳)

"AND YOSEF WAS BROUGHT DOWN TO EGYPT." (*Braishis* 39:1)

Anyone viewing the scene of Yosef being brought down to Egypt as a slave would have considered it a major tragedy. His brothers sold him into slavery and he was being taken far away from his father and his homeland. But the reality was that this was the first step towards his being appointed the second in command of Egypt. He would eventually be in charge of the national economy of Egypt and would be the mastermind behind the complex program to prepare for the years of famine during the years of plenty.

Later on when Yaakov, Yosef's father, went down to Egypt, anyone viewing the scene would have considered it a very positive one. Yaakov was going to be reunited with his favorite son after so many years of separation. His son was a powerful leader and he would be treated with all the honors of royalty. But what was the total picture. This was the first stage in the exile of the Children of Israel. Their enslavement in Egypt was beginning at this very moment, although the entire process would take some time until it was finally felt.

No human being has the omniscience to know what the final consequences of any situation will actually be. Therefore, when a situation seems to be extremely negative, do not despair. This could lead to wonderful things for you. Conversely, when things seem to be going extremely well, do not become complacent or arrogant. One can never tell what the future has in store. (Heard from Rabbi Leib Lopian, late Rosh Hayeshiva of Gateshead)

Internalizing this attitude will prevent you from excessive pain when things seem to be going wrong. Tell yourself, "Perhaps in the near future I will see how I have gained from this." On the other hand, extreme euphoria when things seem to be going very well can possibly lead to depression when the tide of events seem to change. By avoiding extreme reactions you will be able to cope better with the vicissitudes of life.

The Chofetz Chayim's son wrote that his father told him how mistaken people are when they complain about events that take place in their lives. If they have patience, they will see how things are really for their benefit. The Chofetz Chayim related how a certain Rabbi had to leave one city because of a quarrel that arose. That Rabbi ended up in a small town. Years later it was clear that his moving to that town had a powerful positive influence on his children who were not behaving properly in the larger city. Although at first it appeared to be a misfortune, the move turned out for the best. (*Michtevai Chofetz Chayim*, p.15)

MIKAITZ

When you feel joy for what you have you will be free from envying what anyone else has.

והנה מן היאר עלת שבע פרות יפות מראה ובריאת בשר ותרעינה באחו.
(בראשית מ״א ב׳)

In Pharaoh's prophetic dream:
"AND BEHOLD FROM THE NILE ROSE UP SEVEN COWS, WHICH LOOKED GOOD AND HEALTHY OF FLESH AND THEY GRAZED IN THE PASTURE." (*Braishis* 41:2)

Rashi comments that their looking good was a sign of the years of plenty, for then people look good to one another and are not envious of each other.

The idea that Rashi expresses is important for happiness in life. When you allow what someone else has to rob you of your own happiness, you will frequently suffer. But if you learn to appreciate what you have to its fullest, you will be so filled with good feelings yourself that you will not be disturbed by what anyone else has. The more you focus on the good in your life the less it will make a difference to you if anyone else has more than you. When you master this attribute of feeling joy for what you have, your whole life is a life of plenty.

Rabbi Yechezkail Levenstein once noticed that a *chasan* felt badly that he had just a plain watch and not a gold watch as many other people received. Rabbi Levenstein approached him and traded his own gold watch for the plain watch. When he came home, he explained, "Besides the color of the watches there is no practical difference between them. They both tell time with the same accuracy. Why should this person suffer needlessly when I can help him out?" (*Mofes Hador*, p.17)

Never despair, since liberation from difficulties can come at any moment.

וישלח פרעה ויקרא את יוסף ויריצהו מן הבור. (בראשית מ"א י"ד)

After Pharaoh heard that Yosef was able to interpret dreams:
"AND PHARAOH SENT AND HE CALLED YOSEF, AND THEY RAN WITH HIM FROM THE PRISON." (*Braishis* 41:14)

The Chofetz Chayim takes note that when the time came for Yosef's liberation, he wasn't let out of prison slowly. Rather he was rushed out of his captivity with the greatest of speed. This is the way the Almighty brings about redemption. The moment it is the proper time not even one second is lost. This is how it will be with the final redemption, said the Chofetz Chayim. As soon as the right time comes we will immediately be delivered from our exile. (*Chofetz Chayim al Hatorah*, p.49)

In every difficult life situation realize that in just one moment the entire picture can change. Yosef had no deadline by which he could count on being set free. But his imprisonment and freedom were not dependent on the whims of his mortal captors. Rather, the Almighty gave him a set time to remain in prison. As soon as the time was reached Yosef was immediately saved from his plight. This awareness can give you encouragement in difficult times. Even in those situations where you can make no change for improvement and you do not see the situation changing in the future, your liberation can still come in the next moment.

Remove opposition to your ideas by having others gain from them.

ועתה ירא פרעה איש נבון וחכם וישיתהו על ארץ מצרים. יעשה פרעה
ויפקד פקדים על הארץ וחמש את ארץ מצרים בשבע שני השבע.
(בראשית מ״א ל״ג-ל״ד)

After explaining the interpretation of Pharaoh's dream, Yosef said:
"NOW LET PHARAOH LOOK FOR A MAN WHO HAS
UNDERSTANDING AND IS WISE, AND SET HIM OVER THE LAND OF
EGYPT. LET PHARAOH DO THIS, AND LET HIM APPOINT OFFICERS
OVER THE LAND, AND TAKE UP THE FIFTH PART OF THE LAND OF
EGYPT IN THE SEVEN YEARS OF PLENTY." (*Braishis* 41:33,34)

Why did Yosef give Pharaoh advice on the solution to the
problem? All he was asked to do was to explain the dream, he was
not asked to find solutions.

The Dubner Maggid explained that Yosef was afraid that if he
would just give an interpretation of the dream, the regular advisers
of Pharaoh would belittle his interpretation. They might feel
envious of this young prisoner and ridicule what he had to say.
Therefore Yosef added to his interpretation the suggestion that
Pharaoh appoint an adviser to be in charge of the entire operation
of gathering food. Also, many officers would be needed to
implement the plans. Upon hearing the need for new important
positions, the advisers to Pharaoh would each think that they
would be chosen. They would therefore encourage Pharaoh to
accept Yosef's interpretation as being accurate. This is what we see
in verse 37, that all of the servants of Pharaoh actually agreed with
Yosef's interpretation and it became accepted as truth. (*Ohel
Yaakov*)

This strategy of Yosef's will prove invaluable at times. When you
want other people to accept an idea of yours for a project, include
ways for them to gain from your plans. Not only will this remove
potential opposition, but they will become advocates for your
proposal.

Look for even minor virtues in others.

ויאמר פרעה אל יוסף אחרי הודיע אלקים אותך את כל זאת אין נבון
וחכם כמוך. (בראשית מ"א ל"ט)

Pharaoh liked Yosef's interpretation of his dream and then appointed him to be in charge of the economy of Egypt:
"AND PHARAOH SAID TO YOSEF, AFTER THE ALMIGHTY HAS INFORMED YOU OF ALL THIS THERE IS NO ONE WHO IS AS UNDERSTANDING AND WISE AS YOU." (*Braishis* 41:39)

How could Pharaoh have trusted Yosef to such a degree that he appointed him to be the main administrator of the plans to save Egypt from the shortages of the forthcoming famine? True, Yosef was understanding and wise, but how could Pharaoh trust someone who was just released from prison and was previously a slave?

Rabbi Chayim Shmuelevitz, the late Rosh Hayeshiva of Mir, replied that Pharaoh saw Yosef's extreme honesty in something he said before he related the interpretation of the dream. Yosef began by saying to Pharaoh that he had no power to interpret dreams on his own. It was entirely a gift from the Almighty. Yosef didn't want to take credit even for a moment. This total honesty in one minor point showed that Yosef could be completely trusted.

Note what happened here. Pharaoh saw one minor positive point in Yosef's character and extrapolated from this to see the good on a large scale. This should be our model in viewing people. Keep finding minor strengths and good qualities in others and then give the person positive feedback. This can help someone build a positive self-image. The more a person sees himself as having positive attributes the more motivated he will be to utilize those strengths for further growth.

Unfortunately there are people who have a tendency to notice minor faults and weaknesses in others and then keep telling them that they have major character problems. While it is imperative to help people overcome their faults and weaknesses, the main emphasis for most people should be on their strengths. If someone is arrogant, this is not the appropriate approach. But for anyone who has low self-esteem this positive approach is crucial.

There are some counselors who are experts at interpreting people's behavior as problematic. For example, if someone comes late, they say he is showing passive-aggressive behavior. If he is exactly on time, they say he is an obsessive-compulsive. If he is early, they say he fears disapproval and is too concerned with what others think about him. But these same situations can be looked at quite differently. If someone is late, there is the possibility he was detained through no fault of his own. If someone is punctual, it shows that he is orderly and has good time management. If someone is early, it shows that he does not want to inconvenience another person by causing him to wait.

By choosing to focus on the positive aspects of what people do, you will look at others in a favorable light. This way you will be a source of encouragement to others. When a person views himself in a positive light, he will have the strength to deal constructively with his faults.

People respect someone who has the courage to say that he made a mistake.

ויאמרו איש אל אחיו אבל אשמים אנחנו על אחינו אשר ראינו צרת נפשו בהתחננו אלינו ולא שמענו על כן באה אלינו הצרה הזאת. (בראשית מ"ב כ"א)

"AND THEY SAID ONE MAN TO HIS BROTHER, WE ARE GUILTY ABOUT OUR BROTHER. WE SAW THE SUFFERING OF HIS SOUL WHEN HE PLEADED TO US AND WE DID NOT LISTEN TO HIM. THEREFORE THIS MISFORTUNE HAS BEFALLEN US." (*Braishis* 42:21)

Rabbi Dovid of Zeviltov commented: If a person did something wrong and recognizes that he has done wrong, he will be forgiven. But if a person does something wrong and denies it, there is no atonement for him. When Yosef's brothers said previously that they were innocent, Yosef responded by calling them spies. When they said that they were guilty, however, Yosef was full of compassion for them and cried. (cited in *Otzer Chayim*)

Many people deny their faults and the things they have done wrong because they mistakenly think that others will respect them more by their doing so. But in reality people admire someone with the honesty and courage to admit his mistakes. It takes a brave person to say, "Yes, I was wrong." This kind of integrity will not only build up your positive attribute of honesty but will also gain you the respect of others. When you apologize to someone for wronging him, he will feel more positive towards you than if you denied that you did anything wrong. This awareness will make it much easier for you to ask forgiveness from others.

Patience will prevent you from prematurely evaluating a situation as negative.

ויאמר ישראל למה הרעתם לי להגיד לאיש העוד לכם אח. (בראשית מ״ג ו׳)

"AND ISRAEL SAID, WHY DID YOU CAUSE ME BAD BY TELLING THE MAN THAT YOU HAD ANOTHER BROTHER." (*Braishis* 43:6)

The Midrash (*Braishis Rabbah* 91:13) censures Yaakov for evaluating the situation as bad. The Almighty said, "I am involved in having his son rule in Egypt and he says, 'Why did you cause me bad.'"

There are many events in each person's life that might appear to be negative when they first happen. But if a person were to know the entire picture of the consequences of these events, he would readily see how the Almighty planned them for good. What is needed is patience. When an event that seems to be against your interests happens, ask yourself, "How can I be certain that this will turn out bad in the end?" The answer is that you never can. It is always premature to evaluate non-tragic life situations as bad. Acquire a "wait and see" attitude towards events. This will prevent you from much needless suffering in your life.

To internalize this principle make a list of events that happened in your own life that at first seemed to be negative but which you later saw were positive.

Feel joy when you see yourself improving.

וישא משאת מאת פניו אלהם ותרב משאת בנימין ממשאת כלם חמש
ידות וישתו וישכרו עמו. (בראשית מ"ג ל"ד)

"AND [Yosef] TOOK AND SENT PORTIONS TO THEM FROM BEFORE
HIM; AND BINYAMIN'S PORTION WAS FIVE TIMES AS MUCH AS ANY
OF THEIRS. AND THEY DRANK, AND BECAME INEBRIATED WITH
HIM." (*Braishis* 43:34)

Rashi comments that from the day that Yosef's brothers sold
him they didn't drink wine, but on this day they drank.

They didn't recognize Yosef and were unaware that the Egyptian
administrator whom they were dealing with was Yosef, so why did
they drink?

One answer is that the brothers saw that although Binyamin
received five times as much as they did, they did not feel envious of
him. From this they understood that they had corrected the main
fault that had led to their selling their brother Yosef. They were
previously envious of Yosef and this led to their hating him.
Because they had overcome the trait of envy they were able to
drink wine again. (*Kav Chain*; cited in *Maayanah Shel Torah*)

Whenever you see improvement in your character traits, feel
great joy. This joy will motivate you to continue improving. Be
aware of what harm your negative traits caused you in the past and
feel grateful for overcoming them. Knowing that you have already
been successful will give you the encouragement to work on
correcting other faults.

VAYIGASH

To influence someone speak with deep sincerity and make certain that he is giving you a real hearing.

ויגש אליו יהודה ויאמר בי אדני ידבר נא עבדך דבר באזני אדני ואל יחר אפך בעבדך כי כמוך כפרעה. (בראשית מ"ד י"ח)

"AND YEHUDAH APPROACHED [Yosef] AND HE SAID, PLEASE MY MASTER, ALLOW YOUR SERVANT TO SPEAK IN THE EARS OF MY MASTER AND DO NOT BECOME ANGRY AT YOUR SERVANT FOR YOU ARE LIKE PHARAOH." (*Braishis* 44:18)

Yehudah was under the impression that this Egyptian leader who was really Yosef did not understand Hebrew and needed an interpreter. Why then did he ask to speak in his ears?

My Rebbe, the late Rosh Hayeshiva of Brisk in Yerushalayim, explained this in two ways. One, even though Yehudah thought Yosef did not understand the language he was speaking, he wanted him to hear the depth of feeling behind his words. Even if one does not speak the language, sincerity will come through. "Words that come from a person's heart enter the heart of the listener."

This happened to the Chofetz Chayim once when speaking to a high government official to remove a harmful decree against the Jewish people. Even before the interpreter translated the Chofetz Chayim's words from Yiddish, the listener said that no translation was necessary. He understood the language of feeling that permeated each word that came from a pure heart.

The second idea of Rav Yosef Dov was that when you try to influence someone, it is imperative that he be open to what you have to say. If a person is close-minded and has made up his mind not to pay attention to you, nothing you say will influence him. You can give all kinds of rational arguments for your position, but the person will be as if deaf. Therefore, Yehudah asked Yosef to at least give him a fair hearing. "Keep your ears open to the possibility that what I will say has merit."

These two ideas are important to keep in mind when trying to influence someone. Speak with sincerity. When you speak from the bottom of your heart, your words have tremendous force and power. Secondly, make certain that the other person is open to hearing what you have to say. For instance, you might start by saying, "If what I say makes sense, are you willing to change your mind?"

Learn communication skills from Yehudah.

ויגש אליו יהודה ויאמר בי אדני ידבר נא עבדך דבר באזני אדני ואל יחר
אפך בעבדך כי כמוך כפרעה. (בראשית מ״ד י״ח)

"AND YEHUDAH APPROACHED [Yosef] AND HE SAID, PLEASE MY MASTER, ALLOW YOUR SERVANT TO SPEAK IN THE EARS OF MY MASTER. AND DO NOT BECOME ANGRY AT YOUR SERVANT FOR YOU ARE LIKE PHARAOH." (*Braishis* 44:18)

We can note a number of communication principles from Yehudah's strategy in talking to the Egyptian leader who unbeknown to him was Yosef. First, he started by asking Yosef not to become angry. When you think that what you say will be irritating to the person you are talking to, you can defuse his potential anger by mentioning right at the start that you hope that what you say will not get the other person angry.

In this one verse, Yehudah called the other person master twice, while referring to himself as "your servant" twice. He had his goal in mind and in order to make the other person more open to listen to what he had to say he spoke with great respect to him while at the same time putting himself down. One loses nothing by doing this, but gains much. Only pride prevents people from using this approach more often. But it is a very powerful tool.

On the words, "For you are like Pharaoh," Rashi comments that Yehudah had four different levels of meaning in his communication. There is a progression here we can learn from. The first meaning is that Yehudah said, "In my eyes you are as important as a king." Start off with praise. Everyone wants a feeling of importance. If a person sees that you respect him, he will more readily listen to your requests.

The second meaning Rashi cites is that Yehudah said to him, "Just as Pharaoh was smitten by the Almighty when he caused difficulties for Avraham and Sarah, so too He will smite you." On this level, Yehudah was speaking as a friend and giving warning that he should be careful or else he would suffer consequences.

The third meaning Rashi cites is that Yehudah was giving him *mussar*. He rebuked him for not keeping his word. "Just as Pharaoh is inconsistent so are you." In this approach Yehudah was making a plea for him to act in an ethical way. Yehudah pointed out that what he was doing was wrong and censured him for it.

The final meaning cited by Rashi is that Yehudah threatened him. If you do not allow Binyamin to go free, I will kill both Pharaoh and you. If nothing else works to influence the other person, in extreme situations one might need to resort to threats. But even in those situations such an approach must be used only as a last resort. First try to accomplish your goals with diplomacy. Only if lighter strategies are not effective, use the heavier approach.

When traveling in a wagon driven by horses, Rabbi Wolf Zbarazer would not allow the driver to whip the horses. He would tell the drivers, "When you know how to speak to them in the right way, you do not need to use force."

If this is true of animals, how much more so with people.

The right words can have a powerful and instantaneous influence on another person.

ויאמר יוסף אל אחיו אני יוסף העוד אבי חי ולא יכלו אחיו לענות אתו כי
נבהלו מפניו. (בראשית מ"ה ג')

"AND YOSEF SAID TO HIS BROTHERS, I AM YOSEF. IS MY FATHER STILL ALIVE? AND HIS BROTHERS COULD NOT ANSWER HIM BECAUSE THEY TREMBLED BEFORE HIM." (*Braishis* 45:3)

These words of Yosef were rebuke to his brothers. They had thought evil of Yosef and now they realized that his prophetic dreams of rulership and power were true. They instantaneously realized that they were previously wrong in their judgment of him. A mistake they had lived with for many years was cleared up with just one sentence from Yosef. The two Hebrew words "*Ani Yosef*" - I am Yosef - were sufficient to change their minds in just one moment.

When you try to influence someone to see the truth, how long must it take? This, of course, is impossible to answer. It depends on so many factors that are impossible to predict in advance. But we see here there is no minimum. When what you say is powerful enough, at times you can give people great awareness very quickly. Timing and circumstances are crucial. The right two words can sometimes make long-lasting changes.

Rabbi Yisroel Salanter used to relate that a single sentence he heard from Rabbi Zundel of Salant made a total change in him. Rav Zundel called him over and said simply, "Yisroel! Study *mussar* and become a person who fears the Almighty." Rabbi Yisroel Salanter said, "When I heard my Rebbe order me to study *mussar*, it entered my heart like a burning flame." These few words which had a tremendous impact on Rav Yisroel greatly affected the lives of all of the future disciples of Rav Yisroel and their students until this very day.

Rabbi Yeruchem Levovitz's first *mussar* lecture was in the Chofetz Chayim's yeshiva in Radin on the topic of *Emunah*, awareness of the Almighty. His disciple Rabbi Yechezkail

Levenstein, the future *mashgiach* of Mir and Ponevez, testified that he was so influenced by that single talk that from then on he constantly thought about *Emunah* for the rest of his life. After this lecture, Rav Yechezkail would always speak about this topic to himself and to others and this had a great influence on many people. (*Marbitzai Torah Umussar*, vol.2, p.63)

Finding meaning in difficult life events makes them easier to cope with.

ויאמר יוסף אל אחיו אני יוסף. (בראשית מ"ה ג')

"AND YOSEF SAID TO HIS BROTHERS, I AM YOSEF." (*Braishis* 45:3)

The Chofetz Chayim commented that from the time the brothers first came to Egypt to get food and Yosef spoke to them roughly and accused them of being spies, they were very puzzled about what exactly was happening. In both encounters with Yosef they had many questions about their experiences. But as soon as they heard the words, "I am Yosef" all their questions were answered. The difficulties they had in understanding the underlying meaning of the events they experienced were now completely clarified.

Similarly, said the Chofetz Chayim, when the entire world will hear the words "I am Hashem" all the questions and difficulties that people had about the history of the world with all of its suffering will be answered. The entire matter will be clarified and understood. Everyone will see how the hand of the Almighty caused everything for our benefit. (*Chofetz Chayim al Hatorah*)

When one realizes that the Almighty has a plan and a purpose for all the events that occur, it gives meaning to hardships and suffering. When a person sees meaning in suffering, it becomes easier to cope with. One need not wait until the final redemption to be aware that the Almighty has a purpose behind each event. Even if you do not know the exact meaning of a particular event, the knowledge that there is an ultimate meaning will enable you to view the situation in a positive, albeit painful, manner.

The Chazon Ish mastered a positive attitude towards all kinds of suffering. He viewed them as, "The Almighty's messengers that strengthen the connection between the Creator and those He created. Suffering elevates a person to a world that is full of light. It elevates a person above his body's natural tendencies and this is the essence of man." (*Kovetz Igros Chazon Ish* 1:201; *P'air Hador*, vol.3, p.23)

Try to lessen other people's feelings of guilt when they ask your forgiveness.

ועתה לא אתם שלחתם אתי הנה כי האלקים וישמני לאב לפרעה ולאדון לכל ביתו ומשל בכל ארץ מצרים. (בראשית מ"ה ח')

"SO NOW IT WAS NOT YOU WHO SENT ME HERE BUT THE ALMIGHTY, AND HE MADE ME A FATHER TO PHARAOH AND A MASTER OVER ALL OF HIS HOUSE, AND RULER OVER ALL THE LAND OF EGYPT." (*Braishis* 45:8)

Rabbi Yeruchem Levovitz stated that the nature of many people is that when they do an act of kindness for someone, they do not want to receive anything in return. This is not necessarily because they have such a deep desire to do kindness. Just the opposite. They want the other person to feel indebted to them forever. Therefore they take nothing in return to prevent the other person from feeling that he has already repaid the debt. But the obligation to do a complete act of kindness requires that when you do someone a favor you should allow him to give you something or do something for you in return. In this manner you are freeing the person from his debt of gratitude.

Similarly, when someone wrongs another person there is a tendency for that person to want him to feel guilty for ever after. This gives the wronged person a feeling of being "one-up" and the other person of being "one-down." There is an elevated level of forgiving someone even though you know that he is not entirely sincere when he asks you for forgiveness. Just by the fact of his asking forgiveness you can allow him to feel the pleasure of thinking that you believe he is sincere. This is an act of kindness on your part towards that person.

We see this principle with Yosef and his brothers. Yosef wanted to do an act of kindness so that they should not feel guilty for what they had done to him. Therefore Yosef said to them that they were not the ones who sent him to Egypt. Rather it was the Almighty who sent him to become a leader over all of Egypt. They should not think that what they did was harmful. They did him the greatest kindness possible. He was saying to them that he was even grateful to them for all the good that he gained from their selling him. (*Daas Torah: Braishis*, pp.259-60)

When someone asks you for forgiveness, be sensitive to his feelings of guilt and regret. Show him how you did not really lose so much. This is the opposite of what some people do in keeping grudges against others for a very long time. Your goal should be to save other people from emotional stress and suffering. Always ask yourself, "What can I do or say now that will help make this person feel better?"

The Chofetz Chayim's son wrote that his father once received a letter from someone who asked the Chofetz Chayim to pray for him because he was ill. He mentioned in the letter that he erred in the past by speaking against the Chofetz Chayim and belittling his books. The Chofetz Chayim answered him immediately and wrote that he felt suffering for his suffering. Moreover, he asked his forgiveness because of the added suffering he had caused him. Even though he did not believe that the man's illness was because of his speaking against him, he apologized that the person suffered by thinking that this was so. The Chofetz Chayim concluded with a blessing for a speedy recovery. (*Michtevai Chofetz Chayim*, p.12)

A student of Rabbi Nochum Perchovitz, Rabbi Berel Eisenstein, related that before he started to learn with Rav Nochum as a *chavrusa*, Rav Nochum told him that he would agree only under two conditions.

"At first I was concerned about what those conditions would be. I thought that maybe he would demand that I should master the section we would study in advance or that I should study the entire tractate on my own before we began. But the conditions were quite different."

"I want you to guarantee me two things," said Rav Nochum.

"One, if it is difficult for you to come one evening, do not feel at all uncomfortable about it. Do not apologize or give me any reasons. Simply don't come. The second condition is that if you are no longer interested in studying with me let me know right away. Don't continue just because we started. Only if you agree to these two conditions will we begin." (*Yetaid Neaman*, 17 Kislev, 5747, p.6)

Identifying with a cause or project influences a person to make a greater effort.

והקל נשמע בית פרעה לאמר באו אחי יוסף וייטב בעיני פרעה ובעיני עבדיו. (בראשית מ״ה ט״ז)

"AND THE NEWS WAS HEARD IN THE HOUSE OF PHARAOH SAYING, THE BROTHERS OF YOSEF HAVE COME. AND IT WAS GOOD IN THE EYES OF PHARAOH AND IN THE EYES OF HIS SERVANTS." (*Braishis* 45:16)

Sforno comments that Pharaoh was pleased with Yosef's family coming to Egypt because he said to himself that now Yosef's supervision over the land would be even greater than before. Previously he was a stranger to the country. But now he would be a regular citizen in the land together with his entire family. This will give him even greater motivation to be concerned with all his heart for the benefit of the country and all of its inhabitants.

We see two ideas here. One that if you identify with a place, you will devote much more time and energy thinking about the welfare of that place. Even if you are kindhearted, when you personally consider yourself as part of that place you will do much more than if you considered yourself an outsider. Learn to identify with other people. The more you identify with them the greater will be your efforts to help them in many ways.

We also see an important principle for people who want to influence others to devote time and effort for the benefit of a community, cause, or project. Make those other people feel at home. Have them personally identify with the community, cause, or project. When a person feels that he is doing something for a cause that he is part of, he will use more of his talents, skills, and energy for that cause.

When you want to influence someone who might be reluctant, take care of as many preparations as possible for him.

ואתה צויתה זאת עשו קחו לכם מארץ מצרים עגלות לטפכם ולנשיכם
ונשאתם את אביכם ובאתם. (בראשית מ"ה י"ט)

Pharaoh said to Yosef:
"NOW YOU ARE COMMANDED, DO THIS, TAKE WAGONS OUT OF THE LAND OF EGYPT FOR YOUR CHILDREN, AND FOR YOUR WIVES, AND BRING YOUR FATHER AND COME." (*Braishis* 45:19)

Sforno explains that Pharaoh told Yosef to send wagons for the entire family to his father in order that Yaakov should see that everything was already prepared for his journey to Egypt. Since everything would be ready for the trip, he would not refuse to come.

This is a useful lesson to remember when you want to motivate someone to do something that he might not be interested in doing. You should make all the preparations for him. For example, when you write to a very busy person, send him an addressed and stamped return envelope to ensure a reply. You can even add a sheet of paper. When you want someone to make a trip he is not interested in making, take care of all the preparations yourself. Think of ways you can presently utilize this idea.

Channel feelings of love to increase your love for the Almighty.

ויאסר יוסף מרכבתו ויעל לקראת ישראל אביו גשנה וירא אליו ויפל על
צואריו ויבך על צואריו עוד. (בראשית מ"ו כ"ט)

"AND YOSEF HARNESSED UP HIS CHARIOT, AND WENT UP TO
GOSHEN TO GREET YISROEL, HIS FATHER, AND HE APPEARED TO
HIM AND FELL ON HIS NECK, AND WEPT ON HIS NECK
CONTINUOUSLY." (*Braishis* 46:29)

Rashi cites the comment of the Sages that Yaakov did not fall on
the neck of Yosef and kiss him because he was reciting the *Shma
Yisroel* at that moment.

I recall vividly how my father, Rabbi Shmuel Pliskin, of blessed
memory, lived with this reality. He was in Johns Hopkins Hospital
in Baltimore after major surgery for cancer. I flew in from
Yerushalayim to visit him after having been away for seven years.
As I walked into his hospital room, he immediately said *Shma
Yisroel.* Then he said the following: "Why did Yaakov choose this
moment to recite the *Shma*? Why not earlier or later? The answer is
that after not having seen his beloved son for so many years he was
overwhelmed with profound feelings of love and joy. These feelings
can be channeled for love of the Almighty. That is exactly the right
moment to say *Shma Yisroel.* Moreover, for ever after the reciting
of the *Shma* will bring out these feelings over and over again."

While this is a concept I had heard before, I learned from my
father how to internalize a *Dvar Torah* into a living reality. Torah
insights are not merely ideas to be repeated, but are meant as
instructions for living. As I write this I can once again feel the love
my father had for me and the love which we should all feel for our
Heavenly Father.

**By having a greater appreciation for life itself you will be free
from complaints.**

ויאמר פרעה אל יעקב כמה ימי שני חייך. ויאמר יעקב אל פרעה ימי שני
מגורי שלשים ומאת שנה מעט ורעים היו ימי שני חיי ולא השיגו את ימי
שני חיי אבתי בימי מגוריהם. (בראשית מ"ז ח-ט)

"AND PHARAOH SAID TO YAAKOV, HOW MANY ARE THE YEARS OF YOUR LIFE? AND YAAKOV SAID TO PHARAOH, I HAVE LIVED ONE HUNDRED AND THIRTY YEARS. THE YEARS OF MY LIFE WERE FEW AND BAD AND THEY HAVE NOT REACHED THE YEARS OF MY FATHERS." (*Braishis* 47:8-9)

Daas Zkainim cites the Midrash that Yaakov was punished for saying that the days of his life were few and bad. Because of this lack of appreciation for life which was manifested in Yaakov's words, he lived thirty-three years less than his father Yitzchak. These 33 years correspond to the 33 words in verses 8 and 9.

Rabbi Chayim Shmuelevitz would frequently cite this Midrash and explained that we should gain such a great appreciation for life itself that even if we have many difficulties in life, we will still live a life of joy. Experiencing this daily joy of living, we would be unable to say that our life was bad. The ultimate level to strive for is that you should feel tremendous joy in living, and then trivial matters will not cause you to complain.

This concept, said Rav Chayim, is what the Midrash to *Eichah* meant when it stated that life itself is sufficient that we should have no complaints in this world. An illustration of this is someone who was drinking from a glass which fell and broke. The person might be irritated about the inconveniences involved. But imagine the scene if at the exact moment the glass fell and broke, someone would run in and tell this person that he had just won a huge sum of money in the national sweepstakes. He would be so overwhelmed with his good fortune that he would be oblivious to the loss of a glass and the bother of having to sweep it up. Similarly, someone who feels the joy inherent in life itself will have no complaints when things do not work out the way he would wish. He feels so high that nothing will be able to take away his positive feelings.

My father, Rabbi Shmuel Pliskin, lived with this concept. The day after he had major surgery for cancer, someone came into his hospital room and asked him how he was feeling. This is not the appropriate question to ask someone who has six pipes in his stomach twenty-four hours after an operation, and the person immediately regretted having asked the question. But my father's reply was, "*Baruch Hashem*, thank the Almighty, no complaints, I'm alive." When someone lives with this concept every single day, minor irritations are so trivial that they are hardly felt. Living with this reality for many years helps a person master this attitude and even major problems can be dealt with without complaint.

A question arises why Yaakov lost 33 years because of the 33 words in these two verses. Verse 8 consists of Pharaoh's asking Yaakov his age. What does this have to do with Yaakov's saying that his days were short and few? Rabbi Chayim Shmuelevitz replied: As the *Daas Zkainim* writes, Yaakov looked extremely old. Pharaoh thought that Yaakov was older than he actually was and this was the reason he asked him his age. Because Yaakov lacked joy in his life, said Rav Chayim, his suffering caused the aging process to quicken. There are many psychosomatic difficulties caused by painful emotions that would be alleviated if a person were to master the attribute of joy in living. Therefore Yaakov was held accountable for allowing the difficulties in his life to cause him so much stress that he aged prematurely. The amount of stress one experiences in any situation is dependent on one's attitude. The greater one's joy in life the less one will experience stress while going through life's journey.

To remind us that we should feel joy in being alive and to express our gratitude to the Almighty the Sages have formulated the *Modeh Ani* which is the first thing we say when we arise in the morning. It is not sufficient just to rattle off the words of the *Modeh Ani*. Rather we should reflect for a moment that it is wonderful to be alive today and therefore we will be free of complaints this entire day. Each time you repeat the *Modeh Ani* with enthusiasm and joy you are increasing its power to enable you to get off to a positive start each morning.

VAYECHI

Unity creates love and love brings forgiveness.

ויקרא יעקב אל בניו ויאמר האספו ואגידה לכם את אשר יקרא אתכם
באחרית הימים. (בראשית מ"ט א')

Before Yaakov's death:

"AND YAAKOV CALLED TO HIS SONS, AND HE SAID, GATHER TOGETHER AND I WILL TELL YOU WHAT WILL BEFALL YOU IN THE END OF DAYS." (*Braishis* 49:1)

Yaakov told his sons to gather together, to have *achdus*, unity. Only when there is unity among the descendants of Yaakov can there be redemption. If there is not yet unity, it is not yet time for redemption. With this we can understand what Yosef's brothers meant when they said to him later on (50:16-7) that before Yaakov's death he requested that Yosef forgive them. Commentators are puzzled on the issue of where he requested this. The answer can be seen in our verse. Yaakov asked for unity and the deep love that comes from unity. Where there is love, there is forgiveness. (*Shaloh, Torah Shebiksav, Parshas Vayechi*)

This is a crucial issue for our time. People are very different from one another in many ways. But if all the descendants of Yaakov realize how important it is to have *achdus*, this unity will bring about a love that transcends the specific complaints one person has against another.

Work on yourself not to act impulsively.

פחז כמים אל תותר. (בראשית מ"ט ד')

When Yaakov was on his deathbed, he said to Reuven:
"UNSTABLE AS WATER, YOU SHALL NOT HAVE PRE-EMINENCE."
(*Braishis* 49:4)

Rabbi Yeruchem Levovitz commented that the Torah does not usually give metaphors as it does here. The Torah's metaphor is showing us the living reality of the trait of impulsivity. Impulsive as water. Just as water flows quickly, so is the behavior of the person who acts impulsively without carefully thinking about what he is about to do. If you do not weigh the consequences of your behavior, you will make many harmful mistakes and will cause much damage. The Torah's metaphor of water serves as a constant reminder of the dangers of being impulsive. Whenever you see water flowing, tell yourself thoughts that will slow down your reactions. (*Daas Torah: Braishis*, p.275)

Rabbi Simcha Shlomo Levin, son of Rabbi Aryeh Levin, recalled: Once I accompanied my father when he went visiting the prisons. At the prison in Ramle the warden joined us to take us around and said, "Look, in that cell over there is a man who murdered his neighbor on the day before Yom Kippur, after an angry quarrel with him over some garbage cans. He was sentenced to life-imprisonment. Now he is in the grip of a strong, gloomy depression, and we fear for his mental health."

Reb Aryeh went over to the prisoner to talk with him, and asked how he was. "I am unfit for you to talk to me," answered the man. "I am a murderer. I hate myself, because I could not control my evil impulses and my terrible anger. If only one of the people around me during the quarrel would have seized my hands and stopped me. What I did is unforgiveable!" And with that he burst into tears and tore his hair in grief.

Reb Aryeh saw that in his depression this man was losing all hope and giving way to despair, with not a drop of self-esteem left. So he went to work to rebuild his shattered self.

"Look, you are not a murderous type at all. You did not decide to kill in cold blood. You have only one defect: that you cannot control yourself. Well, that is what you have to work on. This is

your life's task now, to repair and correct that defect." Then Reb
Aryeh added, "Believe me, all is not lost for you. Strive to improve
your character, and eventually you will be fit to live among people
again."

For a while the two sat together, silent and thoughtful. Then
Rabbi Levin spoke again: "When our father Yaakov lay on his
deathbed and gave his twelve sons his final blessing, he said to
Reuven, his eldest son, 'Unstable as water, you shall not have pre-
eminence.' Our Sages explain that Reuevn was punished; he lost his
rights as the firstborn son because he interfered in his father's
personal life after Rochel died. Yet the Talmud states, 'Whoever
says that Reuven sinned is only making an error' (*Shabbos* 58b).
How can that be?

"The answer is that Reuven had a bad trait, a defect in his
character: he was 'unstable as water.' He was not bad by nature or
personality; he just had the one unfortunate trait, that he was
quick-tempered. As the eldest son he should have had certain
privileges. He should have been the ancestor of the kings of Israel,
not his brother Yehudah. But because of the defect in character he
lost all that. So this is really what Yaakov told him: Reuven my
son, it is not that you are a sinner or a criminal; but your
problematic character trait has prevented you from fulfilling the
tasks and enjoying the privileges that were destined for you."

From the time he heard this, the prisoner's mind was calmed. (*A
Tzaddik in Our Time*, pp.186-8)

All traits must be utilized in appropriate amounts.

אחלקם ביעקב ואפיצם בישראל. (בראשית מ"ט ז')

Yaakov said about the tribes of Shimon and Levi:
"I WILL DIVIDE THEM AMONG THE REST OF YAAKOV AND I WILL
SPREAD THEM AMONG ISRAEL." (*Braishis* 49:7)

The Chasam Sofer explains that the dividing and spreading in this verse refers to the previously mentioned anger of the tribes of Shimon and Levi. Shimon and Levi overreacted with violence. But the other tribes did nothing for the benefit of Dinah. This was improper for they should have taken some action. Therefore Yaakov said, "I'll take away some of the anger of Shimon and Levi and spread it among the other brothers for they need more than they have now. Then they will all have this trait in a proper amount." (*Toras Moshe*)

Every trait is necessary. The only question is how much and in which situations it should be used. Someone without anger or zealousness will fail to take action to protest against injustice. On the other hand, excessive anger is extremely harmful. It causes quarrels, hurt feelings, much pain and suffering. What is needed is the proper balance to be used according to the directives of the Torah. When one is angry, one is more likely to take action. Anger causes inner physiological reactions that give one more physical strength and energy. But this should only be used in situations when this physical strength is needed for self-defense or to defend others. In daily situations anger is wrong and harmful. Even when anger is appropriate it must be used in the proper amounts. An overreaction will cause more harm than good. The Hebrew word for trait is *midah*, which means measure. One must study each trait from Torah sources to clarify the right time, place, and amount for each trait. To be a complete person every trait must be used. Fortunate is the person who has mastered a proper balance.

Power over oneself is real power.

גור אריה יהודה מטרף בני עלית. (בראשית מ"ט ט')

"YEHUDAH IS A LION'S WHELP, FROM THE PREY, MY SON, YOU HAVE GONE UP." (*Braishis* 49:9)

Rashi comments that Yehudah elevated himself by two actions. One, he stopped his brothers from killing Yosef. Two, he publicly embarrassed himself to save Tamar.

Rabbi Yeruchem Levovitz cited the Kuzari that the righteous person is one who rules over himself and all his impulses. Such a person is worthy of being a ruler over others because he will rule over them with the same righteousness as he rules over himself. This, said Rav Yeruchem, is the reason Yehudah merited being the tribe of the future kings of Israel. In saving Yosef, he ruled over himself not to be influenced by the behavior of others. He was so self-confident that his brothers listened to him. This is the power of ruling over oneself. Such a person can be a ruler because of his own inner strength and not merely because other people happened to choose him. Similarly, when he willingly caused himself public embarrassment it took much self-discipline. This ability to rule himself made him a true king. (*Daas Torah: Braishis*, p.278)

True peace of mind comes from being able to maintain it under all circumstances.

וירא מנחה כי טוב ואת הארץ כי נעמה ויט שכמו לסבל. (בראשית מ״ט ט״ו)

About Yissachar, Yaakov said:

"AND HE SAW THAT REST WAS GOOD, AND THE LAND THAT IT WAS PLEASANT; AND HE BOWED HIS SHOULDERS TO BEAR." (*Braishis* 49:15)

Rabbi Yeruchem Levovitz noted: The Torah was given to the Israelites at Mount Sinai in the wilderness. Some people find this difficult to understand. To acquire Torah one must be in a calm state. One needs peace of mind, without any disturbances. The Torah therefore should have been given in *Eretz Yisroel* when everyone had a home of his own and they were settled in a peaceful environment. Why was the Torah given in a wilderness, a place empty of all physical comforts? Just as the Torah itself contains instructions for living, so too the manner in which the Torah was given serves as an important lesson for us. It teaches us how we can make ourselves fit for accepting the Torah.

For Torah study one needs peace of mind, said Rav Yeruchem. But the Almighty taught us the true definition of peace of mind by giving the Torah in the wilderness. People who do not have a proper understanding of character traits mistakenly think that the way to have peace of mind is for a person to have physical comforts. But the reality is just the opposite. Peace of mind that is dependent on physical comforts and meeting all of one's needs is the source of confusion. A person who becomes used to having peace of mind only when nothing is missing in his life will be broken by unusual circumstances. A person who seeks peace of mind by having physical comforts is similar to a person who throws oil on a fire to extinguish it, or to a person who drinks salt water to quench his thirst. For a moment it appears to him that he is putting the fire out or quenching his thirst, but very soon he will see that the fire is burning with more energy and his thirst is even stronger than before. This is exactly what happens to the person who tries to find peace of mind through physical comforts. When a person is able to have peace of mind even though he is missing comforts and pleasures, then he has acquired the peace of mind necessary for accepting the Torah.

How can a person gain this peace of mind? The way, said Rav Yeruchem, is to be aware of your ultimate goals in life. When you are aware of what life is really about and keep your focus on this, you are constantly in one situation: traveling towards your goal. When you internalize this awareness you will never be overly disturbed or broken. The reason people are broken is because they live in different life situations and feel much stress because of the changes. When a person experiences one stressful situation after the other, they add up and become overwhelming. But the person who views all life situations as means to reach his ultimate goals experiences less stress and will be able to cope with difficulties.

Soldiers are trained to be prepared for battle. A prerequisite for this is for them to have peace of mind even though all around them is chaos and their lives are in danger. The training exercises for this, said Rav Yeruchem, do not include having all their physical needs met. They are not given the most comfortable quarters nor the best foods. Just the opposite. The main exercises are for them to be able to cope with situations when all the comforts of home are missing. They are taught not to allow even the most difficult circumstances to disturb them. There is only one goal in all their training: to fight like a hero for the homeland and to defeat the enemy. With a lack of all comforts, they become conditioned to having the necessary peace of mind even though the situation is very difficult.

Similarly when it comes to studying Torah. The peace of mind that is necessary remains constant even though one is undergoing hardships and deprivation. When one reaches the proper level of training, nothing will be able to take away his serenity. Therefore in reference to Yissachar the Torah states, "He saw that rest was good." Yissachar is the tribe that was devoted to Torah study. He knew that rest and peace of mind were necessary to master the Torah. What did he do? "He bowed his shoulder to bear" - by training himself to bear any difficulties he was able to reach the highest levels of peace of mind in all situations.

There is a mistake that so many people in the world make, said Rav Yeruchem. They seek peace of mind by trying to obtain physical peace. But this is exactly what creates so much stress and tension in people's lives. There are many people who get married and on their wedding day if even one small detail goes wrong this upsets them greatly. They become so agitated that they do not know which world they are in. There is a common expression people use. After someone is married they say he enters "a new life." This way of looking at things is only because they consider every new situation as a change in their life itself. They therefore consider being single and being married as different lives. But that is not the reality. There is only one real life situation and that is the journey towards one's ultimate purpose in life. Fortunate is the person who sees before him only the main goal. When a person reaches this level no occurrence will be able to shake him. He is directed towards his singular goal. One will always find him in a state of tranquility. (*Daas Torah: Braishis*, pp.279-82)

SHMOS

Self-respect leads to having respect for others and to behaving in a more elevated manner.

וימת יוסף וכל אחיו וכל הדור ההוא. (שמות א' ו')

"AND YOSEF DIED, AND ALL HIS BROTHERS, AND THAT ENTIRE GENERATION." (*Shmos* 1:6)

Ohr Hachayim explains that the enslavement of the Israelites by the Egyptians occurred in three stages. First Yosef died, the Israelites lost their power. Then the brothers died. As long as even one of the brothers was alive, the Egyptians still honored them. Even afterwards as long as the members of that first generation were alive, the Egyptians considered them important and were not able to treat them as slaves.

Rabbi Chayim Shmuelevitz, the Mirrer Rosh Hayeshiva, commented on this that there are two aspects here. One is on the side of the Egyptians. They were unable to treat the Jewish people as slaves as long as they considered them important. The other aspect is on the side of the Jewish people themselves. As long as they were considered important and worthy of respect by themselves, the Egyptians were not able to treat them in an inferior manner. Only when they personally considered themselves in a lowly manner could they be subjugated by others.

This, said Rav Chayim, is the way in which the evil inclination deals with people. First, the evil inclination tries to have a person feel inferior and guilty. Once a person feels a sense of guilt and worthlessness then he is easy prey for being trapped by the evil inclination in many ways. What is the antidote? A person should strive to internalize elevated feelings about himself. When a person has those feelings of elevation, he will be careful not to do anything that will lower his level. If feelings of self-respect and importance are an inherent part of a person's self-image, they will prevent him from sinning.

We find this principle in the Talmud (*Sanhedrin* 37a) in reference to the manner in which the judges of a court try to motivate witnesses to refrain from giving false testimony. In capital punishment cases the witnesses are told, "In the beginning only one man was created. This is to teach us that whoever causes the death of one person is considered as destroying an entire world. Therefore each person is obligated to say, 'The world was created for me.'" (See Rambam *Hilchos Sanhedrin* 12:3 that this is part of the warning to the witnesses.) Rashi explains the latter part of this statement: "That is, I am as important as an entire world. Therefore I will not cause myself to be destroyed for one transgression." This, says Rashi, will prevent him from delivering the false testimony. We see from here, said Rav Chayim, that the awareness of the greatness of each person - the greatness of being an entire world - will stop a person from transgressing. He will not want to be lowered from his high level. Even these witnesses who were about to kill someone by means of their false testimony, as soon as they reflect on the greatness of man will back away from committing this crime.

When witnesses were warned not to give false testimony in monitary matters, the Talmud (*Sanhedrin* 29a) states that the judges told them, "False witnesses are considered cheap in the eyes of those who hire them." These witnesses who we suspect of being ready to perjure themselves for profit, and the severity of the transgression of giving false testimony does not frighten them, the way to influence them is by an appeal to their self-respect. They are told that they will be looked at with disgust and disdain by the very same people who they are trying to help with their lies. This, said Rav Chayim, is the most powerful message to influence someone to refrain from doing wrong. This feeling of self-respect will prevent a person from transgressing.

From this entire thought of Rabbi Chayim Shmuelevitz we see how crucial it is for parents and educators to build up the self-esteem of children. The more elevated they see themselves, as long as it is a healthy self-esteem and not arrogance, the more elevated will they behave.

Doing acts of kindness for infants elevates you.

ויאמר מלך מצרים למילדת העברית אשר שם האחת שפרה ושם השנית
פועה. (שמות א' ט"ו)

"AND THE KING OF EGYPT SPOKE TO THE HEBREW MIDWIVES, ONE WAS SHIFRAH AND THE NAME OF THE SECOND WAS PUAH." (*Shmos* 1:15)

Rashi states that Shifrah was a second name for Yocheved, Moshe's mother. She was called Shifrah because she did things for the betterment of the infants in her care. Puah was another name for Miriam, Moshe's sister. She was called Puah because of the comforting sounds she would make to the infants as mothers do to calm a crying baby.

Rabbi Yeruchem Levovitz commented that when the Torah calls someone by a certain name it is because that name represents the essence of the person. The fact that Yocheved and Miriam were called by the names that show how they helped the infants both physically and emotionally means that this was an integral part of their very being. We see from here that what might appear to be minor actions can be part of an elevated level that will comprise the entire person.

This is a point that needs to be spoken about frequently, said Rav Yeruchem. In the creation there is nothing that is in itself small or great. Everything depends on the person himself who is doing any action. The great person will do great acts even in seemingly minor behaviors. On the other hand, a small person will take matters that could be exalted and make them into garbage.

One example is money. This can easily be a poison, said Rav Yeruchem. Money can be the most negative thing in the world. On the other hand, high levels of loving the Almighty can be obtained through a wise use of one's money. The Talmud (*Bava Basra* 10a) states that Turnusrufus, the evil, asked Rabbi Akiva, "If your G-d loves the poor why does he not support them?" Rabbi Akiva replied, "In order that we should be saved from *Gehinom*." We see from this that the same thing that could be poison can be utilized as a purification machine. Money can help a person obtain high levels of *chesed* and kindness.

Great people's lives are full of greatness, Rav Yeruchem concluded. In everything they do they see greatness and elevation. Even in the tiniest things they do they reach great heights. From playing with small infants and saying, "Poo poo" they merited the highest levels. Yocheved and Miriam have a special place in the sacred Torah as Shifrah and Puah for their compassion for babies. (*Daas Torah: Shmos*, pp.5-7)

When you experience love and compassion for others, you are emulating the attributes of the Almighty. The greater your act of kindness the more elevated you become. An infant or young child who experiences warmth and love grows up to be a more loving person. This early conditioning will have life-long positive effects. Such a child will find it much easier to feel love for the Almighty and love for his fellow man. Whenever you make a young child feel good, be aware of the extent of your kindness. The deeper your appreciation for the *chesed* you are doing the more elevated you become.

I heard from a relative of the Chazon Ish that the Chazon Ish would bend over and have his toddler nephews ride on his back. I heard from a student of Rabbi Chayim Shmuelevitz that he once came to Rav Chayim's house and saw him playing hide-and-seek with his grandchildren. When a great person plays with young children, he is not engaging in something trivial or frivolous. Rather he himself is emulating the Almighty and is developing a child who will grow up to have love and compassion for others.

Rabbi Tzvi Broide, son-in-law of Rabbi Simcha Zissel of Kelm, suffered from strong headaches. Once during a painful headache, some young children were playing loudly near him. Someone wanted to tell the children to be quiet, but Rav Tzvi would not allow him to do so. He always wanted to give people pleasure and joy and did not want to do anything that would decrease the happiness of these children. (*Tnuas Hamussar*, vol.2, p.113)

Try to help others even if you do not think you will succeed. Frequently you will accomplish more than you imagined.

ותרד בת פרעה לרחץ על היאר ונערתיה הלכת על יד היאר ותרא את התבה בתוך הסוף ותשלח את אמתה ותקחה. (שמות ב' ה')

"AND THE DAUGHTER OF PHARAOH CAME DOWN TO WASH HERSELF AT THE NILE, AND HER MAIDENS WALKED ALONG BY THE SIDE OF THE NILE; AND SHE SAW THE BOX [containing Moshe] AMONG THE RUSHES, AND SHE STRETCHED OUT HER ARM AND SHE TOOK IT." (*Shmos* 2:5)

Rashi cites the Sages that Pharaoh's daughter's arm stretched out very long and she miraculously was able to save the infant Moshe.

A number of communal activists were at a meeting which was headed by Rabbi Meir Shapiro, Rosh Hayeshiva of Lublin. The matter at hand concerned saving people's lives. There were some people at the meeting who said, "What needs to be done is simply impossible. There is no way that we could possibly be successful."

Rabbi Meir Shapiro cited the Sages who explained our verse that a miracle happened to enable Pharaoh's daughter's arm to stretch so far as to reach Moshe and save him. The question arises, "Why did she stretch out her arm in the first place? Didn't she realize that it was impossible for her to reach Moshe?" The Kotzker Rebbe replied that a person must always try to do everything he can to save someone. Even if you think that your efforts on behalf of others cannot possibly succeed, still make a sincere effort to try anyway. You will be surprised to find that you will frequently accomplish much more than you imagined. "This applies to us," said Rabbi Shapiro. "We must do everything we can even if we do not really believe that we will be successful. The Almighty often helps and the efforts put in prove to be fruitful." (*Otzer Chayim*)

To achieve greatness one must have a highly developed positive self-image.

ויגדל הילד ותבאהו לבת פרעה ויהי לה לבן ותקרא שמו משה ותאמר כי מן המים משיתהו. (שמות ב' י')

"AND THE LAD GREW UP. AND SHE BROUGHT HIM TO THE DAUGHTER OF PHARAOH AND HE WAS TO HER AS A SON. AND SHE CALLED HIS NAME MOSHE. AND SHE SAID, BECAUSE HE WAS DRAWN FROM THE WATER." (*Shmos* 2:10)

Ibn Ezra (to verse 3) states that it is possible the Almighty had Moshe raised in the palace of the king in order for him to experience a royal manner of behavior. He would both see it firsthand and get into the habit of acting this way. We see how this early training helped Moshe develop into a dynamic personality. He killed an Egyptian in order to defend a person he was attacking. He rescued the maidens in Midian and enabled them to water their flocks.

Rabbi Yeruchem Levovitz commented on this that we see here a powerful lesson on the importance of learning and habit in the development of a person and in preparing him for greatness. Even someone with the inherent greatness of Moshe needed a total environmental learning experience of royalty to integrate the personality necessary to be a great leader. The attribute of dynamic leadership is not easy to acquire. One needs much effort and many learning experiences to obtain this attribute. (*Daas Torah: Shmos*, p.8)

Moshe was the most humble of all men. In his personal life he mastered the ability to ignore any slights or insults. But he was a powerful leader who accepted responsibility upon himself to save people in difficulties. One's self-image is a key factor in one's behavior. Moshe's self-image was of a prince growing up in the palace of an absolute monarch. This allowed him to take any action necessary to do what was right.

The most precious gift you can bestow upon any child is a positive self-image. Constant criticism and fault-finding knocks away at one's self-esteem. A child growing up with inferiority feelings is handicapped. This will limit him in many ways. The key focus of anyone dealing with children must be, "How can I elevate this child's self-image?" Yes, humility must be taught, but the humility of a Moshe Rabainu. This is an awareness of one's greatness with the realization that all is a gift from the Almighty.

When Rabbi Simcha Zissel of Kelm would wake up his young children in the morning, he would gently say to them, "Children you are sleeping away when you have a kingdom to rule. The Almighty gave man rulership over the entire creation." (*Meoros Hagdolim*, p.79)

Develop the attribute of seeing the suffering of others.

ויהי בימים ההם ויגדל משה ויצא אל אחיו וירא בסבלתם. (שמות ב' י"א)

"AND IT WAS IN THOSE DAYS AND MOSHE GREW UP AND HE WENT OUT TO HIS BROTHERS, AND HE SAW THEIR SUFFERING." (*Shmos* 2:11)

Rashi adds that Moshe made a special effort that his eyes should see and his heart should feel the suffering of the Children of Israel.

Rabbi Chayim Shmuelevitz used to say that sight is the means by which you are able to feel for another person. Only by seeing can a person have a strong degree of empathy for the suffering of others. Just a plain seeing alone is not sufficient. Rather a person needs to make a "special effort" to observe carefully. When a person observes carefully, he will be able to feel for another person from the depths of his heart.

This is the reason why the Sages said that a blind person is considered as if he were dead, said Rav Chayim. Without being able to see, one cannot feel for another person. He is as if he were alone in the world. When a person is alone, there is an aspect of not being fully alive.

This attribute of becoming more sensitive to the suffering of other people is a basic trait to develop. Make an effort to truly "see" people. Some people are experts at seeing the faults of others. When one works on seeing the suffering of others, one's focus is on helping them. This prevents seeing the negative, and leads to many acts of kindness. This was the trait of Moshe and it is incumbent upon us to use this as our model for our own behavior.

When the time came in the morning for the young children at Aitz Chayim in Jerusalem to enter the classroom for their daily lessons, Rabbi Aryeh Levine would stand at the doorway or at a window, and he would study each small boy - to the puzzlement of the children, who would not understand his reason.

One day his son asked him, "Why do you always stand at the entrance waiting for the pupils, and then you look at them so closely as they enter?"

"You come and stand with me and take a close look at them," said Reb Aryeh. "What do you see?"

"It is quite interesting to watch them go in," his son commented. "You can see how eager they are to study Torah. There I saw a boy pushing ahead of another. He has a zest for learning. That one over there, though, is not at all anxious to enter. His mind is still on the games he was playing."

"I look at different things altogether," said Reb Aryeh. "That child's pants are torn. This one's shoes are quite tattered and worn. That boy over there is definitely hungry; how will he be able to study?"

Rabbi Levine then did all that he could to help those children who were needy. (*A Tzaddik in Our Time*, p.319)

Rabbi Moshe Mordechai Shulsinger was once approached by someone who asked him to travel from Bnai Brak to Tel Aviv to request a certain person to help his son out financially. Rabbi Shulsinger did not know the person he was asked to approach and felt certain that the person would not be willing to help out. The man was persistent in his request and finally agreed that they would consult the Steipler and follow his opinion. The man went to the Steipler himself, and the Steipler replied to Rabbi Shulsinger in a letter, "Even though the chances of actually getting financial assistance are very slight, nevertheless this person is very hopeful that your trying will be beneficial. If you don't go, you will cause this person much disappointment because he will think that you aren't concerned with helping him. Therefore your going is a fulfillment of the great *mitzvah* of doing an act of kindness. Not that you will be able to get him money, but in order to relieve him from the anxiety he experiences until you go." (*Peninai Rabainu Hakehilos Yaakov*, pp.32-4)

You ultimately help yourself when you help others.

ויקם משה ויושען. (שמות ב׳ י״ז)

"AND MOSHE STOOD UP AND SAVED THEM." (*Shmos* 2:17)

The Torah tells us here how Moshe saved Tziporah, who at that time was a complete stranger. Later on we read in the Torah how measure for measure she saved Moshe's life (*Shmos* 4:24-5). We see from this, said the Chofetz Chayim, that all the kindness that a person does for someone else eventually is repaid to him. (*Chofetz Chayim al Hatorah*)

Whenever you do a favor for someone else, you benefit yourself. Definitely, the highest level is to do kindness for others for the sake of a *mitzvah* without thinking of personal gain. But whenever you find it difficult to do kindness for others, at least do it for pragmatic reasons. When you are kind to others, they will be kinder to you. If not right away, then in the course of time you will eventually be repaid.

The Steipler related that when he was a young student in Europe he wrote a letter to the author of the *sefer Imrai Moshe* and asked if he could purchase his book at a cheaper price since he lacked money. The author then sent him a copy of the book for free. Years later, in *Eretz Yisroel* after the Second World War when the students of the *Imrai Moshe* wanted to reprint his book, they searched for a copy and only found the one that the Steipler had. From this single copy they reprinted it. On this it could be said the verse (*Koheles* 11:1), "Cast your bread upon the waters, for you will find it after many days." (*Peninai Rabainu Hakehilos Yaakov*, p.111)

Serve the Almighty by acting in an elevated manner in difficult situations.

המקום אשר אתה עומד עליו אדמת קדש הוא. (שמות ג' ה')

The Almighty told Moshe:
"THE PLACE UPON WHICH YOU ARE STANDING IS SACRED LAND."
(*Shmos* 3:5)

When a person finds himself in a situation with many distractions and difficulties, he is likely to say, "When the Almighty improves my situation, then I will be able to study Torah and fulfill more *mitzvos*. But not right now. Now all I can think about is my problems." In these situations, said the Chofetz Chayim, this verse of the Torah applies. "The place upon which you are standing," that is, the exact situation in which you find yourself is sacred. If your life situation is difficult, it is exactly in that difficult situation that the Almighty wants you to serve Him. As the Sages have said, "According to the difficulty is the reward." (*Chofetz Chayim al Hatorah*, p.61)

Our goal in life is to serve the Almighty. The exact details of how we will serve Him is dependent on how our life unfolds. Many people have an imaginary picture of how they would want their life to be. Unless their life is the way they want it to be, they feel as if they are not really living until they can improve their situation. But we see here the proper Torah perspective. Definitely we can take action to improve conditions. But no matter what life is like, our mission in life is to study Torah and fulfill *mitzvos*. The more difficulties that arise, the more elevated we become when we overcome those difficulties.

The Chofetz Chayim used to say, "A fool makes mud out of gold. But a wise person makes gold out of mud." (*Michtevai Chofetz Chayim; Sichos HaC.C.*, part 2, p.39)

Greatness is utilizing your potential regardless of what that potential is.

ויאמר בי אדני שלח נא ביד תשלח. (שמות ד' י"ג)

When Moshe was told by the Almighty that he would be the leader to approach Pharaoh to demand freedom for the Israelites, Moshe replied:
"PLEASE MY MASTER SEND ANYONE ELSE." (*Shmos* 4:13)

The Ramban explains that Moshe told the Almighty to send anyone else because there is no other person in the world who is not more fitting than me for this mission.

At first glance this is puzzling. How could Moshe sincerely have thought of himself as unworthy. Rabbi Chayim of Volozhin explained that even if a person is very intelligent and wise and has accomplished very much, he nevertheless might not be working as hard as he should. With his talents and abilities he might have accomplished very much if he tried harder. On the other hand, a person who seems to be very lowly perhaps is doing all he can. The lowly person is reaching his potential, while the great person might be far from it. For this reason Moshe felt he was unworthy. In his humility, he thought that he was more distant from being all that he could be than everyone else. (*Ruach Chayim, Avos* 4:1)

This is a lesson for two types of people. Those who feel arrogant and conceited because of their great intellect and accomplishments should be aware that perhaps they are far from reaching their potential and this should lessen their inflated feelings about themselves. For this exact same reason, those who are trying very hard to act in an elevated manner and put in much effort should not feel envious or disheartened when they see others apparently accomplishing more than them. One's true spiritual level cannot be measured by any mortal. There is no accurate objective means of evaluating any person. The true level of each person is based entirely on effort and this only the Almighty can measure.

VAAIRAH

To give encouragement to others speak in a way they can relate to.

וידבר משה כן אל בני ישראל ולא שמעו אל משה מקצר רוח ומעבדה
קשה. (שמות ו' ט')

"AND MOSHE SPOKE SO TO THE CHILDREN OF ISRAEL AND THEY
DID NOT LISTEN TO MOSHE FOR ANGUISH OF SPIRIT AND HARD
WORK." (*Shmos* 6:9)

Rabbi Meir Simcha Hacohen explains that they did not listen to
the previous message that Moshe gave them which was that they
would come into the Land of Israel. This can be understood that
when someone is suffering very much, all he wants to hear is that
his suffering will be removed. He is not yet ready to hear that he
will have good fortune and much success in the future. If someone
paints a too positive picture of the future, it is so far removed from
his present reality that he will not be able to relate to it. Therefore
we read in verse 13 that the Almighty told Moshe to just tell them
that they will be taken out of Egypt, without any mention of a
bright future. (*Meshech Chochmah*)

This is an important principle when trying to give people
emotional support and encouragement. If you give them a picture
that is beyond their present ability to relate to, your words will not
be comforting even if you have very good intentions. Telling
someone who is in deep emotional distress, "Don't worry all will
be well in the future" might not have a positive effect. Show the
person how to get out of the present pain and only then will you be
able to give more optimistic messages.

Anyone in a leadership position must develop the traits of patience and tolerance.

וידבר השם אל משה ואל אהרן ויצום אל בני ישראל. (שמות ו' י"ג)

"AND THE ALMIGHTY SPOKE TO MOSHE AND AHARON AND HE COMMANDED THEM ABOUT THE CHILDREN OF ISRAEL." (*Shmos* 6:13)

Rashi comments that the Almighty commanded Moshe and Aharon to lead them gently. They were told to have patience in dealing with the Israelites. This, writes the *Shaloh*, is a lesson for any person in a position of leadership. Whenever you are in a position of authority, be very careful not to get angry at the people you are dealing with. Watch out that you do not scream and shout. The reward for a leader who has this patience is very great. (*Shnai Luchos Habris, Vaairah*)

There are two possible attitudes for a person in a position of leadership. One is personal power. The person seeks leadership for his own ego. He demands that people listen to him because of his selfish vanity. Such a leader will become angry when people do not follow his orders: "How dare them to disobey me." His entire focus is on his own success. The only reason he cares about other people is because that is how he will be successful. The people he deals with are not his goal, but just a means to an end. The end being his own self-aggrandizement and power. Such a leader will get angry easily.

But the Torah ideal of leadership is just the opposite. The entire goal of leadership is to help as many people as you can. The focus is on the benefit of the people you are dealing with. Such a leader's focus is on being of service to others. When they are suffering, he realizes that they are likely to be moody and complaining. The more difficult they are to deal with, the greater the need for patience and tolerance. That was the Almighty's command to the first leaders of the Jewish people. This is the model for all future leaders. Regardless of whether you have authority over a large amount of people or just a small group such as a class or your own children, this lesson applies to you. Every difficult encounter is a tool for growing in the trait of patience.

Someone who consulted the Chazon Ish very frequently once spoke to him in a manner that he thought would get the Chazon Ish angry. He therefore asked the Chazon Ish not to became angry at him.

The Chazon Ish replied, "In my store this product does not exist." (*P'air Hador*, vol.3, p.49)

Feel joy when you plan to fulfill a good deed.

ויעש משה ואהרן כאשר צוה השם אתם כן עשו. (שמות ז' ו')

"AND MOSHE AND AHARON DID AS THE ALMIGHTY COMMANDED THEM. SO THEY DID." (*Shmos* 7:6)

Rabbi Yosef Karo, author of the *Shulchan Aruch*, commented on this verse that Moshe and Aharon did not yet do what the Almighty commanded. Only later would they approach Pharaoh on behalf of the Jewish people. The reason why the Torah states that they did as commanded is because they accepted upon themselves to do it. This sincere acceptance is considered as if they actually followed through and took action.(*Droshos Maharika*; cited in *Biurai Hamekubalim Beniglah*)

Whenever you sincerely plan to do a good deed, feel the joy of doing a *mitzvah*. Just planning without taking action will not accomplish very much. But when you feel joy in positive planning, you will be motivated to take action. The joy of actually doing the *mitzvah* will be even greater because of your anticipation of performing it. This joy is a manifestation of your appreciation of the opportunities to fulfill the Almighty's commandments and will increase the amount of *mitzvos* you do.

Rabbi Yeshayah Cheshin used to pray in the syngogue in the Nachalas Shivah section of Jerusalem. Once on *Simchas Torah* during the *hakofos* when there was much joyous singing and dancing in the synagogue, there were a number of laborers who were sitting in a corner and did not take part in the festivities. Rav Yeshayah approached them, and with his face radiating from joy, he pleasantly invited them to join in the dancing.

"You who study Torah have what to be joyous about," they said to him. "But we did not study Torah a whole year, why should we have joy?"

"You should know," Rabbi Cheshin said to them, "on *Simchas Torah* there are two *chasanim*: *Chasan Torah* and *Chasan Braishis*. Why is there two? *Chasan Torah* represents those who studied Torah the entire year and have joy for what they have already learned. *Chasan Braishis* represents those who have not studied Torah the past year, but have accepted upon themselves to study Torah the coming year. They have joy for what they are planning to do. Now you can come and join us and experience joy for the future."

Those people felt very positive about this, and said, "We are willing to accept upon ourselves to study Torah, but who will teach us?"

Rav Yeshayah assured them that he will teach them on a regular basis. Right away they joined the dancing and the joy was noticeable on them. They arranged regular learning sessions and it greatly elevated those people. (*Maidmuyos Yerushalayim*, p.112)

Honor-seeking will cause a person much suffering.

לך אל פרעה בבקר הנה יצא המימה ונצבת לקראתו על שפת היאר.
(שמות ז' ט"ו)

The Almighty said to Moshe:
"GO TO PHARAOH IN THE MORNING. BEHOLD HE IS GOING OUT TO THE WATER [of the Nile], AND YOU SHOULD STAND TO GREET HIM UPON THE EDGE OF THE NILE." (*Shmos* 7:15)

Rashi comments that Pharaoh used to go early each morning to the Nile to relieve himself. He claimed to his people that he was a god and did not have normal bodily needs.

Rabbi Chayim Shmuelevitz used to comment on this that we see how people who seek honor do so even though it leads to much irrational, and almost insane, behavior. One can imagine how much discomfort Pharaoh suffered to keep up this facade of being a god. Each day he suffered physically. What was his actual gain? Very little. He was an absolute monarch and had unlimited power. There was not really any practical difference whether people considered him a human powerful ruler whose slightest word could bring death to an insubordinate subject or whether they considered him a divine being. All he got was a little more honor and approval. But at a very costly price. When one suffers, it is much more difficult to appreciate the good things in one's life.

When we view Pharaoh we can see how ridiculous it is to cause oneself so much pain for such an illusory gain as a bit more approval. Introspect and find ways in which you personally cause yourself needless suffering by seeking honor and approval.

Learn to pay attention to the Almighty.

הירא את דבר השם מעבדי פרעה הניס את עבדיו ואת מקנהו אל הבתים.
ואשר לא שם לבו אל דבר השם ויעזב את עבדיו ואת מקנהו בשדה.
(שמות ט' כ־כ"א)

Moshe warned Pharaoh and the Egyptians that there was going to be a devastating hail that would destroy living creatures who remained out in the open: "THOSE WHO FEARED THE WORD OF THE ALMIGHTY FROM THE SERVANTS OF PHAROAH BROUGHT HIS SERVANTS AND HIS CATTLE INTO THE HOUSES. AND THOSE WHO DID NOT PAY ATTENTION TO THE WORD OF THE ALMIGHTY LEFT THEIR SERVANTS AND CATTLE IN THE FIELD." (Shmos 9:20-1)

The Torah does not state that there were people who did not believe that Moshe's warning was true. Rather, the Torah states that they did not pay attention. This we see is the opposite of fearing the Almighty: lack of attention.

Rabbi Chayim Shmuelevitz used to ask on this: Why didn't the servants themselves flee to safety? They should have feared for their lives and run to find safe places. The answer, said Rav Chayim, is that they did not pay attention. When one does not pay attention to danger, it is as if it does not exist.

All the knowledge in the world will not help a person keep away from danger unless he takes that knowledge to heart. For this reason there are plenty of people who do things that could greatly endanger their spiritual and physical well-being. They do not take the dangers seriously. Lack of paying attention to dangers will lead to all kinds of impulsive behavior that will have painful and damaging consequences.

The wise man is one who *sees* the future consequences of his behavior (*Tamid* 32a). The Chofetz Chayim (Introduction to *Chovas Hashmirah*) writes that the Sages used the term "seeing" to tell us a means of making future events real. One should use one's power of imagination to see the future as if it is actually occurring in the present. When you see something before your eyes, it has a much stronger effect than just hearing about it.

People differ greatly in their ability to mentally make pictures in their minds. But anyone who can mentally visualize the negative consequences of transgressing or of engaging in dangerous practices will find it much easier to guard himself from harm. Make an effort to see the future as a present reality.

View suffering as a tool for self-improvement.

וישלח פרעה ויקרא למשה ולאהרן ויאמר אלהם חטאתי הפעם השם
הצדיק ואני ועמי הרשעים. (שמות ט' כ"ז)

"AND PHARAOH SENT AND HE CALLED MOSHE AND AHARON AND HE SAID TO THEM, I HAVE SINNED THIS TIME, THE ALMIGHTY IS RIGHTEOUS AND I AND MY PEOPLE ARE WICKED." (*Shmos* 9:27)

Rabbi Noson Tzvi Finkel of Slobodka noted that although

Pharaoh verbally admitted his guilt when he was under the pressure of the plague, he reverted to his old ways as soon as the pressure was off. The problem was that he viewed suffering with a limited perspective. He viewed suffering merely as a punishment for wrong. That is why he said, "The Almighty is a righteous judge and his punishment is fair because I have done evil." But the reality of the Almighty's suffering is that there is a strong element of kindness. Suffering is a divine message telling a person that he has something to improve. It is a reminder that one needs to improve oneself. The goal of suffering is to motivate a person to improve his behavior. Because Pharaoh viewed suffering only as a punishment, as soon as the punishment was over he made no changes. (*Ohr Hatzafun, Shmos,* p.30)

When you view suffering as a means to elevate yourself, you will find meaning in your suffering. While there is still pain involved, it is much easier to cope with. Whenever you find yourself suffering, ask yourself, "How can I use this as a tool for self-improvement?"

Remember your resolutions and insights.

העתירו אל השם ורב מהית קלת אלקים וברד ואשלחה אתכם ולא תספון לעמד. (שמות ט' כ"ח)

During the plague of hail Pharaoh said to Moshe:
"ENTREAT THE LORD THAT THERE BE NO MORE MIGHTY THUNDERINGS AND HAIL; AND I WILL LET YOU GO, AND YOU SHALL STAY NO LONGER." (*Shmos* 9:28)

Rabbi Yeruchem Levovitz commented that Pharaoh did not mean to lie when he told Moshe that he will allow the Children of Israel to go free. He honestly meant what he said at the time when he said it. He was not mocking Moshe. Under the influence of the suffering of the plague he was greatly changed. But afterwards when the plague was removed, he completely forgot about his good intentions. This is a general tendency of people. When a person is in the midst of great suffering and under a lot of pressure, he can have very high ideals. He will make all kinds of lofty promises without any limit. But as soon as his situation improves, he is so entirely different that it is hard to recognize him as being the same person as before. (*Daas Torah: Shmos*, pp.80-1)

When you find yourself in a very difficult situation and make resolutions to improve yourself, remember those resolutions later on. Similarly, anyone whose life is in danger thinks that if he will be saved, he will have a greater appreciation for all that he has. But after things return to normal, it is easy to forget your previous insights and awarenesses. Make an effort to grow from difficult situations. Don't forget your resolutions and insights.

Be firm with your principles but flexible in your approach.

והחטה והכסמת לא נכו כי אפילת הנה. (שמות ט' ל"ב)

During the plague of hail:
"THE WHEAT AND SPELT WERE NOT DAMAGED, FOR THEY WERE LATE RIPENING." (*Shmos* 9:32)

Rashi explains that since they were late ripening they were soft when the hail struck and were able to bend with the wind. This flexibility on their part enabled them to bounce back and they were not uprooted.

This idea has practical applications. We find in the Talmud (*Taanis* 20b) the statement that a person should always be as soft as a reed and not as hard as a cedar tree. In *Avos D'Reb Noson* (41:1) we find an elaboration of this theme. When a strong wind comes, a reed bends in the direction of the wind. Because of this ability although it bends it does not become uprooted. Regardless of how strong the wind, it remains in its place. A cedar tree, however, does not bend at all. A soft wind which moves the reed has no effect at all on the mighty cedar. But when there is a powerful wind, the cedar breaks and falls.

I remember hearing this concept frequently from my late Rebbe Rabbi Chayim Mordechai Katz, Rosh Hayeshiva of Telz, in the name of Rabbi Yosef Leib Bloch, author of *Shiurai Daas* and Rosh Hayeshiva of Telz in Lithuania: A person needs to be very strong in his principles and ideals. So strong that no power on earth should make him veer from the truth. Nothing should uproot him from his values. But the way to do this is to be like the reed. A person needs softness and flexibility when talking to others. Talk in a kind and gentle manner. This flexibility in approach should be in conjunction with a firm groundedness in Torah values and ideals. A person who is obstinate and inflexible when talking to others might seem to be stronger. But that is an illusion. Such a person can be broken easier. His lack of flexibility will cause that if he is moved he will be entirely broken. His apparent strength is really a weakness. Softness and gentleness combined with persistence in keeping one's principles is the approach that will be victorious in the end.

BO

Don't allow arrogance to cause you to behave in self-defeating ways.

ויבא משה ואהרן אל פרעה ויאמרו אליו כה אמר השם אלקי העברים עד מתי מאנת לענת מפני שלח עמי ויעבדני. (שמות י' ג')

"AND MOSHE AND AHARON CAME TO PHARAOH AND THEY SAID TO HIM, THIS IS WHAT THE ALMIGHTY, THE LORD OF THE HEBREWS SAID, HOW LONG WILL YOU REFUSE TO HUMBLE YOURSELF BEFORE ME? LET MY PEOPLE GO AND THEY SHALL SERVE ME." (*Shmos* 10:3)

Rabainu Bachya wrote in his commentary that the Almighty requests a person to submit his will to the will of the Almighty and this takes humility. Pharaoh was a very arrogant person and refused to humble himself. Because of this faulty attribute he caused his own downfall.

Unfortunately, there are many people who cause themselves problems in life because of their arrogance. It is their arrogance which makes them retaliate when someone slights them in some manner. A person with humility would remain silent and that would end the matter. But the arrogant person answers in an attacking manner and this serves to prolong the quarrel. A person with humility will ask forgiveness when he has wronged someone, even if he feels that the other person is more to blame than himself. The arrogant person will not ask for forgiveness even when he knows that he is really at fault. A person with humility will reach out to others when he needs help. The arrogant person will feel that it is beneath his dignity to show that he has any weaknesses and will suffer rather than do what he considers belittling himself.

In what ways do you cause yourself needless suffering because of arrogance? What will you do to overcome this fault?

When something bothers another person, try to understand the matter from his perspective.

ויעל הארבה על כל ארץ מצרים וינח בכל גבול מצרים כבד מאד לפניו לא היה כן ארבה כמהו ואחריו לא יהיה כן. (שמות י' י"ד)

"AND THE LOCUSTS CAME UP ON THE ENTIRE LAND OF EGYPT AND THEY RESTED ON THE ENTIRE BOUNDARY OF EGYPT, IT WAS VERY HEAVY, BEFORE THIS THERE WERE NEVER AS MANY LOCUSTS AND AFTERWARDS THERE WILL NEVER AGAIN BE AS MUCH." (*Shmos* 10:14)

Rashi raises the question that in the days of the prophet Yoel there was such a strong plague of locusts that the verse (*Yoel* 2:2) states there were never as many.

The Chasam Sofer replied: it is true that in the days of Yoel there were more locusts than there were in Egypt. But that is only in actual numbers. In Egypt they were already devastated by other plagues that destroyed much of the vegetation, such as by the hail. The relative damage done by the locusts in Egypt was greater than at any other time, even though the amount destroyed by the locusts was greater in the time of Yoel.

The underlying idea expressed by the Chasam Sofer gives us some insight into understanding the difficulties that others are suffering. Or better still, it shows us how we can never completely understand the suffering of another person. When someone suffers because of some event, the actual pain is subjective rather than objective. This means that the pain suffered because of anything that happens is proportionate to what the situation means to the person who is suffering. When someone reacts to a situation with more suffering than you think is justified, there is always the possibility that this situation represents for that person "the straw that breaks the camel's back." Because of things that already happened to this person what occurred caused that person much more pain than you would have experienced if you were in the same situation. When someone reacts very strongly to some matter, ask the person, "What does this mean to you?" This empathetic question will help you understand that person better and possibly help him.

Once when Rabbi Dovid of Lelov was walking in the street, a woman mistook him for her husband who had abandoned her, and started to beat him. As soon as she calmed down, she realized her mistake and apologized profusely.

"I made a mistake out of my deep sorrow and suffering," she cried out. "How will I ever be forgiven for having been violent to a righteous person?"

"Please calm yourself," the Rabbi replied. "You didn't really hit me, but rather your husband and that is understandable under the unfortunate circumstances." (*Dmuyos Hod*, vol.1, pp.107-8)

When speaking to two people at the same time be sensitive not to slight either person.

ועתה שא נא חטאתי אך הפעם והעתירו להשם אלקיכם ויסר מעלי רק
את המות הזה. (שמות י' י"ז)

After suffering from the plague of locusts, Pharaoh called Moshe and Aharon and said to them:
"NOW I BESEECH YOU, FORGIVE MY SIN ONLY THIS ONCE, AND PRAY TO THE ALMIGHTY THAT HE MAY ONLY TAKE AWAY THIS DEATH." (*Shmos* 10:17)

The Ramban comments on this verse: Pharaoh realized that it was only Moshe who could intercede on his behalf with the Almighty. For this reason the first part of this verse is written in the singular. But Pharaoh spoke *derech mussar* (in a polite and tactful manner), wrote the Ramban, and asked both Moshe and Aharon to pray for him and for this reason the latter half of the verse is written in the plural.

Rabbi Simcha Zissel of Kelm, one of the main pillars of the *mussar movement*, cited this statement of the Ramban (*Chochmah Umussar,* vol.1, p.456) and added that anyone with wisdom realizes the importance of a *mussar* approach in dealing wisely with other people. In this matter we should learn from Pharaoh. He was careful to show respect to Aharon. Even though he needed a favor from Moshe, and Aharon was not able to act on his behalf, he still spoke in front of Aharon in a manner that would not imply any slight to Aharon's honor. This sensitivity should be our guide in dealing with other people.

A faultfinder will try to find something wrong in every situation and this causes much harm.

ויאמר משה כה אמר השם בחצת הלילה אני יוצא בתוך מצרים. ומת כל בכור בארץ מצרים. (שמות י"א ד')

"AND MOSHE SAID THIS IS WHAT THE ALMIGHTY SAID, AROUND MIDNIGHT I WILL GO OUT IN THE MIDST OF EGYPT AND ALL THE FIRSTBORN IN THE LAND OF EGYPT WILL DIE." (*Shmos* 11:4)

Rashi comments that the Almighty actually told Moshe that exactly at midnight He would cause the plague of the death of the firstborn. Nevertheless, when Moshe repeated this to the Egyptians, he said "around midnight." Since mortals can easily make an error, if Moshe would have said "at midnight" and the plague took place a moment before or after midnight they would have said that Moshe was a liar.

This is amazing. They had already suffered nine plagues after Moshe's warnings. In this last plague only the firstborn would die. What is the difference if it happened exactly at midnight or a few minutes before or after? We see here the power of a person to find fault with someone else if he seeks to find fault. Moshe was absolutely correct in predicting the nature of this most bizarre and destructive plague. The odds against this being by chance were staggering. He was also very close to the right time even according to the Egytians. Moreover, they should have realized that perhaps they were the ones making the mistake and not Moshe. Nevertheless, since they wanted to find fault with what Moshe said, they would have considered this minor discrepancy a total lie and would have claimed that Moshe was a liar.

There are people who take pleasure in finding fault with others. They are experts at finding inconsistencies in what people say and do. It is almost impossible to meet their standards. Just as the Egyptians were able to call Moshe a liar - an extreme term - for what they considered to be a mistake, so too faultfinders use strong language to condemn and belittle their victims. They do this either because they are perfectionists or as a means of gaining power. Living with such a person can cause suffering especially for someone who is very sensitive. Such a person must learn to find the good in what others do. Even if he is not able to master that wonderful trait, he still needs to develop a sense of proportion. If a person does something which is basically right and proper, acknowledge this even if you do point out the errors that still remain. Realize there is always the possibility that you are making a mistake. Then you will be much more gentle when you correct others. Because of the harm caused by this negative tendency, it is crucial to work on overcoming it.

If it happened that the fire in the stove went out on *Shabbos* and the food was cold, Rabbi Yaakov Yisroel Kanievsky, the Steipler, went out of his way to highly praise the food in order to prevent hurt feelings. (*Peninai Rabainu Hakehilos Yaakov*, p.104)

When someone experiences joy don't say or do anything to decrease it.

ולכל בני ישראל לא יחרץ כלב לשנו. (שמות י״א ז׳)

When the Israelites left Egypt:
"AND TO ALL THE CHILDREN OF ISRAEL NO DOG BARKED." (*Shmos* 11:7)

One can imagine the great feeling of liberation experienced by the Israelites when they were finally freed from slavery after so many years. Would it have been so terrible if a dog had barked at them when they were leaving? We see from here that even though the irritation experienced would have been slight under the circumstances, it would have nevertheless still been a blot on their joy. From here we can learn that when someone is experiencing a joyous occasion, we should be careful not to say or do anything that would decrease his joy.

A person might have just bought a new house and feels very happy about it. At that time don't needlessly point out the drawbacks of that house. A person just got married and is very happy, don't voice any pessimistic comments that could cause a tinge of pain. Some people have a tendency to make statements that deflate a person's high feelings. They might be motivated by envy, or they could be simply insensitive. Allow others to savor their good fortune. Don't be like a barking dog and cause others irritation.

Rabbi Yechiel Mordechai Gordon, Rosh Hayeshiva of Lomzhe, suffered excruciating pain in his old age. Nevertheless, his facial expression was always one of joy. He used to say, "The face of a person is a *reshus harabim* - it is part of the public domain. A person has to be careful not to be one who damages in a public domain." (*Yetaid Neaman*, 17 Kislev, 5747, p.11)

Note: Please do not tell this story to someone who is presently suffering. Empathize with the suffering of others and in this way you will help alleviate their suffering. But this story is appropriate for someone who exaggerates the extent of his suffering and for those who seek to attain elevated levels.

Internalize the awareness that the Almighty runs the world.

החדש הזה לכם ראש חדשים. (שמות י"ב ב')

"THIS MONTH SHALL BE FOR YOU THE FIRST OF THE MONTHS."
(*Shmos* 12:2)

Rabbi Moshe Feinstein commented that the month of Tishrei is the month of the creation of the world. The month of Nisson is the month of the exodus from Egypt. Both months are lessons in our awareness of the Almighty's power. The first lesson is that the Almighty is the Creator of the universe. The second lesson is that of *hashgacha pratis*, Divine Providence. The Almighty controls the events of the world and therefore He is the One who enslaved the Children of Israel and He is the One who freed them. The Torah is telling us in this verse that the lesson of the Almighty's guiding historical events is even more important than the lesson of the creation of the world.

One can believe that the Almighty created the world and this might not make any differences in a person's behavior and attitudes. But once a person is aware of the supervision of the Almighty in daily events, he will improve his behavior. Moreover, his trust in the Almighty will free him from worry. The month of Nisson is the first month of the year and by remembering this we remember all that is symbolized by the Exodus. This will have a major effect on what we do and think.

At a small meeting of close friends and Telz alumni, which had gathered to meet him on his arrival in New York during the Second World War, Rabbi Eliyahu Meir Bloch said, "When Yonoson arranged to signal Dovid that he was in danger because King Saul wished to kill him, he told him, 'If I tell the boy the arrows are beyond you, go, for the Almighty has sent you.' Why didn't he say, 'Flee!' rather than 'go.' The answer is that when one recognizes the Almighty's guidance and supervision in all that occurs, he realizes that when people are compelled to leave a place because of impending danger, this is not a flight but the signal of a mission on which they are being dispatched. We are not refugees! We were

sent by the Almighty to replant the yeshiva of Telz in America."
(*Rabbi Chaim Dov Keller; The Jewish Observer*, Sept. 1977)

When you want to have a positive influence on others make certain to model that behavior yourself.

וילכו ויעשו בני ישראל כאשר צוה השם את משה ואהרן כן עשו. (שמות י"ב כ"ח)

"AND THE CHILDREN OF ISRAEL WENT AND DID AS THE ALMIGHTY COMMANDED MOSHE AND AHARON, SO THEY DID." (*Shmos* 12:28)

Rashi comments that, "so they did" refers to Moshe and Aharon. They also did as the Almighty commanded about the Paschal lamb. The Torah tells us this as a lesson to anyone who wants to have a positive influence on others. It is not enough just to tell others to do good deeds. Your own behavior should serve as a model for them to follow. (*Hagigai Osher*)

Action is much more difficult than words. The best way to influence others is to be the type of person you wish others to be.

Awareness that finding favor in the eyes of others is dependent on the will of the Almighty will allow you to ask anyone for anything when it is appropriate.

השם נתן את חן העם בעיני מצרים וישאלום וינצלו את מצרים. (שמות י"ב ל"ו)

"AND THE ALMIGHTY GAVE THE PEOPLE FAVOR IN THE EYES OF EGYPT SO THAT THEY LENT THEM [the gold, silver, and garments], AND THEY DESPOILED EGYPT." (*Shmos* 12:36)

Rabbi Yaakov Kanievsky, the Steipler, commented that this serves as a lesson that the Almighty determines people's finding favor in the eyes of others. Logic would dictate that after the Egyptians suffered so much because of the Israelites, they would never lend them anything, especially not precious vessels of gold and silver. Nevertheless, the Egyptians were willing to lend their prized possessions without any arguments or negotiations. The Israelites clearly saw that it was solely because of the Almighty that they found favor in the eyes of the Egyptians. (*Chayai Olam*, vol.1, ch.15)

There are people who are hesitant about asking others for favors. They are afraid that the other person might refuse. They would consider this refusal a personal rejection and a blow to their self-esteem. Because they evaluate someone's refusal to help them as a major problem, they are filled with anxiety about the thought of making requests. This prevents them from assertively asking for things they need for themselves, and they are unable to approach others to ask them to contribute to worthy causes. But once you internalize the awareness that whether or not you find favor in the eyes of another person is dependent on the will of the Almighty, your whole attitude changes. You will no longer fear asking any person for anything that is considered proper according to the dictates of the Torah. Especially when you are asking someone to help a worthy cause, you will feel comfortable. You know that even if there seems to be no chance that the person will give you what you ask, the Almighty might still cause him to agree. Of course, you will not make requests that will cause others pain or discomfort. But when it is proper to make a request, fear will never stop you.

You create yourself by your behavior. This allows you to become the person you wish to be.

ועצם לא תשברו בו. (שמות י"ב מ"ו)

"NEITHER SHALL YOU BREAK A BONE OF IT." (*Shmos* 12:46)

The Torah has a whole list of commandments which are reminders of the exodus from Egypt. The *Chinuch* (16) writes that someone might ask why the Torah needs so many commandments to commemorate this event. Wouldn't one have been enough? This is not a wise question, he replies. There is an important principle we may derive from this. Know that a person influences himself by his actions. One's thoughts are linked with one's behavior, both for good and for bad. Even if someone is very wicked and has done much wrong, if he will devote himself to Torah study and the performance of good deeds, he will eventually become a righteous person. His heart will follow in the path of his behavior and his thoughts will become more elevated.

This concept of the *Chinuch* is a basic one for becoming a better person. Even if you are not able to have elevated thoughts at first, force yourself to behave in the way in which you hope to eventually become. If you want to become a giving person, even though you are inwardly very selfish you will eventually succeed if you continue to behave in a giving manner. This is the self-creation principle. You create yourself by your behavior. Awareness of this will enable you to improve yourself in any area in which you are deficient. Make a plan to perform as many actions as possible that would manifest the positive traits you want to integrate. After acting positively for a long enough time, your thoughts will become consistent with those actions and you will become a positive person.

The Torah and the land of Israel are one unit.

לתת לך ארץ זבת חלב ודבש ועבדת את העבדה הזאת. (שמות י"ג ה')

"TO GIVE YOU A LAND FLOWING WITH MILK AND HONEY, AND YOU SHALL DO THIS SERVICE." (*Shmos* 13:5)

The Chofetz Chayim commented on this verse which refers to the Jewish People doing the Almighty's commandments: The

Torah and the land of Israel are one unit. Their relationship is as the relationship between the body and the soul. A soul cannot exist alone in this world. The body alone is just dust from the earth, it needs the soul to give it life. The soul of the Jewish People is the sacred Torah. The body is the land of Israel. There are many commandments that cannot be fulfilled outside the land of Israel. In exile our people suffer. Nevertheless, with all the difficulties involved in living in exile, we as a people are alive. The land of Israel without Torah, however, is like a body without a soul. It is just a piece of land. Only when both exist together is there a complete unit. (*Chofetz Chayim al Hatorah*, p.65)

When Rabbi Eliyahu Eliezer Dessler came to *Eretz Yisroel* in his later years, he spoke with great enthusiasm about how wonderful it was to be in the Holy Land. A relative of his asked him, "How can you give an opinion so fast? You haven't traveled at all yet, you have remained in the Ponevez Yeshiva the entire time."

Rabbi Dessler replied, "Will my impression come from seeing buildings and fields? Definitely not! In two hours I attain in spiritual matters things that outside of *Eretz Yisroel* I had to work on a number of weeks." (*Marbitzai Torah Umussar*, vol.3, p.79)

170

BESHALACH

Just as a person can fall from spiritual levels quickly, so too can you rise quickly.

ויהי בשלח פרעה את העם ולא נחם אלקים דרך ארץ פלשתים כי קרוב הוא כי אמר אלקים פן ינחם העם בראתם מלחמה ושבו מצרימה. (שמות י״ג י״ז)

"AND IT WAS WHEN PHARAOH SENT THE PEOPLE, THE ALMIGHTY DID NOT LEAD THEM BY THE LAND OF THE PHILISTINES, FOR THE ALMIGHTY SAID PERHAPS THE PEOPLE WILL REGRET [leaving Egypt] AND WILL RETURN TO EGYPT." (*Shmos* 13:17)

Rabbi Yehuda Leib Chasman commented on this that it is amazing how the Israelites could have even considered returning to Egypt. They suffered so much in their enslavement. They had seen the miracles the Almighty made and the plagues that befell the Egyptians for harming them. They should have trusted the Almighty since He had already helped them in so many ways He would continue to help them. Why would they entertain the thought of going back?

This can only be understood when one realizes that a person is a mixture of a body and a soul, said Rabbi Chasman. Even when a person is on a very high spiritual level, he can fall. For this reason one needs constant vigilance. At one moment a person can be very elevated and then if he panics he can behave in a very immature way. Although the Israelites had a great awareness, this can be lost in a very short time.

But this exact same concept of the changeability of a person can give one great hope, concluded Rav Yehuda Leib. If you can fall quickly, you can pick yourself up very quickly also. Never despair when you feel that you are on a low level. If you are sincerely resolved to climb spiritually, you have the ability to instantaneously put yourself back on the path of life. (*Ohr Yohail*, vol.2, pp.73-4)

Don't waste time with self-pity if you feel that you are not on the level you want to be. Realize that you can obtain great heights at any moment if you have a deep resolution to do so.

Don't allow your desires to blind you.

ואמר פרעה לבני ישראל נבכים הם בארץ סגר עליהם המדבר. (שמות י"ד ג')

"AND PHARAOH WILL SAY ABOUT THE CHILDREN OF ISRAEL THEY ARE ENTRAPPED IN THE LAND, THE WILDERNESS HAS ENCLOSED THEM." (*Shmos* 14:3)

How could Pharaoh possibly think that after all the miracles the Almighty did for the Israelites to save them from the Egytians that now when they were finally liberated He would foresake them? Anyone with any level of intelligence whatsoever should realize that it would be impossible for the Egyptians to harm the Israelites.

Rabbi Simcha Zissel of Kelm wrote that there is a fundamental principle that a person's will and desires blind his intellect. When a person has a strong will, he will act as irrational as a person who is crazy. His bias will convince him that what he plans to do is sensible even though any simple person could easily tell him that he will be harming himself by his actions. (*Chochmah Umussar*, vol.1, p.316)

Otherwise intelligent people make such stupid mistakes when they are biased by will and desire that afterwards they themselves wonder how they could have been so stupid. The reason is that one's will blinds him. Just as a blind person cannot see, so too a person who is blinded by his will cannot think straight. When he is biased, he will come up with all kinds of reasons and rationalizations why his improper actions and mistaken decisions are logical and worthwhile. Whenever you have a strong will that might be biasing your thinking, consult other people who are unbiased to find out how they think about the matter. Ask yourself what you would think if you would not have such a strong will to do that thing. Just realizing that your desire is likely to bias you will enable you to be more cautious. Be patient and wait. Don't allow your desires to force you to act impulsively.

Be aware of your strengths in order to overcome negative impulses.

ויאמר משה אל העם אל תיראו התיצבו וראו את ישועת השם אשר יעשה לכם היום. (שמות י״ד י״ג)

The Egyptians pursued the Israelites, and when the Israelites saw the Egyptians coming they panicked and complained to Moshe for taking them out of Egypt: "AND MOSHE SAID TO THE PEOPLE, DO NOT BE AFRAID, STAND AND YOU WILL SEE THE SALVATION OF THE ALMIGHTY THAT HE WILL DO FOR YOU THIS DAY." (Shmos 14:13)

The question arises why the Israelites did not fight against the Egyptians. Since the Israelites greatly outnumbered them, why didn't they engage them in battle to defend themselves? The Ibn Ezra replied: The Egyptians had been the masters of the Israelites. The people who went out from Egypt learnt from their youth on to bear the yoke of the Egyptians and they felt inferior to them. Therefore they were unable to fight against their masters.

Rabbi Chayim Shmuelevitz commented on this that the same principle applies to each person in his battle against the evil inclination. If a person views himself as inferior and feels excessive guilt, he will not even try to fight against his negative impulses. Since he does not believe in himself and his abilities, he feels utterly discouraged. Our task is to view ourselves in an elevated manner. Internalize the knowledge that you have great potential. Be aware of your strengths and know that when you are resolved to be victorious over your impulses, you will succeed.

Only by mastering your thoughts will you truly experience freedom in your life.

ויושע השם ביום ההוא את ישראל מיד מצרים. (שמות י״ד ל׳)

"AND ON THAT DAY THE ALMIGHTY SAVED THE ISRAELITES FROM THE HAND OF EGYPT." (*Shmos* 14:30)

The *Ohr Hachayim* comments that the Torah states that on that day they were saved, which was the day the Egyptians who pursued them perished in the sea. Even though they were already liberated on the day that they left Egypt, they were not really considered saved since they did not feel secure in relationship to the Egyptians.

We see from this that even though in actuality a person is free, he is not really considered free unless he personally feels free. A person who worries and feels insecure is a person who is imprisoned even though he is not behind bars and no one will harm him. To be truly free you must feel free and that is up to you. You have a great deal of control over your thoughts if you work on it. If you worry about the future, even though future events might work out exactly as you would have wished, you still suffer in the present. This suffering will be the same as if you actually experienced some misfortune. But all the suffering will be unnecessary. The greater your mastery over your thoughts, the greater freedom you will experience in your life.

Rabbi Simcha Zissel of Kelm had such a mastery over his thoughts that at times at the end of the day he would mentally review his thoughts of the day to see what he could improve. (*Tnuas Hamussar*, vol.2, p.42)

When you feel elevated take some positive action.

זה קלי ואנוהו. שמעו עמים ירגזון. (שמות ט״ו ב׳ י״ד)

"THIS IS MY G-D AND I WILL GLORIFY HIM." "NATIONS HEARD AND THEY TREMBLED." (*Shmos* 15:2,14)

The Sages said that even the maidservants witnessed at the crossing of the Red Sea a mystical vision greater than that witnessed by the prophet Yechezkail.

Rabbi Chayim Shmuelevitz commented on this that the maidservants remained maidservants and did not reach the level reached by Yechezkail. A person can experience the greatest experiences, but if it does not lead him to elevating his behavior, it is nothing.

Similarly, Rav Chayim said, we read in verse 14 how nations trembled when they heard about the splitting of the sea and the drowning of the Egyptians. But what happened to them? They just had a special feeling for a few moments and it did not lead to any major changes in their lives. That is the goal of *mussar*, that a person should internalize his insights and have them become a part of him in such a way that his whole behavior will be improved. Otherwise, a person can have a great awakening with many profound realizations but they will not last. There are many events in our lives when we are shaken and we think that we will never be the same. But after a very short time we revert to our old behavior. Whenever you do feel elevated because of a new awareness, make certain to take some positive action to ensure that you will not remain with just a vague feeling.

A Rabbi once asked the Chazon Ish about how to reach elevated spiritual levels. The Chazon Ish replied, "When you fulfill the Almighty's commandments as written in the Torah and with the details specified by the *halachic* authorities, that itself is the reaching of the elevated spiritual levels. Any attempt to attain elevated spiritual levels in other ways and with greater speed will end up in failure." (*P'air Hador*, vol.3, p.11)

Sweeten your outlook on life.

ויבאו מרתה ולא יכלו לשתת מים ממרה כי מרים הם. (שמות ט״ו כ״ג)

"AND THE CHILDREN OF ISRAEL CAME TO MARAH. AND THEY WERE NOT ABLE TO DRINK THE WATER AT MARAH FOR THEY WERE BITTER." (*Shmos* 15:23)

The Kotzker Rebbe explained the words "for they were bitter" as referring to the people themselves. When someone is bitter himself, everything tastes bitter. (*HaRebbe Maikotzk*, p.94)

This concept holds true in many areas of life. If a person feels bitter, nothing in life appears positive. Anyone looking for faults and defects will always be able to find them. A bitter person makes himself miserable and those in his environment suffer with him. While he thinks that he has valid reasons for considering things to be bitter, the source of the problem is not out there but within himself. By sweetening one's own outlook one will live in a much sweeter world.

As my late uncle Rabbi Moshe Helfan used to say, "When a student studies well, the teachers are wise, the other students are friendly, his room is comfortable, and even the food tastes good. When someone is not studying well, the teachers have many faults, the other students are unfriendly, his room is uncomfortable, and even the food tastes bad."

At a *siyum* on tractate *Yevamos* in Slobodka Yeshiva, Rabbi Yechezkail Abramasky spoke on the final statement of the tractate (122b): Rabbi Eliezer said in the name of Rabbi Chanina, "Torah scholars increase peace in the world." The meaning of peace is the opposite of resentment and anger. A person becomes angry easily when he is not satisfied with his life. He is bitter and does not have satisfaction. Then whatever happens not as he would have wished leads to his becoming angry. He arouses fear in others wherever he goes. But any true Torah scholar is full of happiness, satisfaction, pleasure, and joy. The page of Talmud that he studies gives him greater pleasure than that felt by a wealthy person who obtains a billion dollars. Because he is so full of pleasure and satisfaction from his studies, he does not become frustrated over mundane matters. He considers everything else to be totally inconsequential. This increases peace in the world. (*Peninai Rabainu Yechezkail*, p.15)

Patience decreases worry.

ויבאו אילמה ושם שתים עשרה עינת מים ושבעים תמרים ויחנו שם על המים. (שמות ט״ו כ״ז)

"AND THEY CAME TO EILIM, AND THERE WERE TWELVE SPRINGS OF WATER, AND SEVENTY PALM TREES, AND THEY ENCAMPED BY THE WATER." (*Shmos* 15:27)

The Children of Israel came to Eilim from Marah. At Marah they were unable to drink the water because it was bitter. But shortly after they left Marah they reached Eilim where they had plenty of water. For this reason they were in Marah for only one day, while they stayed in Eilim twenty days (Ibn Ezra).

The Chofetz Chayim commented on this that mortals have limited vision. Because of man's limitations some people are always full of complaints. They whine and fret about things not being as they would wish. There is always something that they are missing. If the Israelites would have been aware that they would soon have water in Eilim, they would not have come with their complaints to Moshe that they were missing water. They just had to be a bit more patient.

The source of people's complaints in this world, said the Chofetz Chayim, is that they are not able to see what will be in a short time.

Many things that people complain and worry about turn out much better than they imagined. (*Chofetz Chayim al Hatorah*)

The best antidote for worrying about the future is past experience. When you are aware of how often things you worried about turned out much better than you thought they would, you will have a more patient attitude. "Wait and see." Don't suffer needlessly by assuming that you will suffer in the future. When you do worry about the future, in contrast to taking practical action to improve a situation, you suffer in the present even if your life works out perfectly. Don't cause yourself a life of misery by assuming the worst. Develop greater trust in the Almighty and master the ability to be patient.

Make an effort to feel the suffering of others.

וידי משה כבדים ויקחו אבן וישימו תחתיו וישב עליה. (שמות י"ז י"ב)

"AND THE HANDS OF MOSHE WERE HEAVY AND THEY TOOK A ROCK AND PLACED IT UNDER HIM AND HE SAT ON IT." (*Shmos* 17:12)

Rashi comments that Moshe did not sit on a comfortable pillow but a rock. There was a battle going on with Amalek and Moshe wanted to feel the suffering of the people. This, said Rabbi Yeruchem Levovitz, is a lesson in feeling for another person's suffering. Not only should we mentally feel their pain, but it is proper to do some action in order to feel some discomfort yourself when someone else experiences pain. This way you actually feel his pain. (*Daas Torah, Shmos,* p.152)

Empathy is such an important attribute that we should make every effort to feel for another person. An egoistical person only cares about his own welfare and is totally uninterested in anyone else's difficulties and problems. He only wants to make certain that he is comfortable. If he is in any distress, he no longer can think about the suffering of others. Here we see that in order to feel someone else's suffering, we should go out of our way to make ourselves a little less comfortable. Our own distress is more real than someone else's. By being aware of how a little discomfort bothers us, we can have greater empathy for others.

One winter, Rabbi Akiva Eger travelled all night to perform a *mitzvah*. On the way, a heavy rain came down, and a back wheel of the carriage skidded into a ditch. The driver alighted, jumped into the water of the ditch, and raised the wagon to the road. When the driver returned to his seat, Rabbi Eger offered him a pair of dry socks to replace his wet ones. The driver was profoundly impressed by this thoughtfulness. Yet he was puzzled, because he knew that the Rabbi's baggage was locked in back of the wagon.

In the morning, when Rabbi Eger alighted from the carriage, the driver noticed that he was without socks. "But Rabbi," he said, "How could you have done this?"

Rabbi Eger smiled, "I couldn't permit you to drive in wet socks while my feet were dry." (*Jewish Leaders*, p.107)

When Rabbi Simcha Zissel of Kelm would walk on the main road of the city of Kelm, he would always think about the suffering of the government's prisoners who were forced to build the road under very harsh conditions. He would say, "How can anyone walk on this road in peace? There are human beings who experienced so much pain to make this road." (*Tnuas Hamussar*, vol.2, p.48)

YISRO

Learn from the negative behavior of others the importance of positive values.

וישמע יתרו כהן מדין חתן משה את כל אשר עשה אלקים למשה
ולישראל עמו. (שמות י"ח א')

"AND YISRO, THE PRIEST OF MIDIAN, THE FATHER-IN-LAW OF MOSHE, HEARD ALL THAT THE ALMIGHTY DID FOR MOSHE AND TO ISRAEL HIS PEOPLE." (*Shmos* 18:1)

Rashi cites the Talmud (*Zevachim* 116a): What did Yisro hear to make him come to join the Jewish people? The miracle of the crossing of the Red Sea and the war with Amalek.

What was unique about what Yisro heard, didn't all the other surrounding nations hear about this also? The answer is, said Rabbi Yehuda Leib Chasman, that they heard and remained the same. Yisro, however, didn't merely hear, he took action. Others were moved and inspired for a few moments but stayed where they were. Yisro picked himself up and changed his life. (*Ohr Yohail*, vol.2, *Vayakhail*, p.139)

Everyone has moments of inspiration. The difference between a great person and an ordinary person is that the great person acts upon his inspirations. When you obtain an important awareness, let it move you to actual changes in your life.

Rabbi Eliyahu Lopian asked on this Rashi: We can understand how the miracles at the Red Sea influenced Yisro. But what was so moving about the war with Amalek? He replied: At times the best way to appreciate Torah values for living is to observe the behavior of those who lack those values. Amalek also heard about the crossing of the Red Sea. They themselves were in no danger from the Israelites, nevertheless they cruelly tried to wipe them out. Hearing this, Yisro was moved. He realized how one needs the Almighty in his life for basic values. (*Lev Eliyahu*, vol.1, p.278)

Rabbi Baruch Ber Leibowitz, Rosh Hayeshiva of Kamenetz, was once attacked by a gang of anti-semitic ruffians who almost killed him. His disciple Rabbi Shlomoh Heiman related that Rav Baruch Ber commented after this traumatic occurrence, "Now we should feel even greater joy when we thank the Almighty for giving us the Torah in the blessing of '*asher bochar banu mikal haamim.*' We see how lowly a person can become without Torah. Without it, we also could become robbers and murderers." (*Marbitzai Torah Umussar*, vol.2, p.144)

Only use criticism when it will be beneficial.

וירא חתן משה את כל אשר הוא עשה לעם ויאמר מה הדבר הזה אשר אתה עשה לעם מדוע אתה יושב לבדך וכל העם נצב עליך מן בקר עד ערב. (שמות י״ח י״ד)

"AND THE FATHER-IN-LAW OF MOSHE SAW ALL THAT [Moshe] DID TO THE PEOPLE AND HE SAID, WHAT IS THIS THING THAT YOU ARE DOING TO THE PEOPLE? WHY ARE YOU SITTING BY YOURSELF AND THE ENTIRE PEOPLE STANDING NEARBY FROM THE MORNING TO THE EVENING?" (*Shmos* 18:14)

Rashi to verse 13 states that Moshe was sitting like a king and the people were standing. This bothered Yisro because it appeared as if Moshe was not showing respect to the people by treating them in this manner. Therefore Yisro rebuked Moshe for this.

Rabbi Yeruchem Levovitz commented that the greatness of Yisro was his powerful critical ability. He was a newcomer to Judaism who just now joined the Jewish people, and right away he criticized the great leader of the Jewish people. This critical eye of his is how he attained his elevated level. Previously Yisro tried out every form of idol worship (Rashi, verse 11). Whatever he saw he analyzed with his talent for criticism and became aware of the emptiness of all the false paths. This led him to the Almighty. This attribute is what caused him to find fault with Moshe. Definitely, Moshe had good reasons for judging everyone himself. He felt it was preferable that they should hear everything straight from him rather than hearing what he had to say from a second-hand source. But Yisro with his attribute of truth-seeking was correct and the Almighty agreed with his view that it was preferable to delegate authority to other people in order to increase the efficiency of the legal system.

The trait of criticalness is a means for coming to truth, said Rav Yeruchem. But one must be very careful in using this powerful tool. While it can be very beneficial it can also be very destructive. There is only a thin line that makes all the difference in whether criticism is very positive or very negative. Before using your critical faculties on others, make certain to be self-critical. Only if you constantly criticize yourself can you be certain that your criticizing others comes from truth-seeking. Fortunate is the person who has the positive type of criticalness. (*Daas Torah: Shmos*)

A person who has the ability to notice contradictions and inconsistencies of thought and action has a very powerful tool. As with all other powerful tools just as they can cause much good they can also cause much harm. The key to using this trait wisely is to know when to use it and when not to use it. Note that Yisro did not merely criticize Moshe, he made suggestions on how Moshe could improve the situation. His motivation was only truth and he had the benefit of Moshe in mind. Only be critical when the same can be said about you.

The Chazon Ish once said to someone who was very close to him who constantly had complaints and criticisms about the behavior of others, "According to my personality I would never become involved in matters concerning other people. It is much easier for me to sit in my own corner. But I do not give in to my *yetzer hara*. I go against my nature and become involved when I think it is appropriate. On the other hand, your *yetzer hara* is that on every possible occasion you love to say what is in your heart. But you should do the opposite. Guard yourself not to look for faults." (*P'air Hador*, vol.4, p.160)

The love a parent has for his or her children will make them more loving towards others.

ויאמר משה לחתנו כי יבא אלי העם לדרש אלקים. (שמות י"ח ט"ו)

"AND MOSHE SAID TO HIS FATHER-IN-LAW, THE PEOPLE COME TO ME TO SEEK THE ALMIGHTY." (*Shmos* 18:15)

The Midrash says that Moshe demanded that the people come to him and therefore Moshe had to walk to the burning bush to come closer to the Almighty. The prophet Shmuel, on the other hand, went to the people, and therefore he merited that the Almighty came to him.

Rabbi Chayim Shmuelevitz always used to comment that this is meant to teach us an important lesson in our lives. One's closeness to the Almighty is dependent on one's love for other people. Shmuel's going to the people showed that he had great love and concern for them and therefore the Almighty rewarded him by coming to him. Where did Shmuel get this great love for other people? The Midrash says that the garment his mother made for him was with him his entire life. This garment, said Rav Chayim, was made with the profound love his mother had for him. This love became such a part of Shmuel that it was manifested in his entire way of dealing with other people.

This is a practical lesson for parents, especially for mothers, Rabbi Shmuelevitz would always point out. The love a mother shows for her infants and young children by getting up in the middle of the night to take care of them implants in them a deep feeling of being loved. When such a child grows older he will have love for others. Any small thing a parent does with love for his children will pay off great dividends. The greater the child becomes the more many people will benefit from that love.

When helping others be careful not to burn yourself out.

נבל תבל גם אתה גם העם הזה אשר עמך כי כבד ממך הדבר לא תוכל עשהו לבדך. (שמות י"ח י"ח)

"YOU WILL SURELY WEAR YOURSELF OUT, ALSO YOU AND ALSO THIS PEOPLE WHO ARE WITH YOU. THIS IS TOO DIFFICULT FOR YOU, YOU CANNOT DO IT BY YOURSELF." (*Shmos* 18:18)

Yisro saw that Moshe took total responsibility for helping the Jewish people in spiritual matters. He foresaw that Moshe would eventually wear himself out. Therefore he advised Moshe to delegate authority and by this means share the burden with others. People who devote their time to helping others need to learn from this. It is very easy for an idealistic person to suffer from burnout by accepting too great a burden on himself. One must be aware of his limitations. If you are not careful and you overextend yourself, you are likely to wear yourself out. Not only will you suffer but all the people you could have helped if you had not burned yourself out will also suffer, as Yisro pointed out to Moshe. If you help others, make certain to schedule yourself in a way that you will be able to help others for many years to come.

Note that Moshe did not come to this awareness himself. Yisro had to point it out to him. When a person is idealistic and feels the obligation to help others, it is very easy to think that what you are doing is not enough and you should even be doing much more than you are. But an outsider is likely to be more objective. He might notice how you are wearing yourself out even though you do not yet feel it. While there are well-meaning people who might try to discourage you even though you are not really burning yourself out, there are times when you might be. If someone points out to you that you will not last if you keep up your present pace, weigh the matter objectively. If you really are doing too much yourself, share the responsibilities you have with other reliable people.

A communal leader who constantly consulted the Chazon Ish once asked him for advice about a difficult matter. The Chazon Ish said to him, "You have no need at the present for any practical advice on this subject."

"Yes, right now it's not a practical issue," the man said. "But theoretically if it were a practical question, how would you advise me to react?"

The elderly Chazon Ish replied, "People make a mistake about me. They think that I just pull out my opinions and advice from my shirtsleeves. It is not so! Every time I need to make a decision from someone it steals a piece of my health. When a matter is necessary for practical reasons, I make the effort. But whenever it is not really necessary, I have an obligation to fulfill the commandment to guard one's health." (*P'air Hador*, vol.4, p.78)

A person of truth will see the falseness of honor.

ואתה תחזה מכל העם אנשי חיל יראי אלקים אנשי אמת שנאי בצע
ושמת עלהם שרי אלפים שרי מאות שרי חמשים ושרי עשרת. (שמות
י"ח כ"א)

Yisro advised Moshe:

"AND YOU SHALL SEE FROM ALL THE PEOPLE MEN OF VALOR, THOSE WHO FEAR THE ALMIGHTY, MEN OF TRUTH, THOSE WHO HATE PROFIT, AND APPOINT THEM TO BE OFFICERS OVER THOUSANDS, OFFICERS OVER HUNDREDS, OFFICERS OVER FIFTY, AND OFFICERS OVER TENS." (*Shmos* 18:25)

Since the people who were chosen to be judges over the others were highly qualified people, wouldn't those who were appointed over few people be envious of those who were appointed over larger amounts of people? This could easily have led to much quarreling and arguments. The Kotzker Rebbe replied that since one of the traits required was the attribute of truth there would be no problem. Those who excel in truth know the falseness of honor. Since they were free from honor-seeking there would be no envy and no quarrels over power.

Honor is based on an illusion. What practical difference is there to most honor? Very little. Yet plenty of people make honor-seeking a major focus in their lives. They constantly worry about what others will think of them. They suffer tremendous pain if they think that someone else is getting more honor than they are receiving. The more you view honor from a perspective of ultimate truth the more you will realize how trivial and unimportant honor really is.

Once at a wedding that Rabbi Isser Zalman Meltzer attended, another distinguished Torah scholar was honored to officiate. A member of the *chasan's* family apologized profusely to the Rosh Hayeshiva for his not receiving this honor. Rav Isser Zalman said to him, "You have no need to feel bad or to apologize. Even when a very young Rabbi receives this honor, it is fine with me. All the more so, in this instance when the Rabbi is truly a great Torah scholar."

This was said with such humility and total acceptance that the person commented, "Rebbe, you have such elevated traits that you are by your very nature not interested in honor. You seem to have been born with these traits."

"Perhaps I truly will not receive reward for this," replied Rav Isser Zalman.

The person then told the Rosh Hayeshiva, "It is said in the name of Rabbi Aharon of Karlin that a person who was born with elevated traits will not receive even one thousandth of the reward of a person who needed to toil and work very hard to improve his traits. Even so, Rabbi Aharon of Karlin said, 'I envy a person who was born with good traits.'"

Rabbi Meltzer was pleased with this comment and said, "The reason I do not take pleasure in honor-seeking is not because of *frumkeit* (piety) but because of the *krumkeit* (irrationality) of honor." (*Bederech Aitz Hachayim*, vol.2, p.380)

Love of others, seeing the good in people, and humility are necessary for accepting the Torah.

ויחן שם ישראל נגד ההר. (שמות י"ט ב')

"AND THE ISRAELITES ENCAMPED THERE NEAR THE MOUNTAIN."
(*Shmos* 19:2)

The word the Torah uses for encamped, *Vayichan*, is in the singular. This, says Rashi, is because they were as one unit: "As one person with one heart."

Rav Yeruchem Levovitz commented that from here we see that love of our fellow man is a prerequisite for accepting the Torah. (*Daas Torah: Shmos*)

Rabbi Yitzchok of Vorki noted that the word *Vayichan* besides meaning encamped also comes from the word *chain*, finding favor. That is, the people found favor in the eyes of one another and therefore found favor in the eyes of the Almighty.

When you just see the faults and shortcomings of another person, you become distant from him. But when you see the good and positive in other people, you become closer to them. This unity is a fundamental requirement for accepting the Torah.

How is this developed? We find in *Nachal Kidumim* that togetherness between people is possible only when there is humility. When the Israelites came to Mount Sinai, which is the symbol of humility, they internalized this attribute.

When you have humility, you do not feel a need to gain power over others or to feel above them by focusing on their faults. When you have the trait of humility you can allow yourself to see the good in others. The traits of love for others, seeing the good in them, and having humility go hand in hand. By growing in these traits you make yourself into a more elevated person who is worthy of receiving the Torah.

When trying to influence a person who is sensitive, be careful not to hurt his feelings.

ומשה עלה אל האלקים ויקרא אליו השם מן ההר לאמר כה תאמר לבית
יעקב ותגיד לבני ישראל. (שמות י"ט ג')

"AND MOSHE WENT UP TO THE ALMIGHTY AND THE ALMIGHTY CALLED TO HIM FROM THE MOUNTAIN SAYING, THIS IS WHAT YOU SHOULD SAY TO THE HOUSE OF YAAKOV AND RELATE TO THE CHILDREN OF ISRAEL." (*Shmos* 19:3)

Rashi comments that *Bais Yaakov* (house of Jacob) refers to the women, and *Bnai Yisroel* refers to the men. To the women you should speak in a softer tone of voice, but to the men you can speak much tougher. (In the Hebrew there is a difference between the terms used for saying and relating.)

Rabbi Yeruchem Levovitz said on this that the difference between men and women here refers to the personalities of the people. When speaking to anyone who is sensitive and his feelings can be easily hurt, you must be careful to speak in a soft manner. Be careful to focus on the positive benefits the person will gain by observing the commandments. Show him the sweetness of the Torah. While each person himself should try to strengthen himself to be able to cope with a heavier approach, when dealing with other people we have to speak to them in the manner appropriate for their emotional makeup. (*Daas Torah: Shmos*)

An educator demanded of the Chazon Ish to protest with strong language against a certain matter. To this the Chazon Ish replied, "The only reason people pay attention to what I say is because I do not speak sharply." Similarly, he told Rabbi Shmuel Vozner, "If I will raise my voice like a *shofar*, I will lose the chance to influence those who are far away." (*P'air Hador*, vol.4, pp.160-1)

Persevere and you will overcome difficulties.

Rashi (*Shmos* 19:5) cites the *Mechilta* that, "All beginnings are difficult." When you try to accomplish for Torah, you might become discouraged when you find yourself running into difficulties. Before you started, you might have been very enthusiastic. But when obstacles and obstructions arise, you can easily become disillusioned. You might tell yourself, "Things are so difficult that I'll never accomplish. I'll never get anywhere even if I do try, so I might as well give up right now." If you ever feel this way, remember that all beginnings are difficult. Expect difficulties when you commence doing something and you won't be discouraged by them. The only way to consistently meet your goals is by being persistent. Regardless of how difficult you find it at first, as long as you consider your original goal worthwhile, keep on trying. That is the only way anyone succeeds. Very frequently, the difficulties are short-lived, and as you persevere you will find things becoming easier and easier.

Care must be taken not to show disrespect to a Torah scholar.

כל הנגע בהר מות יומת. (שמות י"ט י"ב)

"ANYONE WHO TOUCHES THE MOUNTAIN WILL SURELY DIE." (*Shmos* 19:12)

The Chofetz Chayim commented that from this warning forbidding the touching of Mount Sinai because of its sanctity when the Torah was given, we can learn a lesson not to do anything that would be disrespectful to a Torah scholar. The mountain does not have an intellect or any feelings, nevertheless since it became sanctified through the giving of the Torah it was forbidden for anyone to do anything that would desecrate it. All the more so must we be careful with the honor of a person who has mastered Torah knowledge. People have feelings and feel pain when verbally attacked. Someone who slights the honor of a Torah scholar is committing a worse offense than anyone who would have touched the mountain. (*Chofetz Chayim al Hatorah*)

When a person agrees with a Torah scholar, there is no need for a warning not to desecrate his honor. This warning is needed when you disagree with him for some reason or are displeased with some statement or action of his. The honor of the Torah scholar is the honor of the Torah. Therefore it is incumbent upon everyone to refrain from any words or behaviors that could be taken as a slight to a Torah scholar even if he is not the scholar you have designated as your authority in Torah matters.

Once in his house in Jerusalem, Rabbi Yechezkail Abramsky told Rabbi Moshe Mordechai Shulsinger that a few days before, a new immigrant from Russia came to visit him. The person was from Slutsk, where Rabbi Abramsky was the *Rav* when he was younger.

Rav Yechezkail said, "This man came to me on a regular weekday wearing his *Shabbos* garments. This reminds me of the custom of the Jews of Slutsk that when they came to the *Rav's* house to ask a question on any day of the week, they would don their special *Shabbos* garments. They had great respect for Torah." (*Peninai Rabainu Yechezkail*, p.12)

Awareness of the Almighty will give you the positive aspects of bashfulness.

ובעבור תהיה יראתו על פניכם לבלתי תחטאו. (שמות כ' י"ז)

"SO THAT THE FEAR OF THE ALMIGHTY BE IMPRESSED UPON YOUR FACE, SO THAT YOU SHALL NOT SIN." (*Shmos* 20:17)

My Rebbe, Rabbi Mordechai Gifter, Rosh Hayeshiva of Telz, commented, "One of the character traits of the Jewish people is that of *bayshonus* - bashfulness. This trait is a determining factor in much of the conduct of the Jew. What is the source of this bashfulness? Our Sages (*Yevomos* 79a) teach us that it is from the verse, 'So that the fear of the Almighty be impressed upon your face, so that you shall not sin.'"

The bashfulness of the Jew is the identification mark of *yiras shomayim* (fear of Hashem). It signifies his inherent consciousness of imperfection before the Almighty, giving him a sense, a feeling of shame.

"Ours is an age void of G-d-awareness and G-d-consciousness. It is therefore a generation which knows no shame. Thus, the inherent character barrier against crime and violence is lost. Small wonder, therefore, that ours is an age of moral decay." (Rabbi Mordechai Gifter; *Torah Perspectives*, pp. 31-2)

Bashfulness is a trait that many people today view as a fault and a problem to overcome. But as the *Chovos Halvovos* states in *Shaar Habechinah*: without bashfulness people would not do acts of kindness. At first glance, this might appear to be an extremely cynical statement. But I recall very clearly hearing this section from the late Rosh Hayeshiva of Telz, Rabbi Chayim Mordechai Katz, in a weekly *mussar* group he gave in his home. He added, "Someone recently asked me to do him a favor which I said I would do. But I didn't get to do it and he called me up last week to ask again. This time I took care of the matter right away. Why? Because I truly felt an obligation to do *chesed*? No. The real reason I did it right away was because I knew he would call me again, and I would feel embarrassed if I were to say that I didn't do it yet."

I remember my thoughts at the time. Here was our elderly Rosh Hayeshiva who was a great *baal chesed*, a lover of doing kindness, and he had the self-awareness to distinguish between what he did as a pure act of kindness and what he did out of embarrassment. He could have easily told the other person that he was so busy he would be unable to do the favor for him, but the sense of embarrassment motivated him to find the time in his busy schedule. I was also extremely impressed at this openness to us, his young students. Frequently, people feel that by admitting a normal human emotion they will be looked down upon by others. I can personally testify how this added to our already profound respect.

Rabbi Tzvi Broide, son-in-law of Rabbi Simcha Zissel of Kelm, had a picture of his father hanging in his house. He wrote that when he looks at his father's picture, he feels embarrassed to do anything that would be improper. (*Tnuas Hamussar*, vol.2, p.116)

I have met people who feel unable to speak *loshon hora* in the presence of a portrait of the Chofetz Chayim. This is a good technique to remember lessons you have learned from various Torah scholars.

MISHPOTIM

No human can give up on the life of another person.

ורפא ירפא. (שמות כ"א י"ט)

If someone damages another person, he must pay for the doctor bills, as the Torah states:

"AND HE SHALL BE HEALED." (see *Shmos* 21:19)

From this verse the Talmud (*Brochos* 60a) derives the principle that a doctor is permitted to heal.

The Chozeh of Lublin commented on this that a doctor only has permission to heal. He does not have a right to despair about a person's being healed. Even though a doctor might see that from his experience and from all that he was taught people in situations similar to this patient's usually do not recover, the Almighty has the final say about the reality of any person's recovery. Never give up hope. There are plenty of people who have lived for many years after doctors have said that they would not get well.

This is true as regards medical problems, all the more so when it comes to areas pertaining to people's behavior and emotions. While one can never be certain that a person will change for the better, one can never be certain that one will not. While we should not expect miracles to happen, as long as a person is still alive there is always hope for improvement if someone is motivated to make the effort to change.

Learn sensitivity to causing others loss or pain from the laws of damages.

וכי יפתח איש בור או כי יכרה איש בר ולא יכסנו ונפל שמה שור או
חמור. בעל הבור ישלם. (שמות כ״א ל״ג ל״ד)

"AND IF A MAN SHALL OPEN A PIT OR IF A MAN SHALL DIG A PIT
AND NOT COVER IT, AND AN OX OR DONKEY WILL FALL IN IT, THE
OWNER OF THE PIT SHALL PAY." (*Shmos* 21: 33-4)

The Torah tells us in the portion of *Mishpotim* the laws
pertaining to damages caused by one's animals and damages
caused by one's digging a hole in the ground. Rabbi Yeruchem
Levovitz used to say that it is very easy just to look at these laws in
terms of financial obligations. In some instances you are legally
obligated to pay for damages and in other instances you are free
from having to pay. But the proper way to view the laws of
damages is from the perspective of the *Chinuch* (243): the
foundation of the laws pertaining to damages is the *mitzvah* of
loving our fellow man. When you care about others, you will be
careful not to do anything that will cause them damage or
suffering. When kind and compassionate people study these laws
they do not think in terms of how much money they will have to
pay, but in terms of what they can do to avoid causing others any
loss or pain. Studying these sections of the Torah in the proper way
will increase your sensitivity to the possibilities of your harming
others. (*Daas Torah: Shmos*, p.202)

The Chofetz Chayim used to say that after one studies tractate
Bava Kama the way to see if he studied it properly in order to fulfill
what he studied is to see if he is careful to close a window to
prevent the wind from hitting someone in the face. (*Ohr Hamussar*,
vol.2, p.143)

Feel joy if someone tries to humiliate you for doing a good deed.

כי יגנב איש שור או שה וטבחו או מכרו חמשה בקר ישלם תחת השור
וארבע צאן תחת השה. (שמות כ״א ל״ז)

"IF A PERSON STEALS AN OX OR A SHEEP AND SLAUGHTERS IT OR SELLS IT, HE MUST PAY FIVE OXEN FOR AN OX AND FOUR SHEEP FOR THE SHEEP." (*Shmos* 21:37)

Rashi cites the Sages that the reason the thief pays less for a sheep is because when he steals it he has to carry it on his shoulders to run away faster. Running with a sheep on one's shoulders in public is embarrassing, and this embarrassment is a partial punishment in itself.

Rabbi Simcha Zissel of Kelm commented that this is amazing. A thief is usually not the most sensitive of people. Even if he is a very coarse person, the slight embarrassment he experiences lightens the punishment he receives for his crime. All the more so, if you suffer embarrassment or humiliation for doing a good deed, that suffering greatly elevates your action, and your reward will be very great. (*Chochmah Umussar*, vol.1, pp.289-90)

Some people are greatly afraid of the disapproval of others. Even if they are doing something that is very worthwhile and meritorious, they feel suffering if others say anything mocking. If someone were to offer you a large sum of money if anyone would insult you, you would react with joy to that insult. Similarly, when you are performing a *mitzvah*, any insults or putdowns greatly increases your merit and reward. This awareness will enable you to react with joy to any difficulties with other people that arise when you are doing good deeds.

Realize that a person who is sincere can make great changes in a short time.

וגר לא תונה ולא תלחצנו כי גרים הייתם בארץ מצרים. (שמות כ"ב כ')

"YOU SHALL NOT WRONG A CONVERT TO JUDAISM NEITHER SHALL YOU OPPRESS HIM, FOR YOU WERE STRANGERS IN THE LAND OF EGYPT." (*Shmos* 22:20)

The Torah commands us not to insult a convert or hurt his feelings. The Chasam Sofer states on this verse that someone might think that a convert has not yet fully accepted upon himself a wholehearted relationship with the Almighty. Therefore he might say something that is a putdown to this convert. But we need to realize that a person who sincerely accepts upon himself to change has the ability to change in an extremely short time. We see this with Rish Lokish (*Bava Metzia* 84a) who originally was the head of a gang of robbers. When he was resolved to study Torah, an immediate change in him took place. For this reason the Torah reminds us in this verse that we were strangers in Egypt. There were Israelites who reached very low spiritual levels in Egypt. Even so, as soon as they were liberated they entered a covenant with the Almighty and were entirely changed. When someone is sincere in his acceptance of Torah values, we must be very careful not to imply that he has not really changed. (*Toras Moshe*)

Have the courage to be different in order not to do something improper.

לא תהיה אחרי רבים לרעת. (שמות כ"ג ב')

"DO NOT GO AFTER THE MAJORITY TO DO EVIL." (*Shmos* 23:2)

Rabainu Bachya explains that the plain meaning of our verse is that if you see many people doing something that is wrong, you should not follow their example.

It is very natural for a person to imitate the behavior of others. When many people do something that is wrong, it is easy for any individual to tell himself, "So many other people are doing this, it can't be so wrong if I do it also." But in this verse the Torah is telling us the principle that each person is responsible for his own behavior. Even when many others do something that is improper, you have an obligation to be careful with your own behavior. It takes much courage and strength of character to be different from others for one's ideals. But anyone who appreciates that the most important thing in the world is to do the will of the Almighty will not be impressed by the fact that many people are doing something. He will weigh his own behavior against the Torah's standards and not the standards of others regardless of how numerous they are.

Help those who are lost spiritually.

כי תפגע שור איבך או חמרו תעה השב תשיבנו לו. (שמות כ"ג ד')

"IF YOU MEET YOUR ENEMY'S OX OR HIS DONKEY GOING ASTRAY, YOU SHALL REPEATEDLY BRING IT BACK TO HIM." (*Shmos* 23:4)

The Chofetz Chayim commented on this: The Torah is concerned about the money of other people. If someone's animal got lost, we are obligated to exert ourselves to return the animal to its owner. All the more so, we must have compassion for a human being who is spiritually lost. Even if it will take much effort to bring him back to Torah observance, we should make that effort.

The Sages (*Bava Metzia* 31a) say on this verse that if someone's animal gets lost even one hundred times, each and every time we are obligated to make the effort to return the animal to him. Similarly, said the Chofetz Chayim, if it takes one hundred times to speak to someone about returning to Torah we should develop the patience to speak to him one hundred times. Have compassion on people who are far from Torah observance. Most people do not spitefully do wrong. The problem is that they lack the proper awareness. It is a great *mitzvah* to teach such people how to return to the Torah way of life. (*Chofetz Chayim al Hatorah*)

After the death of Rabbi Aryeh Levine, one person told Rabbi Levine's son, "I remember how in your father's presence, without his saying a single word to preach or rebuke, we not only wanted to improve but we actually felt that right there we were becoming better human beings." (*A Tzaddik in Our Time*, p.106)

Bias is a bribe which prevents you from seeing your faults.

ושחד לא תקח כי השחד יעור פקחים ויסלף דברי צדיקים. (שמות כ"ג ח')

"AND BRIBERY YOU SHALL NOT TAKE, FOR A BRIBE WILL BLIND THOSE WHO CAN SEE, AND DISTORT THE WORDS OF THE RIGHTEOUS." (*Shmos* 23:8)

Rabbi Avraham of Sochotchov commented that there is a major difference between a person who is blind and a person who is prejudiced because of some bias. When a person is blind, he realizes it and will ask someone who can see to help him. But if a person has a bias, the bias blinds him to such an extent that he does not even realize that he is blind. He feels that what he perceives is reality and will refuse to listen to others.

There are many types of bribes that distort our judgment. We are not referring to an out and out bribe. Any bias will cause us to view things in a way that will fit our particular bias. This is especially true when someone tries to point out our mistakes and faults. We all want to feel that we are correct. Awareness of our own blindness is the first step in overcoming it. When someone tells you something that goes against your bias, weigh the matter very carefully. Remember that bias blinds. Just because you do not immediately recognize a fault does not mean that you do not have it. If necessary, consult a few other people.

Empathy for others includes both feeling their pain and experiencing their joy.

ויראו את אלקי ישראל ותחת רגליו כמעשה לבנת הספיר וכעצם השמים לטהר. (שמות כ"ד י')

"THEY SAW A VISION OF THE G-D OF ISRAEL, AND UNDER HIS FEET WAS SOMETHING LIKE A SAPPHIRE BRICK, LIKE THE ESSENCE OF A CLEAR SKY." (*Shmos* 24:10)

Rashi comments that the brick was in the presence of the Almighty during the time the Israelites were enslaved in Egypt to remind Him of their suffering since they were forced to build with bricks in their slavery. "The essence of a clear sky," is because once they were liberated there was light and joy before the Almighty.

Rabbi Yeruchem Levovitz commented that whenever the Torah tells us about the attributes of the Almighty the purpose is to teach us how we should strive to emulate Him. When someone else suffers, it is not sufficient for us just to try to feel his suffering in the abstract, rather we should do some concrete action that will clearly remind us of the person's suffering.

Also we see from here, said Rav Yeruchem, that even at the time of redemption and joy it is important to recall the previous suffering that one experienced. This adds an entire dimension to the joy. Many people would just like to forget all their suffering when it is over. But the proper attitude is to remember it, and this will give a person an even greater appreciation for the good that he experiences.

Yet another lesson we see from here is how we should make an effort to feel the joy of another person, just as the Almighty felt the joy of the redemption of the Jewish people. There are many people who outwardly act as if they feel joy for the successes of others. But inwardly they are telling themselves, "I really wish that this person will fail."

People say that there are three possibilities for a businessman, Rav Yeruchem said. When he is the only one who was successful in business and his friend lost everything, this is the ultimate in pleasure. If both he and his friend were equally successful or equally suffered a loss, he will feel pain. But if he had a loss and his friend made a profit, this is the greatest suffering in the world for him. For many people their main joy is not when they are successful, rather when their friend suffers a loss they feel great joy. Many people fool even themselves and are not consciously aware how much they really hate the people they call their friends. To really feel joy for the good fortune of another person takes much work. One must devote much deep thought to master this attribute. (*Daas Torah: Shmos*)

Once in the city of Mir the Mirrer Yeshiva did not have sufficient money to buy food for the students. Rabbi Eliezer Yehudah Finkel, the Rosh Hayeshiva, gave his fur coat that he received for his wedding to the people in charge of the finances of the yeshiva. "It is an expensive coat and make certain to get a high price for it," Rav Lazer Yudel said.

The administrator at first refused to take it. They told him that it's in the middle of a very cold winter and he might become ill if he goes without his coat. But Rabbi Finkel insisted they take it, saying, "If the students are hungry, it is very cold for me even if I am wearing a warm coat. However, if they have enough to eat, I feel warm even without a coat." (*Marbitzai Torah Umussar*, vol.4, p.56)

The Chazon Ish wrote, "I have pleasure when I am able to bring joy to the hearts of people. I feel my obligation to be careful not to cause any unpleasantness to another person even for one second." (*Kovetz Igros*, 1:33)

Because of this the Chazon Ish, who was near-sighted, was careful to wear glasses when he walked in the street, even though he did not wear them when he studied from books. He explained, "I am likely not to notice people who I meet when I am walking and who nod their heads to me in greeting. If I don't reciprocate, they will feel discomfort." (*P'air Hador*, vol.3, p.52)

TRUMAH

Money given to charity must be kosher money.

וידבר השם אל משה לאמר. דבר אל בני ישראל ויקחו לי תרומה. (שמות כ״ה א-ב)

"AND THE ALMIGHTY SPOKE TO MOSHE SAYING, SPEAK TO THE CHILDREN OF ISRAEL THAT THEY TAKE FOR ME AN OFFERING." (*Shmos* 25:1,2)

The portion of *Trumah* follows the portion of *Mishpotim* to teach us an important lesson. The concept of *Mishpotim* is that a person's money must be his according to the dictates of justice and the letter of the law. *Trumah* deals with donations to charity. Before a person gives money to charity, he must be very careful that his money was not acquired by cheating anyone else. If a person gives charity by stealing from others, his charity is not considered charity. A *mitzvah* that someone would fulfill by means of violating other commandments is not considered a good deed. (*Bais Halevi*)

When it comes to doing good deeds, the ends do not justify the means. Both the ends and the means must be in accordance with the dictates of the Torah.

Money you give to charity is the only money that is really yours.

ויקחו לי תרומה. (שמות כ״ה ב׳)

TAKE FOR ME AN OFFERING." (*Shmos* 25:2)

Rabbi Yosef Dov Soloveitchik notes in *Bais Halevi* that the Torah uses the term *take* to refer to the donations to the tabernacle even though the people were giving and not taking. This is because only the money that a person gives away to charity is really his. When a fly is in a box which contains a large amount of sugar one cannot say that because the fly is near the sugar the sugar is really his. He might be able to eat a little bit of the sugar, but he is certainly not its owner. Similarly, the money a person has in his possession does not really become part of him. He merely has use of it for the limited time he is on the earth. Therefore the Torah uses the term "taking" when it refers to giving to worthwhile causes, for by this means you are truly taking. The money you give to charity is your eternal possession. (*ibid.*)

Your motivation is a major factor in the ultimate value of what you do.

Rashi (*Shmos* 25:2) comments that the donations given for the tabernacle should be given for the sake of the Almighty.

What is the difference what a person's intentions are when he does a good deed? Rabbi Yehuda Leib Chasman used to give this illustration. Let us say that we hear about a certain person that he delivers milk to people each morning. He wants to ensure that every child in the community will be able to have wholesome milk for breakfast. He brings the milk to each person's home very early in the morning regardless of the weather. What would you say about such a person? You would surely consider him an outstanding example of the most elevated levels of kindness. But what if you then heard that he gets paid a few pennies a bottle? He is no longer such a great, righteous person but a plain milk delivery man. Similarly in all that you do. When you do something with pure motivations, your action is elevated. Work on your thoughts to have positive motivations when you do positive acts.

The Chazon Ish used to relate this story: Once Rabbi Izel Charif came with his father-in-law to the Rabbi of their city with the following dispute. The father-in-law said, "It is now ten years that I am supporting my son-in-law to enable him to study Torah without any distractions. Now I want him to become involved in business. But he refuses and continues to study Torah. If I could at least be assured that he is studying Torah with the proper motivations, I would remain silent and continue to support him. But how can I really know for sure?"

"What do you have to say about the matter?" the Rabbi asked Rav Izel.

"I am not claiming that I already study Torah with the proper motivations," replied Rav Izel. "But it is my heartfelt desire to do so."

The Chazon Ish concluded, "So, too, I also want to reach this level that I study Torah with the proper motivations." (*P'air Hador*, vol.3, p.15)

Rabbi Moshe Aharon Stern related that he was once walking with Rabbi Eliyahu Lopian in Yerushalayim. Upon seeing someone repairing the street, Rav Elya commented, "See how this person is constantly engaged in a *mitzvah*, the *mitzvah* of *yishuv Eretz Yisroel* (building of the land of Israel). What is missing? Only the motivation for the sake of a *mitzvah*! If someone only thinks about making a livelihood and nothing more, he loses all the wonderful benefits of fulfilling a *mitzvah*." (*Lev Eliyahu*, vol.1 p.30)

Do what you can to help finance the daily running of yeshivas

וידבר השם אל משה לאמר. דבר אל בני ישראל ויקחו לי תרומה. (שמות כ"ה א-ב)

"AND THE ALMIGHTY SPOKE TO MOSHE SAYING, SPEAK TO THE CHILDREN OF ISRAEL THAT THEY TAKE FOR ME AN OFFERING." (*Shmos* 25:1,2)

Rashi comments that in this section of the Torah we find the term *Trumah* three times. They refer to three collections of offerings. One collection was for sockets that would serve as a foundation for the tabernacle. One was an obligation that each person give a certain amount to purchase the animals for sacrifices. And one was for the actual building of the tabernacle which was donated by each person in the amount he wished to donate.

Rabbi Zalman Sorotzkin wrote that once the yeshivas in Europe were in deep financial difficulties and he and a delegation of other prominent rabbis traveled to Warsaw to collect funds. They had invited journalists and editors of papers to come to a meeting and Rabbi Zalman Sorotzkin gave a speech about the importance of their mission. One editor asked him, "Why did Rabbi Meir Shapiro build such a luxurious edifice for his yeshiva? He had to raise large sums of money. Wouldn't it have been preferable to share all the money he raised with the other yeshivas?"

The intention of this journalist was to ruin the fundraising campaign, and Rabbi Sorotzkin answered him thus: Why did the Torah obligate each person to give a half shekel for the sacrifices? Why didn't the Torah rely on the generosity of the people as it did when it came to giving donations for the building of the sanctuary? The reason is that the Torah knew human nature when it comes to giving donations. People are more open to giving their money when it comes to donating for a building than for the daily running expenses of the institution. What is more precious: the sanctuary itself or the sacrifices? Of course, the sacrifices, since the whole purpose of the sanctuary was to be a place in which to offer the sacrifices. We also see that the daily offerings were permissible on Shabbos, but the building of the sanctuary was forbidden on Shabbos. Even though the sacrifices were the key purpose, it was necessary to make it an obligation for people to donate for the sacrifices. However, when it came to donations for the building of the sanctuary the people immediately brought on their own all that was needed.

"The same is true with the yeshivas," said Rabbi Sorotzkin. "The purpose of having yeshivas is for Torah study, the buildings are only a means to an end. Nevertheless, people find it easier to give donations for buildings. They appreciate having parts of buildings named in their honor: rooms, doors, windows, and bricks. It is much more difficult to raise money for the daily upkeep of a yeshiva. I am certain that when Rabbi Shapiro completes his building, he will have difficulties in raising the money necessary for the daily maintenance of the yeshiva just as the other heads of Yeshivas do."

Rabbi Sorotzkin concluded that the money for the sockets also needed to be collected as an obligation by every person. True, people are willing to give for a building, but they want to be certain that the building will be a reality and not merely a dream. Therefore they want to wait and see if the foundation gets started. Only after the foundation is completed do they feel secure that the building will actually be built. Therefore the money for the sockets, which was the foundation, had to be collected as an obligation from each person. (*Oznayim Letorah*)

During a difficult time when the Lomzhe yeshiva was in dire financial need, Rabbi Yehudah Leib Gordon, the elderly Rabbi of the city of Lomzhe, decided to travel to the United States to raise funds for the yeshiva. Rabbi Yechiel Mordechai Gordon, the Rosh Hayeshiva, pleaded with him not to go since in his weak state of health the trip was dangerous. But Rav Yehudah Leib replied, "I feel an obligation to go. If I happen to die on the boat, it is worthwhile to die for the sake of Torah study. I am willing to take the risk in order to help you try to save the yeshiva." (*Marbitzai Torah Umussar*, vol.4, p.23)

Live with the Torah wisdom you speak about.

וְצִפִּיתָ אֹתוֹ זָהָב טָהוֹר מִבַּיִת וּמִחוּץ תְּצַפֶּנּוּ וְעָשִׂיתָ עָלָיו זֵר זָהָב סָבִיב.
(שמות כ״ה י״א)

"COVER [the ark] WITH A LAYER OF PURE GOLD ON THE INSIDE AND OUTSIDE AND MAKE A GOLD RIM ALL AROUND ITS TOP." (*Shmos* 25:11)

The Talmud (*Yoma* 72b) states that here we see symbolized that a Torah scholar must be pure inside as well as outside to be considered a *Talmid Chochom*. That is, just as the ark which symbolized Torah knowledge had gold on both the inside and outside, so too a Torah scholar is not someone who just speaks wisdom on the outside, but he must also internalize his wisdom and live with it.

There have been many intellectuals throughout the ages who have espoused profound philosophical ideals. They have expressed the most elevated thoughts of universal love for humanity. But in their own private lives they have been arrogant and cared only for their ideas but not for the people with whom they actually had to deal on a daily basis. This is not the Torah concept of a *Talmid Chochom*. To be considered a true Torah scholar and not merely someone who carries a lot of book knowledge with him, one must practice the lofty ideals that he speaks about. This has held true for all our revered Torah scholars both in ancient and modern times.

Whenever you speak about lofty thoughts, ask yourself whether you really experience them. In your own behavior do you actually follow the principles you speak about? If not, do not stop speaking about those ideals, but elevate your behavior.

Support Torah study continually.

בטבעת הארן יהיו הבדים לא יסרו ממנו. (שמות כ"ה ט"ו)

"THE POLES SHALL BE IN THE RINGS OF THE ARK; THEY SHALL NOT BE TAKEN FROM IT." (*Shmos* 25:15)

The ark symbolized the crown of Torah. The poles are the means by which the ark was carried. Unlike the altar and the table which also had rings for poles, the poles of the ark remained at all times, even when they were not needed to carry the ark. This symbolizes the connection between those who study Torah and those who financially support Torah study. They are considered as one unit.

Those who financially assist Torah study should continue to do so at all times without ceasing. (*Meshech Chochmah*)

The Torah supporters who develop this attitude will not wait for Torah institutions to call upon them to make donations. Rather they will continuously take the initiative to ask the Torah institutions what they can do to help.

When the new *Bais Medrash* of Slobodka Yeshiva in Bnai Brak was finished, the Rosh Hayeshiva, Rabbi Mordechai Shulman, announced to the students that each one should take his *shtender* and his *Gemora* from the old *Bais Medrash* to the new one. This was done without any fanfare or publicity, but Rabbi Yechezkail Abramsky spoke a few words, "Some will ask why the Rosh Hayeshiva needed to raise the money for this new *Bais Medrash* which took so much effort, traveling, and hardship. Why wasn't the old *Bais Medrash* sufficient? I tell you: all the tremendous effort of the Rosh Hayeshiva to raise the money was worthwhile if even one student will understand the *Gemora* better or will develop more creative ideas because he finds the new *Bais Medrash* more conducive to study." (*Peninai Rabainu Yechezkail*, p.12)

Always realize that you are lacking wisdom.

ועשית שנים כרבים זהב. (שמות כ"ה י"ח)

"AND YOU SHALL MAKE TWO CHERUBS OF GOLD." (*Shmos* 25:18)

The ark symbolized Torah study. The reason two cherubs were placed on top of the ark was to teach us that we should always consider ourselves as young children when it comes to studying Torah. No matter how much you know, compared to what there is still to learn you are as if you have just begun. For this reason a Torah scholar is always called a *Talmid Chochom*, that is, the student of a wise man. The greater wisdom one has the more one realizes that one is lacking wisdom. (*Chochmah Umussar*, vol.1, p.344)

Gorg. Olver Maring

Rabbi Simcha Zissel of Kelm used to say: "There is so much wisdom in even one statement of *Chazal* (the Talmudic Sages) that a person could spend his entire lifetime delving into just that one thought." (*Meoros Hagdolim*, p.81)

One day after the morning prayers when most of the people had already left the synagogue in the Botai Rand section of Jerusalem, a young boy aged five or six jumped from bench to bench and made a lot of noise. When the child was getting really wild, Rabbi Isser Zalman Meltzer approached him in his soft and gentle way and said, "Little boy, why don't you go to school?"

"You go to school," the boy said to the elderly Rosh Hayeshiva.

Rav Isser Zalman Meltzer's response was, "This boy is right. I must go to school to study. When someone gets older he forgets some of the things he learned when he was young. Sometimes we even forget the simple meaning of the Torah that we learned when we were young." (*Bederech Aitz Hachayim*, vol.2, p.417)

Even when serving the Almighty remember to do acts of kindness for people.

והבריח התיכן בתוך הקרשים מברח מן הקצה אל הקצה. (שמות כ"ו כ"ח)

"THE CENTER CROSSBAR SHALL GO THROUGH THE MIDDLE OF THE BEAMS, FROM ONE END [of the tabernacle] TO THE OTHER." (*Shmos* 26:28)

Targum Yonoson states that the center crossbar was made with wood that came from the trees that Avraham planted. I heard Rabbi Mordechai Mann of Bnai Brak comment on this that these trees were planted by Avraham for the purpose of doing kindness for travelers. The center crossbar was placed right in the middle of the tabernacle to remind us that even when we are devoting ourselves to serving the Almighty we should never forget to have compassion for our fellow men, who are created in the image of the Almighty.

A government official who wished to visit Rabbi Akiva Eger wrote to ask when he had some free time. "I have no free time," replied Rabbi Eger, "but I always try to be courteous to my visitors." (*Jewish Leaders*, p.108)

Once on *Erev Yom Kippur* Rabbi Zorach Braverman, the Rebbe of Rabbi Ben Tzion Yadler, heard that a certain Torah scholar needed financial assistance to take care of his health. Just a few hours before *Yom Kippur* Rav Zorach went to the homes of a number of potential donors to ask them for donations. One of them said to him, "There is a *mitzvah* to eat today. Why then are you engaged in other matters?"

Rabbi Braverman replied, "Fasting on *Yom Kippur* itself is pushed aside if it is necessary to save someone's life. All the more so this principle applies to eating and drinking on *Erev Yom Kippur*." (*Betuv Yerushalayim*, p.323)

TETZAVEH

Do acts of kindness without expecting anything in return.

ואתה תצוה את בני ׳שראל ויקחו אליך שמן זית זך כתית למאור להעלת
נר תמיד. (שמות כ״ז כ׳)

"AND YOU SHALL COMMAND THE CHILDREN OF ISRAEL THAT
THEY BRING TO YOU PURE OLIVE OIL BEATEN FOR THE LIGHT TO
CAUSE THE LAMP TO BURN ALWAYS." (*Shmos* 27:20)

The Midrash comments on this verse that the Almighty does not
really need the light but you should nonetheless make a light for
Him just as He makes light for you. The Midrash gives the analogy
of a blind person and a person who could see who were walking
together. The person with sight led the blind person the entire way.
When they came to their destination, the sighted person told the
blind person to make a light. "I want you to do this," he said, "so
you will not feel a debt of gratitude for all that I have done for you.
Now you have done something for me in return."

Rabbi Yeruchem Levovitz commented that from here we see
what total kindness is. There are many ulterior motives a person
can have when he does favors for others. But the ultimate in doing
kindness is to do it without any expectations for something in
return. This Midrash should be our guide when we do a favor for
another person. Our attitude should be totally to help someone and
not to expect even gratitude in return. (*Daas Chochmah Umussar*,
essay 116)

Many people feel strong resentment towards people who do not
show any gratitude for what they have done for them. While a

person should feel gratitude, one who does kindnesses for others for the sake of doing kindness will be free of any negative feelings towards someone who does not reciprocate or express gratitude. Moreover, an elevated person will go out of his way to make the person receiving his kindness feel free of any obligations towards him.

A teacher at Aitz Chayim Yeshiva in Jerusalem recalled a time when a child of his was seriously ill. He and his wife had to stay by the child's bedside at night - until the effects began telling on their nerves and health.

One night Rabbi Aryeh Levin and his wife turned up at their home. "Go to sleep now," said Reb Aryeh. "The two of us will stay with your child." He explained with his own brand of genial, charming apology, "We have to talk something over that is very important and we cannot do so at home where the children may eavesdrop." (*A Tzaddik in Our Time*, p.132)

A Torah institution should focus on sanctity.

ועשית בגדי קדש לאהרן אחיך לכבוד ולתפארת. ואתה תדבר אל כל חכמי לב אשר מלאתיו רוח חכמה ועשו את בגדי אהרן לקדשו לכהנו לי. (שמות כ"ח ב-ג)

"AND YOU SHALL MAKE HOLY GARMENTS FOR AHARON YOUR BROTHER FOR HONOR AND BEAUTY. AND YOU SHALL SPEAK TO ALL WHO ARE WISE HEARTED, WHOM I HAVE FILLED WITH A SPIRIT OF WISDOM, THAT THEY MAKE AHARON'S GARMENTS TO SANCTIFY HIM AND THAT HE SHALL SERVE ME." (*Shmos* 28:2,3)

This verse begins by saying that the purpose of the priestly garments was for honor and beauty, but Moshe was told to relate to the people who would make the garments that they should have the intention that the garments were for sanctifying the priests and to serve the Almighty.

Rabbi Yehuda Leib Bloch explained: The priestly garments had profound spiritual and mystical symbolism. They were to give the priests a special sanctity and relationship to the Almighty. For this reason they had to be made exactly as the Almighty commanded. It was not necessary for this that they should be beautiful in the eyes of man. But human nature demands that something which has great importance should also be externally beautiful. People's feelings towards things are greatly influenced by external appearances. Therefore it was necessary that the priestly garments be beautiful. That is the reason behind the "honor and beauty" stated in the verse. Even though the Almighty wanted the garments to be for honor and beauty and commanded Moshe to make them that way, nevertheless Moshe was told not to mention this to the wise men who would make the garments. They were just told to make the garments to sanctify and serve the Almighty. Those who do the actual sacred work should have an elevated mental attitude. If they were to have in mind that the garments were to be beautiful in the eyes of other people, it would have taken away from their more elevated thoughts.

This, said Rabbi Bloch, has practical ramifications for those who are involved with spiritual matters. Though it is necessary to do some things for physical beauty, the main focus for those who are running a Torah institution should be on sanctity and spirituality. (*Shiurai Daas*, vol.3, essay 5)

The timing and wording of a correction are key factors in its being accepted.

ואלה הבגדים אשר יעשו חשן ואפוד ומעיל וכתנת תשבץ מצנפת ואבנט
ועשו בגדי קדש לאהרן אחיך ולבניו לכהנו לי. (שמות כ"ח ד')

"THESE ARE THE GARMENTS THAT THEY SHALL MAKE: A BREASTPLATE, AN EPHOD, A ROBE, A KNITTED TUNIC, A TURBAN, AND A BELT. MAKE THEM AS SACRED GARMENTS FOR AHARON YOUR BROTHER AND HIS SONS SO THAT THEY SHALL BE PRIESTS TO ME." (*Shmos* 28:4)

The Talmud (*Shabbos* 31a) relates that a non-Jew once passed behind a study hall and heard the voice of a teacher who was reading this verse. He asked some people, "Who wears such garments?" "The High Priest," they replied. The non-Jew said to himself, "I will go and convert to Judaism to be able to become the High Priest."

He went over to Shamai and said to him, "Convert me to Judaism on the condition that I should become the High Priest." Shamai considered his request to be very insolent and pushed him away.

He then went over to Hillel with the same condition and Hillel agreed to convert him. Hillel then said to him, "For a person to be appointed king he must be knowledgeable about the rules and regulations that apply to a king. You must study Torah before you can become a High Priest."

When the person came to the verse, "And the stranger who does the service shall die," he asked, "To whom does this verse apply?" Hillel replied, "This applies even to David, king of Israel."

The convert then said to himself, "The Israelites are called children of the Almighty, and because of the Almighty's love for them he called them His firstborn. Nevertheless if they are not of the priestly family, they are guilty of a very serious offense if they do the priestly services. All the more so I who just recently joined this people cannot do the service that was forbidden to David."

The convert went on to praise Hillel for his wisdom and patience.

From here we see a most important principle in dealing with the unreasonable requests and demands of others. Some people feel that when someone makes a mistake they must immediately correct him. But timing in making corrections is crucial. If you tell a person something that he is not yet ready to hear, you will fail to have the positive influence that you could have had if you were to wait patiently. Always be aware of your goal when you wish to correct someone. When you have the other person's best interests in mind, you will not just blurt out your criticism of him. Rather, you will ask yourself, "What is the best way for me to reach this person? How should I word my comments to him? When will he be most receptive to hear what I have to say?" You can easily blame the recipient of your words of correction for being resistant to your well-meaning rebuke. But if you really want to help someone grow, give much thought to how and when you should make your suggestions.

Rabbi Ezra Atiyah, Rosh Hayeshiva of Porat Yosef, understood people well and knew the points to focus on in order to influence someone to improve his behavior. Once the father of one of his students passed away and the Rosh Hayeshiva went to visit him during the *shivah* period. The brother of his student worked in a store that was open on *Shabbos* and this led to his working on *Shabbos*. He asked Rabbi Atiyah, "Out of mourning I should really not shave for thirty days. But the owner of the store probably won't permit me to be unshaven and I might lose my job. Is it permissible for me to shave during the *shloshim* period?"

Rabbi Atiyah raised his voice and shouted at the fellow who asked the question, "It is not enough that you sold your religion, now you even want to sell your father! When you shave during the mourning period, you are shaming your father."

Upon hearing this, the mourner was taken aback and replied, "I won't sell my father. I will not shave even if I do lose my job because of honoring my father."

Rabbi Atiyah then turned to his student and said to him, "Don't allow your brother to desecrate the honor of your father. Lend him money in order that he should be able to open his own store. This way he will be able to observe *Shabbos*. He will no longer sell his religion or his father."

They followed his recommendation and the brother became a *Shabbos* observer. (*Oros Maimizrach*, pp.230-1)

When making a promise clarify the limitations of that promise.

ועשית חשן משפט. (שמות כ"ח ט"ו)

"YOU SHALL MAKE THE CHOSHEN MISHPOT [one of the eight garments of the High Priest]." (*Shmos* 28:15)

Rashi comments on the word *mishpot* that it clarifies the words and its promise is true.

Rabbi Yeruchem Levovitz commented that Rashi's intention here is to allude to the following. One person makes a claim to another, "You have promised me such and such. Please keep your promise." The second person replies, "Yes, I did say that. But my intention was different from what you thought." This indicates a lack of honesty on the part of the person who made the promise. When you make someone a promise, you should make it clear exactly what you are and are not promising. If you do not clarify and qualify when you make your promise, it is not truth. (*Daas Torah: Shmos*)

It sounds more generous when you make a general promise to someone such as, "Don't worry. I'll help you whenever you need my help." You most likely did not mean that you would do anything and everything for this person. But it sounded wonderful when you said it. Of course, you do want to do him some favors. But your intention was to help him in a limited manner. This shows a lack of integrity. By making false promises to someone, you cause him to rely on you when he really shouldn't. Instead of helping the person this can cause him problems later on. When you make a promise to someone, immediately clarify what exactly you are promising. It is only fair to the other person to do so. On your part, each time you make these clarifications you are becoming a more honest person. You are building up the habit of speaking truthfully.

Do not allow compassion to cause you to distort justice.

ונשא אהרן את משפט בני ישראל על לבו לפני השם תמיד. (שמות כ״ח
ל׳)

"AND AHARON SHALL CARRY THE JUDGMENT OF THE CHILDREN OF ISRAEL ON HIS HEART." (*Shmos* 28:30)

Rabbi Aharon Levine, author of *Hadrash Vehaiyun*, used to say: When a judge has to render a decision in a quarrel between two people, he cannot rely on the feelings of his heart. Following one's feelings can lead to a distortion of justice. When a wealthy person and a poor person are involved in a financial quarrel, one's feelings might be prejudiced in favor of the poor person. But it is possible that the wealthy person is right and justice is on his side. Therefore the Torah states, "Aharon shall carry the judgment of the Children of Israel on his heart," that is, above his heart. The law and justice are the key factors in a dispute and one cannot decide in favor of the person one wants to win. (cited in *Otzer Chayim*)

While the attributes of compassion and mercy are very important to acquire, they are not always appropriate. Just because you feel sorry for one person, you do not have the right to unlawfully cause another person a loss. If you want to help a poor person, do so at your own expense, not at the expense of anyone else.

Once someone came to Rabbi Yaakov Yisroel Kanievsky and asked for a general blessing that he should be successful. The Steipler replied, "How can I give you a blessing when I don't know what you are referring to? Perhaps you have a case before a Rabbinical court today and the truth is that the other party is right. How is it possible then to bless you to be successful? This could be against Torah law."

When the person went out, he told the people who were there that he did in fact have a *Din Torah* that day. (*Peninai Rabainu Hakehilos Yaakov*, p.53)

Be proud of doing the Almighty's will.

ועשית ציץ זהב טהור ופתחת עליו פתוחי חתם קדש להשם. ושמת אתו
על פתיל תכלת והיה על המצנפת אל מול פני המצנפת יהיה. (שמות כ"ח
ל"ו-ל"ז)

"MAKE A FOREHEAD PLATE OF PURE GOLD, AND ENGRAVE ON IT THE SAME MANNER AS A SIGNET RING, [the words], HOLY TO G-D. ATTACH A TWIST OF SKY-BLUE WOOL TO IT, SO THAT IT CAN BE [worn] RIGHT NEAR THE FRONT OF THE TURBAN." (*Shmos* 28:36-7)

The turban, which is on top of the priest's head, atoned for arrogance and conceit. But there is a time and place for pride and that is when a person is proud to do the will of the Almighty. That is alluded to in our verse. When pride is "holy to the Almighty" then it can be on top of a person's head. (*Ksav Sofer*)

When you are proud of your Torah values, you will not be ashamed to fulfill the commandments even if others who do not appreciate them will mock or insult you. Arrogance is a trait that is detrimental to one's spiritual development and causes many difficulties when dealing with other people. But when you are proud of doing good deeds you will be motivated to continue to do good.

KI SISAH

Money can build and can destroy, use it well.

זה יתנו כל העבר על הפקדים מחצית השקל בשקל הקדש. (שמות ל'
י"ג)

"THIS THEY SHALL GIVE, EVERY ONE THAT PASSES AMONG THEM THAT ARE NUMBERED, HALF A SHEKEL OF THE SHEKEL OF THE SANCTUARY." (*Shmos* 30:13)

Rashi comments that the Almighty showed Moshe a coin of fire. This symbolizes that money has similarities with fire. Fire has the potential to give warmth and to help people prepare food. But fire can also destroy property and even lives. Similarly, money can build and it can destroy. A person can ruin his life and the lives of others in his pursuit of money. But if money is utilized properly, one can help many people with it and can build worthwhile institutions. (*Noam Elimelech*, cited in *Maayanah Shel Torah*)

Love of wisdom increases your wisdom.

ובלב כל חכם לב נתתי חכמה ועשו את כל אשר צויתך. (שמות ל"א ו')

"AND IN THE HEART OF EACH PERSON WHO HAD A WISE HEART I HAVE GIVEN WISDOM." (*Shmos* 31:6)

Rabbi Chayim Shmuelevitz used to say that we see from here

that a person needs wisdom to merit acquiring wisdom. What is this wisdom? It is the heartfelt desire for more wisdom. We can have a picture of what this desire is from the desire of Haman for honor. He was second to the king in power and the entire population of 127 countries bowed to him. Nevertheless, when Mordechai refused to bow down to him, he said that all his honor was as nothing since he was missing one person's honor. So too, a person who has a deep love of wisdom feels a strong lack for any wisdom he is missing. When you have this love for wisdom, the Almighty will give you greater wisdom.

Observing Shabbos is a sign of your relationship with the Almighty.

ויאמר השם אל משה לאמר. ואתה דבר אל בני ישראל לאמר אך את שבתתי תשמרו כי אות הוא ביני וביניכם לדרתיכם לדעת כי אני השם מקדשכם. (שמות ל״א י״ב י״ג)

"AND THE ALMIGHTY SPOKE TO MOSHE SAYING, SPEAK TO THE CHILDREN OF ISRAEL SAYING, MY SHABBOS YOU SHALL KEEP, FOR IT IS A SIGN BETWEEN ME AND YOU THROUGHOUT YOUR GENERATIONS, THAT YOU MAY KNOW THAT I AM THE ALMIGHTY WHO SANCTIFIES YOU." (*Shmos* 31:12,13)

The Talmud (*Shabbos* 10b) describes the Shabbos as a special gift the Almighty gave to the Jewish people.

The Chofetz Chayim gave two parables to illustrate how Shabbos serves as a sign of the relationship between the Jewish people and the Almighty. When two people are engaged to be married they send each other gifts. Even if difficulties arise between them, as long as they keep the gifts that they received from each other we know they still plan to get married. But if we see that they have returned the gifts, then we know that the relationship between them is over. Similarly, as long as a person observes Shabbos we see that he still has a relationship with the Almighty. But if a person, as it were, returns this gift of Shabbos, the relationship ceases to exist.

The Chofetz Chayim offered another illustration. When a person opens a new store, he puts a sign outside that tells everyone what kind of store it is. A tailor will have a symbol that shows he is a tailor, and a shoemaker a symbol showing he is a shoemaker. Even if a person travels away for a while, as long as his sign is still on the outside of the store, everyone can expect him to eventually return. But as soon as he takes down his emblem from the store, we know that he no longer plans to return. When you observe Shabbos, you testify that the Almighty created the world in six days and rested on the seventh. By keeping Shabbos you proclaim that you have this awareness. Even if you are not perfect, you are still testifying that you wish to follow the will of the Almighty. A person who fails to keep Shabbos removes this sign. This is the reason for the importance of Shabbos observance and the severity of failing to observe it. (*Chofetz Chayim al Hatorah*, pp.131-4)

Before 1948 members of the Haganah once used an open space near the Chazon Ish's home as a site for target practice. One of the officers approached the Chazon Ish and said to him, "Rebbe, don't worry about the shooting. These shots come from our boys."

"I am more afraid of your shots on *Shabbos*," replied the Chazon Ish, "than I am of the Arabs the other days of the week." (*P'air Hador*, vol.3, p.38)

To have peace of mind on Shabbos you need to have mastery over your traits.

ששת ימים יעשה מלאכה וביום השביעי שבת שבתון קדש להשם. (שמות ל״א ט״ז)

"SIX DAYS WORK SHALL BE DONE, AND ON THE SEVENTH DAY IT SHOULD BE A COMPLETE REST SACRED TO THE ALMIGHTY." (*Shmos* 31:15)

Rashi comments on this that rest on Shabbos should be a permanent rest and not merely a temporary rest. I heard from Rabbi Chayim Shmuelevitz the following explanation: A temporary rest means that a person has not really changed his inner traits, but he merely controls them on Shabbos. He still has a bad temper and has a tendency to engage in quarrels, but because of the elevation of Shabbos he has self-discipline and these traits are not manifest. But the ultimate in Shabbos observance is that a person should uproot those negative traits which are contradictory to peace of mind on Shabbos. One needs to uproot such traits as anger and the tendency to quarrel with others. Only then is your rest on Shabbos a complete rest.

It is not sufficient for a person just to refrain from the formal categories of work on Shabbos. Shabbos is the gift of peace of mind. This is not considered righteousness, but an essential aspect of Shabbos. Only by being a master over your negative emotions can you have true peace of mind.

On Shabbos there are many opportunities to get angry and engage in quarrels that one does not have leisure for on other days. But this can also be an opportunity for growth. By mastering attitudes and approaches conducive to peaceful relationships with others you elevate yourself.

Whenever letters arrived on Friday after the middle of the day, it was Rabbi Aryeh Levin's custom not to open them, so that bothersome thoughts and worries should not trouble him during *Shabbos*, the holy day of rest. (*A Tzaddik in Our Time*, p.100)

One Friday night, a policeman came to the home of Reb Yaakov Yosef Herman: "I just received word that there is a fire in your fur store. The fire department has been alerted and is doing its best to extinguish the flames. It is advisable for you to get there as soon as possible."

Reb Yaakov Yosef thanked the police officer and then said, "It is our Sabbath. I cannot be there until after it ends tomorrow night."

The policeman looked at him in amazement. "Your store is

burning down, and you won't even go there to see what is happening?"

The entire *Shabbos*, Reb Yaakov Yosef showed no anxiety. He sang *zemiros*, said his *dvar Torah* at the table, and did not hurry to make *havdalah* after *Shabbos*.

Saturday night, Reb Yaakov Yosef rode over to Seventh Avenue, where his fur store was situated, expecting to see it in shambles. However, it was the adjoining fur store that had gone up in flames. (*All For The Boss*, p.119)

Try to find favorable intentions for the behavior of others.

ויאמר אלהם אהרן פרקו נזמי הזהב אשר באזני נשיכם בניכם ובנתיכם
והביאו אלי. (שמות ל"ב ב')

"AND AHARON SAID TO THEM, REMOVE THE GOLDEN EARRINGS WHICH ARE ON THE EARS OF YOUR WIVES, SONS, AND DAUGHTERS, AND BRING THEM TO ME." (*Shmos* 32:2)

Daas Zkainim explains that Aharon's intentions were for the sake of heaven. This is what he said to himself: "Now that Moshe has not returned, if I will appoint Kolaiv or Nachshon as the leader in Moshe's absence, when Moshe returns they will not be eager to give up their position of leadership and this will cause a major quarrel. If I do not appoint anyone as a leader, they will choose a leader themselves and this will also cause a major quarrel. If I will make myself the leader until Moshe returns, when he comes back perhaps he will feel that I tried to usurp his leadership. Therefore, until Moshe returns I will keep them busy with talk about making a meaningless golden calf. The women will be reluctant to give up their jewelry and therefore I will be able to stall for time."

At first glance when one reads this verse one might wonder how Aharon could have possibly taken an action that appears to be a form of idolatry. But when we see his real intentions we see that he sincerely tried to avoid doing things that could be problematic. This is a lesson in judging others favorably. You might look at someone's actions and wonder how he could have done something so negative. But if you were to know his true motivations, you would realize that he meant nothing wrong and even tried to prevent something negative from happening. Before condemning someone for his behavior, ask yourself, "What positive motivations and intentions could he possibly have had?"

When you make a mistake have the flexibility to admit it and improve.

ויאמר השם אל משה ראיתי את העם הזה והנה עם קשה ערף הוא.
(שמות ל"ב ט')

"AND THE ALMIGHTY SAID TO MOSHE, I HAVE SEEN THIS PEOPLE AND THEY ARE A STIFF-NECKED PEOPLE." (*Shmos* 32:9)

Rabbi Simcha Zissel of Kelm commented: In the previous verse we read how they made a golden calf, bowed down to it and even brought it offerings. But in this concluding verse we see that the main fault of the people was that they were stiff-necked. That is, they lacked the flexibility to admit that they made a mistake. When someone is flexible, even if he makes many mistakes he will regret them and will change. But if a person is inflexible, when he makes a mistake he will not repent and improve. (*Chochmah Umussar*, vol.1, p.258)

When you do something improper at least do not feel joy over it.

ויהי כאשר קרב אל המחנה וירא את העגל ומחלת ויחר אף משה וישלך מידיו את הלחת וישבר אתם תחת ההר. (שמות ל"ב י"ט)

"AND IT WAS WHEN [Moshe] GOT CLOSE TO THE CAMP AND HE SAW THE CALF AND THE DANCING, AND MOSHE BECAME ANGRY AND HE THREW THE TABLETS FROM HIS HANDS AND HE BROKE THEM BENEATH THE MOUNTAIN." (*Shmos* 32:19)

Sforno comments that Moshe was angry because he saw that they had joy from the wrong they did. If they would have felt suffering when they did wrong, they could have corrected their error and been worthy of the tablets. But their dancing and joy caused Moshe to give up hope.

We see from here that if you have done wrong, you should feel regret about it. These feelings of regret will motivate you to improve your actions. Feeling good about doing something that is wrong is even worse than the negative behavior itself. When you feel bad about some wrong you have done, you can then feel positive about this manifestation of your sense of values.

Forego your personal prejudices for the honor of the Almighty.

ויעמד משה בשער המחנה ויאמר מי להשם אלי ויאספו אליו כל בני לוי.
(שמות ל"ב כ"ו)

"AND MOSHE STOOD AT THE GATE OF THE CAMP AND HE SAID, WHOEVER IS FOR THE ALMIGHTY COME TO ME. AND ALL OF THE DESCENDANTS OF LEVI GATHERED UNTO HIM." (*Shmos* 32:26)

The Chasam Sofer notes that the Torah emphasises the word "all," every member of the tribe of Levi came to Moshe. This included Korach and those Levites who later followed him. Even though they were greatly displeased with Moshe, when it came to the honor of the Almighty they joined him to fight for the Almighty. (*Toras Moshe*)

This has practical applications. There are many times in one's life when one will be called upon to make a similar decision. There will be people whom you might envy or feel have taken a position above others that they do not deserve. But what they presently want to do is clearly positive. You might have mixed feelings about joining with them for a cause or a project. Your only consideration should be whether what you are doing is consistent with the honor of the Almighty. If they are calling upon you to take action for the Almighty, put your personal prejudices aside and join them.

VAYAKHAIL

Do not make calculations to violate Torah commandments.

ששת ימים תעשה מלאכה וביום השביעי יהיה לכם קדש שבת שבתון
להשם. (שמות ל"ה ב')

"SIX DAYS YOU SHALL WORK AND THE SEVENTH DAY SHALL BE
SACRED FOR YOU. IT IS A COMPLETE REST FOR THE ALMIGHTY."
(*Shmos* 35:2)

Rashi cites the Sages that the Torah repeats the prohibition
against working on Shabbos as an introduction to the command to
build the Sanctuary. This is to teach us that working on Shabbos is
forbidden even for the great *mitzvah* of building the holiest of
places (see Sforno).

At times a person might make all kinds of calculations that it is
worthwhile to break Torah commandments because his intentions
are elevated. He might argue that he is not doing this for personal
gain but for the sake of Heaven. Here we can understand the
principle that these calculations are against the Almighty's will.

Rabbi Elchonon Wasserman gave a parable that expresses this
point. An emperor sent his most trusted adviser to a foreign
country on a specific mission. He was told to speak to the king of
that country, but was warned not to make any wagers or bets.
"Remember carefully," the emperor told him, "no matter what the
wager is do not get involved."

When the emperor's adviser was in the midst of his discussion
with the foreign king, the king said to him, "I have never seen

anyone as hunchbacked as you."

"But I am not a hunchback at all," said the puzzled adviser.

"I see clearly that you are," the king insisted. "I'll even make you a wager of a million dollars. Just take off your shirt and undershirt and everyone will see that you are a hunchback."

The adviser was about to enter into the wager with the king. But then he remembered the warning of the emperor not to make any wagers. "But this is different," the adviser told himself. "I can't possibly lose on this one. I know that I am not a hunchback and I'm certain that if I were able to consult with the emperor he would allow me to make this wager."

The adviser made the wager and when he undressed in front of the king and in the presence of all those who stood by, the king gave him the million dollars that he had won.

With great joy the adviser rushed back to the emperor and told him the wonderful news. But instead of being happy with this report, the emperor angrily said to him, "How could you have disobeyed my orders not to make any wagers? You are gravely mistaken. You might have gained one million dollars, but I have just lost ten million dollars. I had a wager with this king that he would not be able to willfully have you undress in front of the members of his court. Your small gain is my great loss."

This, said Rabbi Elchonon Wasserman, is what happens when a person disobeys the commandments of the Torah with calculations that what he is doing is better for the Almighty. The person only thinks there is a gain, but in fact there is only a loss.

When giving a monetary donation, involve your heart.

כל נדיב לבו יביאה את תרומת השם. (שמות ל״ה ה׳)

"WHOEVER IS OF A WILLING HEART, LET HIM BRING IT, AN OFFERING OF THE ALMIGHTY." (*Shmos* 35:5)

Rabbi Simcha Zissel of Kelm explained this verse that those who brought the offerings for the Sanctuary should bring their hearts with their offering. It is not sufficient just to give a monetary donation. The Almighty wants our hearts, that is, our thoughts and emotions. They too should be an expression of our generosity. (*Chochmah Umussar*, vol.2, p.150)

When you just give money to charity or to a worthy institution, you help the cause for which you are giving. But when you give your heart also, you are changing and elevating yourself as a person. Each donation makes you into a more giving person. Whenever you give, reflect for a while on what you are doing.

One evening, the executive of a well-known yeshiva came to the home of Mr. R to request a donation on behalf of the yeshiva. Mr. R immediately interrupted what he was doing, warmly received his visitor, and responded generously to his request. The visitor wished Mr. R well and as he rose to leave apologized for having intruded at an obviously busy time.

Mr. R told him, "You know, Rabbi Yitzchok Hutner calls me at times for donations for his yeshiva. Before I hang up, I always thank him for the call, and I once explained to the Rosh Hayeshiva why he deserves my thanks. I am very organized in my *tzedakah*. I set aside a certain share of my earnings and distribute it to worthy causes. My donation would be the same without a call, but I want my children to see that giving *tzedakah* is not like paying the electric bill. I don't interrupt my dinner to pay bills, but I do when I get a call for *tzedakah*. If the request is made in person, I ask my son to fetch my checkbook for me. So I say the same to you, thanks for coming by." (Rabbi Eliezer Cohen; *The Jewish Observer*, Feb. 1985)

When you have been in a Torah environment it should be noticeable in your behavior.

ויצאו כל עדת בני ישראל מלפני משה. (שמות ל"ה כ')

"AND THE ENTIRE CONGREGATION OF THE CHILDREN OF ISRAEL
WENT OUT FROM THE PRESENCE OF MOSHE." (*Shmos* 35:20)

Rabbi Eliyahu Lopian commented on this verse that it was
noticeable that they were in the presence of Moshe and they were
now parting from him. If you see someone who was at a bar, it will
be noticeable from the way he talks and walks where he was. One
can easily perceive that someone is drunk from his actions and
speech. Similarly, when someone seriously studies Torah in a
yeshiva, it should be noticeable from the way he behaves that he
has been studying Torah. That is what this verse expresses:
everyone could tell from the elevated manner in which the people
behaved that they had just come from Moshe. Whenever you are in
a Torah environment, it should be noticeable from your deeds and
traits that you have been in a spiritual environment. (*Lev Eliyahu*,
vol.1, p.267)

Increase your initiative and you will accomplish much.

ויבאו כל איש אשר נשאו לבו. (שמות ל"ה כ"א)

"AND EACH PERSON WHOSE HEART MOTIVATED HIM CAME."
(*Shmos* 35:21)

The Ramban states that they needed motivation from their
hearts because there was no one who had any previous experience
with the skills necessary for the tabernacle. There were no teachers
available to train them. But there were people who had the courage
to come before Moshe to tell him, "I will do all that you say."
Rabbi Yeruchem Levovitz commented that if we look at the
really wealthy people of the world, we will see that they are people
with great initiative. There are major differences between people

who reach the top by having much initiative and those who stay behind because of a lack of initiative. The Torah notes that the people who were successful in the sacred work of building the sanctuary were successful because of their inner courage to come forth and volunteer to do what was needed. (*Daas Torah: Shmos*, p.348)

Be aware of the moments in your life when you felt a strong desire to accomplish spiritual greatness. Let those memories motivate you in the future to have even more initiative for true accomplishments. Have the courage to accept upon yourself to do what is needed. A person who has a strong drive to accomplish something will find that he has many talents and abilities that would have remained dormant had he lacked that drive.

Be careful not to allow laziness to cause you to procrastinate.

והנשאם הביאו את אבני השהם ואת אבני המלאים לאפוד ולחשן.
(שמות ל"ה כ"ז)

"AND THE HEADS OF THE TRIBES BROUGHT SHOHAM STONES, AND STONES TO BE SET, FOR THE EFOD, AND FOR THE BREASTPLATE." (*Shmos* 35:27)

Rashi cites the words of the Sages who note that the heads of the tribes brought the last donations for the Sanctuary. They said, "We will let the other people donate whatever they will donate, and we will bring whatever is missing." But the people brought all that was needed. The heads of the tribes then asked, "What can we still do?" The only things remaining were the special stones that were needed and this is what they brought. But because they procrastinated at the beginning, the letter *yud* is missing from their name in this verse (in the Hebrew word *nesiim*).

Rabbi Yeruchem Levovitz commented that their original thought appears to have been virtuous. They said they would bring whatever was needed at the end. This appears to be a very generous proposal on their part. But we learn from here that since their behavior touched on the negative trait of laziness, their behavior was considered incorrect and they were censured for it. (*Daas Torah: Shmos*, p.350)

Whenever a negative character trait could be an underlying factor for your behavior, be very careful to clarify what your true motivation is. This applies especially to the trait of laziness. It is easy to give many good-sounding reasons for not doing things. But when laziness could be the real reason for your lack of action, be suspicious that your reasons are actually rationalizations by which you are trying to excuse yourself.

If the Alter of Nevardok had difficulty deciding whether he should go to the *Bais Medrash* to study Torah or to go someplace else, he would first go to the doorstep of the *Bais Medrash*. By this means he would remove the bias of laziness and only then would he reach a decision about what to do. (*Chayai Hamussar*, vol.2, p.201)

Use your creative talents for the Almighty's honor.

ולחשב מחשבת לעשת בזהב ובכסף ובנחשת. (שמות ל״ה ל״ב)
ולהורת נתן בלבו. (שמות ל״ה ל״ד)

"AND TO THINK THOUGHTS TO MAKE WITH GOLD, AND WITH SILVER AND WITH BRASS." (*Shmos* 35:32)

There are two types of skillful artisans. There is an expert in making fancy vessels with intricate designs. But this person is not at all creative and original. After he sees what someone else has done, he learns to make similar things. Because he is so skillful he is able to produce an even better work than the original designer. A truly great craftsman, however, is one who is able to picture new designs in his mind. His fertile imagination enables him to create original works of art. This, wrote Rabbi Shlomo Kluger, is what the present verse is expressing. "And to think thoughts," that is, Betzalel had the ability to visualize entirely new artistic creations. (*Imrai Shafer*)

Whatever creative abilities a person has can be utilized for the honor of the Almighty. Betzalel used his great talent to build the Sanctuary for worshipping the Almighty. Whoever is blessed with creativity should creatively find elevated ways to use it.

Share your knowledge with others.

ולהורת נתן בלבו. (שמות ל"ה ל"ד)

"AND HE PUT IN HIS HEART TO TEACH." (*Shmos* 35:34)

There are people who have special knowledge and skills but do not want to teach them to others. Therefore the Torah praises Betzalel because he was willing to share his knowledge with others. (*Ohr Hachayim*)

A person who desires knowledge only for his own honor will be reluctant to share what he knows with others. The more people who have the same knowledge the less special he will be. But if a person realizes that his knowledge and skills are gifts from the Almighty, he will readily pass them on to others. He wants to accomplish the most that is possible, and if more people have that special knowledge more will be accomplished. Your willingness to share what you know with others is a sign of your true inner attitudes towards your wisdom.

Rabbi Yaakov Yisroel Kanievsky, the Steipler, author of the multi-volume work, *Kehilos Yaakov*, used to say, "I agree with a full heart that anyone who gives a Talmudic lecture can repeat my original thoughts from my books without acknowledging me. I give others permission to express the ideas as if they had thought of them by themselves. The main thing is that Torah ideas should be studied." (*Peninai Rabainu Hakehilos Yaakov*, p.11)

PIKUDAI

Learn to do things in their proper order.

וּבְצַלְאֵל בֶּן אוּרִי בֶן חוּר לְמַטֵה יְהוּדָה עָשָׂה אֵת כָּל אֲשֶׁר צִוָּה הַשֵׁם אֶת
מֹשֶׁה. (שמות ל״ח כ״ב)

"AND BETZALEL THE SON OF CHUR OF THE TRIBE OF YEHUDAH
DID ALL THAT THE ALMIGHTY COMMANDED MOSHE." (*Shmos* 38:22)

Rashi states that Betzalel realized on his own that the proper
order was to make the tabernacle first and only then to make the
vessels. When building a house, people need to build the house first
and then they acquire the furniture to put into the house. Although
at first Moshe told Betzalel what to do in the reverse order, he
agreed that Betzalel was correct in changing the order.

Rabbi Yeruchem Levovitz commented that we see here the
concept of the importance of having things done in their proper
order. One always needs to clarify his priorities and to have the
organizational skills to do things in order. (*Daas Torah: Shmos*,
pp.350-1)

This is an important tool for accomplishing anything in life. One
needs to know what he must do and then he must have an order of
priorities. We will never have enough time to do everything we
would like to. But by being aware of the order of importance of
what you have to do, you will ensure that you will effectively
accomplish the most possible within the limitations of the time
alloted to you. Each day make a list of the various tasks you need
to take care of. Then decide on a proper order in which to do them.

Be grateful to people who enable you to make worthwhile contributions.

וירא משה את כל המלאכה והנה עשו אתה כאשר צוה השם כן עשו
ויברך אתם משה. (שמות ל"ט מ"ג)

"AND MOSHE SAW ALL THE WORK AND BEHOLD THEY DID IT AS THE ALMIGHTY COMMANDED, SO DID THEY DO, AND MOSHE BLESSED THEM." (*Shmos* 39:43)

Rabbi Zalman Sorotzkin related that he was once at the dedication ceremony of an institution for which one Rabbi selflessly devoted an extremely large amount of time and energy. The Rabbi spoke and heaped much praise and many blessings upon the donors whose contributions made the institution possible. Rabbi Zalman Sorotzkin was the next speaker and said, "Really the donors should be the ones to praise and bless the Rabbi. It was his efforts that enabled them to have the merit of contributing to such a worthwhile charity. But he followed in the footsteps of Moshe. After the complete report of everything that was donated to the *mishkan*, Moshe blessed all those who participated in the donations and contributions. They should have blessed Moshe for the opportunity he gave them."

"The same is true when a wealthy person helps a poor person. The wealthy person gains more from the poor person, since he gains spiritual merit. But what do we see in the world? The receiver expresses more thanks to the giver than the giver does to the receiver." (*Oznayim Letorah*)

When someone approaches us for a contribution for a worthy cause, we should appreciate that he is doing us a favor by giving us an opportunity to contribute. This is an important concept for fundraisers to keep in mind. They should be aware that they are doing an act of kindness for the donors. At the same time, they need to show their gratitude to the donors.

Rabbi Yisroel Salanter once asked a wealthy person to donate money for a very worthy cause. The wealthy person, however, did not act as he should have. Rav Yisroel told him, "The truth is that you have an obligation to go around and find people who need your financial assistance. By coming to you in your home we are saving you effort. You should be grateful to us. We are doing you a favor and not you with us." (*Chayai Hamussar* vol.2, pp.196-7)

My late uncle, Rabbi Moshe Helfan, was a fundraiser for the Telzer Yeshiva in Cleveland. There was a Jewish farmer in Pennsylvania who used to give a small yearly donation to the yeshiva. In the 1970's when the price of fuel went up, the cost of gas needed to drive to that person's farm was higher than the amount of that person's usual donation.

Rabbi Helfan said the following, "I can't not go to the person for his donation. His supporting Torah study in the yeshiva is a great merit for him and I can't deprive him of that merit. I can't make the yeshiva pay for the gas because this would cause a loss to the yeshiva. Therefore, I'll drive to his farm, but I'll pay for the gas with my own money."

Everyone can fall prey to envy but one can overcome it.

ומשחת אתם כאשר משחת את אביהם. (שמות מ' ט"ו)

After being told to anoint Aharon, Moshe was told in reference to Aharon's sons: "AND YOU SHALL ANNOINT THEM AS YOU ANNOINTED THEIR FATHER." (*Shmos* 40:15)

Rabbi Meir Simcha Hacohen explained that when Moshe was told to annoint his brother Aharon he was able to do it with a complete heart. Moshe, the younger brother, was the leader of the Israelites and was happy that his brother was the High Priest. But in reference to Aharon's sons, the situation was different. Moshe's own sons were not going to succeed him as leaders. So when it came to annointing Aharon's sons Moshe might have felt envy.

Therefore the Almighty told Moshe to annoint Aharon's sons with the same wholeheartedness and joy with which he annointed their father. (*Meshech Chochmah*)

It is amazing that Moshe would need a special command to overcome envy. We see from here that even the greatest person needs to internalize attitudes that' will help him avoid envy. Moreover, we see that it is possible to feel joy and enthusiasm for another person's success even if that person has something that you do not.

Focus on doing the will of the Almighty.

ויעש משה ככל אשר צוה השם אתו כן עשה. (שמות מ' ט"ז)

"AND MOSHE DID ALL THAT THE ALMIGHTY COMMANDED HIM, THAT IS WHAT HE DID." (*Shmos* 40:16)

Moshe's motivation in all that he did for the Sanctuary was for the Almighty's honor. Even though he personally would gain from the construction of the tabernacle, for the Almighty would communicate with him there, he was not motivated by thoughts of his own glory. Neither was he motivated by thoughts of the honor of his brother, Aharon, who was to be the High Priest. Moshe focused solely on doing the will of the Almighty. (*Haamek Dovor*)

This is a most difficult task. To do something for which you will have great benefit yourself and still to have pure motivations. But the more sacred the work you are involved in the greater the importance of having elevated thoughts and motivations.

Rabbi Yechezkail Abramsky told Rabbi Moshe Mordechai Shulsinger, "Every time I go to deliver a Torah lecture I have in mind that I am now going to serve the Almighty with the *mitzvah* of teaching Torah. At times, to think these thoughts sincerely is even more difficult than any other aspect of giving the lecture." (*Peninai Rabainu Yechezkail*, p.14)

VAYIKRA

Happiness is dependent on closeness with the Almighty.

אדם כי יקריב מכם קרבן להשם. (ויקרא א' ב')

"WHEN A PERSON OF YOU BRINGS AN OFFERING TO THE ALMIGHTY..." (*Vayikra* 1:2)

Rabbi Samson Raphael Hirsch commented on this verse: It is most regrettable that we have no word which really reproduces the idea which lies behind the expression *karbon*. The unfortunate use of the term "sacrifice" implies the idea of giving something up that is of value to oneself for the benefit of another, or of having to do without something of value. Also, the underlying idea of "offering" makes it by no means an adequate expression for *karbon*. The idea of an offering presupposes a desire on the part of the one to whom it is brought which is satisfied by the "offering," which is like a gift. But the idea of a "karbon" is never used for a gift. It is used exclusively with reference to Man's relation to the Almighty, and its meaning can only be understood from its root *karov*, which means to approach, to come near, and so to come into close relationship with somebody. The object and purpose of *hakravah* is the attainment of a higher sphere of life. The one bringing the *karbon* desires that something of himself should come into closer relationship to the Almighty, and the procedure by which this greater nearness to the Almighty is to be achieved is called *hakravah*. Closeness to the Almighty is the highest, and the only conception of what is "good" (see *Tehilim* 73:28). True happiness in life is dependent on closeness to the Almighty. In the halls of the Almighty the problems of life solve themselves. Life's happiness rises and falls in accordance with the proximity or distance of the Almighty. All prosperity loses its attraction if it entails estrangement from the Almighty. Even suffering itself becomes exalted happiness in the nearness of the Almighty to those who have refined their minds in the halls of the Sanctuary in order to get an understanding of true happiness. (Rabbi Hirsch's Commentary)

Acknowledge the gifts you have received from the Almighty.

וכי תקריב קרבן מנחה מאפה תנור וגו'. ואם מנחה על מחבת קרבנך וגו'. ואם מנחת מרחשת קרבנך וגו'. (ויקרא ב'-ד,ה,ז)

"AND IF YOU BRING NEAR A FLOUR OFFERING BAKED IN THE OVEN... AND IF YOUR OFFERING IS A FLOUR OFFERING BAKED IN A PAN... AND IF YOUR OFFERING IS A FLOUR OFFERING BAKED IN A POT..." (*Vayikra* 2:4,5,7)

Rabbi Samson Raphael Hirsch commented: The *Minchah*, flour offering, expresses our acknowledgement to the Almighty in respect to our food, comfort and satisfaction, altogether referring to our happiness in life. *Minchas solas*, the fine flour offering, in its general basic elements expresses various degrees and proportions of the necessities, the comforts and the joys of life. For the conditions of happiness in life are indeed multifarious, although the fundamental conditions out of which they are formed remain essentially the same. If we compare the offerings baked in the oven, baked in a pan, and baked in a pot, they seem to have the relation to each other of bread, cake, and specially prepared dishes. Bread, (*maafeh tanur*) is ordinary food for happy daily life. Cake (*machavas*) signifies the extra enjoyment, the unusual condition of luxury. *Marcheshes* is a dish prepared for a special occasion, the temporary, passing moment of special joy. So that taken all together, they may express our consciousness of the fact that not only the actual necessities for a happy daily life, but also the extras that we could really do without, as well as the passing moments of special joy, are all to be looked upon as gifts of the Almighty's care for us, and we acknowledge Him and give Him homage. (Rabbi Hirsch's Commentary)

Be yourself, but be certain to utilize your full potential.

כל המנחה אשר תקריבו להשם לא תעשה חמץ כי כל שאר וכל דבש לא תקטירו ממנו אשה להשם. וכל קרבן מנחתך במלח תמלח. (ויקרא ב' י"א י"ג)

"EVERY MEAL OFFERING THAT YOU OFFER TO THE ALMIGHTY DO NOT MAKE IT CHOMETZ; FOR YOU SHALL BURN NO YEAST, NOR ANY HONEY, IN ANY OFFERING OF THE ALMIGHTY MADE BY FIRE. WITH ALL YOUR OFFERINGS YOU SHALL OFFER SALT." (*Vayikra* 2:11,13)

Yeast and honey were not permitted in the offerings on the altar. Yeast makes the dough rise higher, but it is an external additive. Honey makes things taste sweet, but it is also an external additive. Salt, on the other hand, brings out the flavor of the food, but only the flavor that is already there. This, says Rabbi Mordechai Gifter, symbolizes a basic principle in spiritual matters. When serving the Almighty you should follow the model of salt. That is, utilize all the abilities and talents that you have to serve Him. Do not be like yeast that causes distortion of what is there. Do not be like honey that is very sweet but is something borrowed from the outside. Be yourself, but make every effort to be all that you can be. (*Pirke Torah*, vol.1, p.111)

This thought can be repeated frequently since there is a custom to dip bread into salt at the beginning of a meal. This is a reminder of the sacrifices. It can also serve as a reminder to be ourselves, but to utilize our potential to its fullest.

When in a position of power have the courage to admit your mistakes.

אשר נשיא יחטא ועשה אחת מכל מצות השם אלקיו אשר לא תעשינה
בשגגה. (ויקרא ד' כ"ב)

"IF THE KING COMMITS A SIN BY UNINTENTIONALLY VIOLATING
ONE OF THE ALMIGHTY'S COMMANDMENTS WHICH HE SHOULD
NOT HAVE DONE..." (*Vayikra* 4:22)

Rashi comments that the first word in our verse *asher* (if) comes
from the word *ashrai* - fortunate. Fortunate is the generation in
which the king brings an offering when he transgresses
unintentionally. All the more so will he regret it if he does
something wrong intentionally.

The question arises why the Torah only states this here in
reference to the king transgressing unintentionally. Why did the
Torah not use this in reference to the High Priest or the Sanhedrin
whose sacrifices are dealt with in previous sections of this portion?
The answer is that the High Priest had a high level of sanctity and
the members of the Sanhedrin were great Torah scholars.
Therefore these factors contributed to their regretting the wrongs
that they did. But the king was a person with much power, and
power gives a person such high feelings about himself that he is
unlikely to admit that he has done anything wrong. For this reason
when the king with unlimited power admits that he has erred and
regrets what he has done, it is fortunate for his generation. (*Maskil
Ledovid*)

People who are power-hungry have a strong tendency to deny
making mistakes. When such a person is in a position of authority,
he is likely to consider himself so perfect that whatever he does and
says must be correct. Admitting that one has erred takes much
courage. The more power you have the greater the importance of
having the intellectual honesty to admit that you have made a
mistake. Take pleasure whenever you are brave enough to admit
that you were wrong. This pleasure will give you the strength to
accept the fact that what you have done was wrong.

Feeling embarrassed for doing wrong is a sign of having positive values.

וכפר עליו הכהן ונסלח לו. (ויקרא ד' ל"א)

When a person brings a female kid of the goats for a sin-offering, the Torah states: "AND THE PRIEST SHALL MAKE ATONEMENT FOR HIM AND HE SHALL BE FORGIVEN." (*Vayikra* 4:31)

The Talmud (*Sotah* 32b) states that when a person brings a female kid of the goats he causes himself embarrassment. Everyone who sees the offering immediately realizes that he is bringing it for his sins. This is unlike the lamb offering (verse 32) which can be offered for other purposes.

Rabbi Naftoli Tzvi Berlin noted that here the Torah's wording is that he shall be forgiven and it does not add the words "for his sin" as it does in verse 35 in reference to the lamb offering. The reason for this, writes the Netziv, is that when a person brings a female goat he accepts upon himself embarrassment for his transgression although he has another alternative. He can offer a lamb and people will not realize that he has transgressed. A person who sins and then feels embarrassment over his sins is forgiven for all his transgressions. Therefore the Torah states "he shall be forgiven," meaning he shall be forgiven for all his wrongs. (*Haamek Dovor*)

When a person feels embarrassed about his transgressions, he can feel positive about these painful feelings. It shows that he has a strong sense of values and that he really wants to refrain from doing wrong. Guilt feelings are problematic if a person feels that it is inappropriate for him to feel guilty. When, however, a person sees the positive aspects of his embarrassment he still suffers, but it is a fruitful suffering and one that can be coped with. This embarrassment will motivate a person to keep away from wrongdoing in the future. Because it leads to improvement and elevation a person will feel positive when he experiences this embarrassment.

Each person is obligated to give charity according to his means.

ואם לא תשיג ידו לשתי תרים או לשני בני יונה והביא את קרבנו אשר
חטא עשירת האפה סלת לחטאת. (ויקרא ה' י"א)

"AND IF HE DOES NOT HAVE THE FINANCIAL MEANS FOR TWO TURTLEDOVES OR FOR TWO YOUNG PIGEONS, THEN HE SHALL BRING HIS OFFERING FOR HIS TRANSGRESSION THE TENTH PART OF AN EPHAH OF FINE FLOUR FOR A SIN OFFERING." (*Vayikra* 5:11)

The Chofetz Chayim commented that we see from here how the Torah established different requirements for a wealthy person and a poor person. A wealthier person's offering must be worth more money for him to fulfill his obligation. If a wealthy person will bring the offering of a poor person, his offering is not valid and he is still obligated to bring a larger offering. The same is true of our obligation to give charity. The more money you have the greater is your obligation to give charity. Every person is obliged to give a tenth of his income to charity. One who earns a hundred times more than someone else must give a hundred times more charity. (*Chofetz Chayim al Hatorah*)

The same concept also applies to other talents. The greater your intellect, for instance, the greater your obligation to share your wisdom with others.

Rabbi Shlomoh Zalman Lipshitz, author of *Chemdas Shlomoh*, would give money to the poor even when he would not be left with any money for himself. When asked why he didn't leave money for his own expenses, he replied, "People trust me and I can always buy what I need on credit. But no one will want to give this poor person credit." (*Maigdolai Hatorah Vehachasidus: Rishonai Horabanim Bevarshah*, vol.15)

Internalize Torah values to such a degree that you will not forget them.

ואם נפש כי תחטא ועשתה אחת מכל מצות השם אשר לא תעשינה ולא
ידע ואשם ונשא עונו. (ויקרא ה' י"ז)

"AND IF ANY PERSON WILL SIN, AND VIOLATE ONE OF THE
COMMANDMENTS OF THE ALMIGHTY WHICH HE SHOULD NOT
HAVE DONE, AND HE DID NOT KNOW, HE IS GUILTY AND SHALL
BEAR HIS INIQUITY." (*Vayikra* 5:17)

The Torah wants us to internalize its values and ideals. It is not
sufficient for a person to have a superficial knowledge of Torah
values. Rather we need to make them a part of our inner being. We
see this concept from the fact that the Torah obliges a person to
bring a sacrifice when he transgresses without willful forethought,
noted Rabbi Eliyahu Eliezer Dessler. At first glance it seems
puzzling that the Torah prescribes an offering as a punishment
when a person transgresses without a conscious intent to
transgress. The principle here is that a person will not forget or
make mistakes in regard to matters that are an integral part of his
very being. If you do forget or make mistakes in some matter, it is a
sign that those values are not yet really a part of you. By bringing a
sacrifice, a person reminds himself to work on internalizing Torah
values. This is our constant task: to integrate Torah values until
they become so much a part of our personality that we will always
remember them. (*Michtav Maieliyahu*, vol.3, pp.138-9)

A person who studied Torah came to the author of the *Chidushai
Harim* and complained that he forgets the Torah that he studied.

"Do you also forget to eat?" the Rebbe asked him.

When the person replied in the negative, the Rebbe asked him,
"Why not?"

"My life is dependent on my eating," the man replied.

"Your life is also dependent on the Torah that you study," said
the *Chidushai Harim*. (*Geonai Polin Hoachronim*, p.19)

TZAV

It is arrogance to demand that everything always be the way you wish.

זאת תורת העלה. (ויקרא ו' ב')

"THIS IS THE LAW OF THE BURNT-OFFERING." (*Vayikra* 6:2)

Our verse can be read: "This" is the principle of the arrogant person, the one who looks at himself as an exalted person (*haolah*). He constantly demands "this." He always wants things to be done his way without taking the needs of others into consideration. (*Vayedabair Moshe*)

An arrogant person always wants to have everything his own way. His thoughts are focused only on what he wants. He is totally inconsiderate of others. This trait causes much strife in interpersonal relationships. If two people in a relationship both demand that things must be their way, they will quarrel all the time. If such a person finds someone who is submissive to him, he will get his way but at the heavy price of causing another human being pain and anguish.

Be aware of the needs and feelings of others. Be willing to compromise on your demands of how things should be. While you need not always give in to others, when you take someone else's needs into consideration you gain spiritually more than you would have by demanding that only your wishes should be met.

View each new day as the first day of your life.

ופשט את בגדיו ולבש בגדים אחרים והוציא את הדשן אל מחוץ למחנה
אל מקום טהור. (ויקרא ו' ד')

"THEN [the priest] SHALL TAKE OFF HIS GARMENTS AND PUT ON OTHER GARMENTS AND CARRY FORTH THE ASHES OUT OF THE CAMP UNTO A PURE PLACE." (*Vayikra* 6:4)

Rabbi Samson Raphael Hirsch commented: The taking out of the ashes that remained on the altar from the previous day expresses the thought that with each new day the Torah mission must be accomplished afresh, as if nothing had yet been accomplished. Every new day calls us to our mission with new devotion and sacrifice. The thought of what has already been accomplished can be the death of that which is still to be accomplished. Woe unto him who with smug self-complacency thinks he can rest on his laurels, on what he has already achieved, and who does not meet the task of every fresh day with full devotion as if it were the first day of his life's work!

"Carry forth the ashes out of the camp." Every trace of yesterday's sacrifice is to be removed from the hearth on the Altar, so that the service of the new day can be started on completely fresh ground. Given these considerations, we can understand the law that prescribes the wearing of worn-out garments when one is occupied with the achievements of the previous day. The past is not to be forgotten. But it is to be retired to the background, and is not to invest us with pride before the fresh task to which each new day calls us. (Rabbi Hirsch's Commentary)

Protect others from embarrassment.

דבר אל אהרן ואל בניו לאמר זאת תורת החטאת במקום אשר תשחט
העלה תשחט החטאת. (ויקרא ו' י"ח)

"SPEAK TO AHARON AND TO HIS SONS SAYING: THIS IS THE LAW OF THE SIN-OFFERING. AT THE PLACE WHERE YOU SLAUGHTER THE

BURNT-OFFERING YOU SHALL SLAUGHTER THE SIN-OFFERING."
(*Vayikra* 6:18)

The *Talmud Yerushalmi* (*Yevamos* 8:3) states that the reason the burnt-offerings and the sin-offerings were slaughtered at the same place was in order to save those who sinned from embarrassment. When people saw the animal they brought being slaughtered, they would not know that it was a sin-offering.

From here we see the principle of not causing others shame or discomfort when they have done something improper in the past and now regret it. Never remind anyone of past misdeeds. Always do whatever you can to protect people from embarrassment.

Publicize your good fortune rather than talking about your misfortunes.

אם על תודה יקריבנו והקריב על זבח התודה חלות מצות בלולת בשמן ורקיקי מצות משחים בשמן וסלת מרבכת חלת בלולת בשמן. (ויקרא ז' י"ב)

"IF FOR THANKSGIVING HE OFFERS IT, THEN HE SHALL OFFER WITH THE SACRIFICE OF THANKSGIVING UNLEAVENED CAKES MINGLED WITH OIL, AND UNLEAVENED WAFERS SPREAD WITH OIL, AND FINE FLOUR SOAKED AND MADE INTO CAKES MINGLED WITH OIL." (*Vayikra* 7:12)

When a person's life was in danger and he was saved, it is incumbent upon him to bring a *karbon todah*, a thanksgiving offering. Together with the offering he also brought forty loaves of bread in four different forms. One of each kind was given to the priest. The remaining thirty-six were his to eat. There was a time limit of the remainder of that day and the following night. After that time they could not be eaten. Sforno comments that the purpose of this extremely short time period was to ensure that he would share the bread with others. This would ultimately publicize the fortunate event.

Note that the only time that such publicity was a part of the offering was in the case of good news. A person felt deep gratitude to the Almighty for His help and in this joyous state he shared his joy with others. When one brought an offering for a sin, this was not publicized. When things were going wrong in one's life, one did not do this. Only when one had an event to be thankful for did one publicize it. This should be our model for choosing topics to speak about. Keep your main focus on the multitude of kindnesses the Almighty does for you. While there is definitely a need to share problems and difficulties with a sympathetic and understanding listener, the main areas to publicize are the good that happens to you.

Do not try to impress others with your humility.

ויעש אהרן ובניו את כל הדברים אשר צוה השם ביד משה. (ויקרא ח' ל"ו)

"AND AHARON AND HIS SONS DID ALL THE THINGS WHICH THE ALMIGHTY COMMANDED THROUGH MOSHE." (*Vayikra* 8:36)

Rashi comments that this is to praise them for not turning right or left.

The *Ksav Sofer* wrote that there are some people who are inwardly very conceited but outwardly try to act as if they were humble. Therefore when they receive some honor they shrug their shoulders to the right and to the left to give others the impression that they are so humble that they do not feel they deserve the honor bestowed upon them. But in their hearts they are really very arrogant. This can be one understanding of Rashi's words: "they did not turn [their shoulders] right or left." While inwardly they were truly humble they did not try to give others the impression that they had humility. (cited in *Otzer Chayim*)

True humility is an inward attitude. The more you make an effort to give other people the impression that you are humble the less sincere humility you actually have.

SHMINI

Don't allow humility to prevent you from accomplishing.

ויאמר משה אל אהרן קרב אל המזבח. (ויקרא ט' ז')

"AND MOSHE SAID TO AHARON: GO CLOSE TO THE ALTAR." (*Vayikra* 9:7)

Rashi cites *Toras Kohanim* that Aharon was afraid to go close to the altar out of embarrassment. Moshe then said to him, "Why are you embarrassed? For this reason you were chosen."

Rabbi Yitzchok of Volozhin explained: Aharon in his humility felt that he was unworthy to be the High Priest of the Jewish people. This is exactly what makes you worthy of being the High Priest, replied Moshe. The attribute of humility is so precious that because you have this trait you were chosen to be the High Priest. (footnote to *Ruach Chayim* 4:1)

When you try to accomplish in spiritual matters as a leader or teacher, you might say to yourself, "I realize how little I know. I am aware of my faults. How can I possibly serve in this position?" But as long as you are sincere in your efforts and are aware of your deficiencies, your humility is exactly the trait that makes you fit for the job. A person with true humility will learn from others, he will ask questions when he has doubts, and will be open to criticism. Never allow humility to stop you from worthy accomplishments.

Consult wiser people and peers before doing things that are questionable.

ויקחו בני אהרן נדב ואביהוא איש מתחתו ויתנו בהן אש וישימו עליה
קטרת ויקריבו לפני השם אש זרה אשר לא צוה אתם. (ויקרא י' א')

"AND THE SONS OF AHARON, NADAV AND AVIHU, TOOK EACH OF THEM HIS CENSER, AND PUT INSIDE INCENSE, AND OFFERED BEFORE THE ALMIGHTY STRANGE FIRE, WHICH HE HAD NOT COMMANDED THEM." (*Vayikra* 10:1)

In *Toras Kohanim* (in the portion of *Acharai Mos*) it is stated that Nadav and Avihu erred by not consulting Moshe for advice on whether it was proper for them to bring this incense. They also erred by not asking each other for advice.

We see two important ideas from this *Braisa*. One, before doing something that is questionable, make certain to consult someone who is older and wiser. You might feel that what you are about to do is the right thing to do. But there are always aspects that you might have overlooked or were unaware of. The second thing we see is that if they were to have consulted each other they might not have erred. At first glance this seems puzzling since they both did the same thing. But we see the principle that at times two people can do something, but if they would have discussed the matter between themselves they might have reached the conclusion that they should refrain from their behavior. Neither one might come to this conclusion on his own. But together they might. Develop the habit of discussing things with peers to see if there are reasons why you should not do some of the things you feel like doing.

Learn to accept the Almighty's will.

וידם אהרן. (ויקרא י' ג')

When Aharon's two sons died, his reaction was:
"AND AHARON WAS SILENT." (*Vayikra* 10:3)

Aharon was greatly praised for his remaining silent. What was the greatness of Aharon for not complaining against the Almighty? Before something happens one might be able to take action to prevent it. But afterwards what can one do? We find later Sages who excelled in accepting the will of the Almighty. Rabbi Akiva always used to say when something apparently negative happened, "All that the Almighty does is for the good." Nochum, *ish gam zu*, used to say, "This, too, is for the good." The Sages required us to bless the Almighty for the bad just as we bless Him for the good. What then was the special praise of Aharon, the first High Priest, for his silence?

When a person says, "All that the Almighty does is for the good" about something that originally disturbed or frustrated him, it implies that at first he was bothered by what happened. But as soon as he realizes the matter bothers him he uses his intellect to overcome his negative reaction. Intellectually he knows that all that the Almighty causes to occur is ultimately for the good and this knowledge enables him to accept the situation. But an even higher level is to internalize the concept that whatever the Almighty does is positive and good. When this is a person's automatic evaluation of every occurrence, he does not have to keep convincing himself that a specific event is good. Such a person accepts with joy everything that occurs in his life. This was the greatness of Aharon. He remained silent because he knew clearly that everything the Almighty does is purposeful. When things consistently go well for a person he feels an inner joy. The more you learn to accept the will of the Almighty the greater joy you will experience in your life. (Rabbi Moshe Hacohen Rice, cited in *Ohr Hamussar*, vol.2, pp.86-7)

Acceptance of the Almighty's will is the most crucial attitude to make part of oneself for living a happy life. The goal to strive for is to accept the Almighty's will as your own. Whatever He wishes is what you joyously accept. Fortunate is the person who has mastered this attitude.

In 1949 when Rabbi Moshe Yechiel Epstein, author of *Aish Dos*, was visiting *Eretz Yisroel*, his only son Reb Avraham Shlomoh died in New York at the age of twenty-one. The family did not want him to hear the news until he came back home. When he arrived at the airport, the Rebbes of Boyan and Kopishnitz, who were very close colleagues of his, carefully told him about his son. His only response to this bitter news were the words, "We are obligated to love the Almighty with all of our soul, even when He takes away our soul. My son was a part of my soul." (*Rishfai Aish Dos*, p.64)

When you can enter a joyous state with your own mind you do not need artificial stimulants.

וידבר השם אל אהרן לאמר. יין ושכר אל תשת אתה ובניך אתך בבאכם
אל אהל מועד. (ויקרא י' ח־ט)

"AND THE ALMIGHTY SPOKE TO AHARON SAYING: WINE AND OTHER INTOXICATING BEVERAGES YOU SHALL NOT DRINK, YOU AND YOUR SONS WITH YOU, WHEN YOU COME INTO THE TENT OF MEETING." (*Vayikra* 10:8-9)

The Netziv, Rabbi Naftoli Tzvi Yehudah Berlin, commented: A regular priest is forbidden to do the service in the Temple when he has just lost a close relative, but the High Priest is permitted to do so. Why? Because one must be in a state of joy to do the Almighty's service. When a regular person loses a relative, he is in a state of grief and therefore lacks the necessary joy. But the High Priest had to be a person who reached the level that his service in the Temple would transcend any personal loss. When he performed the Almighty's service, he was able to be in a joyous state regardless of what events had just occurred. Because joy is necessary, one might mistakenly think that a priest could or even should take wine in order to put himself in a high mood. Therefore the Torah tells us that this joy must come from an awareness of the Almighty. It should not be artificially induced by means of some chemical substance that one ingests. (*Haamek Dovor*)

This thought has practical applications in a generation when people who are miserable and depressed with their daily lives take alcoholic beverages or drugs as a means of elevating their moods. A person who can enter an emotional high state with his own mind has no need for external stimulants.

When you have a strong will for something, the Almighty leads you in that path.

יין ושכר אל תשת. (ויקרא י' ט')

"WINE AND OTHER INTOXICATING BEVERAGES YOU SHALL NOT DRINK." (*Vayikra* 10:9)

The Midrash (*Vayikra Rabbah* 12:1) warns against the harm of alcoholism: "If a person drinks too much wine, he will end up selling all that he owns to keep up his addiction to drinking."

The Midrash then relates the story of a man who spent so much money on his habit of drinking that his children were worried they soon would be penniless. When he was drunk, they tied him up and took him out to a cemetery. They hoped that when he became sober he would be shocked to find himself in the cemetery and would become aware of the dangers of drinking to excess. That day a caravan carrying vats of wine passed near the cemetery. The caravan was attacked and traveled as fast as it could. One of the large barrels it was carrying fell off and landed right next to the head of the drunk man. When he awoke from his drunken sleep, he was surprised to find the faucet of the barrel right next to his face and kept drinking right there in the cemetery.

In a letter to his father, Rabbi Eliyahu Eliezer Dessler commented that we see from this the principle that the Almighty leads a person in the way he wants to go. The events that led the person to find wine in the cemetery were so unusual that they were almost miraculous. If this is so when a person wants to do something that is improper, all the more so is it true when a person has a strong will to do what is good. (*Michtav Maieliyahu*, vol.3, pp.319-20)

The greater your desire to do something the more successful you will be. When you wish to accomplish in spiritual matters, build up a strong desire to accomplish and the Almighty will lead you in that path.

When you love wisdom you have joy for the wisdom of others.

וישמע משה וייטב בעיניו. (ויקרא י' כ')

Moshe was under the impression that Aharon made a mistake and censured him for it. Aharon then told Moshe the reason why his behavior was proper: "AND MOSHE HEARD AND IT WAS GOOD IN HIS EYES." (*Vayikra* 10:20)

Sforno comments on this verse: Moshe felt joy upon hearing the reasoning of Aharon. He had pleasure that Aharon was correct in his decision.

People who love wisdom will derive pleasure when they come up with an original idea or when they find that they are correct in some intellectual matter. But it is a rare quality to have such a love of wisdom that one derives pleasure when another person comes up with a good idea. What was special about Moshe's joy was that he himself made an error and Aharon was right. Many people would feel upset that they had made a mistake. But not Moshe Rabainu. He was joyful that his brother had an awareness of truth, even though this meant that he was wrong. Moshe's love of wisdom should serve as our model to strive for.

Rabbi Mendel Shook, a student of Rabbi Isser Zalman Meltzer in Slutsk, related, "Four other students and I were in a special group that met regularly in Rabbi Meltzer's house for lectures on tractate *Zevachim*. Once in the middle of a lecture on a complex topic, I gave an answer to a difficult question. Over the next few months the Rosh Hayeshiva frequently praised the answer that I gave. Thirty-five years later I visited the Rosh Hayeshiva in *Eretz Yisroel*. He asked me who I was, and as soon as I told him my name, he called out with much joy, 'Reb Mendel, I really liked the answer you gave.'" (*Bederech Aitz Hachayim*, vol.1, p.238)

TAZRIA

Motherhood is the highest and noblest occupation.

דבר אל בני ישראל לאמר אשה כי תזריע וילדה זכר וטמאה שבעת ימים.
(ויקרא י״ב ב׳)

"SPEAK UNTO THE CHILDREN OF ISRAEL, SAYING: WHEN A WOMAN
CONCEIVES AND GIVES BIRTH TO A MALE, THEN SHE SHALL BE IN A
STATE OF TUMAH SEVEN DAYS." (*Vayikra* 12:2)

Rabbi Samson Raphael Hirsch wrote: By the use of the
expression *tazria* here, which only occurs elsewhere in *Braishis*
1:11,12, referring to the activity of plants for the continuation of
their species, the mother's role in producing progeny is looked at as
a purely material, physiological process, and with that one word
the whole idea of *tumah* is shown. The highest and noblest
occupation on which the whole future of the human race is built,
and in which the whole constitution of womanhood finds its
purpose and goal is the process of the production of a new human
being. Man originates, grows and exists like a plant and the noblest
and most glorious name that the human tongue can utter, the name
"Mother," reminds one at the same time of the purely physical
unfree process of human origin. If anywhere, it is surely here that
the fact must be established, that, in spite of this, once he is born,
Man is a morally free agent. Above all, the mother herself, under
the fresh impression of her passively and painfully having to
submit to the forces of the physical laws of nature at the most
sublime procedure of her earthly calling, has to reestablish again
the consciousness of her own spiritual height. And only after this

impression of lack of freedom of will has completely passed away has she, by an offering, to undertake to allow herself of her own free will to give herself up to the whole spiritual height of her calling of Woman and Mother which is now beginning again with all its momentous and often painful moments; and to allow herself to reenter the Sanctuary of holy happy faithfulness to duty. (Rabbi Hirsch's Commentary)

Learn from Aharon to make peace between people even at the price of distorting the truth.

אדם כי יהיה בעור בשרו שאת או ספחת או בהרת והיה בעור בשרו לנגע צרעת והובא אל אהרן הכהן או אל אחד מבניו הכהנים. (ויקרא י"ג ב')

"WHEN A MAN SHALL HAVE IN THE SKIN OF HIS FLESH A SWELLING, A SCAB, OR BRIGHT SPOT, AND IT BE IN THE SKIN OF HIS FLESH THE PLAGUE OF TZORAAS, THEN HE SHALL BE BROUGHT TO AHARON THE PRIEST, OR TO ONE OF HIS SONS THE PRIESTS." (*Vayikra* 13:2)

The Rabbi of Alexander commented on this verse: The Sages state that *tzoraas* is an affliction that comes because a person spoke *loshon hora* against others. When people say negative things about others, they frequently rationalize that it is proper for them to say what they are saying. One common excuse is that they are telling the truth. The other person has done so much wrong that it is important to publicize what a bad person he is. They claim that they would never do this without having elevated intentions and that they are actually performing a *mitzvah*. Although their claims might sound good at first, they cause much hatred, quarrels, and pain. Therefore the person with *tzoraas* was sent to Aharon, the priest. One of the traits of Aharon was that he did everything he could to make peace between people. He even exaggerated and told untruths in order to bring about peaceful relationships between people. Whenever people quarreled, he would tell both sides that the other side was saying kind and positive things about them.

When someone was told that the other person was speaking positively about him, he automatically felt positive about the other person and this greatly improved their relationship. This was the lesson that Aharon would give to the person who spoke against others. Don't justify your harming and wronging others by claiming that you want to publicize the truth. Do all that is in your power to help people feel love for one another.

A certain widow lived in a rented apartment in Bnai Brak. A quarrel arose between her and the owner of the apartment over an amount of 50 lires, which in those days was a very large sum of money. The widow claimed she did not owe the money and refused to pay. The owner of the apartment took her to a secular court which ruled that she must leave the apartment. English policemen immediately forced the widow out and threw all of her furniture onto the street. Some hot-headed people felt sorry for the widow and were ready to beat up the owner of the apartment. But just in time, someone came up with the suggestion that they consult the Chazon Ish.

Both parties agreed to discuss the matter with the Chazon Ish and to follow his directives. The people who accompanied the widow were furious at the lack of compassion of the owner and did not conceal their anger when they spoke up on her behalf. Then the owner gave his version of the situation. He claimed she owed him the money and had no choice but to act the way he did. To the surprise of those standing there, the Chazon Ish's response to the owner was, "You are right. You are right."

Those who came with the widow remained silent even though they were flabbergasted over the Chazon Ish's agreeing with the owner. Then the Chazon Ish called over each of the sides separately and convinced them to give in a little bit in order to work out a compromise. He said that he would hold the money the widow would give him for the owner and would hand it over to him as soon as the widow moved back into the apartment. He did this because he convinced the widow to pay 15 lires, and she thought the owner was willing to give up 35 lires. The Chazon Ish had the owner agree to accept 40 lires which the owner thought the widow would be paying. Meanwhile, the Chazon Ish, who only had five lires himself, borrowed 20 lires which he would pay back little by little. Neither the owner nor the widow realized that the Chazon Ish was paying the money himself.

After the owner and widow left, the Chazon Ish called over those who came with the widow and explained why he appeared to agree with the owner. "The owner has a weak heart and if his integrity would have been questioned, it might have killed him. I was forced to sound as if I agreed with him. Even though he acted improperly, we must still save his life." (P'air Hador, vol.3, pp.161-2)

Suffering is atonement and atonement is joy.

והיה בעור בשרו לנגע צרעת. (ויקרא י"ג ב')

"AND IT BE IN THE SKIN OF HIS FLESH THE PLAGUE OF TZORAAS." (Vayikra 13:2)

In this verse the term vehaya is used which denotes joy. Tzoraas is a very painful affliction, what is the joy of having it? The answer is that all suffering serves as an atonement for one's wrongdoing. When someone atones for his transgressions, it is a great joy. (Rabbi Pinchos Menachem of Piltz; cited in Otzer Chayim)

By internalizing this attitude you will find it much easier to cope with the situations and events in your life that cause you suffering.

A few days before Rabbi Aharon Kotler passed away, he suffered great pain from his illness. His wife tried to give him words of encouragement. "It will be good," she said. Rav Aharon replied, "It is already good right now. All that the Almighty does is for the good." (Marbitzai Torah Umussar, vol.3, p.284)

Find a spiritual guide to assist you if you suffer.

וראהו הכהן ביום השביעי. (ויקרא י"ג ה')

"A.., THE PRIEST SHALL SEE HIM ON THE SEVENTH DAY." (*Vayikra* 13:5)

The Torah requires a priest to be the one to make the decision about whether a person is afflicted with *tzoraas*. This is because the priests were spiritual people who taught wisdom to others. They would be able to advise those afflicted to check through their behavior and to correct their faults. They would also teach the person how to pray to the Almighty for help. Moreover, the priests themselves would pray for the welfare of the person. (Sforno)

This is a lesson for someone who finds that the Almighty has sent him affliction. Find a spiritual guide who will be able to point out areas in which you can improve yourself, ask him for advice on what to pray for and ask him to pray for you. Those who follow this procedure will gain much from their suffering.

When you see a fault in someone else, ask yourself whether you have that fault yourself.

וטמא טמא יקרא. (ויקרא י"ג מ"ה)

"AND [the *metzora*] SHALL CALL OUT: UNCLEAN, UNCLEAN." (*Vayikra* 13:45)

The Shaloh wrote that this verse can be read as, "Unclean," an unclean person says about others. That is, a person who finds fault with others is really projecting his own faults and imperfections onto others. As the Sages (*Kidushin* 70a) have said, "Those who try to invalidate others do so with their own blemishes." (*Shnai Luchos Habris, Tazria*)

One means of finding out your own faults and blemishes is to see what faults you tend to notice in others. If you focus on certain negative aspects of others, it is possible that you have those same tendencies yourself. Also, if you know that if you tell others that someone has a certain fault they will immediately suspect you of having the same fault, you will certainly be very careful before saying negative things about others. For this reason, if you develop the habit that if someone tries to speak negatively about others in your presence you will say when appropriate, "Those who try to invalidate others really do so with their own blemishes," people will definitely refrain from speaking against others when you are around. Even when you are not present, they will be careful because they will be afraid that others, too, will look at them as having the same faults that they are trying to ascribe to others.

During his visit to the United States in 1939 on behalf of his yeshiva, Rabbi Elchonon Wasserman was asked for his impressions of America. Those who posed the question anticipated a zealous condemnation of a G-dless society. He surprised them, saying, "American youth has the greatest potential of any I have met. They are sincere in their search for truth, and once they are taught the Torah view, they develop into the finest *bnai Torah*." (Rabbi Chaim Shapiro; *The Jewish Observer*, Oct. 1973, p.16)

View the irritations caused by other people as the price you pay for companionship.

כל ימי אשר הנגע בו וגו' בדד ישב מחוץ למחנה מושבו. (ויקרא י"ג מ"ו)

"ALL THE DAYS THE PLAGUE IS IN HIM... HE SHALL DWELL ALONE; OUTSIDE THE CAMP SHALL HIS DWELLING BE." (*Vayikra* 13:46)

The Sages (*Erchin* 16b) said that since the *metzora* caused the separation of friends by speaking against others, he too should be separated from others.

Being all alone is a great distress. Everyone needs other people. While some people have a greater need to be around others and some have a lesser need, being in isolation causes much suffering.

Having people around you is a source of many benefits. But there is a price to pay for this. Your friends and relatives are bound to do things that irritate you. If you keep in mind that the alternative to having people around you is being all alone, you will view the drawbacks of having friends and relatives as a price well worth paying. When you purchase an item, you usually focus on what you are gaining not on your giving up money. Similarly, keep your focus on how you gain from other people and you will be free from focusing on how much they annoy you. When you view others in a positive manner, you will be much calmer in your search for strategies to influence them to stop their annoying behavior.

METZORA

Feel pleasure when meeting your responsibilities.

זאת תהיה תורת המצרע ביום טהרתו והובא אל הכהן. (ויקרא י״ד ב׳)

"THIS SHALL BE THE TORAH OF THE ONE STRICKEN WITH TZORAAS ON THE DAY OF HIS PURIFICATION, AND HE SHALL BE BROUGHT TO THE PRIEST." (*Vayikra* 14:2)

Ibn Ezra notes that the Torah states the person will be brought to the priest, not that he will come on his own to the priest. The reason is because after the *tzoraas* clears up, he will not want to bring the offerings that he is responsible to bring.

When a person has *tzoraas*, he will definitely claim that of course he will bring the necessary offerings when the *tzoraas* clears up. But once he is cured, he can easily forget his obligations. Now that nothing is pressing him, he will focus on other things and not on meeting his obligations.

Some people find it difficult to meet their responsabilities. When they need favors from someone or want to impress someone, they might make many promises. But when the time comes to keep their obligations, they do all they can to avoid meeting them. A person with integrity will derive pleasure from meeting his responsibilities and will not need others to coerce him to keep them. The more pleasure you feel when meeting your obligations, the more motivated you will be to meet them.

Think before you speak.

וצוה הכהן ולקח למטהר שתי צפרים חיות טהרות ועץ ארז ושני תולעת
ואזב. (ויקרא י"ד ד')

"AND THE PRIEST SHALL COMMAND TO TAKE FOR HIM WHO IS TO
BE PURIFIED TWO BIRDS ALIVE AND PURE." (*Vayikra* 14:4)

Rashi states the reason birds were taken for the process of
purifying the *metzora* was because birds constantly chirp. Since
tzoraas comes from speaking *loshon hora*, which is a matter of
chattering, the *metzora* needed birds for his atonement.

Rabbi Yeruchem Levovitz commented on this that the Torah is
giving us a key insight into what lies behind a person's speaking
against others. A root of the problem is that the person keeps on
talking without thinking about what he is saying. Just as birds keep
making noises, so too is this person just making a lot of noise. A
person needs to think about the goals of what he is about to say.
Before speaking you need to ask yourself, "What is the purpose of
what I am about to say? What will it accomplish? What effects will
it have?" Once you get into the habit of asking yourself these
questions, you will always think before you speak. This will enable
you to overcome the tendency of speaking against others. (*Daas
Torah: Vayikra*, pp.109-10)

Rabbi Avraham Chanoch Hoffman of Yerushalayim was a close
friend of Rabbi Ben Tzion Yadler. They would discuss ways they
could work on self-improvement, especially regarding their speech
at home. Rav Avraham Chanoch would say that when a husband
comes home and asks his wife, "What is there to eat?" or "What
did you cook today?" his question is superfluous. Why do you need
to ask this question? Whatever has been prepared is what you will
soon see. These types of questions can easily lead to anger and
quarrels. (*Betuv Yerushalayim*, pp.391-2)

Focus on your own faults and you will not speak against others.

וצוה הכהן ולקח למטהר שתי צפרים חיות טהרות ועץ ארז ושני תולעת
ואזב. (ויקרא י"ד ד')

"AND THE PRIEST SHALL COMMAND TO TAKE FOR HIM WHO IS TO
BE PURIFIED TWO BIRDS ALIVE AND PURE, AND CEDAR WOOD,
AND SCARLET, AND HYSSOP." (*Vayikra* 14:4)

Rashi cites the Sages that the cedar symbolizes arrogance
because *tzoraas* comes from arrogance. What is the cure for the
person that he shall be healed? He should humble himself, which is
symbolized by the scarlet that comes from the lowly worm and by
the small hyssop.

The Chofetz Chayim commented on this that one of the major
reasons a person speaks *loshon hora* is because of arrogance.
Someone who speaks against others views himself as above other
people and therefore feels that he has a right to say negative things
about them. If he were aware of his own faults and limitations, he
would not seek out the faults of others. (*Shmiras Haloshon*, part 2,
Metzora)

The greater your awareness of your own errors and negative
traits the less you will focus on the faults of others. When you focus
on the faults of others, you gain nothing yourself. By becoming
more aware of your own faults, you will keep improving your
character and you will free yourself from speaking against others.

Arrogance implies a lack of awareness of the Almighty.

ולקח הכהן את הכבש האחד והקריב אתו לאשם. (ויקרא י"ד י"ב)

"AND THE PRIEST SHALL TAKE ONE LAMB AND OFFER IT FOR A
GUILT OFFERING." (*Vayikra* 14:12)

The offering that the *metzora* brought was an *asham*, a guilt offering. This is the offering one brings when one is guilty of desecrating that which is holy. The reason for this is that *tzoraas* comes for speaking negatively against others and for arrogance. Both are aspects of desecrating the Almighty. When someone speaks against another person, he usually does so in private and wants to make certain that he is not overheard by other people. This is a lack of awareness that the Almighty overhears all that he says. Similarly, when a person is arrogant, it implies a lack of awareness of the Almighty. When one is truly aware of the infinite greatness and power of the Almighty, it is impossible to be arrogant. One is so small in comparison that as soon as one reflects on this, he will automatically have humility. By bringing the offering of the *asham*, the *metzora* gives thought to how he has previously lacked a proper awareness of the omniscience and omnipotence of the Almighty and will begin to internalize this understanding. (based on Sforno)

Although we do not have offerings in our time, by reading about the offerings we should internalize the messages that they teach us. The message here is that we should be very careful with what we say about others because the Almighty hears us. Similarly, we should be aware of how small and powerless we all are in comparison to the Creator and this will prevent us from becoming arrogant. Arrogance comes from comparing oneself with others who have less talents, abilities, knowledge, etc. All one needs to do is compare oneself to the Almighty and the arrogance will disappear.

Once a disciple of Rabbi Chayim Meir Yechiel Shapiro, grandson of the Maggid of Koznitz, came to him and said that he had the trait of arrogance and sought advice on how to change this negative trait.

Rabbi Shapiro replied, "When you ask advice from someone you need to consult someone who has knowledge about the matter. I really don't have any knowledge about arrogance, I don't know what it is. I really can't understand how anyone could possibly be arrogant." (*Maigdolai Hatorah Vehachasidus: Bais Koznitz*, vol.18)

Develop the habit of saying, "It appears as if," instead of making dogmatic statements.

ובא אשר לו הבית והגיד לכהן לאמר כנגע נראה לי בבית. (ויקרא י״ד
ל״ה)

"AND HE THAT OWNS THE HOUSE SHALL COME AND TELL THE PRIEST, SAYING, IT SEEMS TO ME AS IF THERE IS A PLAGUE IN THE HOUSE." (*Vayikra* 14:35)

Rashi comments: Even if the person is a Torah scholar and feels certain that what he sees is actually *tzoraas*, he should still say, "It appears to me as if it is *tzoraas*," rather than saying, "It is definitely *tzoraas*."

Rabbi Yeruchem Levovitz noted that practically speaking it made no difference whether the person said "it is" or "it appears as if." A priest is needed to render the house impure. But we have a practical lesson on how we should speak in all situations. The Sages (*Brochos* 4a) say that we should become accustomed to saying, "I do not know." Similarly, we should develop the habit of saying, "It appears to me," and "I think that perhaps," instead of making absolute statements. (*Daas Torah: Vayikra*, p.112)

Very frequently people think that what they are saying is correct. But in reality they make many mistakes. At times their perceptions are wrong, or their inferences are mistaken, or the information they heard from others is incorrect. When you realize how often you make mistakes, you will see the necessity of wording your statements as "to me it seems." By doing this you will find it easier to concede that someone else is correct. Moreover, when you word your opinions as "to me" statements, others might find it easier to agree with you. Of course there are times when it is appropriate and necessary to make strong statements. But in many instances you will gain by saying, "To me it appears..."

Rabbi Reuven Grozovsky said: Whenever Rabbi Isser Zalman

Meltzer gave an opinion and someone argued with him and gave an opposite opinion, he would turn to the side and repeat to himself out loud, "I say such and such, and this person says such and such." He would carefully weigh both opinions as if he personally were not involved. He was totally objective in searching for the truth rather than trying to be competitive. (*Marbitzai Torah Umussar*, vol.3, p.19)

Be careful not to cause others financial loss.

וצוה הכהן ופנו את הבית בטרם יבא הכהן לראות את הנגע ולא יטמא כל
אשר בבית ואחר כן יבא הכהן לראות את הבית. (ויקרא י"ד ל"ו)

"THEN THE PRIEST SHALL COMMAND THAT THEY EMPTY THE HOUSE, BEFORE THE PRIEST GOES INTO IT TO SEE THE PLAGUE, SO THAT ALL THAT IS IN THE HOUSE WILL NOT BE MADE UNCLEAN, AND AFTERWARDS THE PRIEST SHALL GO IN TO SEE THE HOUSE." (*Vayikra* 14:36)

Rashi cites the Sages that the main reason the Torah tells the owner of the house to remove all that is inside is because of the earthenware vessels. Even if the house is rendered impure, other vessels besides those made of earthenware can be purified. But once earthenware vessels become impure they remain in that state. We see here how the Almighty has compassion for a person even if only a very small amount of money is involved.

This is a lesson for us to be careful not to cause other people any financial loss. *Tzoraas* of the house comes because of a person's transgressions. Even so, the Almighty is careful not to cause the person any unnecessary loss. Having this awareness will make us much more careful with the money and property of others.

Before the holiday of *Sukos* the Steipler once went into a store that sold *lulavim*. He checked all the *lulavim* in the store, but did not find any that were satisfactory to him. He walked out of the store, but suddenly he returned. He again searched through them. This time he took one and paid for it. When he walked outside, he explained to his relative who accompanied him, "If I were to have walked out of the store without purchasing a *lulav*, it is likely that a rumor would start that Rabbi Kanievsky didn't find even one *lulav* that was *kosher* in this store. And then other people will not enter and it would come out that I caused this person a loss of money. Therefore I made certain to buy a *lulav*." (*Peninai Rabainu Hakehilos Yaakov*, p.125)

ACHARAI MOS

Cite concrete examples to illustrate points.

וידבר השם אל משה אחרי מות שני בני אהרן. (ויקרא ט"ז א')

"AND THE ALMIGHTY SPOKE TO MOSHE AFTER THE DEATH OF THE TWO SONS OF AHARON." (*Vayikra* 16:1)

Rashi cites the thought of Rabbi Eliezer ben Azarya that this is analogous to an ill person who was visited by a physician. The doctor said to him, "Do not eat such and such foods, and do not sleep in a damp place." Then another physician came to him and said, "Do not eat such and such foods and do not sleep in a damp place in order that you should not die like this certain person did." The second doctor will have a stronger effect than the first doctor. Therefore, the Torah emphasizes that the Almighty spoke to Moshe after the death of the two sons of Aharon. When involved in any of the services of the Tabernacle, great care must be taken not to make errors for they could be fatal.

From this Rashi we see an important lesson in how to make our communications more effective. It is not sufficient to convey to others abstract ideals and general warnings. Rather, we must try to add practical illustrations from everyday life describing the effects of negative behavior. Just telling someone that smoking is dangerous is not as effective as pointing out how a specific person died from disease caused by smoking. Whenever appropriate, give examples of how others have lost out by engaging in counterproductive behavior. (Note: Familiarity with the laws of *loshon hora* are necessary for this.) Similarly, for the good. When you tell someone about the benefits of proper behavior, bring examples from the lives of people who have gained much from having positive traits and doing good deeds.

Use techniques to overcome excessive concern about what others think of you.

וכל אדם לא יהיה באהל מועד בבאו לכפר בקדש. (ויקרא ט"ז י"ז)

"AND THERE SHALL BE NO MAN IN THE TENT OF MEETING WHEN HE GOES IN TO MAKE ATONEMENT IN THE SACRED PLACE." (*Vayikra* 16:17)

When the High Priest performed the special service on Yom Kippur, it could have been very easy for him to feel conceited. He had been the only one chosen from the entire nation to perform the sacred service on this most holy of days. He might easily focus on the honor he was receiving from others and how other people would be thinking of him with respect and even awe. Therefore the Torah tells him, "There shall be no man," that is, the High Priest should mentally view the world as if there were no other people in existence. He should do this when he enters the tent of meeting to make atonement in the sacred place. By having this mental attitude, he frees himself from any thoughts of seeking honor and approval. (*Degel Machaneh Ephraim*)

This mental technique is a very useful one for people who are overly self-conscious and constantly worry about what other people are thinking of them. They should imagine for a while that other people do not exist. If others do not exist, one does not need to be concerned with what anyone thinks of him. Even if you are only able to do this for a short while, it will enable you to decrease your worrying about what others think of you. A large part of the concern for the approval of others is based on illusion. In truth, others do not think about you as much as you think they do. Even if they are thinking about you, much of what they think makes absolutely no practical difference in your life. The illusion that there are no other people around will enable you to free yourself from the harm and pain caused by that other illusion.

Feel joy when cleaning up after serving guests.

בא אהרן אל אהל מועד. (ויקרא ט"ז כ"ג)

"AND AHARON SHALL COME INTO THE TENT OF MEETING." (*Vayikra* 16:23)

Rashi explains that Aharon went this time into the tent of meeting to remove the spoon and the censer in which he previously burned the incense.

The Baal Shem Tov brought a proof from here that when someone serves food to a Torah scholar, after the food is already eaten and the empty plates and used silverware need to be removed, removing them is part of the *mitzvah* of serving the Torah scholar. Just as removing the vessels was considered part of the service on Yom Kippur, so too when removing any vessels that were previously used for a *mitzvah* their removal is included in the good deed. (*Mayanah Shel Torah*)

This has practical applications for those who are hospitable to guests. Just as serving guests is part of the *mitzvah* of *hachnosas orchim*, so too all the work that is necessary in cleaning up afterwards is part of the *mitzvah*, and therefore can be done with the joy of doing acts of kindness. It is usually easier to feel this joy while serving, and often the work of cleaning up is considered just plain drudgery. But since both the serving and the cleaning up are integral parts of the *chesed*, they both are considered aspects of the *mitzvah* and this should be one's internalized attitude.

For many years the Steipler was *Chasan Torah* in Lederman's Shul on *Simchas Torah*, and he would give a *kidush* in his house after prayers. Every year when the holiday was over, he would don an apron and spend the next few hours washing every dish and cleaning every table until the house was spotless. "Just because I make a *simchah* doesn't mean that the household has to suffer." He would then study through the night to compensate for the time taken from learning. (*The Jewish Observer*, Nov. 1985)

Be careful not to wrong others to avoid needing their forgiveness.

כי ביום הזה יכפר עליכם לטהר אתכם מכל חטאתיכם לפני השם
תטהרו. (ויקרא ט״ז ל׳)

"FOR ON THIS DAY YOU SHALL RECEIVE ATONEMENT TO PURIFY YOU FOR ALL YOUR TRANSGRESSIONS, BEFORE THE ALMIGHTY YOU SHALL BE PURIFIED." (*Vayikra* 16:30)

The Sages (*Yoma* 85b) comment on this that Yom Kippur atones for transgressions between man and the Almighty. But as regards transgressions between man and man Yom Kippur can only atone if a person first attains the forgiveness of those whom he has offended or harmed.

From this principle we see the importance of being careful not to cause other people harm, either financial, physical, or emotional. While it is proper to forgive those who ask for our forgiveness, not everyone is sincerely ready to forgive others. There are some people who are hypersensitive and even though they would wish to forgive others, it is very difficult for them to do so. Even though they might say that they forgive, deep down they feel resentment and have not truly forgiven. Some might say, "Well if this person is so sensitive and nonforgiving, it is his problem." Yes, it is true that he has a problem and he will suffer from this, but if you have harmed him you will still not be forgiven without his forgiveness. The best way to ensure that you will be forgiven is to be especially careful in advance not to cause pain or suffering to others. Our main reason for not hurting others should be out of compassion and caring. But at least we should be careful not to harm others out of our own self-interest.

Do something for growth every day.

את משפטי תעשו ואת חקתי תשמרו ללכת בהם אני השם אלקיכם. (ויקרא י"ח ד')

"MY ORDINANCES YOU SHALL DO, AND MY STATUTES YOU SHALL OBSERVE, TO WALK WITH THEM, I AM THE LORD, YOUR G-D." (*Vayikra* 18:4)

The Ksav Sofer commented on the words, "to walk with them": a person needs to walk from one level to the next level. That is, a person should constantly keep on growing and elevating himself.

It is not enough to keep on the same level that you were on the previous day. Rather, each day should be a climb higher than the day before. When difficult tests come your way, you might not always appreciate them. But the only way to keep on elevating yourself is to keep passing more and more difficult life-tests. View every difficulty as a means of elevating yourself by applying the appropriate Torah principles. At the end of each day, ask yourself, "What did I do today to elevate myself a little higher?" If you cannot find an answer, ask yourself, "What can I plan to do tomorrow to elevate myself?"

Do good deeds with energy and enthusiasm.

ושמרתם את חקתי ואת משפטי אשר יעשה אתם האדם וחי בהם אני השם. (ויקרא י"ח ה')

"AND YOU SHALL KEEP MY STATUTES AND MY ORDINANCES,

WHICH A MAN SHALL DO AND LIVE BY THEM, I AM THE ALMIGHTY." (*Vayikra* 18:5)

On the words, "And live by them," the Shaloh comments: When you do good deeds they should be done with life, that is, with a lot of energy and enthusiasm. (*Shnai Luchos Habris, Acharai Mos*)

When you fulfill good deeds with enthusiasm, your whole being becomes alive. There is no comparison between doing a good deed with a feeling of being oppressed and forced and doing the same thing with joy and excitement. The life of a person who constantly does good deeds with joy is a life of pleasure and elevation. Not only do you gain very much yourself by this, but you will also motivate others. When others see how much enjoyment you have from doing good deeds, they too will be motivated to follow in your footsteps and their positive behavior will be a merit for you.

If you would like to experience enthusiasm but do not as yet, the *Mesilas Yeshorim* (ch. 7) advises you to act as if you were enthusiastic and your outer behavior will influence your inner feelings.

"The Almighty can testify that my biggest pleasure in life is praying with enthusiasm," said the Koznitzer Maggid. "This pleasure is my reward for the few good deeds that I have done." (*Niflaos Hamaggid Maikoznitz*, p.15)

KDOSHIM

Introspect to gain self-knowledge to strengthen areas that need strengthening.

איש אמו ואביו תיראו. (ויקרא י"ט ג')

"EACH PERSON, HIS MOTHER AND FATHER SHALL HE FEAR."
(*Vayikra* 19:3)

Rashi cites the Sages that here the Torah states mother before father because a child usually fears his father more than his mother. In the Ten Commandments (*Parshas Yisro*) the Torah tells us to honor our father and mother. As regards honor, the father is mentioned first since a child usually honors his mother more because of the gentle manner in which she speaks to him.

Here the Torah reveals to us the inner tendencies of people. Awareness of your inner tendencies is crucial in order to have greater control over your behavior. (Rabbi Yeruchem Levovitz; *Daas Torah: Vayikra*, p.174)

Self-knowledge is a prerequisite for a total fulfillment of our Torah obligations. An awareness of your natural tendencies lets you know on what you need to put your emphasis. Here the Torah tells us that we have a strong tendency to honor our mother and fear our father. This knowledge allows you to work on increasing your honor for your father and your reverence for your mother. Introspect to gain greater self-awareness of your natural tendencies. Then make an effort to behave in a manner that will strengthen those areas that need strengthening.

If someone wrongs you, don't waste time feeling resentment.

לא תלין פעלת שכיר אתך עד בקר. לא תקלל חרש. (ויקרא י״ט י״ג-י״ד)

"DO NOT LEAVE THE WAGES OF YOUR EMPLOYEE WITH YOU OVERNIGHT UNTIL THE MORNING. YOU SHALL NOT CURSE THE DEAF." (*Vayikra* 19:13,14)

The Torah puts these two commandments one after the other to teach us that even if your employer refuses to pay your wages, you shall not curse him. Rather you should take him to court to receive the money coming to you. (*Baal Haturim*)

When someone wrongs you in some manner, it is easy to get angry at him and to curse him. But what do you gain from this? Absolutely nothing. All you do is lose out with your anger and resentment. Cursing him lowers you spiritually and gives you nothing. It is an outlet for your frustration, but a very negative outlet. Be practical. If someone wrongs you and you have a practical means of helping yourself, do what you legally can to protect yourself from loss. But do not needlessly focus on this person's negative behavior. Brooding about it and indiscriminately telling others about it does not help you. Do not waste your precious time on this earth with resentful thoughts, and do not defile your mouth with any kind of curse. Fill your mind with elevating and joyous thoughts and free yourself from negative thoughts about others. Take action to help yourself when that action is appropriate. But both before and afterwards utilize your time wisely.

Someone wrote a *sefer* in which he attacked Rabbi Moshe Feinstein's responsa in disrespectful and even vulgar terms. The typesetter-printer called to ask Rav Moshe whether he should refuse to accept the job. Rav Moshe urged him to do the assignment, explaining that both the author and the printer had to earn a livelihood. Presumably, the author felt that he had to curry favor with elements whose opinions he supported. As far as Rav Moshe personally was concerned, he had no right to stand in the way. (Rabbi Nosson Scherman, *The Jewish Observer*, Oct. 1986, p.25)

Only rebuke others with a sincere concern for their welfare.

הוכח תוכיח את עמיתך. (ויקרא י"ט י"ז)

"YOU SHALL REBUKE YOUR FELLOW MAN." (*Vayikra* 19:17)

When someone tries to criticize or rebuke another person, it is obligatory for those words to come from the depths of his heart. The Sages have said that only those words that come from the heart will enter the heart of the other person. Therefore, if your words of correction are not an expression of your inner feelings of care and concern for the welfare of the other person, they will not have a positive influence on the person you are speaking to. But there is yet another aspect here. If your rebuke does not come from a sincere caring for the other person, then you have personal reasons for that rebuke and your motives are not entirely pure. If that is the case, you are guilty of slighting the honor of another person and of causing him pain with words for your personal pleasure. This is a very serious offense. (Rabbi Eliyahu Eliezer Dessler; *Michtav Maieliyahu*, vol.3, p.139)

Before correcting someone, ask yourself, "What are my true motives in trying to correct this person?" Can you honestly say that your sole motivation is that you are so concerned about his welfare that you feel a need to make certain he does only good and refrains from evil? To what degree do you want to rebuke him because you feel a sense of power in telling someone off? To what degree do you want honor from others? To what degree do you derive personal pleasure from making someone else feel uncomfortable? We do have a *mitzvah* to correct others. But here motivation is an essential ingredient. Build up your inner feelings of love for others. Then your motivation will be pure and you will be able to have a positive influence on others.

In the last lecture Rabbi Nachum Perchovitz gave before *Yom Kippur* he ended by saying, "I ask forgiveness if I offended anyone or spoke harshly. Together with this I ask forgiveness from those I censured less than I should have." (*Yetaid Neaman*, 17 Kislaiv, 5747, p.10)

Rabbi Eliyahu Klatzkin was easily moved to tears by the suffering of any Jewish community and the mishaps which visited anyone, near or far. When he preached about the desecration of the *Shabbos* or dishonesty in business practices, he would be so choked by sobs that his voice became inaudible to the members of the audience, who would themselves be deeply stirred by his grief. (*Jewish Leaders*, p.333)

Rabbi Simcha Zissel of Kelm once found out that a student of his read his private letters. He did not censure him right away. Rather, he waited two full months until he was certain that his own anger had subsided. Then he approached that student and gave him a very stern lecture on how improper his behavior had been. (*Meoros Hagdolim*, p.77)

Even if you are only successful one time in a hundred, keep trying to have a positive influence on others.

הוכח תוכיח את עמיתך. (ויקרא י״ט י״ז)

"YOU SHALL REBUKE YOUR FELLOW MAN." (*Vayikra* 19:17)

The Talmud (*Bava Metzia* 31a) states that we are required to try to correct others even one hundred times. This, said the Chofetz Chayim, teaches us that we should not refrain from trying to help someone improve even if we think that the person will not listen to us.

Not only should we keep trying to influence the same person, we should also try to reach out to as many people as possible. The

Chofetz Chayim gave an analogy of a person selling apples on a busy streetcorner. Even if many people pass by without purchasing any apples, the vendor will still keep calling out, "Apples for sale." You might ask the person, "Why do you keep calling out that you are selling apples when so many people pass by without buying from you?" The apple-seller will reply, "True, most people do not buy any apples from me. But every once in a while someone does. It is from those individuals who do buy from me that I earn my livelihood."

When selling to people who pass by, even if only one in a hundred makes a purchase, it is worthwhile to keep trying. So too when it comes to having a positive influence on others. Even if only one person in a hundred improves because of what you tell him, it is worthwhile to make every effort to have a positive influence on others. (*Chofetz Chayim al Hatorah*, pp.160-1)

An idealistic person who tries to have a positive influence on others might feel very discouraged when he spends much time and energy trying to influence someone and that person remains the same as before. But if a person knows that he will make an enormous profit from making a sale or negotiating a deal he will keep trying even if he is frequently unsuccessful. All he needs to do is to be successful a few times and he will become wealthy. He need not focus on the times that things did not go well. Rather he should focus on his previous successes and this will motivate him to keep trying in the future. The merit for having a positive influence on others is so great that even if you are only successful a few times your entire life, all your efforts are worthwhile. Keeping this in mind will make it much easier for you to keep trying.

Reb Yaakov Yosef Herman placed an ad in the *Jewish Morning Journal* inviting anyone interested in free Torah courses to come to the Bais Medrash Hagodol on Norfolk Street in New York at 8 P.M. on a certain day.

He waited, expecting many people to answer his request. The advertisement brought no one at all. He advertised again, without any results. He did not give up, and once more placed the same ad.

This time, one teenager, wearing a lumber jacket, showed up.

This young man became one of Reb Yaakov Yosef's disciples, and is now a hidden *tzaddik*. (*All for the Boss*, p.426)

Stress the positive benefits of good behavior.

הוכח תוכיח את עמיתך ולא תשא עליו חטא. (ויקרא י"ט י"ז)

"YOU SHALL REBUKE YOUR FELLOW MAN, AND YOU SHALL NOT BEAR SIN BECAUSE OF HIM." (*Vayikra* 19:17)

The Chofetz Chayim frequently told public speakers to focus on the great value and beauty of following the Torah way of life. Most people suffer enough already and it is improper to add to their suffering by arousing guilt feelings. What needs to be stressed is the great blessing one will find in following the Torah and the elevation and enrichment of performing good deeds and improving one's character traits. (*Hachofetz Chayim*, cited in *Gateway to Happiness*, p.224)

It is a mistake to think that the way to correct others is by embarrassing and humiliating them. This is clearly forbidden even when trying to correct someone (*Erchin* 16b). In trying to motivate someone to do something, there are two possible patterns. You can try to show the person how he will benefit by doing it and therefore he will want to do it for the positive gain. The other choice is to threaten a person with dire warnings of the harm in not doing it. The Chofetz Chayim, who was imbued with great love for the Almighty and love for people, stressed focusing on the positive. Let this be your guide.

Rabbi Eliyahu Eliezer Dessler would never censure any of his students in a personal way. Rather he would give general talks on the benefits of having positive traits and on the harm and loss of negative traits. Someone once complained to the Chazon Ish that Rabbi Dessler was not showing toughness towards his students. But the Chazon Ish agreed with Rabbi Dessler's approach, saying, "*Meshichah* is a stronger *kinyan* than *chazakah*." (This is a concept borrowed from *halachah* and meant in this context that it is preferable to draw someone to positive qualities by influencing him to want to have the positive trait rather than forcing someone to act positively.) (*Marbitzai Torah Umussar*, vol.3, p.81)

Rabbi Levi Yitzchok of Berditchev once heard an itinerant preacher rebuking his listeners in a very harsh and stringent manner. The speaker strongly condemned the people for all kinds of transgressions and wrongdoings. Rav Levi Yitzchok, who always found merit for people, said the following to the Almighty, "Almighty, this person is not really speaking. It is really his problems and suffering that are talking. He needs to marry off his daughter and this is how he makes his living. Please Almighty, send him enough money to pay for the wedding so he will not have a need to find fault with Your people." (*Horav Maiapte*, p.9)

Feel love for other people because it is the Creator's wishes.

ואהבת לרעך כמוך אני השם. (ויקרא י"ט י"ח)

"LOVE YOUR FELLOW MAN AS YOURSELF, I AM THE ALMIGHTY."
(*Vayikra* 19:18)

The Chasam Sofer commented: The commandment to love our fellow man is a concept that anyone can relate to with his own intellect. Nevertheless, the Torah tells us to love our fellow man because it is the Almighty's will. (*Toras Moshe*)

If your love of other people is based only on your own feelings, there could easily be a lack of consistency. One day you might feel positive towards someone and on the next day your feelings can change. But the Torah states that the Almighty commands us to love others. We need to develop positive attitudes towards others by focusing on their virtues whether it comes easily to us or whether it is difficult.

Very often I am asked how it is possible to feel love towards someone when you meet him for the first time. Once when I was giving a lecture to beginners in Yeshiva Aish Hatorah in the Old City of Jerusalem a cute little dog walked into the room. Everyone turned to the dog and smiled at it. I then asked, "Did anyone ever see this dog before?" No one had. I pointed out that even though this was the first time they had seen this dog, they all felt positive about it and their positive feelings were noticeable on their faces. If we would internalize the awareness that each human being is created in the image of the Almighty and the Almighty Himself wishes that we feel love for him, we would automatically have positive feelings for others.

If an extremely wealthy and generous person who was the source of your entire income would tell you to be kind and friendly to his relative, you would find it quite easy to do so. In your dealings with other people keep in mind that your Creator and the Sustainer of the universe is the Creator of this individual and He wants you to be kind and loving to him.

Before Rabbi Isser Zalman Meltzer would deliver his weekly lecture in his yeshiva, he would first go for a few minutes to one of the rooms of the yeshiva and close the door behind him. Once one of the students wanted to know what the Rosh Hayeshiva did during those few minutes before the lecture. Very carefully, the student opened the door just a little bit and peeked inside the room. To his surprise, he saw how Rav Isser Zalman walked back and forth repeating to himself over and over again the verse, "Love your fellow man as yourself." (*Bederech Aitz Hachayim*, vol.1, p.249)

Anyone who interacts with other people should learn from this. By repeating this verse to yourself you will relate to other people in a much more elevated manner.

Rabbi Moshe Feinstein used to recite Psalms in his yeshiva on *Shabbos* afternoon. One *Shabbos*, as he was reciting the Psalms, a mildly retarded child stood watching him. The boy went over and turned Rav Moshe's *Tehillim* on an angle to the right, and Rav

Moshe continued reciting. Then the boy turned the *Tehillim* to the left and Rav Moshe continued reciting. The boy took the *Tehillim* and turned it completely around and Rav Moshe continued reciting. Not satisfied, the boy turned a page, but the Rosh Hayeshiva still was not fazed. A gentleman had watched all this and, although people went out of their way to be patient with the boy, the man had seen too much. He snapped, "Stop it already! Let the Rosh Hayeshiva alone!"

Rav Moshe turned to the man and said, "He is only playing with me. I enjoy it when he plays with me. I love him like my own child!" With that, Rav Moshe embraced the boy and kissed him. (Rabbi Nosson Scherman, *The Jewish Observer*, Oct. 1986, p.29)

Share your Torah knowledge.

ואהבת לרעך כמוך אני השם. (ויקרא י״ט י״ח)

"LOVE YOUR FELLOW MAN AS YOURSELF, I AM THE ALMIGHTY."
(*Vayikra* 19:18)

Rashi cites the words of Rabbi Akiva that this verse is a great principle in Torah. The Chasam Sofer explains that this means we are obligated to take time from our own Torah studies to teach others Torah. Love your fellow man as yourself, just as you want to gain Torah wisdom yourself, feel the need to help others gain Torah wisdom also. Ultimately, you do not lose from this because you become more elevated by sharing your knowledge with others. (*Toras Moshe*)

Even if someone is not a formal teacher, there are many opportunities to share one's Torah knowledge with others. Keep looking for these opportunities.

Your behavior towards others should be a manifestation of your love towards them.

ואהבת לרעך כמוך אני השם. (ויקרא י"ט י"ח)

"LOVE YOUR FELLOW MAN AS YOURSELF, I AM THE ALMIGHTY."
(*Vayikra* 19:18)

The Talmud (*Shabbos* 31a) relates that a non-Jew came to Hillel and said to him, "Convert me on condition that you will teach me the entire Torah while I stand on one foot." Hillel accepted his condition and told him, "What you dislike, do not do to your friend. This is the entire Torah."

Since Hillel was referring to the commandment of love your neighbor, why didn't he just mention the words of this verse? Rabbi Yeruchem Levovitz explained that this is to teach us an important principle. From the words "love your fellow man" one might think that as long as one feels the emotion of love towards others one fulfills this commandment. But the truth is that just feeling love alone is not sufficient. Rather this love must motivate us to do positive things for others and to refrain from any actions or words that could cause someone any pain or suffering. The Torah definitely requires us to feel deep love for others in our hearts. But even more than that, our behavior towards others must manifest this love. Therefore, Hillel explained to this man that a basic Torah principle is that the same commandment which requires us to have a profoundly positive feeling for others also requires us to behave in an elevated manner in our daily encounters with them. (*Daas Torah: Vayikra*, p.175)

It is very easy to just repeat the slogan that we should love others. To actually feel this in your heart is much more difficult. But even after you sincerely feel this love, your entire behavior towards others should be an expression of it. Constantly be on the lookout for acts of kindness you can do for other people. When you look for them, you will constantly find things to do and words to say. Similarly, be very careful not to do anything that will harm others or cause them any pain or suffering. This is a lifelong challenge, but it is a cornerstone of the Torah.

Rabbi Baruch Ber Leibowitz, Rosh Hayeshiva of Kamenetz, used to say, "When my time will come to stand before the Heavenly court I will be asked, 'What merits do you have?' What will I reply? If I want to say, 'With my Torah,' do I truly have enough Torah? With my fear of Heaven? Do I really have sufficient fear? There is really only one merit that I can say for myself. I have profound *ahavas Yisroel*. Whenever I am walking in the street and see someone coming in my direction, I immediately say to myself, 'A blessing on his head.'" (*Marbitzai Torah Umussar*, vol.2, p.151)

The Chazon Ish would listen patiently to the problems of anyone who came to him. This was quite a feat since people would come to him at all hours of the day and night. A relative of the Chazon Ish was amazed at how he was able to listen to a certain "nudnick" who spoke in a loud tone of voice and in a very long-winded and roundabout manner. The Chazon Ish explained, "A person who owns a mill is used to the noise of the mill. On the contrary, if the mill would stop it would give him a headache." (*P'air Hador*, vol.4, p.20)

Rabbi Chayim Koledetzky related to his family how he was a guest at the home of the Chofetz Chayim. The Chofetz Chayim personally made the bed for him and prepared the pillow and blankets. Reb Chayim was startled to see that after preparing the bed the Chofetz Chayim laid down on the bed for a few seconds to check if it would be sufficiently comfortable for his guest. (*Bederech Aitz Hachayim*, vol.1, p.61, f.n.)

EMOR

Make peace between people, but do not be negatively influenced.

ויאמר השם אל משה אמר אל הכהנים בני אהרן ואמרת אלהם לנפש לא
יטמא בעמיו. (ויקרא כ"א א')

"AND THE ALMIGHTY SAID TO MOSHE, SPEAK TO THE PRIESTS, THE SONS OF AHARON, AND SAY TO THEM, FOR A PERSON HE SHALL NOT DEFILE HIMSELF AMONG HIS PEOPLE." (*Vayikra* 21:1)

The Chozeh of Lublin explained this verse that Moshe was told that the priests should be worthy of being the descendants of Aharon. That is, just as Aharon had the trait of loving and pursuing peace, so too, they also should work on acquiring this trait. Therefore the latter part of this verse warns them that even though they should try to make peace between people whenever they can, they must be very careful not to defile themselves in the process. At times they might come into contact with very aggressive and violent people and they should not become too close to them lest they become negatively influenced by their faults.

The good you do should be complete.

ושמרו את משמרתי ולא ישאו עליו חטא. (ויקרא כ"ב ט')

"AND THEY SHALL OBSERVE MY CHARGE, AND THEY SHALL NOT BEAR SIN FOR IT." (*Vayikra* 22:9)

Rashi explains that this verse is a warning to the priests not to eat *trumah* while they are in a state of *tumah*.

Even though eating *trumah* is the fulfillment of a *mitzvah* for the priests, they must be very careful not to do so in a manner that will transform the potential good into a transgression. Rabbi Yeruchem Levovitz commented that we see here an important principle: even when a person is involved in doing the Almighty's service, he must be very careful that no transgressions should come from it. On the practical level, whenever you are engaged in doing a good deed or involved in a worthwhile project, be on guard that the good you do is complete and does not include any transgressions. (*Daas Torah: Vayikra*, p.210)

A person who studies Torah must strive to interact with others on an elevated level.

ושמרתם מצותי ועשיתם אתם אני השם. ולא תחללו את שם קדשי
ונקדשתי בתוך בני ישראל אני השם מקדשכם. (ויקרא כ"ב ל"א-ל"ב)

"AND YOU SHALL OBSERVE MY COMMANDMENTS AND DO THEM, I AM THE ALMIGHTY. AND YOU SHALL NOT DESECRATE MY HOLY NAME AND I WILL BE SANCTIFIED AMONG THE CHILDREN OF ISRAEL, I AM THE ALMIGHTY WHO SANCTIFIES YOU." (*Vayikra* 22:31,32)

The Chasam Sofer commented that verse 31 is an introduction to verse 32. Rashi states that "you shall observe my commandments" refers to studying Torah," (the only way to observe is to study first). Therefore the Torah immediately warns those who study Torah against *chilul Hashem*, desecration of the Almighty's name, and obliges those who study to make a *kidush Hashem*, a sanctification of the Almighty's name. The behavior of anyone who studies Torah should be on such a level that it will be an expression of the sanctity of the Almighty. People who observe those who study Torah should be able to say that the Torah gives those who study it much wisdom and promotes excellence in their daily behavior. (see *Yoma* 86a; *Toras Moshe*)

Rabbi Yeruchem Levovitz used to stress, "Everyone who studies Torah must excel in his love for other people, in showing honor and respect to other people, and in the pleasant manner with which he should always speak to others. His elevated behavior should be on such a level that everyone will say about him, 'How fortunate is his father who taught him Torah. How fortunate is his teacher who taught him Torah. How unfortunate are those who have not studied Torah. This person who has studied Torah see how pleasant are his ways.'" (*Daas Torah: Vayikra*, p.209)

This statement of Rabbi Yeruchem Levovitz should be repeated over and over again. Based on the Talmudic statement of *Yoma* 86a, it stresses three points: (1) love for other people, (2) honor and respect for others, (3) a pleasant manner of speaking. Not everyone can appreciate the genius of deep Torah thoughts. But everyone does appreciate being spoken to with kindness and respect. Whenever someone who studies Torah speaks to another person he has an opportunity to make a *kidush Hashem*. On the other hand, he is in danger of making a *chilul Hashem*. The more Torah knowledge one has or that others think one has, the greater the obligation to be nicer to other people. Talking to others in a rough, insolent, or even impatient manner is a *chilul Hashem*. This idea has been emphasized by Torah educators throughout the ages, and Torah teachers today continue to stress it.

This obligation is especially important when talking to people who are far away from Torah observance. They will judge the value and effect of Torah study and observance by the behavior towards them of those who observe *mitzvos*. Have in mind that each encounter is an opportunity for the great *mitzvah* of *kidush Hashem*. Even if at first someone is very hostile, a persistent showing of politeness and kindness on your part will eventually change the other person's attitude. Do not use the other person's negative manner towards you as your guide for how you speak to him. Consistently use the Torah ideal of *kidush Hashem* as your guide.

In short, if you study Torah, make certain to talk to everyone you meet in a manner that will cause them to say, "I'm really impressed with this person. I want my children and relatives to study Torah also if this is the way they will behave."

Look forward to studying Torah.

וספרתם לכם ממחרת השבת מיום הביאכם את עמר התנופה שבע
שבתות תמימת תהיינה. (ויקרא כ"ג ט"ו)

"AND YOU SHALL COUNT FROM THE DAY AFTER THE DAY OF REST, FROM THE DAY THAT YOU BROUGHT THE WAVING OMER, SEVEN COMPLETE WEEKS THEY SHALL BE." (*Vayikra* 23:15)

The Torah gives us a *mitzvah* to count the days from the second day of Pesach until the holiday of Shavuos. The root of this commandment, wrote the Chinuch, is that the essence of the Jewish People is the Torah, and for the Torah the entire world and Israel were created. The Israelites were redeemed from Egypt in order to accept the Torah at Sinai and to fulfill it. The counting of the days from the exodus from Egypt until the day of the accepting of the Torah is an expression of the importance of the Torah for the Jewish People. Just as a person who is enslaved and knows that he will be liberated on a certain day will count each day until he finally gets his freedom, so too, we count the days until we receive the Torah. Counting the days shows that our entire being has a strong desire to finally reach the end of the time we are counting. (*Sefer Hachinuch* 306)

The greater your appreciation of the Torah the more you will study it. Realizing how important the Torah is for us as a nation and for each of us individually we will have great joy and pleasure when we devote ourselves to studying and mastering it. Every year when we count the days between Pesach and Shavuos we once again repeat this message daily for forty-nine days.

Commentators mention that each of those days is for working on one of the 48 tools for acquiring Torah that are listed in the sixth chapter of *Pirke Avos*. In their totality they comprise the traits and attributes that make up the complete person.

Rabbi Baruch Ber Leibowitz, Rosh Hayeshiva of Kamenetz, once remarked, "What can compare to my situation? I wake up in the morning, and it's as though I have the *Shaagas Aryeh*, *Ketzos Hachoshen*, and *Rabbi Akiva Eger* (all classical commentaries) waiting for me at my bedside! I can't wait to wash my hands and arise to my riches!" (Rabbi Chaim Shapiro; *The Jewish Observer*, Oct. 1980)

Our normal mood should be one of happiness.

וידבר השם אל משה לאמר. דבר אל בני ישראל לאמר בחמשה עשר יום לחדש השביעי הזה חג הסכות שבעת ימים להשם. (ויקרא כ״ג ל״ג-ל״ד)

"AND THE ALMIGHTY SPOKE TO MOSHE SAYING, SPEAK TO THE CHILDREN OF ISRAEL SAYING: ON THE FIFTEENTH DAY OF THE SEVENTH MONTH IS THE FESTIVAL OF TABERNACLES, SEVEN DAYS DEDICATED TO THE ALMIGHTY." (*Vayikra* 23:33,34)

Rabbi Samson Raphael Hirsch noted that Rosh Hashanah in Torah law is only one day (Rabbinical law renders it two days), and Yom Kippur is only one day, while Sukos is seven days. Rosh Hashanah is a day of shaking us out of ways of life displeasing to the Almighty. Yom Kippur is a day of fasting and awareness of our faults and mistakes. Sukos, however, sets us up afresh in living to achieve the highest earthly possession: joy and happiness before the Almighty. There is only one day for the mood of Rosh Hashanah, and only one day for the fasting of atonement, but seven days, a whole cycle of days, for the joyful building of our huts, and for enjoying our possessions before the Almighty. This is what is most characteristic of Torah law, it teaches that the normal mood of one's life should be, not the bowed down, broken feeling, but the joy of life which runs equally throughout the year of a life faithfully devoted to duty. (Rabbi Hirsch's Commentary)

To live a joyous life avoid quarreling.

ולקחתם לכם ביום הראשון פרי עץ הדר כפת תמרים וענף עץ עבת וערבי
נחל ושמחתם לפני השם אלקיכם שבעת ימים. (ויקרא כ"ג מ')

"AND YOU SHALL TAKE ON THE FIRST DAY A FRUIT OF THE
CITRON TREE, BRANCHES OF PALM TREES, MYRTLE BRANCHES,
AND WILLOWS OF THE BROOKS, AND YOU SHALL REJOICE BEFORE
THE ALMIGHTY SEVEN DAYS." (*Vayikra* 23:40)

True joy is only possible when there is peace among people.
Quarrels cause so many difficulties and problems that joy is
impossible when there is strife and conflict. This is symbolized in
our verse. The four species we take in our hand on the holiday of
Sukos symbolize the various types of people who make up the
Jewish nation. Holding them together is a sign of peace and unity.
Only when there is togetherness can the latter part of the verse, joy
before the Almighty, be fulfilled. (*Kli Yokor*)

Quarrels destroy people's lives. Both on the national level and on
the personal level peace is essential for a good life. Even if a person
has many positive things in his life, if he is argumentative and
quarrelsome he will not be able to enjoy what he has. Many
quarrels can easily be avoided by just thinking sensibly about how
irrational and counterproductive it is to waste time and energy in a
quarrel that really makes no practical difference. Before becoming
involved in a quarrel ask yourself, "What are the potential benefits
of this quarrel? What are its potential losses? Is it really worthwhile
to be involved in this quarrel?"

Joy and happiness are necessary traits for living a good life.
Quarrels are destructive and cause much pain and suffering. By
avoiding quarrels whenever possible, you will enable yourself to
live a much more joyous life.

Rabbi Eliyahu Klatzkin, Rabbi of Lublin and later of Jerusalem,
once told his son that some people had taken his seal without
permission and affixed it to proclamations without consulting him.
His son asked him why he had not refuted them in the press, and he

answered, "I am afraid that if I protest against the forgery, I shall arouse the anger of these troublemakers and I shall be forced to make controversial statements. In any case they will surely be bold enough to besmirch the motive behind my denials, and I shall be forced to issue a protest. As a result, my time will be wasted in controversy and I shall be unable to spend it in studying Torah." (*Jewish Leaders*, p.327)

A relative of Rabbi Shlomo Heyman (who served as Rosh Hayeshiva of Mesivta Torah Vodaath in the late 30's and early 40's) once offered him one of the apartments in his summer home, where the two couples would share a kitchen and eating area. Rav Shlomo asked his wife to figure out if their modest income would cover the expenses of such a venture. She made the computations and announced that the apartment would be within their means. Rav Shlomo asked to see the figures, an unusual request for him.

He checked them over and then told his wife, "You forgot to add in one expense: *Shalom Bayis Gelt*."

"*Shalom Bayis Gelt*?" his wife asked puzzled.

Rav Shlomo explained, "When two parties share living facilities there are bound to be some questions as to how much each side should contribute to the expenses. Who used more electricity, who used the telephone more and so on. When those questions come up, each party often finds it difficult to part with their hard-earned money, and that is where arguments begin. To avoid this, one should set aside some money from the start, in the event such problems arise. Then he will have no difficulty in surrendering the money." (Rabbi Eliezer Cohen, *The Jewish Observer*, Feb., 1985)

Sukos and guests are both reminders of our temporary status.

בסכת תשבו שבעת ימים כל האזרח בישראל ישבו בסכת. (ויקרא כ"ג מ"ב)

"YOU SHALL DWELL SEVEN DAYS IN BOOTHS, EVERY MEMBER OF ISRAEL SHALL DWELL IN BOOTHS." (*Vayikra* 23:42)

The Chofetz Chayim said that the *mitzvah* of being hospitable to guests benefits the host in a spiritual way. The guest serves as a reminder to the host that every person is only a guest in this world. The holiday of Sukos, also, is a reminder that we are only in this world temporarily. Just as the booths we sit in are temporary dwellings, so too our entire sojourn in this world is only a temporary dwelling. Therefore, on Sukos, said the Chofetz Chayim, we should be especially careful to invite guests. For then we have a double reminder of our temporary status in this world. This awareness will increase our motivation to make the best use of our time to accomplish as much good as we can.

Rabbi Sholom Eisen came to Rabbi Isser Zalman Meltzer and invited him to his son's *bar-mitzvah* which would be a long distance from Rabbi Meltzer's home. When Rav Isser Zalman heard about the *bar-mitzvah* of his student's son, he said with great emotion, "It is already the *bar-mitzvah* of your son. Time passes by so quickly. It's amazing how time flies." These thoughts were repeated a few times.

At the time, Rabbi Meltzer was already elderly and it was difficult for him to walk a long distance. Therefore, on the *Shabbos* of the *bar-mitzvah* Rabbi Eisen was very surprised to see Rabbi Meltzer walking into the synagogue where the *bar-mitzvah* was being held, and he ran to greet his Rebbe.

"It is hard for me to walk so much," Rabbi Meltzer said. "But I felt an obligation of gratitude to come. When you invited me to the *bar-mitzvah* of your son, I started thinking about how fast time flies. I gained from these thoughts, and therefore I felt it proper to join in your *simchah*." (*Bederech Aitz Hachayim*, vol.2, p.418)

BEHAR

Shabbos and shmitah remind us that the Creator is our ruler.

כי תבאו אל הארץ אשר אני נתן לכם ושבתה הארץ שבת להשם. (ויקרא
כ"ה ב')

"WHEN YOU COME TO THE LAND WHICH I GIVE YOU, THE LAND
SHALL REST, A REST FOR THE ALMIGHTY." (*Vayikra* 25:2)

Rashi notes that the Torah explicitly mentions that the rest on
the Sabbatical year is for the Almighty, just as the Torah states this
in reference to the weekly Shabbos.

Rabbi Yeruchem Levovitz cites the Raavad (Introduction to
Baalai Nefesh) that a fundamental principle behind the
commandments is that: "they are to remind us constantly that we
have a Creator who is our Ruler." The Almighty gave us this earth,
but after using the earth for some time a person can mistakenly
think that the earth belongs to him, and he can forget that the
Almighty is the real owner. Therefore in all that we do there are
commandments that contain restrictions to show that the Creator
is above us. For this reason, said Rav Yeruchem, the Torah stresses
in this verse that the commandment to rest on the seventh year
applies to the land which the Almighty gave us. The Almighty gave
us a commandment to refrain from work on the land on the
seventh year to help us internalize the awareness that He is the true
boss of the earth.

This is also the lesson we learn from the weekly Shabbos, said
Rav Yeruchem. It shows a person that the Almighty is the One who
gives him the power to work on the other days of the week. This is

a weekly reminder that we have a ruler who is our ultimate authority. (*Daas Torah: Vayikra*)

When you realize that others also suffer, you will find it easier to cope with your own suffering.

וְהַעֲבַרְתָּ שׁוֹפַר תְּרוּעָה בַּחֹדֶשׁ הַשְּׁבִעִי בֶּעָשׂוֹר לַחֹדֶשׁ בְּיוֹם הַכִּפֻּרִים תַּעֲבִירוּ שׁוֹפָר בְּכָל אַרְצְכֶם. וְקִדַּשְׁתֶּם אֵת שְׁנַת הַחֲמִשִּׁים שָׁנָה וּקְרָאתֶם דְּרוֹר בָּאָרֶץ לְכָל יֹשְׁבֶיהָ יוֹבֵל הִוא תִּהְיֶה לָכֶם וְשַׁבְתֶּם אִישׁ אֶל אֲחֻזָּתוֹ וְאִישׁ אֶל מִשְׁפַּחְתּוֹ תָּשֻׁבוּ. (ויקרא כ"ה ט-י)

"YOU SHALL BLOW THE SHOFAR ON THE TENTH DAY OF THE SEVENTH MONTH, ON THE DAY OF ATONEMENT SHALL YOU SOUND THE SHOFAR THROUGHOUT ALL YOUR LAND. AND YOU SHALL SANCTIFY THE FIFTIETH YEAR, AND PROCLAIM LIBERTY THROUGHOUT ALL THE LAND TO ALL ITS INHABITANTS; IT SHALL BE A JUBILEE FOR YOU, AND YOU SHALL RETURN EVERY MAN TO HIS POSSESSION, AND YOU SHALL RETURN EVERY MAN TO HIS FAMILY." (*Vayikra* 25:9,10)

On the fiftieth year, the *yovail* (Jubilee year), there is a *mitzvah* to blow the *shofar*. The reason for this is that on the *yovail* the servants were set free. When a master had a servant for a long period of time, it was difficult for him to lose the helping hand. The *shofar* was blown for the master to realize that he was not the only one freeing his servant. Rather, the same was happening to everyone else who had servants. The knowledge that others are also suffering in the same way makes it much eaiser to accept hardships. (*Sefer Hachinuch* 331)

There are many difficulties in life that people subjectively make worse for themselves because they feel that they are the only ones who are suffering. The more you realize that each person has his own life-problems, the easier you will find it to cope in a positive way with your own. While not everyone will have the same problems as you do, everyone does have hardships and tests. Gain greater awareness of the suffering of other people and you will be able to put your own suffering in a perspective that will decrease the pain.

The Creator does not want you to cheat His children.

וכי תמכרו ממכר לעמיתך או קנה מיד עמיתך אל תונו איש את אחיו
(ויקרא כ"ה י"ד)

'AND WHEN YOU SELL ANYTHING TO YOUR FELLOW MAN OR BUY FROM YOUR FELLOW MAN, YOU SHALL NOT CHEAT ONE ANOTHER." (*Vayikra* 25:14)

Sforno (to verse 17) comments that the Almighty is the G-d of the buyer and the G-d of the seller and He does not want anyone to cheat a buyer or a seller.

When selling something to another person or when buying from someone, if you keep in mind that the Creator is his G-d you will be very careful not to deceive him in any manner. If the son of an emperor or of a president of a powerful nation would purchase something from you or sell you something, you would be extremely careful not to cheat him. Either you would have respect for his father and out of that respect you would be honest with him. Or else you would fear retribution if you would deceive him and his father found out about your deception. This should be our attitude in our monetary dealings with other people. The Almighty is their Heavenly Father and He commands you to be honest with them. Either out of respect for the Almighty or out of fear of Him you should be meticulously careful not to cheat another person in any way.

Rabbi Nachman of Kossov was once asked, "How is it possible to think of the Almighty when someone is involved in business?"

Rav Nachman replied, "People find it quite easy to think about business matters when they are involved in praying. Similarly, if someone really wants to, he can think of the Almighty while engaged in financial matters."

Be very careful not to cause people pain with your words.

ולא תונו איש את עמיתו ויראת מאלקיך. (ויקרא כ״ה י״ז)

"AND YOU SHALL NOT HURT THE FEELINGS OF ONE ANOTHER AND YOU SHALL FEAR THE ALMIGHTY." (*Vayikra* 25:17)

In this verse the Torah commands us to be careful not to say anything to another person that will cause him emotional pain (see *Love Your Neighbor*, pp.326-31, for details of this commandment). Rabbi Shlomo Kluger commented: Some people are careless with the feelings of other people and think that they only have to be careful to observe those commandments which involve man's obligation to the Almighty. But the truth is that if a person is not careful with his obligations to his fellow men and speaks against them and hurts their feelings, he will eventually be careless with the commandments between man and the Almighty. Therefore in the same verse that the Torah warns against hurting the feelings of other people the Torah adds "and you shall fear the Almighty." Failure to observe the first half of the verse will lead to failure to observe the latter half of the verse. (*Imrai Shaifer*)

Since verbal abuse can cause so much suffering, much care must be taken not to say things to people that will hurt their feelings. The more sensitive someone is the greater care we must take when speaking to him that we do not cause him pain with our words. Not only is it important to watch what you say to someone, but also your tone of voice is crucial. If you shout at someone or speak in an angry voice, this causes hurt feelings and is included in the prohibition of this verse of the Torah. Every time you speak to someone you have a choice of saying things that will make him feel good which is the fulfillment of an act of *chesed*, or you might say something that will hurt him which is a violation of this prohibition. Utilize your power of speech to build people up, not to tear them down.

The Chazon Ish understood the specific things that bothered those who came to consult him. "I request that you do not ask this patient any personal questions," the Chazon Ish wrote to a doctor who was treating a certain patient. "It will cause him much discomfort if others try to enter his private domain." (*P'air Hador*, vol.4, p.36)

Do acts of kindness without any ulterior motive.

את כספך לא תתן לו בנשך. (ויקרא כ"ה ל"ז)

"YOUR MONEY YOU SHALL NOT GIVE HIM UPON INTEREST." (*Vayikra* 25:37)

Rabbi Chayim Shmuelevitz used to explain the Torah's prohibition against taking interest when lending money to others by saying that the Torah wants to train us to do acts of kindness for others without any gain at all. Not only is it forbidden to receive money for lending money, but the person who borrowed the money is not allowed to do any special favors for the person who lent him the money. When you lend someone money, you are doing so only because you want to help this person and you know that you will not be receiving anything material in return. (Heard from Rabbi Chayim Shmuelevitz)

There is a strong tendency for people to keep asking, "What's in this for me?" When they do not see any personal profit or benefit in what they are doing, they are frequently not motivated to take action. But the Torah ideal is that we should develop the attribute of helping others for no ulterior motive. Do kindness for the sake of the kindness itself. This is the Torah's lesson in the commandment to lend others money without any form of personal gain.

One day members of the Chazon Ish's family came running to his room when they heard him crying out in great anguish. What happened? Someone whom the Chazon Ish didn't really know had borrowed a sum of money and now he came to repay the loan. Before the Chazon Ish had a chance to count the money, the man left the house. As soon as the Chazon Ish counted the money, however, he found that the person had given him more than he had borrowed.

With deep grief the Chazon Ish pleaded with members of his family, "Please have mercy on me, and search for that person. He paid me back evil in place of good. I lent him money to help him out of his financial difficulties, but in return he caused me this great misfortune."

He had no rest until his relatives made a thorough search for the stranger. Eventually they found him and brought him back to the Chazon Ish who returned the extra money. (*P'air Hador*, vol.3, p.41)

Feel an inner respect for other people.

לא תרדה בו בפרך ויראת מאלקיך. (ויקרא כ"ה מ"ג)

"YOU SHALL NOT RULE OVER HIM WITH RIGOR BUT YOU SHALL FEAR THE ALMIGHTY." (*Vayikra* 25:43)

Rashi cites *Sifra* that this verse is a prohibition against giving a servant work that is not really necessary. For example, a master is forbidden to tell his servant to warm things up when he really does not need it. Perhaps the master will say, "No one knows whether this is really necessary or not, and I will tell him that this is necessary." This is a matter which is given over to his heart, therefore it is stated, "And you shall fear the Almighty."

Since the servant does not know that the work the master is giving him is not really needed, why does the Torah prohibit it? The principle we see here is that the Torah wants us to feel an inner respect for others. A master who gives his servant work just to keep him busy is expressing a lack of respect for the dignity of the person who is working for him. People are created in the image of the

Almighty and have a spark of divinity in them. As such they must be treated with great respect. Even if the other person does not feel that you are treating him with a lack of respect, your inner thoughts and attitude towards him must be respectful. Your inner feelings will be the roots of your actions. When you master an inner respect for others, your entire behavior in dealing with them will be on a much higher level.

BECHUKOSAI

Toiling in Torah gives one joy.

אם בחקתי תלכו ואת מצותי תשמרו ועשיתם אתם. (ויקרא כ"ו ג')

"IF YOU SHALL WALK IN MY STATUTES AND OBSERVE MY
COMMANDMENTS, AND DO THEM..." (*Vayikra* 26:3)

My Rebbe, Rabbi Mordechai Gifter, Rosh Hayeshiva of Telz,
commented: "Our Rabbis teach us: '*Im bechukosai teileichu*, if you
shall walk in My statutes, refers to *amailus baTorah*, labor in
Torah.' This concept of toiling in Torah is inherent in the study of
Torah. *Amal Hatorah* means the complete engrossment of the
student in Torah to the exclusion of all else. It signifies the ability
to find in Torah study all the joy and pleasure which one could
wish for. It means finding in Torah the joys and benefits 'of bread
and meat, of wine and oil, of fields and vineyards, of milk and
honey, of precious stones and pearls.'"

Amal HaTorah does not mean life impoverished by complete
removal from human joys and pleasures but rather the sublime
contentment of the most intimate contact with the source of all joy
and pleasure.

"This is the content of the two blessings recited daily upon the
study of Torah. One, *laasok bedivrai Torah*, not merely to study
Torah, but that study becomes an *esek*, a complete involvement.
The second blessing, *vehaarev na* (let it be pleasant), helps us find
the *mesikus haTorah*, the sweetness of Torah."

"*Amal Hatorah*, this unique characteristic of Torah study creates a unique world for the Torah student. His greatest sorrow is the *kushya* - a difficult passage which he cannot master, a difficult Rambam attacked by the critique of a Raavad. The greatest joy of the Torah student is the *terutz*, the answer; he has seen the light, he has felt the truth and with the Psalmist he sings forth: 'Unveil my eyes and I shall see the sublime wonders of Your Torah.'" (Rabbi Mordechai Gifter; *Torah Perspectives*, p.25)

Rabbi Shaul Kagan, a student of the late Rabbi Aharon Kotler, Rosh Hayeshiva of Lakewood, wrote about his Rebbe: "Rav Aharon's love for Torah study was phenomenal. As he studied, his face strained with concentration, smiling, even laughing, out of rapture. This love was extended to whoever was engaged in Torah and expressed itself in the boundless pleasure he drew from seeing others learn." (Rabbi Shaul Kagan; *The Jewish Observer*, May, 1973)

Rabbi Chaim Dov Keller wrote that he realized the boundless love of Torah of his Rebbe Rabbi Eliyahu Meir Bloch from his last visit with him in the hospital when the Rosh Hayeshiva was very weak and suffered greatly: "After some conversation, I mentioned an observation I had made on a passage of the *Ketzos Hachoshen*. As soon as I mentioned the *Ketzos*, the Rosh Hayeshiva underwent a remarkable change. His eyes lit up, his face evinced his old warmth, a smile crossed his face, and his voice became strong and clear, as if the old Rav Elya Meir had been revived. 'I made the same observation in one of my lectures,' he said, and proceeded to discuss the *Ketzos* with a liveliness which so entranced me that, to my everlasting regret, I could not concentrate on his words." (Rabbi Chaim Dov Keller; *The Jewish Observer*, Sept. 1977)

In a Talmudic lecture in Slobodka Yeshiva in Bnai Brak, Rabbi Yechezkail Abramsky cited a concept from *Chidushai Rabainu Chayim Halevi*. At the end of the lecture Rabbi Abramsky, who was a student of Rabbi Chayim Soloveitchik, said to his students, "You should study Reb Chayim Brisker's *sefer* very well. He merited that scholars should delve into his book. Why? Because of his tremendous toiling in Torah study."

"I remember," said Rabbi Abramsky, "seeing Rav Chayim in a synagogue in Minsk during the First World War. Once, he stood on his feet six hours straight with his hands behind his back deeply immersed in a Torah thought. During those six hours hundreds of people went in and out of the synagogue but Rav Chayim did not notice anything that went on because of his total concentration. After six hours he suddenly awoke from this state and cried out, 'What is this hanging behind me?' He was referring to his hands which were behind him, but he did not feel them until that moment." (*Peninai Rabainu Yechezkail*, p.10)

Rabbi Moshe Mordechai Shulsinger related that he once came to Rabbi Yechezkail Abramsky and asked him, "How does the Rebbe feel?" Rav Yechezkail replied "When I woke up this morning I did not feel well. But *Baruch Hashem* I feel so much better now. I studied seven pages of Talmud in tractate *Airchin* and this transformed me into a different person." (*ibid.*, p.6)

Utilize traveling time for Torah study.

אם בחקתי תלכו. (ויקרא כ"ו ג')

"YOU SHALL WALK IN MY STATUTES." (*Vayikra* 26:3)

The *Ohr Hachayim* comments: Since this part of the verse refers to toiling in Torah, it states the term "walking" because we should become used to studying Torah even when we are walking and traveling.

There are many opportunities to study Torah that frequently are not utilized properly. When you travel, remember to take along a *sefer* to study from. Even if a person does not have that much travel time, there are light topics that one does not always have a chance to study and the time waiting for transportation to arrive and the actual time traveling can be used very productively. Even if you do have interruptions and are not able to study the entire time, whatever you are able to study is a great benefit.

Many people listen to Torah tapes in their cars when traveling. Besides benefiting the driver, it gives those traveling with him a chance to listen to lectures that they otherwise would not have heard.

Be happy for the good fortune of others.

ונתתי שלום בארץ. (ויקרא כ"ו ו')

"AND I WILL PLACE PEACE IN THE LAND." (*Vayikra* 26:6)

Rashi states: "If there is no peace, there is nothing." There are many people who would really feel satisfied with what they themselves already have. But because they see that others have more, they feel envious of those people. They actually feel pain when they see that someone else has what they do not. But when a person feels sincere love for someone else, he is not envious of that person and it does not bother him if that person has more than him. Therefore the only way for people to really experience a total blessing with what the Almighty has given them is for there to be true peace among people. This is the peace in which people feel love for one another and are happy for their good fortune. (*Ksav Sofer*)

The only way you will be able to enjoy what you have is to master the attitude of feeling good for the good fortune of others. Envy prevents you from living life to its fullest. The more joy you feel for others, the better your own quality of life.

Reb Bainish Rosenbaum who spent many hours studying with the Noviminsker Rebbe, Rabbi Nochum Mordechai Perlow, wrote, "His face would light up with joy whenever he learned of the success of someone else's undertaking: a Rebbe attracted a host of new followers - marvelous! A Rosh Yeshiva expanded his institution - wonderful! Another's triumph was the most precious of occurrences." (*The Jewish Observer*, Dec. 1976)

Be aware of the dangers in rejecting the Torah.

ואם בחקתי תמאסו. (ויקרא כ״ו ט״ו)

"AND IF YOU SHALL REJECT MY STATUTES..." (*Vayikra* 26:15)

The Chofetz Chayim used to say that there are people who are afraid to read this section of the *Tochocho*, the warning of retribution for failure to keep the Torah. In some synagogues the person who reads the Torah in public reads this in a very low voice, and some people even walk out of the synagogue when this section is read. But they are very mistaken.

The Chofetz Chayim gave an analogy of someone who had to travel on a dangerous path. It was on a very high and extremely narrow mountain and he could eaily trip and harm himself. Besides, there were many wild animals stalking in the area and the whole path had many pitfalls. One person who was aware of the serious dangers involved in traveling on that path was very nervous about it. After thinking the matter over, he came up with an original solution to his fears. He would walk blindfolded. This way he would not be able to see the great dangers that surrounded him from all sides and he would then be able to remain calm. Anyone with a drop of sense can easily see how this "solution" just adds to the problem without solving anything at all. He is now in even greater danger than before since he will be unaware of his true situation.

Similarly, said the Chofetz Chayim, we must become aware of the dangers of not behaving properly. By realizing the consequences of transgressions and the failure to do good, you will watch your behavior and will gain immensely. (*Chofetz Chayim al Hatorah*)

While the Chofetz Chayim used to stress that our main emphasis should be on the benefits of Torah observance and the joy and pleasure of following the Torah, it is still very important to realize the harmful consequences of failure to observe the Torah. While our main focus should be on the positive aspects of doing what is right, an awareness of the harm of doing evil will motivate us to keep from doing wrong.

Don't just confess your sins, actually improve.

והתודו את עונם ואת עון אבתם במעלם אשר מעלו בי ואף אשר הלכו עמי בקרי. אף אני אלך עמם בקרי והבאתי אתם בארץ איביהם. (ויקרא כ"ו מ-מ"א)

"AND THEY SHALL CONFESS THEIR INIQUITY AND THE INIQUITY OF THEIR FATHERS, IN THEIR TREACHERY WHICH THEY COMMITTED AGAINST ME, AND ALSO THEY HAVE WALKED CONTRARY UNTO ME. I ALSO WILL WALK CONTRARY UNTO THEM, AND BRING THEM INTO THE LAND OF THEIR ENEMIES." (*Vayikra* 26:40,41)

At first glance it seems difficult to understand the continuity of these two verses. The Torah tells us that they will confess their sins. This is a positive thing for them to do. Why then does the next verse say that they will receive more retribution? The Chofetz Chayim explained that here the Torah teaches us that just confessing one's wrongdoings without sincerely regretting the wrong one has done and without accepting upon oneself to improve in the future is not worth anything. The most important aspect of repentance is to improve oneself from now on. Only positive changes in one's actual behavior is true repentance. (*Chofetz Chayim al Hatorah*)

This principle applies to all aspects of Torah. Saying *viduy* is easy. All you do is read off a list of sins and transgressions. But you stay the same. You still have all of your old faults. True change is very difficult. It takes much work and effort. But that is what is demanded of us. For example, if you keep getting angry at other people and insult or shout at them, you might regret your outbursts afterwards. Therefore you keep saying that you are sorry. It is definitely better to say that you are sorry than not to say it. But just saying the words without actually feeling regret will just make the other person feel worse. Moreover, even if you are sincere in your regret, the other person wants you to stop your abusive language and behavior. Don't just confess your sins, change and improve.

Act in an elevated manner at home.

ואיש כי יקדש את ביתו. (ויקרא כ"ז י"ד)

"A PERSON WHO SANCTIFIES HIS HOUSE..." (*Vayikra* 27:14)

The Kotzker Rebbe commented on this verse: When a person is involved in spiritual matters, it is relatively easy for him to do so in a sanctified state. But true holiness is when a person sanctifies the seemingly mundane daily activities of running his house. When one behaves in an elevated manner in his own house, he is truly a holy person. (*Amud Haemes*)

Torah ideals and principles are not only for when one is in a yeshiva or synagogue. Rather Torah principles and values apply to all areas of our lives. At home one has many opportunities for acts of kindness to one's own family. Also, behaving properly towards members of one's own family at home is frequently more difficult than behaving properly towards strangers. But the more difficult it is to apply Torah principles the greater the reward. The more sanctified your behavior at home the greater you become.

BAMIDBAR

Humility enables you to learn from everyone and to teach everyone.

וידבר השם אל משה במדבר סיני. (במדבר א' א')

"AND THE ALMIGHTY SPOKE TO MOSHE IN THE WILDERNESS OF SINAI." (*Bamidbar* 1:1)

The Midrash (*Bamidbar Rabbah* 1:7) states on this verse: "Whoever does not make himself open and free like a wilderness will not be able to acquire wisdom and Torah." This, comments *Matnos Kehunah*, refers to having the trait of humility which enables a person to learn from everyone and to teach everyone.

A person with arrogance will only be willing to learn from someone if he feels that it is fitting to his honor to do so. If, for example, someone much younger than he has Torah knowledge that he is lacking, he will not ask that person to teach him for he feels that would lower his status. If there is something he does not understand, he will be very careful before he asks anyone to explain it to him. He has to size up the situation to see if it is fitting for him. Similarly, he will only be willing to teach someone if he feels that he will gain honor from teaching this person.

But the humble person's thoughts are solely on gaining Torah knowledge. He is willing to learn from anyone who knows something that he does not, even though he might have much more overall Torah knowledge than the other person. Similarly, he wants to spread Torah knowledge to everyone he can. He does not focus on his own ego but on gaining and sharing wisdom.

When Rabbi Eliyahu Klatzkin settled in Jerusalem, his tiny room became a crowded center for people of all classes and parties. There were scholars, but there were also many vagrants and miscellaneous hangers-on. Once his son asked him why he permitted everyone to come to his house without discrimination. He answered, "You must admit that it is logical to assume that all who come here are decent people. Ask yourself - for what purpose would anyone come to me? Certainly not for any material benefit, for everyone knows that I am penniless and cannot give them any help. Shall we say they come to be honored by me? Everyone knows that I am far from flattery and even sparing in words of praise when phrasing endorsements of the works of great Torah scholars. Therefore you will be forced to admit that my visitors must come to hear my words of Torah, and it is self-evident they must be men of some spiritual worth or at least of good intentions." (*Jewish Leaders*, pp. 329-30)

Make your descendants proud of you.

ואתכם יהיו איש איש למטה איש איש לבית אבתיו הוא. (במדבר א׳ד׳)

"AND WITH YOU SHALL BE ONE MAN FROM EACH TRIBE, EACH MAN SHOULD BE THE HEAD OF HIS FAMILY." (*Bamidbar* 1:4)

A simple and boorish person who came from distinguished lineage was arguing with a wise scholar who came from a very plain family. The coarse ignoramus boasted about his illustrious ancestors. "I am a scion of great people. Your ancestors are nothing compared to mine," he arrogantly said. The scholar wanted to put him in his place and said to him, "True, you come from a long line of great people. But unfortunately the line ends with you. My family tree begins with me."

This, said Rabbi Moshe Chaifetz, author of *Meleches Machsheves*, is the idea of our verse. Each man should be the head of his family's lineage. He should be an elevated person in his own right and his descendants should be proud to consider him their ancestor.

Rather than boasting about one's prominent lineage, one should focus on making oneself into an elevated person.

When the Maggid of Mezeritch was a young boy of five, fire destroyed his parent's house. The young boy saw that his mother was sitting in deep anguish, and he asked her why she felt so bad.

"I am not in pain because of the loss of the house," his mother told him. "But we had a document which traced our lineage back to great scholars."

"In that case, you need not worry," her five-year-old son comforted her. "The distinguished lineage will now start from me." (*Rabbi Meir Yechiel Maiostrovtze*, p.33)

Keep away from listening to loshon hora.

אֵךְ אֶת מַטֵּה לֵוִי לֹא תִפְקֹד וְאֶת רֹאשָׁם לֹא תִשָּׂא בְּתוֹךְ בְּנֵי יִשְׂרָאֵל. (במדבר א' מ"ט)

"BUT YOU SHALL NOT NUMBER THE TRIBE OF LEVI, NOR TAKE THE SUM OF THEM AMONG THE CHILDREN OF ISRAEL." (*Bamidbar* 1:49)

Rashi cites the Midrash that one of the reasons the tribe of Levi was not counted was because the Almighty foresaw that everyone over twenty years of age would die in the forty years the Israelites were in the wilderness. Therefore He said, "The Levites should not be counted among the others in order not to be included with them. They are Mine since they did not transgress in the sin of the Golden Calf."

The question arises: The decree of dying in the wilderness was for the transgression of accepting the negative report about *Eretz*

Yisroel from the spies. Rashi should have said that the Levites did not transgress in the episode of the spies rather than saying that they did not transgress with the Golden Calf. The answer, wrote the *Sifsai Chachomim*, is that the Levites also accepted the negative report of the spies. But the decree of dying in the wilderness was because of the double transgressions of the Golden Calf and the spies. Since the Levites were not guilty in the incident of the Golden Calf, they were not included in the decree.

Rabbi Baruch Sorotzkin, the late Rosh Hayeshiva of Telz, commented that we see from here the dangers of listening to *loshon hora*, a negative report about others. Even though the Levites had the strength of character not to sin when others did in the incident of the Golden Calf, they still fell prey to accepting the *loshon hora* about the land of Israel. From this we should learn how far we need to keep from listening to *loshon hora*.

There are some people who rationalize their listening to *loshon hora* by claiming that they will never really believe the negative information they hear about others. They will only listen but they will not accept what they hear as the truth. Even if this is accurate, merely listening to *loshon hora* without believing it is forbidden. But in reality most people do in the end believe the negative things they hear about others. If you are unable to stop someone from saying negative things about others, walk away.

Influence others to study Torah.

מטה זבולן. (במדבר ב' ז')

"THE TRIBE OF ZEVULUN..." (*Bamidbar* 2:7)

Baal Haturim notes that in reference to certain of the tribes that were together with other tribes the Torah adds the letter "vav" - which denotes that they are separate but together. But as regards the tribe of Zevulun there is not a "vav." This is because the tribe of Yissochor, which is mentioned right above, devoted themselves to Torah study, while the tribe of Zevulun worked to support both of them. Because they enabled the tribe of Yissochor to study Torah they are considered as one tribe and their reward is the same.

Rabbi Chayim Shmuelevitz used to comment on this that just as those who support Torah study financially have the merit of the Torah study of those they support, so too anyone who influences another person to study Torah shares in the merit of that person. Every student in a yeshiva has many opportunities to be a positive influence on others. Frequently by just studying with diligence oneself others will use that diligence as a model and this will increase their Torah study, which is an added merit for the diligent student.

Parents who influence and enable their children to study Torah have this merit, as do wives who enable their husbands to study Torah.

Don't become involved in a quarrel about seating arrangements.

ויעשו בני ישראל ככל אשר צוה השם את משה כן חנו לרגליהם וכן נסעו איש למשפחתיו על בית אבתיו. (במדבר ב׳ ל״ד)

"AND THE CHILDREN OF ISRAEL DID ALL THAT THE ALMIGHTY COMMANDED MOSHE, THAT IS THE WAY THEY ENCAMPED ACCORDING TO THEIR FLAGS, AND THAT IS THE WAY THEY TRAVELED, EACH PERSON TO HIS FAMILY TOGETHER WITH THE HOUSE OF HIS FATHER." (*Bamidbar* 2:34)

What is the greatness of the Israelites listening to Moshe in this matter? Why would anyone have thought that they would not have listened? This comes to teach us that they did not quarrel about whose place would be at the head and who would be at the end, who would be at the east and who at the west. They accepted the will of the Almighty and did not complain or argue. Unfortunately, in many places arguments do arise when people are not satisfied with the seating arrangements. (*Oznayim Letorah*)

Arguments and complaints about this matter are usually based on arrogance and honor-seeking. If a person has a practical reason for wanting a certain place, his request could be quite reasonable. But if the root of his dissatisfaction is based on honor, he is making a big mistake. The Sages (*Taanis* 21b) have said, "It is not the place that honors the person, but the person who honors the place." If a person is honorable because of his own wisdom and behavior, then regardless of where he sits he remains honorable. If, however, a person lacks his own virtues, the place where he sits will not miraculously make him into a more honorable person. A person who places a great emphasis on external symbols demonstrates a lack of appreciation for his own value. Focus on spiritual growth, and not on superficial signs of status.

Respect the privacy of others.

ויפקד אתם משה על פי השם כאשר צוה. (במדבר ג' ט"ז)

"AND MOSHE COUNTED THEM ACCORDING TO THE WORD OF THE ALMIGHTY, AS HE COMMANDED." (*Bamidbar* 3:16)

Rashi cites the Midrash that since the Levites were counted from the age of thirty days, Moshe asked the Almighty, "How can I enter the private tents of other people to know how many infants each family has?" The Almighty replied, "You do what is required of you, and I will take care of the rest." Therefore when Moshe walked in front of each tent, a Divine voice announced the number of people who lived in that tent.

Rabbi Chayim Shmuelevitz used to note the importance of observing the principles of *derech eretz*. Although Moshe had a *mitzvah* to count the people, he felt it was wrong to invade the privacy of others. Each person's tent belongs to him and one must respect the privacy of the individual. Therefore the Almighty arranged a supernatural method of counting the Levites. Rav

Chayim cited this as he censured people who in trying to protest against the behavior of others failed to respect their private property. (Heard from Rabbi Chayim Shmuelevitz)

A person's privacy is a very important emotional need. Even if a person is not doing anything wrong, he does not want other people to pry into his private matters out of curiosity. Even Moshe, the leader of the people, refrained from entering other people's homes when he felt that this would cause them discomfort or uneasiness. Do not allow your curiosity to cause any suffering to others.

NASO

Act with love and kindness towards converts.

ואשמה הנפש ההוא. (במדבר ה' ו')

"TO DO A TRESPASS AGAINST THE ALMIGHTY." (*Bamidbar* 5:6)

Sforno comments that this refers to one who steals from a convert to Judaism. Harming him is considered a trespass against the Almighty because this person had the idealism to come to the Almighty's Torah. One desecrates the Almighty's name in his eyes by deceiving him.

A person who comes to Torah on his own volition does so because of the beautiful and elevated ideas he hears about Torah principles. He made his decision on the assumption that those who follow the Torah will act towards him in accordance with all the Torah laws pertaining to interpersonal relations. If someone cheats him financially or in any other way wrongs him, he will not only suffer a monetary loss. Rather, he might also feel disillusioned with his decision to accept the Torah way of life. He has usually given up very much because of his ideals and will experience much pain from his disappointment that the people he is in contact with do not meet the Torah standards he expected of them. The importance of not harming a convert can be seen from the fact that the Torah warns us about this in numerous places. From the negative we can learn the positive. The merit of acting with love and kindness towards a convert is very great. Go out of your way to be especially friendly towards converts.

Know the difference between self-discipline and self-denial.

מיין ושכר יזיר. (במדבר ו' ג')

"FROM NEW WINE AND OLD WINE HE SHOULD SEPARATE HIMSELF." (*Bambidbar* 6:3)

Sforno (verse 3) notes that when the Torah discusses abstaining from physical desires it refers only to refraining from drinking wine. This is a desire that is not a basic need for one's health and well-being and abstention will not weaken a person. But a person should not subject himself to fasting for this will have a negative effect on his health and will decrease his ability to devote himself to spiritual activity. In the previous verse Sforno states that the purpose of the abstention from physical pleasures is to enable a person to devote himself entirely to the Almighty: to delve into Torah study and to perfect his character so that he walks in the ways of the Almighty (being compassionate and merciful).

We see here an important concept. One must be very careful not to refrain from those things one needs for one's health. There is no goal of causing oneself needless pain. Those pleasures that would be detrimental for a person and would cause him to waste precious time can be eliminated, and it is an act of holiness to do so. The focus should always be on increasing Torah knowledge and perfecting one's character. Self-discipline that leads to this is a *mitzvah*; but self-denial that weakens a person is forbidden.

A young married fellow started to fast and cause himself other suffering in order to atone for any wrongs that he did. Because of this his physical health declined and he was in a general state of depression. Rabbi Shmuel Houminer, author of *Ikrai Dinim* and a great *tzadik*, noticed this and went with the young man to Rabbi Isser Zalman Meltzer in order for the Rosh Hayeshiva to influence him to refrain from this negative behavior.

When Rabbi Meltzer heard the details, he spoke strongly to that person, saying, "If from today on you stop fasting and causing yourself needless pain and you improve your ways, I accept upon myself all of your past transgressions, from now on they are mine." Eventually this person became an outstanding Torah scholar in Yerushalayim. (*Bederech Aitz Hachayim*, vol.1, p.283)

The true king is one who is free from desires.

כי נזר אלקיו על ראשו. (במדבר ו' ז')

"FOR THE CROWN OF THE ALMIGHTY IS ON HIS HEAD." (*Bamidbar* 6:7)

Ibn Ezra writes: "The term *nozir* (the person who takes a vow to abstain from wine) comes from the Hebrew word meaning crown. You should know that almost all people are slaves to the pleasures of the world. The only person who is truly a king and has the royal crown on his head is someone who is free from desires."

People who are addicted to pleasures might mistakenly view themselves as fortunate that they have so much pleasure. But the truth is that they are enslaved by those pleasures. When they don't have them, they feel the suffering of deprivation. Their thoughts are fixated on what they can do to obtain their desires. They spend more time worrying about how they can obtain pleasures than actually enjoying themselves. Seeking pleasure is an illusory goal. A pleasure-seeker will never be fulfilled. Happiness is a much more sensible goal than pleasure, and the way to acquire happiness is by being in control of one's desires. When you derive pleasure from self-discipline, your situation is reversed. You will be free from worrying about obtaining desires and you will constantly experience the pleasure of being the ruler over yourself.

Every time you experience self-discipline view yourself as a king: you are obtaining mastery over yourself. The pleasure you have from self-discipline will enable you to rule over your desires.

The Chazon Ish told someone close to him, "To me there is no difference between before and after I eat. I actually don't feel any difference at all. But if members of my family place food before me, I rely on them that probably it is before I have eaten." (*P'air Hador*, vol.3, p.12)

Elevate all that you do.

ואחר ישתה הנזיר יין. (במדבר ו' כ')

"AND AFTERWARDS THE NOZIR MAY DRINK WINE." (*Bamidbar* 6:20)

After the *Nozir* completed the entire process described by the Torah, he may drink wine once again. Why does the Torah still call the person a *nozir* in this verse since he is no longer in the state of being a *nozir*? The *Alshich* explained that when a person goes through a period of thirty days of being a *nozir*, he elevates himself to a high level of spirituality. He is now on such a level that even if he drinks wine it is the drinking of a person on the level of a *nozir*.

Two people can drink wine and the meaning behind their behavior can be totally different. The following two incidents illustrate this clearly.

My Rebbe, Rabbi Mordechai Gifter, Rosh Hayeshiva of Telz, was on an airplane from Cleveland to Boston traveling to the wedding of one of the yeshiva's students. In the middle of the flight, passengers could see that one of the airplane's engines was on fire, and there was an announcement that the plane would have to make an emergency landing in a nearby city. One of the passengers called out to a stewardess, "Give me one last drink before I die." Fortunately, the plane landed safely and this incident was the topic of the next *mussar* lecture in the yeshiva. A person who identifies himself entirely with his body and not with his soul keeps this attitude even at the very last minute of his life.

This is in contrast to a similar story told about a very righteous scholar. This scholar always lived a very ascetic life and denied himself many pleasures. When he was on his deathbed he said to someone standing near him, "Please bring me a glass of wine before I die. My entire life I denied my body physical pleasures. Now I want to ask my body forgiveness and I wish to appease it with a glass of wine." This righteous man identified himself entirely with his soul. His request for a final drink of wine was with the spirituality of a *nozir*.

With unity there is a blessing.

יברכך השם וישמרך. (במדבר ו' כ"ד)

"THE ALMIGHTY SHOULD BLESS YOU AND GUARD YOU." (*Bamidbar* 6:24)

The blessings of *Birchas Kohanim* (the priestly blessings) are all in the singular rather than in the plural. Rabbi Moshe Leib of Sassov said that this is to teach us that the greatest blessing is togetherness. When we feel as if we are one unit, in this itself there is a great blessing.

It is easy to focus on the differences among people and to consider yourself as separate from others. Truly no two people are exactly alike. But there are many common factors among people. By focusing on the fact that every human being is created in the image of the Almighty you will have greater identification with others and this will lead to greater unity.

Avoid oneupmanship in spiritual matters.

ויהי המקריב ביום הראשון את קרבנו נחשון בן עמינדב למטה יהודה. (במדבר ז' י"ב)

"THE ONE WHO BROUGHT HIS OFFERING ON THE FIRST DAY WAS NACHSHON, SON OF AMINODOV, OF THE TRIBE OF YEHUDAH." (*Bamidbar* 7:12)

During the twelve days of the dedication of the Tabernacle the heads of the twelve tribes each brought an offering. Although the offerings of the twelve leaders were the same, the Torah repeats them over and over with all of their details. The Ralbag comments that this is to teach us the lesson that one person should not try to outdo another in order to boast or to feel above him. Therefore the Torah elaborates on how each one brought the same thing.

The goal in spiritual matters is to serve the Almighty, not to compete with anyone else. Competition has its motivating factor, but it also has many drawbacks. Oneupmanship has no place in the fulfillment of Torah principles. A person who feels that he needs to be above others will be motivated by the thought that he needs to outdo them in order to get honor or to feel that he is the best. This is contrary to the concept of fulfilling *mitzvos* with pure intentions. When there is togetherness in accomplishment, everyone gains.

When Rabbi Yisroel Salanter was just fourteen years old, he wrote an original Talmudic monograph. Upon the suggestion of his teacher, Rabbi Tzvi Broide, the Rabbi of Salant, he sent it to Rabbi Akiva Eger. Rabbi Eger, however, did not reply. Awhile afterwards, a resident of Salant visited Posen, and upon the request of Rabbi Broide went to Rabbi Eger to give him the Rabbi's regards. Rabbi Akiva Eger told this person that he received a monograph from a youth from Salant and it was a work of exceptional genius. But he did not send back a letter of praise, although it truly deserved great praise. Rabbi Eger was surprised that the lad wrote to him when in his own city there was a brilliant scholar, Rabbi Tzvi Broide. Not aware that Rabbi Broide himself had told him to send the monograph, Rabbi Eger was apprehensive that perhaps the lad would utilize a reply from him as a means of oneupmanship over Rabbi Broide. (*Tnuas Hamussar*, vol.1, pp.140-1)

BEHAALOSCHO

Learn to keep up your enthusiasm.

ויעש כן אהרן. (במדבר ח' ג')

"AND AHARON DID SO." (*Bamidbar* 8:3)

Rashi comments: "This is to tell the praise of Aharon that he did not change."

The *Sfas Emes* explained that usually when a person starts something new, he feels very enthusiastic about what he is doing. He is excited about the good he is doing and feels very motivated. But after some time passes the enthusiasm and excitement get lost. This was the praise of Aharon. Every time he lit the lamp in the Tabernacle he did so with the same enthusiasm as on the first day.

There are many projects that people start with much enthusiasm. There is a special excitement in starting something new. But after doing the same thing over and over, people get bored and often give up in the middle. In order to accomplish anything, one needs to master the ability of sustaining enthusiasm. The more enthusiastic one is the more motivated one will be to continue. Always focus on the value of what you are doing and view it as if this were the first time.

Be aware that the Almighty is your place.

על פי השם יסעו בני ישראל ועל פי השם יחנו. (במדבר ט' י"ח)

"ACCORDING TO THE WORD OF THE ALMIGHTY THE CHILDREN OF ISRAEL TRAVELED AND ACCORDING TO THE WORD OF THE ALMIGHTY THEY ENCAMPED." (*Bamidbar* 9:18)

The Talmud (*Shabbos* 31b) in discussing the various forms of work that are forbidden on Shabbos states that the main prohibition against breaking down a building applies only when it is planned to rebuild it on the same spot. The Talmud asks on this that in the wilderness when the Tabernacle was taken apart it was rebuilt on a different spot. Since we learn the prohibition against work from the work that was done at the Tabernacle, the same law should apply when rebuilding in a different place as for rebuilding in the same place. The Talmud answers that since they traveled and encamped according to the word of the Almighty it is considered as if it were in the same place.

Rabbi Chayim Shmuelevitz explained thus: When a mother travels with an infant from Jerusalem to Tel Aviv one cannot say that the infant has really gone from one place to another. The place of the infant is with its mother. As long as it is with its mother there is no difference to the infant what city it is in. Similarly, with the Israelites in the wilderness. Since they did everything according to the word of the Almighty, they were totally with Him. He was their place and even though they moved from one spot in the desert to another, their place was really always the same: with the Almighty.

When one has a constant awareness that he is always with the Almighty, the exact place where he is will not make a major difference. His main focus is on the Almighty and not on the superficial differences between one spot and another.

Even when traveling be careful to observe Torah values.

על פי השם יחנו ועל פי השם יסעו. (במדבר ט' כ"ג)

"ACCORDING TO THE WORD OF THE ALMIGHTY THEY SHALL ENCAMP AND ACCORDING TO THE WORD OF THE ALMIGHTY THEY SHALL TRAVEL." (*Bamidbar* 9:23)

When a person is in his usual place, it is relatively easy to keep higher standards of Torah observance. But when a person travels, said the Chofetz Chayim, there are many tests that arise. When in a strange place, away from one's familiar environment, one is faced with new difficulties. A person needs to make a special effort to observe Torah values.

This is hinted to in our verse. Both when a person is at rest and when he travels, all that he does should be in accordance with the will of the Almighty. (*Chofetz Chayim al Hatorah*)

Rabbi Yaakov Kamenetzky was about to take his place at the end of a long line waiting to board a bus, when someone in front of the line who knew him called out, "Rebbe, you can come here in front of me!"

"I'm not permitted to," replied Rav Yaakov. "It would be stealing."

"I give you permission. I don't mind."

"But what about everybody else behind you?" said the Rosh Hayeshiva. "I would be stealing their time and choice of seat by moving them back one. Who says they allow me to?"

And Rav Yaakov took his place at the end of the line. (*The Jewish Observer*, Nov., 1985)

Do not allow opposition to stop you from spreading Torah.

ויהי בנסע הארן ויאמר משה קומה השם ויפצו איביך וינסו משנאיך מפניך. (במדבר י' ל"ה)

"AND IT WAS WHEN THE ARK TRAVELED, MOSHE SAID, ARISE ALMIGHTY AND DISPERSE YOUR ENEMIES. AND THOSE WHO HATE YOU WILL FLEE FROM YOU." (*Bamidbar* 10:35)

Rabbi Yosef Chayim Sonnenfeld was the guest speaker at the opening of a yeshiva in Yerushalayim. He cited this verse and said that there is a special reason this is recited every time we open the ark in the synagogue to take out the Torah scroll. Whenever someone wants to start some worthwhile Torah institution or project there are always people who will try to stop him. Therefore when we take out the Torah we ask that the Almighty should disperse the enemies of Torah and prevent them from causing trouble. (*Mara Deara Yisroel*, p.155)

When you realize in advance that difficulties are likely to arise when you try to spread Torah, you will not be taken by surprise. Rather you will make plans to overcome those difficulties and you will pray for the Almighty's assistance. Do not allow opposition to prevent you from spreading Torah.

Focus on the good instead of complaining about what is wrong.

ויהי העם כמתאננים רע באזני השם. (במדבר י"א א')

"AND THE PEOPLE WERE COMPLAINING IN A BAD WAY IN THE EARS OF THE ALMIGHTY." (*Bamidbar* 11:1)

Rashi comments that when the people were complaining they had no real cause to complain, they were just looking for an excuse to separate themselves from the Almighty. By finding what would sound like a complaint they felt justified in keeping a distance from the Creator.

When someone realizes all that the Almighty does for him, he will not have a complaining attitude. There are times when a person is missing things and times when he is suffering. That is a time for action and prayer. But complaining is wrong. The underlying theme behind a complainer is not necessarily that he wants the situation to be improved, but that he wants to have the benefits of complaining. The payoff here is that if I have complaints against someone, I can tell myself that I am free from the obligations I have towards him for all the good that he has done. Ultimately, a person who goes through life complaining does not appreciate the good in his life. By keeping his focus only on what he is missing, he blinds himself to what he does have. No matter how much you do have, there will always be something to complain about if you look hard enough. This attitude is not merely a means by which a person causes himself a miserable existence. It is a direct contradiction to our obligation to be grateful to the Almighty. Anyone having this negative trait must make a concerted effort to build up the habit of appreciating what he has. This is crucial both for spiritual reasons and for one's happiness in life.

This same principle that we see in Rashi also applies to relationships between people. When a person wants to keep an emotional distance from someone with whom he should be close, a ploy used is to have complaints against that person. By complaining about what the person does wrong or what he does not do enough of, you try to free yourself from gratitude to him for what he has done for you. This fault causes much misery in both the life of the complainer and the life of the person he complains about. The Sages have said that when a person does not appreciate what another person has done for him, he will eventually deny the good that the Almighty has done for him. Show appreciation for everyone who helps you. Make an effort to verbalize your gratitude for all favors and kindnesses that others do for you.

One of the harms of complaining is that this attitude is contagious (see Rashi to verse 4). When you complain, you build up a complaining attitude in the minds of the people who hear your complaining. Even though they previously might not have thought that they had anything to complain about, after they hear you complaining they are likely to "catch" this fault from you. For this reason you owe it to others not to be a complainer (unless it is necessary to take action to rectify a situation).

In case you are around other people who have a habit of complaining about things, be very careful that you do not model them. Instead make an effort to be a person who sees the good in situations and hopefully others will learn from you. (A note of caution: this must be done with common sense and tact or else the effect could be negative.) Even if others do not learn from you to be more positive, by verbalizing your positive evaluations you will at least prevent yourself from learning from them.

SHLACH

When Torah values are involved remain steadfast.

ויקרא משה להושע בן נון יהושע. (במדבר י״ג ט״ז)

"AND MOSHE CALLED HOSHEA, THE SON OF NUN, YEHOSHUA."
(*Bamidbar* 13:16)

Rashi states that Moshe called him Yehoshua because Moshe prayed that the Almighty should save him from the plans of the other spies. *Targum Yonoson* comments on this verse that Moshe called him Yehoshua when he saw his humility.

Rabbi Avraham Mordechai of Gur explained that the nature of a person with humility is not to be stubborn about his own opinions and wishes. He is compliant and will easily give in to the opinions and wishes of others. The other spies were all very distinguished and important men. Moshe feared that Yehoshua might concede to their opinions and be swayed by them even though he felt differently. Therefore Moshe especially prayed for Yehoshua not to be negatively influenced by the others.

When a question of Torah ideals is involved, one must not budge. That is when it is appropriate to resist. When dealing with basic principles, remain steadfast and do not allow others to sway you. One needs wisdom to know the difference between situations when it is proper to give in to others and when it is not. For this we need the Almighty's assistance. (cited in *Maayanah Shel Torah*)

When the time came that Rabbi Moshe Feinstein alone had the

stature to decide controversies in the Torah world, he took the initiative in calling the parties to judgment. In one such instance, a party complained that it was not Rav Moshe's business, to which he replied matter-of-factly and without any anger, "I am the father of all *yeshivos*." This most modest of men was the last to impose his will on others; it was unpleasant for him. But when he realized the burden had fallen upon him, he felt he had no right to refuse it. (Rabbi Nosson Scherman, *The Jewish Observer*, Oct. 1986, p.19)

A person who tends to lie will lie even if he does not really need to.

ויספרו לו ויאמרו באנו אל הארץ אשר שלחתנו וגם זבת חלב ודבש הוא
וזה פריה. (במדבר י״ג כ״ז)

"AND THEY TOLD HIM, AND THEY SAID, WE CAME TO THE LAND WHERE YOU SENT US. AND IT IS FLOWING WITH MILK AND HONEY, AND THIS IS ITS FRUIT." (*Bamidbar* 13:27)

Rabbi A.M. Shimanowitz, a *mussar* personality, used to comment: "Rashi cites the Sages on this verse that, 'Every falsehood that does not start with some truth will not last.' Unfortunately, today there are many people who mistakenly feel that every truth that is not mixed with some falsehood will not last." (cited in *Chayai Hamussar*, vol.1, p.71)

Rabbi Eliyahu Meir Bloch, the late Rosh Hayeshiva of Telz, related in a lecture on the subject of speaking the truth about an incident that took place when he was visiting *Eretz Yisroel*. On the shores of Yam Kineret he had the urge to immerse himself in the sea. On a stony deserted stretch, Rav Elya Meir prepared himself to enter the water and walked barefoot over the sharp stones towards the water.

"What are you doing?" asked his startled companion.

"I want to be able to say that I bathed in the Kineret," he replied.

The man looked at him incredulously, "But why go to all the trouble? Who's to stop you from saying it?"

Rav Elya Meir was astonished by the question, "It used to be said, 'If you can tell the truth, why tell a lie?' Now people say, 'If you can tell a lie, why bother with the truth?'" (Rabbi Chaim Dov Keller; *The Jewish Observer*, Sept. 1977)

Beware of false conclusions from the facts you observe.

אפס כי עז העם הישב בארץ והערים בצרות גדלת מאד וגם ילדי הענק ראינו שם. והאנשים אשר עלו עמו אמרו לא נוכל לעלות אל העם כי חזק הוא ממנו. (במדבר י״ג כ״ח-ל״א)

"THE PEOPLE WHO DWELL IN THE LAND ARE EXTREMELY FIERCE AND THE CITIES ARE FORTIFIED AND VERY GREAT, AND WE ALSO SAW THE CHILDREN OF ANAK THERE." "WE CANNOT GO UP TO THE PEOPLE BECAUSE THEY ARE STRONGER THAN US." (*Bamidbar* 13:28,31)

The *Akaidah* explains that the report of the spies itself was appropriate. They were told to see the land and report back on the conditions of the land itself and of the people who lived there. But their task was just to observe and relate what they saw. Their mistake was in rendering a decision that they should not attempt to enter the land. It was not up to them to come to any final conclusions, only to report the facts.

They were wrong about their not being able to conquer the land. The Almighty has the power to help against all odds. Just because in their minds they did not think it was possible for them to successfully take over the land of Israel did not mean that it was really not possible.

Very often people see factors in a situation and come to erroneous conclusions based on their perceptions. Even if someone's observations are correct, there could always be factors that he didn't take into consideration or that he was unaware of. It is a special talent to be able to reach correct decisions based on the facts. This is especially true when having to make judgments about other people. Some people have a strong tendency to reach negative conclusions about others that are inaccurate. Even if what you see about another person is basically true, always keep in mind that your conclusions could be wrong and the other person should still be judged favorably.

Use strategy when trying to influence others.

If someone you try to influence sees you as biased, have someone else speak to him.

ויהס כלב את העם אל משה ויאמר עלה נעלה וירשנו אתה כי יכול נוכל לה. (במדבר י״ג ל׳)

"AND KOLAIV STILLED THE PEOPLE TOWARDS MOSHE AND SAID, WE SHOULD CERTAINLY GO UP AND POSSESS THE LAND FOR WE ARE WELL ABLE TO TAKE IT." (*Bamidbar* 13:30)

Kolaiv spoke to the people on behalf of Moshe and said that they would be successful when they tried to conquer the land of Israel. Why didn't Yehoshua speak up? He was also one of the spies and he and Kolaiv agreed about the positive qualities of the land and about how they would certainly be able to conquer the land. Why did only Kolaiv speak to the people now and not Yehoshua?

The Ari, z.l., explained that Yehoshua preferred that Kolaiv speak to the people because he felt that if he spoke up, the people would respond, "You only want to enter the land because of your desire for power. You are only concerned about your own welfare. You want leadership for yourself. But it is not in our best interests to go to the land." (cited in *Biurai Hamekubalim Beniglah*, p.188)

When you try to influence others to do something, it is important that they view what you say as being for their welfare. If someone you are trying to influence feels that you are motivated by self-interest, he will not heed you. Even if you are truly concerned with the other person's welfare, be aware of the possibility that since you might gain from the other person's listening to you, he will not trust you. In such instances it is preferable to ask someone else who is wholly unbiased to speak to the person instead of you.

There is another important lesson to be learned from Kolaiv's speaking to the people. Rashi explains that the first few words that Kolaiv said gave people the impression that he was going to speak against Moshe. Since after hearing the negative report of the spies they were feeling resentment towards Moshe, they eagerly listened to someone whom they thought would also be speaking against Moshe. This gave Kolaiv the opportunity to praise Moshe for all the wonderful things he did for them.

This strategy needs to be used in many instances. Very often when a listener is not open the speaker immediately starts out with a statement that is a direct attack on the listener's point of view. This just creates more hostility and the listener does not pay any attention to what the speaker has to say. Learn to start by speaking to people in a way that seems to agree with them. (Note that Kolaiv did not say anything that was not true. He just said, "Is this the only thing that Moshe did to us?" Although they thought he was going to say something negative, he said positive things about Moshe.) Then, when they are open to what you have to say, you can tell them how you disagree with them. If you start by attacking them, they will frequently not give you a hearing at all. Be aware of your goal which is to have a positive influence on others and use strategy to reach that goal.

Rabbi Moshe Leib of Sassov was once walking and saw something awful. A non-Jewish nobleman was sitting in a carriage with his wife and child and an entire Jewish family was harnessed to the carriage and were forced to pull it. To increase their speed the nobleman kept lashing them. Rav Moshe Leib, who was very distinguished looking, stopped the carriage and held the nobleman's young boy. He expressed great praise for the beauty of the child and even kissed him. After giving the child a blessing, Rav Moshe Leib told the nobleman that the cries of the family were harmful to the child's emotional well-being. Rav Moshe Leib advised the nobleman to free the family for his son's sake. Upon hearing this, the nobleman allowed the Jewish family to go free. (*Eser Tzichtzachus*, p.52)

Do not allow guilt feelings to prevent you from doing good.

והאנשים אשר עלו עמו אמרו לא נוכל לעלות אל העם כי חזק הוא ממנו. (במדבר י"ג ל"א)

"AND THE PEOPLE WHO WENT UP WITH HIM SAID, WE CANNOT GO UP TO THE PEOPLE BECAUSE THEY ARE STRONGER THAN US." (*Bamidbar* 13:31)

The Chofetz Chayim used to say that the evil inclination tries in every possible way to prevent a person from doing good deeds. At times a person is arrogant and feels that he is already on the highest level and need not do any more. At other times, when a person tries to do something good, he starts feeling sad and guilt-ridden. He tells himself that the good thing he wants to do is only for people on a much higher level than he. He immediately remembers all the bad things he has done in his life. Even though he might have already regretted those things and repented, he forgets this and starts feeling so inferior that he loses all desire to accomplish anything positive.

This, said the Chofetz Chayim, was their mistake in being afraid to enter the land of Eretz Yisroel. They remembered the things they did wrong in the past and said that they were unworthy to enter the land. Especially since the people who lived there before were very mighty, they would need a special merit to be victorious and they felt too lowly for this. But we should never be deterred from doing what is good out of misplaced humility. Do not allow guilt feelings to prevent you from doing the will of the Almighty. (*Shmiras Haloshon*, vol.2, *Shlach*)

In Eretz Yisroel there is a special obligation to keep growing spiritually.

ארץ אכלת יושביה הוא. (במדבר י"ג ל"ב)

"A LAND WHICH DEVOURS THOSE WHO DWELL IN IT." (*Bamidbar* 13:32)

Rabbi Yitzchok of Vorki said that this verse can be understood that the land of Israel is a land which devours those who sit in one place. That is, in *Eretz Yisroel* it is especially important to keep rising higher and higher in spiritual levels. Those who try to stay in one place will not only not rise higher but will start deteriorating. (*Bais Yitzchok: Shlach*)

Realize your own value as a person.

ונהי בעינינו כחגבים וכן היינו בעיניהם. (במדבר י"ג ל"ג)

"AND WE WERE IN OUR OWN SIGHT AS GRASSHOPPERS, AND SO WE WERE IN THEIR SIGHT." (*Bamidbar* 13:33)

The Kotzker Rebbe said that the mistake of the spies was in the words "and so we were in their sight." It should not bother a person how others view him. (*Otzer Chayim*)

A person who worries about how others view him will have no rest. Regardless of what he does or does not do he will always be anxious about receiving the approval of others. Such a person makes his self-esteem dependent on the whims of others. It is a mistake to give others so much control over you. Keep your focus on doing what is right and proper. Work on mastering the ability to have a positive self-image regardless of how others view you. If people give you constructive criticism because of things you are doing wrong, you should appreciate the opportunity to improve. But do not allow your self-image to be dependent on the arbitrary approval and disapproval of others.

The Chofetz Chayim (*Hachofetz Chayim*, vol.3, p.1060) commented: When you view yourself as inferior, you will assume that others also view you in this manner. But the truth could very well be that the other person views you in a much higher manner. As the *Yalkut Shimoni* states, "The Almighty said, 'Who says that you were not in their eyes as angels?'"

The more inferior you consider yourself the lower you feel that others consider you. This can be extremely painful and can prevent a person from accomplishing anything in life. Realize your intrinsic value as a being created in the image of the Almighty and you will feel much more comfortable around other people.

Humility allows a person to be satisfied.

טובה הארץ מאד מאד. (במדבר י"ד ז')

"THE LAND [of Israel] IS VERY, VERY GOOD." (*Bamidbar* 14:7)

Someone who lived in *Eretz Yisroel* once came to Rabbi Moshe of Lelov and was extremely critical of the land. Rabbi Moshe censured him and said, "The Torah tells us that the land is very, very good. When does someone find the good of the land, when he fulfills the *Mishnah* (*Pirke Avos* 4:4) of, 'Be very, very humble.' When someone has the trait of arrogance, he will not be satisfied and will complain about the land." (cited in *Otzer Chayim*)

An arrogant person demands that everything should be exactly as he wishes. He lacks patience and this causes him much frustration and suffering. But a person with humility finds it easy to accept things not being the way he would have wished them to be. He focuses on the positive in each situation and circumstance. He appreciates the spiritual dimension of *Eretz Yisroel* and thus feels great joy in living there.

KORACH

Keep your focus on the goal of doing for the Almighty.

ויקח קרח בן יצהר בן קהת בן לוי. (במדבר ט״ז א׳)

"AND KORACH, THE SON OF YITZHOR, THE SON OF K'HOS, THE SON OF LEVI, TOOK ..." (*Bamidbar* 16:1)

Rashi explains that the key reason for Korach's rebellion against Moshe was that he was envious of another relative who received honor while he didn't.

Envy is destructive. It prevents a person from enjoying what he himself has. When you focus on the success of another person and feel pain because of it, you are likely to do things that are highly counterproductive. Envy is one of the three things that totally destroy a person (*Pirke Avos* 4:28). The downfall of Korach was because of this trait. Not only did he not get what he wanted, but he lost everything he already had.

How does one overcome envy? The key is to focus on what you yourself have and on what you yourself can accomplish in this world. Envy arises when a person looks at others and compares himself to them. The ultimate that anyone can have in this world is happiness. When you master this trait by focusing on those things conducive to happiness, you need never envy any other person.

Rabbi Levi Yitzchok of Berditchev (*Kdushas Levi*) commented that a truly righteous person's main goal in all that he does is to give pleasure to the Almighty. To such a person there is no difference if he or another righteous person causes that pleasure.

But if a person's main focus is on his personal reward, he wants to do everything himself. Therefore our verse states that Korach took. He wanted to take for himself and therefore felt resentment about the attainments of others.

This concept is an important tool for overcoming envy in spiritual matters. Keep your focus on the ultimate goal of doing for the Almighty. When this is your focus, you will feel pleasure when others accomplish spiritually and will be free from envy.

When someone speaks against others realize that he could be just projecting his own faults.

ויקהלו על משה ועל אהרן ויאמרו אלהם רב לכם כי כל העדה כלם
קדשים ובתוכם השם ומדוע תתנשאו על קהל השם. (במדבר ט"ז ג')

"AND THEY GATHERED AGAINST MOSHE AND AHARON. AND THEY SAID TO THEM, YOU HAVE TAKEN TOO MUCH POWER FOR YOURSELVES. THE ENTIRE CONGREGATION IS HOLY, AND THE ALMIGHTY IS IN THEIR MIDST. WHY DO YOU TAKE LEADERSHIP OVER THE CONGREGATION OF THE ALMIGHTY?" (*Bamidbar* 16:3)

The Kotzker Rebbe commented that people who quarrel with the righteous try to find complaints in ways that are the exact opposite of truth. Moshe was the most humble of men, and Aharon's relationship with others was always to pursue peace which takes much humility. Nevertheless, this did not stop Korach and his followers from claiming that Moshe and Aharon were acting arrogantly and were taking too much power for themselves. (cited in *Maayanah Shel Torah*)

This is an important lesson in our being careful not to believe *loshon hora*. Some people have the attitude that if someone is critical of another person, what is said must have at least some truth to it. No! People can have the audacity to find fault with others even though the person excels in the exact traits that are being referred to. Here the motive of Korach was personal envy and he was projecting his own drive for power unto Moshe.

Remember that the Sages say that when a person finds fault with others he frequently is just mentioning his own faults which he can wrongly assume someone else has. Be very careful not to accept negative information about others as the truth without a careful examination.

Don't take it personally if someone who verbally abuses others insults you.

לכן אתה וכל עדתֶּך הנעדים על השם ואהרן מה הוא כי תלינו עליו. (במדבר ט"ז י"א)

"THEREFORE YOU AND YOUR CONGREGATION WHO GATHER TOGETHER ARE AGAINST THE ALMIGHTY; AND AHARON WHO IS HE THAT YOU COMPLAIN AGAINST HIM." (*Bamidbar* 16:11)

Rabbi Shlomo Kluger wrote that when someone verbally abuses a very distinguished and elevated person and then does the same to a simple person, the simple person will not take offense because of what was said. This is what Moshe said to Korach. Since you are really complaining against the Almighty, how can your words hurt Aharon? He will easily remain oblivious to what you say since he sees that you also have complaints against the Almighty. (*Imrai Shaifer*)

When coming into contact with a very critical person or with a coarse person who speaks roughly and with insolence to everyone, you need not take offense at what he says. He does not only speak this way towards you but does so to others also. There is therefore no reason to take what he says against you personally. Realize that the problem is his, not yours, and free yourself from any possible hurt feelings because of what he says.

Keep trying to make peace.

וישלח משה לקרא לדתן ולאבירם בני אליאב ויאמרו לא נעלה. (במדבר ט"ז י"ב)

"AND MOSHE SENT TO CALL DASAN AND AVIRAM THE SONS OF ALIAV, AND THEY SAID, WE WILL NOT GO UP." (*Bamidbar* 16:12)

Rashi cites the Talmud (*Sanhedrin* 110a) that from here we see the principle that one should not keep up a quarrel. Moshe took the initiative to go after them to make peace.

Rabbi Yitzchok of Vorki commented: The Sages said there is no *chazakah* in a quarrel. A *chazakah* means that since a situation is a certain way we assume that it was that way before and will remain that way. But if you try to make peace when there is a quarrel, never say that since you have already tried and have not been successful it will be impossible for you to make peace. Even if you have not been successful in the past, there is always the possibility that you will be able to make peace now.

Even if someone seems very obstinate and many people have tried to reason with him and have failed, it is always possible that a new approach or a new strategy might work to bring about peace. There is no guarantee that any two people will be able to be the best of friends, but at least from a distance people should be on peaceful terms with each other. Disputes and feuds are so destructive that it is always worthwhile to keep doing all you can to make peace.

One very important principle for bringing about peace is a willingness to apologize to someone. There are some people who refuse to apologize to others even if they are clearly wrong. They are very stubborn about the matter and this keeps quarrels going for much longer than necessary. Other people are willing to say they are sorry when they realize they have made a mistake. But they still refuse to apologize if they feel that they are right and the other person is wrong. This, too, can needlessly prolong disputes. A person who sincerely loves and seeks peace will be willing to apologize to someone who feels hurt even if he thinks that he really did not do anything wrong. While this should not be done in situations when someone will take advantage of you, in most instances you lose absolutely nothing and gain much in terms of harmony and peaceful relationships by saying, "I am sorry."

True humility is to show honor and respect to everyone.

ויחר למשה מאד ויאמר אל השם אל תפן אל מנחתם לא חמור אחד מהם
נשאתי ולא הרעתי את אחד מהם. (במדבר ט״ז ט״ו)

"AND MOSHE WAS VERY PAINED AND HE SAID TO THE ALMIGHTY,
DO NOT TURN TO THEIR OFFERINGS. I DID NOT TAKE EVEN ONE
MULE OF THEIRS. AND I DID NOT HARM EVEN ONE OF THEM."
(*Bamidbar* 16:15)

Rabbi Meir Simcha Hacohen explained that if a person has false
humility, he will be willing to act in a humble manner when
interacting with people who are much lower than him in stature or
intellect. He knows that everyone realizes he is above those people
and is not worried about losing honor in the eyes of others. But
with those who are equal to him in stature or above him he will not
act humbly at all. He fears that others will think that he is below
these people and since he is really an honor-seeker he does not
want people to think he is lower than anyone else. With these
people he will do everything he can to show that he is above them.
This is what Moshe, the truly humble man, said. I did not do
anything negative to anyone, even those who are distinguished. I
did nothing to belittle the stature of any person. (*Meshech
Chochmah*)

When a person is able to show honor and respect to competitors,
that is a sign of true humility. The arrogant person thinks, "If I
honor this person, what will people think of me? Will it raise or
lower my stature in the eyes of others?" But the humble person
makes no calculations of this kind. He treats each person according
to the Torah ideals of how people should be treated. Ultimately
this only elevates a person's true stature regardless of how other
people might react.

Rabbi Isser Zalman Meltzer used to give a weekly Talmudic
lecture in his yeshiva. One of the students who usually remained
silent during the lecture once spoke up and said, "The *Sfas Emes*

explains this section differently than what was just said." The Rosh Hayeshiva replied, "If the *Sfas Emes* explains the *Gemora* differently, I should really stop my lecture right away. But I ask of you a favor. I worked hard to prepare this lecture. Do me a *chesed* and give me permission to continue the lecture which I prepared with so much effort."

The statement of Rabbi Meltzer seemed a bit strange. Even if another scholar explained the passage differently, he had a right to offer his own interpretation. As Rabbi Meltzer frequently said about similar situations, "He explains his way and I explain my way."

Immediately after the lecture, one of the top students ran to the yeshiva's library and looked up the *Sfas Emes's* commentary. He saw that the *Sfas Emes's* explanation was really consistent with the Rosh Hayeshiva's interpretation. The student ran over to Rabbi Meltzer and told him this. "I am familiar with what the *Sfas Emes* wrote," said Rav Isser Zalman, "and you are right, there is no contradiction there to what I said."

The student was very curious about the Rosh Hayeshiva's reaction and walked him home. On the way Rav Isser Zalman explained, "During the lecture I noticed a businessman who never before came to my lectures. Also, this fellow who asked the question usually does not ask questions during the lecture. I assumed that there might be a possible *shiduch* between the young man and the businessman's daughter. I'm not certain that this man has a daughter but most likely he does. Probably the fellow asked the question to impress the businessman that he knows how to learn. I replied the way I did to raise this student in the eyes of his prospective father-in-law."

A few weeks later this young man actually became engaged to that person's daughter. (*Bederech Aitz Hachayim*, vol.1, pp.223-4)

At times kindness requires that we use harsh measures.

ויאמר משה בזאת תדעון כי השם שלחני לעשות את כל המעשים האלה כי לא מלבי. (במדבר ט"ז כ"ח)

"AND MOSHE SAID, WITH THIS YOU SHALL KNOW THAT THE ALMIGHTY SENT ME TO DO ALL THESE THINGS, I DID NOT MAKE THEM UP." (*Bamidbar* 16:28)

Moshe goes on to tell Korach and his followers that they would soon die unnatural deaths (verses 29-35). This might appear to be very cruel on Moshe's part. To explain Moshe's reaction, the Alshich gives the analogy of a doctor who sees a need to amputate a person's hand or foot in order that a disease should not spread. Although this might seem cruel, it is really an act of kindness because it saves the person's life. Similarly, Moshe saw that Korach's rebellion was spreading and he had 250 followers already. In order to save the rest of the nation, Moshe, with his compassion for everyone else, had to use stringent measures. (*Toras Moshe: Alshich*)

True kindness at times will obligate us to use approaches that might appear very strict. But the key factor is always our motivation and the entire situation. If someone sees a young child playing with matches and grabs them from him, the child will most probably cry and think that this person is very cruel. But only a person who is apathetic or callous would allow the child to continue playing with matches. Using harsh measures when they are not absolutely needed is cruel. But failing to use harsh measures when they are the only approach available in order to help someone is also cruel. The person who is truly kind will weigh each situation carefully to see what is needed. People who lack compassion use this concept as a rationalization to be cruel, which is very wrong. But misplaced softness also has negative consequences. Much wisdom and compassion are needed to apply the appropriate methods in each situation.

During the Eichmann trial, a certain Jew announced that he was willing to serve as a witness for the defense of this enemy of the Jewish people. Apparently he was promised a large sum of money for his services. That person traveled from out of the country to Jerusalem to deliver his testimony. Although members of his family tried to persuade him to refrain from testifying, they were unsuccessful. They had a lot of pain from this and on the day that person was supposed to deliver his testimony they came to Rabbi Dov Bairish Wiedenfeld, the Rav of Tshabin, and poured out their hearts about the *chilul Hashem* their relative was going to cause.

The Tshabiner Rav was ill at the time and felt very weak. Nevertheless, he sent a messenger to the person who was already on his way to testify in court and told him to come to his house at once. "I am notifying you that it is forbidden for you to testify," Rabbi Wiedenfeld said to him. That man tried to argue that he already made a commitment that he would testify and he couldn't back down. Although the Tshabiner Rav was a very kindhearted and gentle person, he spoke strongly, "I am telling you another time that you should not go to testify. And if you do not listen to me, I will entirely destroy you from your roots." He said this with great emotion and his entire body was shaking while his face became white. When he finished these words he immediately left the room without waiting for a reply. The deep emotion with which these words were said had their effect and at the last moment the person refrained from his evil intentions. (*Rabosainu*, p.258)

During a quarrel focus on making peace not on blaming.

ולא יהיה כקרח וכעדתו. (במדבר י"ז ה')

"THERE SHALL NOT BE LIKE KORACH AND HIS CONGREGATION." (*Bamidbar* 17:5)

Rabbi Chayim Shmuelevitz commented that this verse tells us an important principle about quarrels. The verse is definitely a prohibition against being involved in quarrels (see *Love Your Neighbor*, pp.349-51). But the verse can also be read: There will not be other quarrels like that of Korach and his followers. In this instance Moshe was one hundred percent right, and Korach was one hundred percent wrong. But in most arguments and feuds even if one side is more correct than the other both sides are usually making some mistakes. (Heard from Rabbi Shmuelevitz)

When two people quarrel, each person usually tries to blame the other for what he did or said. But it is more productive for both people to ask themselves what they did to contribute to the quarrel. Even if it is ninety percent the other person's fault, if things you said or did contributed ten percent, you should make every effort to eliminate your ten percent in the future. For example, you might have spoken in a slightly angry tone or could have been a bit sarcastic and then the other person greatly overreacted. Most outside observers might blame the other person for what he did or said in his rage. But if you sincerely want to bring about peace, you will have to work on your tone of voice and the content of what you say to stop provoking that person. This is especially true for family quarrels.

Moreover, in many family quarrels neither side is really right or wrong. The personalities of the parties involved are different. Each person can be one hundred percent right from his point of view and according to his personality. But together there is a strong clash. When you stop blaming and condemning the other party, you will be calm enough to work out peaceful solutions.

When involved in a personal quarrel, do not focus on who is right and who is wrong, but focus on peace. Ask yourself, "What can be said or done so that all the people involved can be satisfied?"

CHUKAS

When necessary to correct a fault behave in the extreme opposite manner.

זאת חקת התורה אשר צוה השם לאמר. (במדבר י"ט ב')

"THIS IS THE STATUTE OF THE TORAH WHICH THE ALMIGHTY COMMANDED SAYING..." (*Bamidbar* 19:2)

Sforno notes the paradox involved in the purification of the *Parah Adumah* (the Red Heifer). A person who became spiritually impure through contact with a corpse became pure through the process described in this section of the Torah. While this process purified the person who underwent it, it also caused people who were previously pure to become impure. Moreover, in verse 6 we see that wood from a cedar tree was used, which denotes strength and power, and also a hyssop which is a humble leaf. This whole section symbolizes the concept that when a person has a fault he needs to go to the opposite extreme in order to correct his fault. Normally the proper way to behave is the middle path in all traits, and it is considered a fault if someone is too extreme in any area. But when a person has a fault, which is symbolized by the scarlet that was used (verse 6), he should behave in the extreme opposite manner. This extreme behavior is wrong for the average person but is correct for him. This is symbolized by the fact that the same thing that can cause impurity for one person brings about purity for someone else.

Be aware of what traits you need to correct. For a limited amount of time act in a manner that is diametrically opposed to your usual way of behaving until you find yourself automatically behaving appropriately. For example, a person who has a bad temper and frequently gets angry should for a while ignore anything that happens that he does not like. If a person finds that he speaks *loshon hora*, he should make an effort not to speak at all about other people even those things which are really permissible.

Rabbi Simcha Zissel of Kelm noticed that one of his young daughters had a tendency to like money. In order to prevent this trait from taking root, each day he would give her some money and took her over to a charity *pushka* where she would place the money she was given. In this way he trained her to be generous. (*Tnuas Hamussar*, vol.2, p.92)

Love for others necessitates making sacrifices.

וטמא הכהן עד הערב. (במדבר י"ט ז')

"AND THE PRIEST IS IMPURE UNTIL THE EVENING." (*Bamidbar* 19:7)

Rabbi Yitzchok of Vorki said that the essence of the *Parah Adumah* (that is, the whole procedure of purifying those who were spiritually impure) is the concept of "Love your neighbor." His grandson, Rabbi Mendel of Vorki explained that this is because the priest who was involved in the purification process became impure himself by the same process that purified the person who came to him. When someone loses out himself in order to help someone else, that is the ultimate in love for one's fellow man. (*Bais Yitzchok: Chukas*)

A person who is not willing to make any sacrifices for other people will always find reasons why it is too difficult for him to do acts of kindness for others. To help others takes time, energy, and money. But when someone truly loves another person, he feels pleasure in all the sacrifices that he makes for him. The greater your love for someone, the more sacrifices you are willing to make. Therefore the test of your level of love for your fellow man is the amount of sacrifices you are willing to make. A person who is not willing to make any sacrifices shows that he lacks love for others. Where do you stand?

Rabbi Moshe Leib of Sassov married a girl who was poor, lacked intelligence, and was ugly. He was a person with great compassion and he said, "If I don't marry her, who will?" (*Horav Maiapte*)

Always find time to study Torah.

זאת התורה אדם כי ימות באהל. (במדבר י"ט י"ד)

"THIS IS THE TORAH, IF A PERSON DIES IN A TENT..." (*Bamidbar* 19:14)

The Sages (*Brochos* 63b) state that the Torah only lasts with those who die over it. This seems very puzzling since the Torah is for living, as it states (*Vayikra* 18:5), "And you shall live with them (the commandments)."

The Chofetz Chayim gave the following analogy. A very successful merchant was so busy taking care of the customers who came to his store that he had no time for Torah study. He noticed one day that his hair was turning gray and he realized that he was getting older. He knew that the day he would leave this world was getting closer. He therefore decided that he would go each morning to the synagogue to pray with a *minyan* and to study Torah for a couple of hours.

When he came late to the store, his wife was frantic. People would have come to his store if he were there and they were losing customers. He calmly told his wife, "What would I do if the Angel of Death came to me and told me that my time in this world was up? Could I tell him that I can't go yet since I'll miss out on customers? If I were already dead I would not be able to come to the store. Therefore each day let us imagine for a couple of hours that I have already died. This way I am able to study Torah each day."

This, said the Chofetz Chayim, is what the Sages are advising us. You might be very busy and feel that you do not have any time to study Torah. But if you will just view yourself as if you were already dead, you will find the time to study Torah which gives life to those who study it. (*Chofetz Chayim al Hatorah*)

When doctors told Rabbi Akiva Eger that he might not live much longer if he continued his intensive study of Torah, he replied, "If I study Torah, I may not live much longer; if I discontinue my studies of Torah, I certainly will not live much longer. Doubt must not prevail against certainty!" (*Jewish Leaders*, p.111)

Join others who are involved in good deeds.

ויאמר השם אל משה ואל אהרן יען לא האמנתם בי להקדישני לעיני בני ישראל לכן לא תביאו את הקהל הזה אל הארץ אשר נתתי להם. (במדבר כ' י"ב)

"AND THE ALMIGHTY SAID TO MOSHE AND TO AHARON, BECAUSE YOU DID NOT BELIEVE IN ME TO SANCTIFY ME IN THE EYES OF THE CHILDREN OF ISRAEL, THEREFORE YOU WILL NOT BRING THIS CONGREGATION TO THE LAND WHICH I GAVE THEM." (*Bamidbar* 20:12)

Rashi comments: If Moshe were to have spoken to the rock (instead of hitting it) and it would have given forth water, the Almighty would have been sanctified in the eyes of the congregation. The people would say, "If this rock which does not speak and does not hear fulfills the word of the Almighty, all the more so should we."

We see here that the essence of sanctifying the Almighty's name is not merely that someone should be impressed by another person's righteous behavior. It is not sufficient for someone to just think that you are acting in an elevated manner. Rather the key factor is that other people should be influenced to improve their own behavior. Whenever you behave in a manner that influences others to follow the Almighty's will, you have sanctified His name.

Midrash Tanchuma says on this verse that although Moshe was the main one who erred, since Aharon was with Moshe he was also included in the punishment. Rabbi Yehuda Leib Chasman (*Ohr Yohail*, vol.2) commented that since the Sages (*Sotah* 11a and *Tosfos*) say that for the positive a person is rewarded five hundred times more than he is punished for doing something wrong, we can see how great it is to be together with someone who fulfills a *mitzvah*. In this instance Moshe's transgression was based on a slight error on his part; nevertheless both he and Aharon were punished strongly in their not being able to enter the land of *Eretz Yisroel*. Therefore even when someone is involved in a small *mitzvah* joining with him brings great reward. All the more so, when someone is involved in a very large *mitzvah* the reward for being part of it is immense.

Whenever you have a chance to join someone who is involved in a good deed, do so. Even if the other person is the main one who is accomplishing the good deed, joining with him is such a wonderful thing that it should give you great joy.

The Almighty causes suffering for our benefit.

ויאמר השם אל משה עשה לך שרף ושים אתו על נס והיה כל הנשוך וראה אתו וחי. (במדבר כ"א ח')

"AND THE ALMIGHTY SAID TO MOSHE. MAKE FOR YOURSELF THE IMAGE OF A SNAKE AND PLACE IT ON A POLE. AND IT WILL BE THAT EVERYONE WHO WAS BITTEN SHALL SEE IT AND WILL LIVE." (*Bamidbar* 21:8)

Commentators note that the snakes bit the people and the image of the snake was the cure. Rabbi Chayim Shmuelevitz explained that when a person hits someone, it comes from anger and hatred, but when he helps another person, it comes from compassion and love. With the Almighty, however, even when He causes a person to suffer, it comes from His compassion and love. In the overall scheme of things a person gains from that suffering. It is either atonement, it serves as a lesson to teach a person to improve, or it elevates a person. Therefore the smiting and the cure can be from the same thing because they both come from the attribute of love. (Heard from Rabbi Shmuelevitz at the Kiddush on the Shabbos before the wedding of Rabbi Heshy Weissman, Rosh Kollel of Meshech Chochmah)

While being smitten hurts regardless of the motivation of the one who smites you, it is much easier to cope with when you know that it is ultimately beneficial for you and comes from love. When a dentist removes a rotten tooth, it is less painful than if a gangster knocks out a tooth. Realizing the Almighty's love for you will render all the suffering in your life as meaningful and purposeful. When you find meaning in your suffering, it is much easier to accept it with a positive attitude.

Be joyous for the good fortune of others.

ויעש משה נחש נחשת וישמהו על הנס והיה אם נשך הנחש את איש והביט אל נחש הנחשת וחי. (במדבר כ"א ט')

"AND MOSHE MADE A BRASS SNAKE, AND HE PLACED IT ON A POLE, AND IT WAS THAT IF A SNAKE BIT A PERSON HE WOULD GAZE AT THE BRASS SNAKE AND WOULD LIVE." (*Bamidbar* 21:9)

The term *vehayah* denotes joy (*Midrash Rabbah: Esther* Intro.:11). Why then does the Torah use it in this verse since being bitten by a snake is painful and not something that one would feel joy over? Rabbi Meir Simcha Hacohen explained that in the previous verse (21:8) the Almighty said that everyone who was bitten would live when he gazed at the brass snake on the pole. This includes someone who was deathly ill from a previous disease. If he was bitten by one of the snakes, he would be totally cured from everything by gazing at the brass snake. Therefore such a person would experience joy if he were bitten by a snake, for this would now make him eligible to regain his total health. For this reason the Torah uses the term *vehayah*, it was a joyous occurrence. (*Meshech Chochmah*)

But one can ask on this: The joy was only for those specific people who were previously seriously ill. Why is this considered joyous for everyone? We see here the idea that everyone who was bitten by a snake could experience the joy of those specific people who gained greatly. Those bitten by the snake suffered pain but had a means of being cured hence the bite was painful but not fatal. Even though they themselves suffered they could empathize with those who were gaining greatly. Since they could view the situation as positive because of those who gained, everyone had a joyous reaction.

Set aside time for a daily accounting of your behavior.

עַל כֵּן יֹאמְרוּ הַמֹּשְׁלִים בֹּאוּ חֶשְׁבּוֹן תִּבָּנֶה וְתִכּוֹנֵן עִיר סִיחוֹן. (במדבר כ"א כ"ז)

"BECAUSE OF THAT, THEY WHO SPEAK IN PARABLES SAY: COME TO CHESHBON. LET THE CITY OF SICHON BE BUILT AND ESTABLISHED." (*Bamidbar* 21:27)

The Talmud (*Bava Basra* 78b) states on this verse: "*Hamoshlim* refers to those who rule over their impulses. *Bo-ooh cheshbon*, come and make a calculation of your behavior. Think about what you lose by performing a good deed and weigh that against all that you gain from it. Think about what you gain from transgressing and weigh that against what you lose. If you do this, you will be built up in this world, and will be established in the world to come."

In reference to keeping an account of one's behavior, Rabbi Moshe Chayim Luzzatto wrote that a person needs to keep an eye on all that he does. A person should work on overcoming all of his negative habits and negative traits. Successful businessmen keep close track of all of their investments and constantly weigh their financial situation. So too a person should make an accounting of his behavior each day to work on self-improvement. Set aside special times for this accounting for the benefits are very great.

Rav Moshe Chayim Luzzatto goes on to explain the Talmudic statement cited above, that those who rule over their impulses advise everyone to make an accounting of their behavior. He uses as a metaphor the mazes that very wealthy aristocrats used to have on their property. These mazes were formed from bushes and shrubbery and were very complex. It was difficult for a person to find the correct path since so many of the paths led the wrong way. Only someone who successfully found the correct path and stood on the high area above the entire scene could give another person advice on how to avoid the traps and get to the destination. Similarly, only someone who is successful in mastering his impulses can advise others on how to do it. What is their advice? Constantly weigh your behavior and see the benefits of doing good and the harm of doing evil. (*Mesilas Yeshorim*, ch.3)

When you do make an accounting of your behavior, feel joy in every bit of improvement. Do not allow yourself to become discouraged when you see your faults and mistakes. When you keep your focus on how you have already done something positive, you will be motivated to keep on improving.

BALAK

An arrogant person tries to fool others to give him more honor.

ויאמר בלעם אל האלקים בלק בן צפר מלך מואב שלח אלי. (במדבר כ"ב י')

"AND BILAAM SAID TO THE ALMIGHTY: BALAK, THE SON OF TZIPOR, THE KING OF MOAV SENT TO ME." (*Bamidbar* 22:10)

Rashi explains that Bilaam was saying to the Almighty, "Even though I am not considered distinguished in Your eyes, I am still considered distinguished in the eyes of kings."

My late Rebbe, Rabbi Yosef Dov Soloveitchik of Brisk in Yerushalayim, noted that Rashi to verse 8 states that Bilaam told the messengers who came to call him to go to Balak that perhaps the Almighty would not allow him to go with people who were not of high stature. He must consult with the Almighty who might only allow him to travel with people who were more distinguished than they were. We see here how an arrogant person plays games with others, even with the Almighty. Bilaam kept trying to build himself up in the eyes of others. He therefore told the messengers that the Almighty considered him more important than they did. And later he told the Almighty that Balak considered him more distinguished than the Almighty did. The arrogant man tries to fool even the Almighty into giving him more respect and honor.

The arrogant person tries to escape from reality. He considers it of utmost importance to be considered distinguished in the eyes of others. Even if no one truly respects him, he will cunningly try to trick people into believing that he is more worthy and elevated than he really is. Instead of trying to convince others by means of subterfuge of one's importance, a person should rather focus on improving his behavior and making himself a truly elevated person.

Bias blinds a person from fulfilling the Almighty's will.

ויאמר אלקים אל בלעם לא תלך עמהם לא תאר את העם כי ברוך הוא. (במדבר כ״ב י״ב)

"AND THE ALMIGHTY SAID TO BILAAM, DO NOT GO WITH THEM. DO NOT CURSE THE NATION FOR THEY ARE BLESSED." (*Bamidbar* 22:12)

Rabbi Chayim Shmuelevitz commented that any unbiased person who heard that the Almighty said here not to go with the messengers would understand that the Almighty did not want Bilaam to curse the Jewish people. We see here the power of bias to blind a person from seeing what any unbiased person could see. What did Bilaam report back to the messengers of Balak? That the Almighty considered him so distinguished that He would not allow him to go with them. It is quite possible that Bilaam did not merely lie to them. Rather his own arrogance led him to fool himself about what he thought were the Almighty's intentions. A person always hears what he wants to hear.

Each person has a similar tendency, said Rav Chayim, to interpret the Torah according to his own bias even though his conclusions might be opposite the Torah's true intentions. By being aware of your own biases, you will be able to avoid this trap.

Nothing stands in the way of a strong will.

ויבא אלקים אל בלעם לילה ויאמר לו אם לקרא לך באו האנשים קום לך אתם. (במדבר כ״ב כ׳)

"THE ALMIGHTY CAME TO BILAAM AT NIGHT AND SAID TO HIM: IF THESE PEOPLE CAME TO CALL YOU, ARISE, GO WITH THEM." (*Bamidbar* 22:20)

The Talmud (*Makos* 10b) takes note that previously in verse twelve the Almighty told Bilaam not to go with Balak's messengers who requested that he accompany them to curse the Jewish people. From here the Talmud derives the principle, "In the way a man wishes to go, he is led."

If a person wants to do evil, he will be able to do so. But he will have to pay a heavy price for his successful completion of his evil wishes. Conversely, someone who wishes to study Torah and fulfill the Almighty's commandments will be successful. When you wish to travel along a certain path in life, you will be divinely assisted.

"Nothing stands in the way of a strong will." There are many things that we wish for half-heartedly, but when you strongly set your mind on a particular goal, you will have the strength and abilities necessary to meet that goal. What a person truly wants in life, he will usually obtain. (*Alai Shur*, pp.120-1)

Rabbi Avigdor Miller comments (*Rejoice O Youth*, p.1) that the Almighty guides the person who seeks wisdom, and the amount of guidance is in proportion to the earnestness of the seeker.

When you feel a strong need for something, you will not feel the difficulties which you encounter even though you might have to work very hard to accomplish your goals. When you are not strongly motivated to do something, you will procrastinate and it will take you a very long time. Moreover, you will not do a very good job. (*Chochmah Umussar*, vol.2, p.180)

It is up to you to intensify your will to do good. The stronger your will, the more you will actually accomplish. Lack of spiritual accomplishment does not come from lack of ability, but from lack of will. Work on developing a strong desire for spiritual growth and you will be amazed at the positive changes you will experience.

Rabbi Ben Tzion Yadler used to quote the Alter of Nevardok, "There is no such thing as 'I cannot.' What happens is that a person is missing the will and then he claims that he can't." (*Betuv Yerushalayim*, p.116)

True compassion is based on seeing the entire picture.

ויחר אף אלקים כי הולך הוא ויתיצב מלאך השם בדרך לשטן לו. (במדבר
כ"ב כ"ב)

"AND THE ALMIGHTY WAS ANGRY THAT [Bilaam] WENT, AND AN ANGEL OF THE ALMIGHTY STOOD IN THE WAY FOR AN ADVERSARY AGAINST HIM." (*Bamidbar* 22:22)

Rashi explains that the angel that stood in Bilaam's way was an angel of mercy that wanted to prevent him from transgressing so that he should not be lost. In verse 31 we read that the angel had a drawn sword. Rabbi Zalman Sorotzkin commented on this that at times an angel of mercy who is trying to save a person will appear to him as an adversary who is out to harm him. (*Oznayim Letorah*)

When a person has many faults, he will often have friends and relatives who keep trying to influence him to improve. He is likely to view their nagging as extremely irritating and painful and will consider them as his enemies. But the truth is that they have his best interests in mind. He should not only not be angry at them but should even be appreciative and grateful that they are concerned about his welfare. When someone tries to have a positive influence on you, thank him for it.

Rabbi Zalman Sorotzkin also commented that from here we see that at times an angel of mercy has to be willing to take an aggressive stance in order to prevent someone from destroying himself and others. (*ibid.*)

True compassion is based on seeing the entire picture. For instance, a parent who allows his child to do whatever he wants just because he does not want his child ever to cry, might allow his child to do all kinds of things that are destructive both spiritually and to his physical well-being. When you really care about someone, you do not want him to harm himself and will be willing at times to be strict in order to protect him from his own ignorance or foolishness.

When someone acts against your wishes, look for how you might be acting against the Almighty's wishes.

ותרא האתון את מלאך השם נצב בדרך וחרבו שלופה בידו ותט האתון מן הדרך ותלך בשדה ויך בלעם את האתון להטתה הדרך. (במדבר כ"ב כ"ג)

"AND THE DONKEY SAW THE ANGEL OF THE ALMIGHTY STANDING ON THE ROAD AND HIS SWORD WAS DRAWN IN HIS HAND AND THE DONKEY TURNED ASIDE OUT OF THE WAY AND WENT INTO THE FIELD. AND BILAAM HIT THE DONKEY TO TURN HER TO THE ROAD." (*Bamidbar* 22:23)

The Midrash (*Bamidbar Rabbah* 20:14) comments: "This wicked person is going to curse an entire nation which did nothing at all against him, and he hits his donkey to prevent it from going off the road and onto the field."

This teaches us a lesson about the great lack of insight a person can have about himself. Bilaam, the wicked, is now traveling to go and curse the Jewish people even though his going is against the will of the Almighty. At the same time, when his own donkey does a minor thing against his will how does he act? He is very angry and smites it. He was only thinking about how his donkey was acting against his will and was oblivious of how he himself was going against the will of the Almighty at that very moment. (*Nachalas Yosef*, vol.2, p.324)

Whenever you become irritated at someone else for going against your wishes, use that as a cue to try to find ways that you are going against the Almighty's wishes. This way you will be able to utilize those otherwise irritating situations as opportunities for self-improvement. This is especially true when you shout at another person for not listening to you. If you would listen to the Almighty's wishes about how to treat another person, you would talk politely and respectfully to him.

Honor-seeking causes a person to act in a ludicrous and counterproductive manner.

ויאמר בלעם לאתון כי התעללת בי לו יש חרב בידי כי עתה הרגתיך.
(במדבר כ״ב כ״ט)

"AND BILAAM SAID TO THE DONKEY: BECAUSE YOU HAVE MOCKED ME, IF I WERE TO HAVE A SWORD IN MY HAND RIGHT NOW I WOULD KILL YOU." (*Bamidbar* 22:29)

My Rebbe, Rabbi Yosef Dov Soloveitchik of Brisk in Yerushalayim commented on this: Usually why does a person hit a donkey? Because he wants it to go faster. But Bilaam was a pursuer of honor. Therefore when the donkey caused him irritation he considered it a slight to his honor and wanted to kill it. When a person seeks honor, he doesn't realize how ridiculous he is and how he hurts himself. Bilaam said that he wanted to kill the donkey right now. He should have said that he would wait until he reached his destination and only then would he kill it. His seeking honor prevented him from thinking straight. Moreover, the donkey started speaking. This was a miraculous event and Bilaam should have been overwhelmed with amazement. But what does Bilaam focus on? Only one thing: his honor. He seems totally unaware of how unusual the talking of the donkey is and only thinks about how the donkey has slighted his honor. Also, from whom does Bilaam want honor? From a donkey! Every honor-seeker has aspects of this in him. Because of the negativity of this trait one must do all one can to overcome it. The Chofetz Chayim used to say that true honor is when one seeks wisdom. Gaining more wisdom is honorable in itself and when one seeks it one will free oneself from seeking superficial signs of honor that are only illusions.

Be sincere when you regret what you have done wrong.

ויאמר בלעם אל מלאך השם חטאתי כי לא ידעתי כי אתה נצב לקראתי
בדרך ועתה אם רע בעיניך אשובה לי. (במדבר כ"ב ל"ד)

"AND BILAAM SAID TO THE ANGEL OF THE ALMIGHTY: I HAVE
SINNED, FOR I DID NOT KNOW THAT YOU WERE STANDING BEFORE
ME ON THE ROAD, AND NOW IF IT IS BAD IN YOUR EYES I SHALL
RETURN." (*Bamidbar* 22:34)

The Midrash (*Bamidbar Rabbah* 20:15) comments on Bilaam's
saying that he had sinned: "Bilaam was a cunning evil person and
realized that he had to admit that he had sinned in order to be
saved."

That is, Bilaam was totally insincere in saying that he had made a
mistake. True repentance is when a person sincerely regrets the
wrong that he has done. But Bilaam cared not one bit about being
a truly good person. He was full of negative traits and only cared
about gratifying his desires. Therefore he was even willing to say
that he was sorry for what he did if that would get him off the
hook. He had no interest in true self-improvement.

There are two ways that a person can admit that he was wrong.
One is a sincere wish to do what is right and to avoid doing what is
wrong. When a person with integrity sees that he has erred, he truly
regrets what he has done wrong and resolves to improve in the
future. But a person who just says that he realizes he has done
wrong in order to save himself from punishment does not truly
regret the wrongs that he has done, and he will not be resolved to
stop doing wrong in the future. If he feels that he can get away with
doing wrong, he will continue to do it. Do not just say that you are
sorry when you have erred. Rather try to experience sincere regret
and be resolved to actually improve your behavior. If you tell
another person whom you have wronged that you are sorry and the
person sees that you are just saying it so he will leave you alone, he
will not accept your apology. The Almighty is the same. Be sincere
when you tell Him that you are sorry.

Faulty character traits prevent a person from living up to his ideals.

תמת נפשי מות ישרים ותהי אחריתי כמהו. (במדבר כ"ג י')

Bilaam said:
"LET ME DIE THE DEATH OF THE RIGHTEOUS, AND LET MY END BE LIKE HIS." (*Bamidbar* 23:10)

We see from this statement of Bilaam that he realized the truth that one should lead a righteous life. Why then did he himself not live righteously and only wished that he could die and be rewarded as the righteous? Rabbi Simcha Zissel of Kelm explained that although Bilaam had an intellectual awareness of the proper way to live, in his own life he found this too difficult. Because he had faulty character traits, he was not able to live according to the ideals and principles he knew were true. (*Chochmah Umussar*, vol.1, p.78)

We see from here the importance of correcting one's character traits. Without an awareness of what is proper and what is improper one cannot live righteously. But even after one has studied and knows what is good and what is evil, he must be able to follow through in his daily behavior. A person needs to be in control of his impulses. Having this mastery over one's natural tendencies will enable a person to live according to his ideals. Lacking this, one will do all kinds of improper actions. The problem is not one of knowledge, but of self-discipline. For this reason we must work on improving our character traits for only then will we be able to act righteously. It is just wishful thinking to believe that one can do all kinds of evil and still die as a righteous person. The only way to die as a righteous person is to live as one, and to do this takes much self-discipline. But as cited earlier, when a person has a strong will to live a certain way, he will be successful. By building up a strong will to live righteously your entire behavior will be elevated.

In *mussar* circles they used to say it would have been worthwhile for someone to come from great distances to witness the death of Rabbi Nochum Zev Ziv, son of Rabbi Simcha Zissel, to learn from him how one should die. Even though he suffered great pain during his final illness, he was in a state of complete serenity until the very end. His doctor who was not Jewish, a Dr. Grozad, revealed to him that he only had a few days left, but he was prepared for this without any signs of anxiety. The doctor was asked why he told Rabbi Ziv the true nature of his condition since this could have a negative effect on his health. The doctor's reply was, "I know Rabbi Ziv and his elevated spiritual level. He has an internalized awareness that death is just traveling from one world to the next. Therefore he will be able to accept his death with equanimity." (*Tnuas Hamussar*, vol.2, p.105)

PINCHOS

Be willing to do the right thing even if it is not popular.

וידבר השם אל משה לאמר. פינחס בן אלעזר בן אהרן הכהן השיב את
חמתי מעל בני ישראל בקנאו את קנאתי בתוכם ולא כליתי את בני
ישראל בקנאתי. (במדבר כ"ה י-י"א)

"AND THE ALMIGHTY SPOKE TO MOSHE SAYING: PINCHOS THE SON
OF ELIEZER, THE SON OF AHARON THE PRIEST HAS TURNED AWAY
MY ANGER FROM THE CHILDREN OF ISRAEL IN THAT HE WAS
ZEALOUS FOR MY SAKE AMONG THEM, SO THAT I DID NOT
CONSUME THE CHILDREN OF ISRAEL IN MY JEALOUSY." (*Bamidbar*
25:10,11)

The Alshich makes note of the word "among them." Pinchos's
zealous action was not very popular and there were those who were
ready to kill him for his zealousness. Nevertheless, Pinchos was
ready to sacrifice everything to do the will of the Almighty. He
took action even though many people disapproved of what he did.
(*Toras Moshe: Alshich*)

There are many instances in life in which the correct thing to do
is not always the most popular. For example, if a group of people
are speaking *loshon hora* against others, they usually do not
appreciate someone's telling them to stop talking negatively. But a
person whose focus is on doing the will of the Almighty will not be
deterred even if others will insult him for his behavior. In these
matters there is always a thin line between what is proper and
elevated and what is wild, impulsive, and counterproductive. A
Torah scholar should be consulted whenever questions arise.

If you need to act aggressively on occasion be careful that this does not become a habit.

לכן אמר הנני נתן לו את בריתי שלום. (במדבר כ"ה י"ב)

"THEREFORE SAY: I AM GIVING HIM MY COVENANT OF PEACE."
(*Bamidbar* 25:12)

Rabbi Naftoli Tzvi Berlin (the Netziv) commented: Pinchos did a zealous act that could cause someone to become aggressive even when it would not be appropriate. Therefore the Almighty blessed him with a covenant of peace. In all other areas of his life he should be a man of peace. (*Haamek Dovor*)

Our usual state should be one of peace. There are times when it is proper and even necessary to be aggressive. But since this trait is so destructive one must be very careful that it does not become part of one's nature. We become molded by our behavior. If we keep acting a certain way it becomes part of our usual personality. There is a danger that a trait which is frequently negative and sometimes positive depending on the circumstances will be used negatively if it becomes a part of our character. To prevent this from happening with the trait of aggression, someone who has to be aggressive on occasion should go out of his way to be extremely kind and compassionate in other instances.

Although the Chazon Ish was an extremely gentle person who always avoided quarrels and arguments, whenever it was necessary he could act as if he were angry. But even so he remained inwardly calm. Once he spoke with a person who was very active in communal affairs. Suddenly the Chazon Ish looked at him in a very stern manner. He banged his hand on the table and spoke very sharp words. All of this was incongruous with the Chazon Ish's usual behavior. When that person left the room, the Chazon Ish had a wide smile on his face and looked as if he were not at all angry. He told those who were close to him, "What can I do? This person does not listen when you speak to him in any other manner." (*P'air Hador*, vol.3, p.46)

Zealousness with negative motivations is a crime.

והיתה לו ולזרעו אחריו ברית כהנת עולם תחת אשר קנא לאלקיו ויכפר על בני ישראל. (במדבר כ"ה י"ג)

"AND IT SHALL BE FOR HIM AND HIS DESCENDANTS AFTER HIM A COVENANT OF AN EVERLASTING PRIESTHOOD, BECAUSE HE WAS ZEALOUS FOR HIS G-D, AND HE ATONED FOR THE CHILDREN OF ISRAEL." (*Bamidbar* 25:13)

The Torah uses the words, "for his G-d," to tell us that Pinchos's zealousness was entirely with pure intentions, said Rabbi Yehuda Leib Chasman. He had no other motivation whatsoever but to do the will of the Almighty. Without pure intentions an act of zealousness can be a crime in itself. Therefore one must be very certain of one's true motivations before acting zealously. (*Ohr Yohail*, vol.2)

There are many personal motives that could transform an act of zealousness from a *mitzvah* to a transgression. For example, someone might want glory and therefore he acts zealously to be in the limelight. Another person might enjoy excitement. He is bored and wants to be involved in some action. Yet another person might have a grudge against someone or feel envy or personal hatred. He therefore views this moment as an opportunity to embarrass the other person. A fourth person might see some financial gain for himself. Regardless of what the personal motivation is it renders an act of zealousness a sin for personal gain. Frequently it could cause a *chilul Hashem* - a desecration of the Almighty's name. This is especially so when irresponsible youths take action without consulting Torah scholars. (See *Maishiv Dovor*, vol.1, no.44, that the matter is very complex and depends greatly on the time, place, and other factors.) Because of the potentially negative side-effects of zealousness it must be used with great care.

Family ties help a person have greater love for others.

ראובן בכור ישראל בני ראובן חנוך משפחת החנכי. (במדבר כ"ו ה')

"REUVEN WAS THE FIRSTBORN OF ISRAEL. THE SONS OF REUVEN WERE CHANOCH, THE FAMILY OF CHANOCHI..." (*Bamidbar* 26:5)

The Torah (*Braishis* 2:18) tells us that "it is not good for a person to be alone." This, said Rabbi Zalman Sorotzkin, teaches us that we should choose family life over living by ourselves. Besides the joys of a family and the many practical benefits, a family serves as a training ground for a person to build up his love for other people. A person has a natural love for his father and mother, his wife and children and other relatives. Through this love he learns to feel and express love through acts of kindness for his friends, acquaintances, and other people. When the entire Jewish People were in the wilderness it was as if they were one big family living in one place. The only separation was the division of the people into tribes even though they all lived close together. For this reason when the Torah gives us an accounting of the nation in the portion of *Bamidbar*, there is no mention of families, only of tribes. But in Arvus Moav, they were counted right before the division of the land of Israel. They would now be spread out throughout the land and would be separated from each other. Now they were counted according to their families. This was to hint to them that they should keep their family ties even though each person had his own property. By this means they would live in peace and harmony and their love for others would spread. (*Oznayim Letorah*)

When Reb Yaakov Yosef Herman was questioned about the countless tasks that were beneath his dignity which he performed for the guests whom he invited to his home, he answered, "The guests are my children. Is there anything too low or too difficult for a father to do for his children?" (*All for the Boss*, p.434)

Patience is necessary to understand the depth of Torah and to review what you have studied.

לישוב משפחת הישבי. (במדבר כ"ו כ"ד)

"TO YASHUV THE FAMILY OF YASHUVI." (*Bamidbar* 26:24)

The *Ohr Hachayim* commented that the tribe of Yissochor was the tribe devoted to the study of Torah. Therefore among the families of this tribe there are hints to different concepts pertaining to Torah study. The word *yishuv* in this verse refers to the quality of reflecting patiently on Torah ideas. One must spend much time on each detail of the Torah until one fathoms a bit of its depth.

Racing through the Torah in order to read it as fast as possible will lead to a person making many mistakes, or one will miss many insights and concepts that one could gain by a more careful study. The trait necessary for this is patience. The goal is to understand as well as possible. Not only will this trait enable you to concentrate longer on any single idea, but it will also allow you to spend more time reviewing what you have learned. The more you review, the better you will understand and the longer you will remember. When you have been patient and have gained greater comprehension, you will see the benefits of this trait and this will motivate you to continue having this intellectual patience in your Torah studies.

The first time Rabbi Chayim of Volozhin visited the Vilna Gaon he was just nineteen years old. At this young age, Rav Chayim was already well-known as a brilliant scholar. He had a very clear mind, studied diligently, and had a fantastic memory.

"I reviewed all of the Talmudic tractates dealing with the holidays fourteen times," the young genius said. "And still I do not feel that I have sufficient clarity."

"With just 14 times how can you expect to have clarity," replied the Vilna Gaon.

"How many times are necessary?" Rav Chayim asked.

"There is no limit to the amount of times you must review what you have studied," the Vilna Gaon taught him. "Your entire life you must continuously keep on reviewing." (*Hagaon Hachasid Maivilna*, p.195)

You can be successful even if you have less than others.

אלה בני דן למשפחתם וגו'. ארבעה וששים אלף וארבע מאות. (במדבר כ"ו מ"ב-מ"ג)

"THESE ARE THE CHILDREN OF DAN ACCORDING TO THEIR FAMILIES... SIXTY-FOUR THOUSAND AND FOUR HUNDRED." (*Bamidbar* 26:42,43)

The Chofetz Chayim noted that the total population of the tribe of Binyamin was forty-five thousand and six hundred. Dan's population was sixty-four thousand and four hundred. What is so remarkable about this is that Binyamin, the patriarch of the tribe of Binyamin, had ten sons, while his brother Dan had only one son, Chushim (see Ibn Ezra, verse 42). What is even more amazing is that Chushim was handicapped; he was deaf. Although Dan had only one son and Binyamin had ten, Dan had more descendants than Binyamin.

From here we can learn, said the Chofetz Chayim, that if the Almighty wants a person to be successful, he will succeed even if it appears at first that he has less than someone else. It is possible that from one son a person can have more than from ten sons. Similarly, as regards wealth and possessions. There are some people with only a limited amount of money and possessions but they feel happy with what they have and live very cheerful lives. On the opposite side, there are wealthy people who lack true success in life even though they own a lot. (*Chofetz Chayim al Hatorah*)

Some people see that others have more than they do, and they feel so bad about this that they fail to enjoy what they themselves have. This envy is a mistake. You can live a very joyous life even if you appear to have less than others. Pray for the Almighty's blessing with what you have. Quantity is not always a valid measurement for success in life. The person who masters taking pleasure with what he has is guaranteed a life of happiness.

MATOS

Anger is an improper motivation for a vow.

איש כי ידר נדר להשם. (במדבר ל' ג')

"WHEN A PERSON MAKES A VOW TO THE ALMIGHTY..." (*Bamidbar* 30:3)

When do people most frequently make a vow or an oath? When they become angry. Out of anger they swear that they will or will not do something (a *shvuah*) or that something should be forbidden to them (a *neder*). But anger is not the proper motivation for a vow or oath. Rather, the vow should be "to the Almighty." That is, if a person sees that his negative impulses might lead him to transgress, then out of a calculated, willful decision it is proper to make a vow or oath that will motivate him to refrain from transgressing. (*Toras Moshe*: Alshich; also see *Kli Yokr*)

The same actions can be done with various motivations. Depending on your motivation that act will either be a manifestation of a loss of control or an elevated act of self-discipline. When you impulsively do or say things out of anger, you are the servant of your temper. On the other hand, when you decide that doing something can be spiritually harmful for you and therefore you are willing to set up self-restraints, you are becoming the master over your impulses.

Do not remain silent if your silence can be mistaken for agreement with something that is wrong.

ואם החרש יחריש לה אישה מיום אל יום והקים את כל נדריה או את כל אסריה אשר עליה הקים אתם כי החרש לה ביום שמעו. (במדבר ל' ט"ו)

"IF HER HUSBAND WILL REMAIN SILENT FOR A COMPLETE DAY, THEN SHE MUST FULFILL ALL OF HER VOWS OR ALL OF THE BANS WHICH ARE UPON HER. HE HAS ESTABLISHED THEM BECAUSE HE REMAINED SILENT ON THE DAY THAT HE HEARD THEM." (*Bamidbar* 30:15)

Sforno comments: When a person has the ability to protest and remains silent, his silence is similar to verbal consent. When you do not say something to disagree, it is as if you agree with what was said or done.

This concept has many practical applications. Very often, someone might say something in your presence that is improper and you feel that you cannot really influence the person to change his mind or to stop what he is saying. Should you speak up or remain silent? Whenever your silence can be understood by others as agreement with what was said, you have an obligation to speak the truth. This way no one will mistakenly think that you agree with what was said. Moreover, you can never tell; perhaps you will be successful in influencing others to make positive changes. A person who is not very assertive might find this difficult. But learn from the person who says things that should not be said. If he is able to say something that he shouldn't, you certainly have a right to say those things that should be said. He is not afraid to say something improper, you should have the courage to speak up out of idealism.

Speed in doing something difficult is praiseworthy.

וידבר משה אל העם לאמר החלצו מאתכם אנשים לצבא ויהיו על מדין לתת נקמת השם במדין. (במדבר ל"א ג')

"AND MOSHE SPOKE TO THE PEOPLE SAYING: DETACH FROM YOU MEN FOR THE ARMY, AND THEY SHALL BE AGAINST MIDIAN TO TAKE THE ALMIGHTY'S VENGEANCE AGAINST MIDIAN." (*Bamidbar* 31:3)

Rashi cites the *Sifri*: Even though Moshe heard that he would die after this battle, he nevertheless acted with joy and did not procrastinate.

We see here two important traits in doing the will of the Almighty even though we might find it difficult. One trait is joy, the other is acting with alacrity. The more difficult it is to do a good deed the greater the reward (*Pirke Avos* 5:23). The most precious thing a person has is life itself. Knowing that fulfilling the will of the Almighty will cost one's life is the greatest difficulty possible. Exactly because of this Moshe experienced joy in fulfilling this act and he did it with great speed. The more difficult it is for you to do a good deed, the greater joy you can experience. Moreover, speed in such matters is going against one's nature and is highly praiseworthy. The next time you have an opportunity to do a difficult good deed, do it as fast as you can and with inner pleasure.

The Chofetz Chayim used to say, "There are people who complain, 'These days it is so hard to keep the Torah.' They need to learn from workers who are ambitious. They purposely look to find more difficult work in order to earn more money." (*Michtevai Chofetz Chayim: Sichos Hachofetz Chayim*, part 2, p.37)

When someone has complaints against you, try to find some positive aspect to his complaint.

וימסרו מאלפי ישראל אלף למטה. (במדבר ל"א ה')

"AND HE GAVE OVER FROM THE THOUSANDS OF ISRAEL, ONE THOUSAND FROM EACH TRIBE..." (*Bamidbar* 31:5)

Rashi comments on this verse: This is to teach us how cherished their leaders are to the Jewish People. Previously the people were complaining against Moshe to the extent that he said they would soon stone him. Now that they heard that Moshe would die as soon as they fought against the Midianites, they did not want to wage war against them and Moshe had to coerce them to give over the soldiers who would fight.

The question arises: Since Rashi is talking about the praise of the Jewish People why did he have to mention that they previously had strong complaints against Moshe. The Shaloh replied that when a person complains against someone else it can come from a positive quality. Because the Israelites considered Moshe to be their loving leader who was like a father to them, they demanded of him the same support that one would have demanded of a father. From the fact that they wanted Moshe to continue being their leader and did not want to do anything that would hasten the moment of his departure, it showed that their previous complaints came out of the closeness they felt towards him. (*Shnai Luchos Habris*)

When someone has complaints against you, it frequently can be quite painful. But if you find positive aspects to those complaints, you will be able to cope with them much more effectively. For example, if someone complains that you did not do more for him than you actually did, it shows that he considers you a compassionate and capable person from whom he has a right to expect more. He does not have this complaint against a complete stranger, nor against someone whom he thinks is incompetent. In general, when someone finds fault with you or complains against you, try to find some positive aspect in what he is saying. Mastery of this ability to reframe potentially negative statements will free you from much emotional pain in your life.

When trying to make peace between members of a family, show them how their frustration and anger is really based on their care and concern for each other and on a belief in the strengths of the other person. For instance, when a child views his parent's anger towards him as concern for his well-being, he will find it easier to fulfill the commandment of honoring his parents.

If you have done wrong in the past, do an equal amount of good in the present.

ויאמר אלעזר הכהן אל אנשי הצבא הבאים למלחמה זאת חקַת התורה.
אַך את הזהב ואת הכסף וגו'. (במדבר ל"א כ"א-כ"ב)

"AND ELIEZER THE PRIEST SAID TO THE MEN OF THE ARMY WHO WERE COMING TO THE WAR: THIS IS THE STATUTE OF THE TORAH... BUT THE GOLD AND THE SILVER..." (*Bamidbar* 31:21,22)

This section of the Torah deals with the kashering of vessels that were previously used for unkosher food. It was imperative to remove any unkosher food that was absorbed in the vessel before using it for kosher food. First it was necessary to clean out the vessels very well and to remove any rust. Then the vessels were kashered by the same method as they were previously used. If they were used directly on the fire, they needed to have direct contact with fire to render them fit to be used. If nonkosher food was cooked in them with boiling water, they now needed to be immersed in boiling water to remove what was absorbed.

The Chofetz Chayim commented on this that the same applies to purifying people from their spiritual impurities and defects. First a person must remove the "rust" of his transgressions by means of repentance; regretting what one has done wrong and accepting upon oneself not to continue doing those things in the future. Afterwards you need to be careful that the positive actions you will do to replace the negative behavior will be on the same level as the negative things you have done. So if you were enthusiastic and energetic in doing wrong, you should now have similar enthusiasm and energy when doing good. Moreover, you should now use what you have erred with to make amends. If you have used your ability to speak to relate *loshon hora*, you should now utilize speech for studying Torah. If you have done much wrong in your life, you should presently make a special effort to engage in a large amount of *mitzvos*. (*Chofetz Chayim al Hatorah*)

If you are impulsive, work on becoming more patient.

ויבאו בני גד ובני ראובן. (במדבר ל"ב ב')

"AND THE MEMBERS OF THE TRIBE OF GAD AND THE TRIBE OF REUVEN CAME..." (*Bamidbar* 32:2)

The tribes of Reuven and Gad had large herds of cattle and wanted the land on the other side of the Jordan as their territory. When they approached Moshe to make this request, the tribe of Gad came first even though Reuven was the oldest of the twelve brothers and his tribe is mentioned first in the previous verse. The descendants of Reuven were embarrassed to go first because Reuven's rebuke from his father Yaakov was that he was impulsive as water. By their refraining from acting impulsively they rectified the previous fault. (*Sifsai Cohen*)

A person who is impulsive will make many errors. The negative trait can cause both oneself and others much harm. The Rambam writes that the way to overcome any negative trait is to act in a manner that is diametrically opposed to that trait. If you tend to be impulsive make a resolution to act in a patient and thoughtful manner. By working on the positive trait of patience you will eventually overcome your tendency to be impulsive.

Your good deeds are a spiritual monument that is everlasting.

ונבח הלך וילכד את קנת ואת בנתיה ויקרא לה נבח בשמו. (במדבר ל"ב מ"ב)

"AND NOVACH WENT AND CAPTURED KENAS AND ITS SURROUNDING VILLAGES AND HE CALLED IT NOVACH AFTER HIS NAME." (*Bamidbar* 32:42)

Rashi cites Rabbi Moshe Hadarshan that this name did not last, and this is implied in the verse through a grammatical point (see Rashi).

What is the purpose of the Torah's writing this? Rabbi Samson Raphael Hirsch said that this teaches us an important principle. Throughout the world powerful leaders have wanted to leave monuments to themselves through statues and buildings named after them. Kings and conquerors have even named large cities after themselves. But names can very easily be changed and then nothing is left, as happened to Novach. The good deeds of a person and his spiritual attainments are the only true everlasting monuments. (cited in *Otzer Chayim*)

When you view the good that you do as your eternal monument, you will feel greater motivation to accomplish as much as you can. Any material monument will eventually deteriorate. Others might remember you for a while, but eventually all will be forgotten. A life of spiritual attainments is everlasting. Why put one's focus on something that is temporary when you have the choice of building up a spiritual structure that is forever? Feel joy in every positive act you do, for it gives greater splendor to your monument.

MASAI

Take pleasure in not hurting others with words.

פי החירת. (במדבר ל"ג ז')

"PI HACHIROS" (*Bamidbar* 33:7)

According to *Sefer Glilai Zahav* this was a form of idolatry that proclaimed total freedom of the mouth (the Hebrew words can be translated as such). That is, a person can say whatever he happens to feel like saying; he should be able to slander and insult others whenever he wants. (cited in *Otzer Chayim*)

There are people who feel that to be true to themselves they must say anything that comes to their minds. This leads them to be blunt and tactless when speaking to others. They only think of themselves and what they want, but are oblivious to the pain and suffering they cause others by their verbal abuse. This tendency is antithetical to the whole concept of loving one's fellow man. If you have even a minimum amount of kindness and concern for the suffering of others, you will feel pleasure in guarding your tongue from hurting anyone emotionally. You will experience joy every time you control an impulse to say something that could cause another person pain.

If you have caused people pain with words in the past, go out of your way to give people strength and encouragement from now on. Elevate your power of speech by helping others with it.

Realizing your true purpose in this world will eliminate violence.

ויסעו מאילם ויחנו על ים סוף. (במדבר ל"ג י')

"AND THEY TRAVELED FROM AILIM AND THEY ENCAMPED BY YAM SUF." (*Bamidbar* 33:10)

Ailim hints to the word *alimus* which means violence. *Yam Suf* hints to the word *sof*, the end. They traveled from the trait of violence. How? By coming to the trait of looking at the end of a person. (*Toras Avos*)

Violence includes both actions and words. There is the physical violence of hitting or pushing someone, and there is the verbal violence of shouting at someone or putting him down. Any form of violence not in self-defense is against the principles of Torah. What is the main cause of violence? Frustration and anger! When you become frustrated and angry, you are likely to lash out at someone. When you remember your true purpose in this world, most things that get other people angry will not affect you very strongly. Also, the more you appreciate life and the more joyous you feel the less angry you will become. By remembering the end of each person you will gain a greater appreciation for life. You will value your time and utilize every opportunity for growth. This awareness will keep you far away from any form of violence.

Do not allow temporary desires to harm you.

ויסעו מקברת התאוה. (במדבר ל"ג י"ז)

"AND THEY TRAVELED FROM KIVROS HATAAVAH." (*Bamidbar* 33:17)

Rabbi Yitzchok of Vorki said that the Torah hints to us here to keep a distance from desires. *Kivros* comes from the word *kever*, a burial site. *Taavah* is desires. A person needs to be on guard that his desires do not cause him an early burial. How does one overcome his desires? By remembering that "they traveled." Our stay in this world is only temporary, so do not allow temporary desires to destroy your life.

Desires can destroy someone, both spiritually and physically. The Torah gives us instructions for living that guide us to avoid those things that are spiritually harmful. The Torah also includes a commandment to guard our health. Giving in to desires to overeat, to eat unhealthy food, to smoke, etc., can cause an early death. Be in control of your desires and do not allow your desires to control you.

Keep your environment free from spiritual dangers.

וידבר השם אל משה בערבת מואב על ירדן ירחו לאמר. (במדבר ל"ג נ')

"AND THE ALMIGHTY SPOKE TO MOSHE AT ARVOS MOAV BY THE JORDAN AT YERICHO SAYING." (*Bamidbar* 33:50)

The Torah previously listed all the places the Israelites traveled during their forty years in the wilderness. Now the Almighty gave them the commandment to dwell in the land of Israel (verse 53, see Ramban). But before they were told about dwelling in the land they were commanded to destroy all forms of idolatry. Note that the Hebrew word *kol*, meaning every last one, is used four times in verse 52. No form of idolatry should be left; they must be totally eradicated. Failure to do so could lead to people following some of the idolatrous practices of those who dwelt there previously. Here we see the principle of removing all forms of temptation before a problem arises. It is important to avoid an environment that is potentially dangerous to one's spiritual well-being. Even if there are many positive aspects to some environment, no one would want to live there if it were dangerous to his physical health. All the more so, we must make certain that there is no danger to our spiritual health.

When you feel regret for harming someone, the pain is the cure.

עָרֵי מִקְלָט תִּהְיֶינָה לָכֶם וְנָס שָׁמָּה רֹצֵחַ מַכֵּה נֶפֶשׁ בִּשְׁגָגָה. (בְּמִדְבָּר ל"ה
י"א)

"CITIES OF REFUGE THEY SHALL BE FOR YOU, AND THE
MURDERER WHO KILLED SOMEONE UNINTENTIONALLY SHALL
FLEE THERE." (*Bamidbar* 35:11)

The *Chidushai Harim* commented that if a member of *Klal
Yisroel* killed someone, even though it was unintentional he will
feel extremely broken and guilty. He will be so shattered that he
has no place in the world to go or to hide. Then the Almighty tells
him, "I will give you a place." Go to the exile of the refuge city and
you will be saved. There you can find peace of mind. But this only
applies to someone who has a depth of understanding of what
damage he has caused. If a person does not feel this deep regret and
still feels he has a place in the world, then the city of refuge is not
for him. (cited in *Mayanah Shel Torah*)

When you harm another person and feel regret about it, it is
positive that you experience this pain. The pain itself is purifying. It
will motivate you to improve. Someone who causes another person
a loss or suffering and does not feel guilty manifests a lack of caring
about others. We need a balance. Lack of guilt is even a worse
problem than too much guilt. But excessive guilt is also a problem.
The ideal is to feel regret when you harm someone. But then do
what you can to make amends and do *tshuvah*. When your
repentance is sincere, you can feel joy that you are fulfilling a
mitzvah.

Someone once came to the Steipler and told him that he had a
legal problem that concerned a violation of a traffic law and now
he had to appear at a trial. He asked the Steipler for a blessing that
he should be found innocent in court.

Instead of a blessing, the Steipler censured him, "If you violate a
traffic law, you are endangering the lives of other people. You are

therefore deserving of the biggest punishment."

The person explained that in this situation it was more a question of the prestige of the policeman rather than any actual danger. "Nu, then you should only get a small fine," said the Steipler. And that is what occurred, he received only a small fine. (*Peninai Rabainu Hakehilos Yaakov*, p.126)

Awareness of the suffering of others is a partial consolation.

כי בעיר מקלטו ישב עד מות הכהן הגדל ואחרי מות הכהן הגדל ישוב
הרצח אל ארץ אחזתו. (במדבר ל״ה כ״ח)

If a person kills someone unintentionally, a relative of the deceased might try to kill him and he must stay in a refuge city.
"FOR HE SHALL STAY IN HIS CITY OF REFUGE UNTIL THE DEATH OF THE HIGH PRIEST, AND AFTER THE DEATH OF THE HIGH PRIEST THE MURDERER SHALL RETURN TO THE LAND OF HIS POSSESSION." (*Bamidbar* 35:28)

The Rambam offers this explanation for the death of the High Priest being a time of release for the person who killed someone unintentionally. The nature of a person who suffers a serious misfortune is that his own suffering becomes somewhat alleviated if he sees that others have also suffered in a similar manner. The death felt most strongly was the death of the person holding the exalted position of High Priest. Therefore when the High Priest died, it was a partial consolation to the relatives of the deceased and they would no longer feel the passion for revenge. (*Moreh Nevuchim*)

This is a very important idea for helping us cope with our own suffering. When you personally are in some emotional pain, your suffering is increased by the thought, "I am the only one who suffers so much." But if you will just open your eyes and ears to the suffering of other people in the world, you will gain a more realistic perspective on your own suffering. Regardless of what your problems are there are many people suffering just as much as you and many are suffering even more. This awareness takes away the feeling that you are exceptional. While it is true that even though others are suffering, your own pain still hurts, nevertheless the degree you feel pain is based on your subjective evaluation of it. By being aware of the suffering of others your evaluation of your own suffering makes it much easier to cope with.

A strong word of caution. When someone is suffering, he will usually hate to hear, "But so and so is suffering more than you," or "You are not the only one with problems." Feel empathy for the suffering of others. When someone sees that you personally feel the pain he is experiencing, it makes the burden lighter. A most important rule to remember in communication is that the meaning of what you say is the results you get. Do not just think about what you would like to say when someone is suffering. Be aware of the reaction of the person you are talking to. If what you say is helpful, wonderful. If not, you could be causing the person even more pain. If in doubt, ask the person, "Is what I am saying helpful?" A person might say yes out of embarrassment, so note his non-verbal reactions to what you say.

DVORIM

Utilize the hints of others for self-improvement.

אלה הדברים אשר דבר משה אל כל ישראל. (דברים א' א')

"THESE ARE THE THINGS WHICH MOSHE SPOKE TO ALL OF ISRAEL." (*Dvorim* 1:1)

Rashi cites the *Sifra* that this section contains Moshe's words of rebuke to the Jewish People before he died and he listed all the places where they transgressed. Out of respect for the people, Moshe only hinted at their transgressions and did not mention them explicitly.

Rabbi Yehuda Leib Chasman commented on this that a person who is sincerely interested in self-improvement and growth only needs a slight hint that he has done something wrong in order to realize that he needs to improve. Such a person looks for opportunities to make positive changes in himself and uses his own ability to think to fill in the details when someone gives him a hint that he has made a mistake. (*Ohr Yohail*)

Many people try to avoid hearing any criticism at all. Even if someone explicitly tells them that they have done wrong, they find all kinds of rationalizations to deny the criticism. But when you truly want to become a better person, your goal is overcoming faults. You appreciate it when someone points out ways you can improve. A person who is interested in becoming wealthy will utilize any tips and suggestions he hears if he thinks they will be financially beneficial. In the same way, utilize any tips and suggestions that can be spiritually beneficial.

Rabbi Yisroel Salanter would utilize every opportunity to gain *mussar* insights and to motivate himself to further self-improvement. There were many occurrences when most people would think nothing of them, but Rav Yisroel would gain some lesson for growth. Rav Yisroel once was in the home of a shoemaker late at night and observed how he was doing his work by the light of the candle that was almost going out. "Why are you still working?" Rav Yisroel asked him. "It is very late and soon the candle will be extinguished."

The shoemaker replied, "As long as the candle is still burning it is still possible to accomplish and to mend."

Rabbi Salanter was very moved by this, and said, "If for our physical needs as long as the candle is burning one keeps mending, all the more so for our souls, as long as the light of the soul is still going we must make every effort to accomplish and mend."

After this he would frequently repeat to himself, "As long as the candle is lit, accomplish and mend." (*Tnuas Hamussar*, vol.1, p.315-6)

Before he became a Rebbe, Rabbi Bunim of Parshischo was a merchant. He once went to the market to purchase grain. The Polish farmer asked for a higher price than Rav Bunim wanted to give. "Do better," the farmer said to him. Even though it was clear that the farmer was referring to a higher price for his grain, Rav Bunim used this saying as a reminder to improve his entire behavior. (*Siach Sarfai Kodesh*, vol.1, p.33)

When censuring others include praise and encouragement.

השם אלקי אבותיכם יסף עליכם ככם אלף פעמים. (דברים א' י"א)

Moshe said to the Jewish People:
"THE ALMIGHTY, THE G-D OF YOUR FATHERS, SHOULD INCREASE YOU ONE THOUSAND TIMES SIMILAR TO YOU." (*Dvorim* 1:11)

Why did Moshe need to say that the increase should be "similar to you"? Rabbi Leibel Eger explained that since Moshe was rebuking the people for their errors, he wanted to make certain that they would not feel depressed and discouraged by his criticism. Therefore he told them that they shouldn't think he considered them to be evil. Rather, he wished there would be a thousandfold more just like them. (cited in *Al Hatorah*)

This is an important concept to keep in mind when censuring someone. If you give a person the impression that he is an awful person, he will not be motivated to improve. Even if he does decide to become better, inwardly he will feel devastated and inferior. But if you show the person that you really consider him to be a fine person but that he has some faults that he needs to correct, he will feel good about himself and is more likely to have the energy and enthusiasm necessary to make positive changes. Whenever you criticize someone, make certain to add some positive words of praise and encouragement.

This can also serve as a lesson to someone who is very sensitive and whenever someone criticizes a detail of what he has done, he automatically assumes that the person is totally condemning him. If you point out a minor mistake that he has made, he might say to himself, "This means that the person considers me a total failure and absolutely no good." The truth frequently is that the person knows that you have many virtues but he is just trying to correct your mistakes. You need not cause yourself unnecessary pain by adding to what the person has said. For example, a teacher might wish that he had many more students similar to you but he still feels it is important for you to improve in a few areas. This realization will save you much needless suffering.

When Rabbi Aharon of Belz would see the need to rebuke someone, he would first elaborate on the greatness of the soul of the person he was talking to. These words were said with tremendous love until the person felt that he was standing in the presence of a compassionate father. Only afterwards would he speak about the severity of what the person did wrong and the importance of correcting the matter. (*Horav Hakodosh Maibelz*, p.254)

Whenever Rabbi Yitzchok Zev Yadler met someone who took a yeshiva student for a son-in-law, he would highly praise the young man to the father-in-law. He used to do this even if he personally did not know the fellow. "How fortunate you are to have merited a son-in-law who studies Torah," he would say. The father-in-law would repeat this to his wife and they would both show respect to the young man. When the yeshiva student would find out about this he would approach Rav Yitzchok Zev to thank him for what he said. Rabbi Ben Tzion Yadler, who related this, added that his father would always utilize this opportunity to encourage the young man, "Make certain that all the praise I said will be true." (*Betuv Yerushalayim*, pp.285-6)

Master the art of seeing the good in others.

איכה אשא לבדי טרחכם ומשאכם וריבכם. (דברים א' י"ב)

"HOW CAN I CARRY BY MYSELF ALL OF YOUR BOTHERSOMENESS, AND YOUR BURDEN, AND YOUR QUARRELS." (*Dvorim* 1:12)

Rashi cites the Sages: If Moshe came out of his house early they would say, "Why is Moshe early? Perhaps he is having family problems at home." If Moshe came out late from his house, they would say, "Moshe stays home longer in order to devise negative plans against you."

It is amazing how someone with a tendency to judge people negatively will always find ways to see faults in others. The reality is that whatever someone does or does not do you can always find some negative motivation or interpretation. But there are always positive ways to interpret the behavior of others. For instance, if Moshe came early they could have said, "Look at Moshe's willingness to make great sacrifices for the welfare of others. He is even ready to minimize the amount of time he is at home with his family in order to give his time for others." If Moshe was late, they could have said, "He wants to prepare himself properly in order to be most effective in giving good advice to the people."

The way you interpret events has more to do with your character traits than it does with the reality of what someone else is like. There is a commandment in the Torah to judge people favorably. Of course, we are allowed and even obligated to guard ourselves from harm. But in most instances our judgments of others will not have practical effects on us. The more good you see in others the better you yourself will feel. Your entire world will be much sweeter. Moreover, people frequently live up to your expectations of them. Assume that someone is inconsiderate towards you and he probably will act that way. But if you assume the good in others, they will feel positive towards you and act accordingly. Be resolved to master the art of seeing the good in others.

Treat others as close relatives.

ואצוה את שפטיכם בעת ההוא לאמר שמע בין אחיכם. (דברים א' ט"ז)

"AND I COMMANDED YOUR JUDGES AT THAT TIME SAYING, LISTEN AMONG YOUR BROTHERS." (*Dvorim* 1:16)

Rabbi Zalman Sorotzkin writes that some judges may see themselves as elevated people and the litigants who come to them as wicked. Therefore the Torah states, "Listen among your brothers." That is, consider anyone who comes to you as a brother and treat him accordingly. (*Oznayim Letorah*)

This concept applies to anyone in a position of authority. It is very easy to treat people as objects. But our attitude towards others should be, "How would I feel, act and talk if this person were my brother?" This is especially important for anyone who is in a position where people in financial need or emotional pain come to him for assistance. The person you are talking to is suffering and often might feel embarrassed that he needs to come to someone for help. Be extremely sensitive to his feelings. If you are able to make him feel that you feel towards him as a close relative, it is a great kindness.

Two middle-aged Torah scholars, whose fathers were butchers on the East Side, remember frequently being sent to Rabbi Moshe Feinstein with *she'eilos* (questions, in this instance pertaining to the *kashrus* of the chickens). As children they knew him as the nice, friendly man who never made them feel unimportant intruders. As they grew older, they realized with a shock that their "friend" was one of Jewry's greatest people. It is not surprising that one woman used to call him every Friday afternoon about the time to light candles; he would answer and pleasantly wish her a *Gutten Shabbos*, as he would have done as a young rabbi. (Rabbi Nosson Scherman; *The Jewish Observer*, Oct. 1986, p.18)

When trying to settle quarrels remember that every life situation is different.

ואצוה את שפטיכם בעת ההוא לאמר שמע בין אחיכם. (דברים א' ט"ז)

"AND I COMMANDED YOUR JUDGES AT THAT TIME SAYING, LISTEN AMONG YOUR BROTHERS." (*Dvorim* 1:16)

Rashi cites the *Sifri* that Moshe told the judges to be patient and deliberate in each case that came before them. Even if they had similar cases in the past, they should discuss the present case thoroughly.

Every case is different from any other, and each case should be viewed as entirely new and every detail considered. This applies whenever you become involved in settling quarrels between people. Of course, there are patterns that anyone with experience will recognize. But there will always be factors that make this situation unique. Do not jump to conclusions. Rather, listen carefully to both sides. Just because one solution worked in a past situation does not mean that it will automatically be effective in a situation that is quite similar but a little bit different. One needs to be creative and flexible. Whenever you try to help people settle quarrels, give the matter your full attention to see what needs to be said and done in this specific situation. By doing this you will have the merit of bringing peace to many more people than if you rigidly try the exact same approach each time.

Make certain to start any project with derech eretz.

וֹ:קרבון אלי כלכם ותאמרו נשלחה אנשים לפנינו ויחפרו לנו את הארץ.
(דברים א' כ"ב)

"AND ALL OF YOU APPROACHED ME, AND YOU SAID, LET US SEND PEOPLE BEFORE US TO EXPLORE THE LAND FOR US." (*Dvorim* 1:22)

Rashi states that they came to Moshe in a disorderly manner. Children were pushing the elders and the elders were pushing the leaders.

At first glance this lack of orderliness seems to be just a small lack of *derech eretz* (proper manners), why was it mentioned together with the severe offense of the acceptance of the slander of the spies and the refusal to listen to the Almighty's will to enter the land? Rabbi Naftoli Tzvi Berlin cited the reply of his father-in-law, Rabbi Yitchok of Volozhin. This lack of *derech eretz* of the people is attached to the transgression of the spies to increase the severity of their offense. The people might have tried to lessen the offense by saying that their original plan to send the spies was correct, but that later on they were negatively influenced by the evil report of the spies. Therefore Moshe showed them that right from the start something was seriously wrong. When people are involved in a project that is really proper, they will have appropriate *derech eretz* at the very beginning of the venture. Since in the matter of sending the spies they acted rudely and unruly they should have realized that they were doing something wrong. (*Haamek Dovor*)

Derech eretz is so important that if you lack it, it shows that all that follows is not proper. If you want your teachers or parents to agree with a project you wish to engage in, make certain to speak to them with proper honor and respect. Failure to do so is not merely a minor character flaw, but a manifestation that your entire motivation is not on the right level. Getting off to a good start is crucial in spiritual matters for it is a strong sign of your true inner attitudes towards what you are planning to do.

When consulting a Torah scholar clarify his true opinion.

וייטב בעיני הדבר. (דברים א' כ"ג)

Moshe said to the Israelites:
"AND THE MATTER WAS GOOD IN MY EYES." (*Dvorim* 1:23)

If Moshe said that the matter was good in his eyes, why did he list the sending of the spies here when he was enumerating things that the Israelites did wrong? Rashi explains with an analogy. This is similar to someone who asked his friend to sell him his donkey and the person agreed. "Will you allow me to test it out?" the potential buyer asked his friend. "Of course, I will," replied the seller. "Can I even try it out on hills and mountains?" the buyer asked. "Anywhere you wish," the seller confidently said. Once the buyer saw that the seller had total confidence in the strength and health of his donkey, he realized that he would not find any defects in it and said, "Take your money. I do not need to test out the animal any further." Similarly, Moshe really did not want them to send spies. But he felt that as soon as they saw he was willing to allow them to send spies they should have realized that the land was good and they had no further need to send anyone to check on it.

There are two different attitudes someone can have when he

consults a Torah scholar about whether or not he should do something. One attitude is a serious will to do the right thing. Such a person wants to know what the opinion of the Torah scholar really is and is willing to do exactly as the scholar feels he should do. But there are people who consult with a scholar only to hear the reply that they want to hear. They will ask their question in such a manner as to get the answer they want. If at first they do not hear what they wish, they will persistently argue until they get at least tacit consent. Then they will tell others that they have the approval of the scholar. The correct attitude to adopt is the will to do what is right even if it is not exactly what you would have preferred. The people who took Moshe's saying that they could send spies as permission to actually send them should have asked him to tell them what he truly wanted them to do. This should be our approach when consulting a Torah scholar or in fulfilling the commandment of honoring our parents.

There are some people who do even worse than the above. They could even know that the scholar does not want them to do something but they try to give others the impression that he agrees with them. Rabbi Simcha Wasserman, Rosh Hayeshiva of Ohr Elchonon, told me about an instance where someone involved in communal matters did something that was very controversial. When asked how he could have done it, he replied that he had spoken the matter over with Rabbi Aharon Kotler, Rosh Hayeshiva of Lakewood. Most people were impressed with this and assumed that Rabbi Kotler had agreed that he could do it. But Rav Simcha said to himself it was impossible that Rav Aharon would agree. He then asked the person, "And what did Rabbi Kotler say?" "Well, he said that I should not do it," replied the man. Remember this incident and do not always accept at face value someone's saying that he has the agreement of such and such a scholar.

Be careful that your positive statements do not contain negative messages.

ויאמרו טובה הארץ אשר השם אלקינו נתן לנו. (דברים א' כ"ה)

"AND THEY SAID, THE LAND WHICH THE LORD, OUR G-D, IS GIVING US IS GOOD." (*Dvorim* 1:25)

Saying that the land is good is a positive statement and Rashi understands these to be the words of Yehoshua and Kolaiv who praised the land. But the Chasam Sofer said that these could also be the words of the other spies who were against them trying to enter the land. They said that the land is so good that those who presently inhabit it will not easily allow others to take it away from them. They will fight to the end for this land because no other place will be so good. (*Toras Moshe*)

From here we see that it is possible for someone to say something that on the surface seems to be a positive statement, but when taking the entire situation into account is meant to have a negative effect. There are people who frequently do this. They do not want to appear as if they are attacking others. Therefore they say things that at first sound as if they are compliments or praise but are intended to cause pain. Such as telling someone, "You finally did a good job." This might be meant as praise and encouragement. But it could also be meant as an emphasis on all the times the person did not do satisfactorily. When someone praises you, do not assume he means anything negative. But when you speak to others be careful that your positive statements will not be taken in a negative way. It goes without saying that you should not use a subterfuge to make statements that could cause others harm or pain.

A distinguished Torah scholar began construction of a community in *Eretz Yisroel*. The Steipler sent him a letter with blessings in honor of the groundbreaking. He then commented to members of his family, "There is a statement of the Sages that would be appropriate for this occasion. The Talmud (*Sanhedrin* 102b) states, 'Why did Imri merit becoming a king? Because he added a city in *Eretz Yisroel*.' But since Imri was an evil person, I was afraid that perhaps it would show a lack of respect to write this." (*Peninai Rabainu Hakehilos Yaakov*, p.108)

If you feel love towards others, you will assume they have love for you.

ותרגנו באהליכם ותאמרו בשנאת השם אתנו הוציאנו מארץ מצרים לתת אתנו ביד האמרי להשמידנו. (דברים א' כ"ז)

"AND YOU COMPLAINED IN YOUR TENTS, AND YOU SAID, BECAUSE THE ALMIGHTY HATED US HE TOOK US OUT OF EGYPT TO HAND US OVER TO THE EMORITES TO DESTROY US." (*Dvorim* 1:27)

Rashi comments on this verse that the Almighty really loved the Israelites but because they felt hatred towards Him, they mistakenly felt that He hated them. This is what people say, writes Rashi (see *Sifsai Chachomim*), "What you feel about someone else you assume he feels about you."

There is a strong tendency for people to project their own feelings towards others onto those people. If you constantly think that other people should not be trusted, it could show that you feel that others should not really trust you. If you always think that everyone will disapprove of you, it shows that you do not approve of others or that you do not approve of yourself. Conversely, if you feel love and compassion for others, you will assume that others feel positive about you. Unless you are a person who is totally out of touch with how others react, this will have positive effects on others. When they see that you smile when greeting them and show signs that you care about them (which is how you will react because of your assumption that they feel positive about you), they will increase their positive feelings towards you. Therefore you gain both in increasing your own positive inner feelings and also by the practical benefits of influencing people to be more positive towards you.

VAESCHANAN

Be persistent in spiritual matters.

ואתחנן אל השם בעת ההוא לאמר. (דברים ג' כ"ג)

Moshe wanted to enter the land of Israel which he was told he could not enter: "AND I PRAYED TO THE ALMIGHTY AT THAT TIME SAYING." (*Dvorim* 3:23)

Moshe prayed to the Almighty, say the Sages, as many prayers as the numerical value of the word *vaeschanan* (the first word in this verse). This amounts to 515 prayers, so strong was Moshe's desire to enter the Holy Land. Let us picture this. If someone asks another person for something and the other person refuses to meet his request, it is possible that he will ask again. But after a few times, he will give up. There is a limit to how many times one person will ask another for something. But here we see that Moshe continued to ask five hundred and fifteen times. This is truly amazing. The principle we see is that the way to elevation is persistence and even stubbornness. In spiritual matters one needs to adopt the attitude, "I don't care about anything else. This matter is crucial and I'll keep trying and trying." (Rabbi Yeruchem Levovitz; *Daas Torah: Braishis*, p.187)

The key to accomplishment is persistence. If you ask someone for something that is very important and the person refuses, you might say to yourself that he will never give in. But eventually people do give in if the other party keeps repeating his request often enough. Most young children are experts at this, as any parent can attest. It is only a question of what you are willing to be persistent about. For example, if someone does not want to sell a possession of his that you would like to have, it is wrong to keep on nagging him until he gives in. But in important spiritual matters keep on trying.

Love of Eretz Yisroel necessitates Torah observance.

אעברה נא ואראה את הארץ הטובה אשר בעבר הירדן ההר הטוב הזה
והלבנן. (דברים ג' כ"ה)

Moshe prayed to the Almighty:
"ALLOW ME PLEASE TO GO TO THE OTHER SIDE AND I WILL SEE THE GOOD LAND WHICH IS ON THE OTHER SIDE OF THE JORDAN, THIS GOOD MOUNTAIN AND THE LEVONON." (*Dvorim* 3:25)

Ibn Ezra (verse 24) writes: The purpose of this section of the Torah is to enable us to cherish the land of Israel. If the land of Israel will be dear to us, we will observe the Almighty's commandments to prevent our being exiled from it.

We see from here that only if a person observes the Torah's commandments can he say that he truly loves *Eretz Yisroel*. Failure to keep the Torah's commandments in *Eretz Yisroel* implies a lack of love for the land.

Bring sanctity into all aspects of human endeavor.

ראה למדתי אתכם חקים ומשפטים כאשר צוני השם אלקי לעשות כן
בקרב הארץ. (דברים ד' ה')

"SEE THAT I HAVE TAUGHT YOU STATUTES AND LAWS AS THE LORD, MY G-D, COMMANDED ME, TO DO SO IN THE MIDST OF THE LAND." (*Dvorim* 4:5)

There have been philosophers who taught that if a person wants to live a life of sanctity and perfection of the soul, he must flee from inhabited places and live alone in a wilderness. There he will separate himself from other people and from all worldly pursuits. But this is not the path of the Torah. Moshe told the people, "I have taught you to follow the commandments in the midst of the land." That is, you should live an elevated life among other people. True sanctity and perfection is to live among people and behave both towards G-d and towards your fellow men in a manner consistent with Torah values. (*Arvai Nachal*)

The ideal of Torah is to bring sanctity and idealism into all aspects of human endeavor. If you live alone, you will be free from anger, envy, causing other people pain, etc. But you will be missing opportunities for kindness, compassion, and love. Moreover, not becoming angry at others when you are alone on an island or among people who speak a foreign language is no challenge. Not becoming angry when you are living among members of your family or acquaintances who do things you find irritating is a test of your true level. Not deceiving others is no problem if there is nobody around to deceive. But the true test of honesty is when you have to deal with others. Only when you are in the company of other people can you fulfill all aspects of the Torah.

Guarding your health is a mitzvah.

ונשמרתם מאד לנפשתיכם. (דברים ד' ט"ו)

"AND YOU SHALL GUARD YOUR SOULS VERY MUCH." (*Dvorim* 4:15)

The Torah commands us in this verse to guard our health. The Chofetz Chayim noted that the Torah uses the term *nefesh*, which refers to the soul, and does not say guard your body. This comes to teach us that whenever you are involved in matters pertaining to the welfare of your body such as business matters or eating, you must be very careful not to do anything that will be harmful to your soul. Before doing anything for your body's needs, give careful thought not to do anything against the will of the Almighty.

A person is sent to this world by the Almighty to do His will, and this should be one's motivation in all that one does. Even when you are engaged in the needs of your body realize that what you are involved in is part of your mission in this world. It is the will of the Creator that you guard your health. (*Chofetz Chayim al Hatorah*, pp.226-7)

The Chofetz Chayim would constantly stress the importance of guarding one's health. In his yeshiva he would insist that his students get enough sleep. He used to say that at times the evil inclination will try to have someone study late into the night on a consistent basis in order that he should weaken himself and become unable to study Torah later on. The Chofetz Chayim would say, "Even if the evil inclination advises you to study more and more, do not listen to him. His intention is to prevent you from Torah study." (*ibid.*, p.227)

One must guard one's physical and emotional health. It is important to keep in mind that different people have very different needs. One person might need much more sleep than the average, and someone else might need much less. If you need more sleep and relaxation than someone else, do not try to imitate him if he stays up half the night and never takes any breaks. Conversely, a person who feels much joy and excitement in his Torah studies will need less sleep and his Torah study itself is his enjoyment, hence he will not have a need for other forms of recreation. Be aware of your true needs and act accordingly.

Rabbi Avraham of Sochotchov, author of *Avnai Nezer*, used to say to anyone who was ill, "A person who is sick has to keep his main focus on fulfilling the commandment of guarding his health. The evil inclination does all that he can that a person should not fulfill this *mitzvah*." (*Maigdolai Hachasidus: Hoadmor Maisochotchov*, p.115)

There is a well-known saying of Rabbi Chayim Soloveitchik of Brisk, who could have appeared to be lenient in permitting medical needs to be taken care of on *Shabbos* and permitting people to eat on *Yom Kippur* when they were ill, "I am not lenient as regards the laws of *Shabbos* and *Yom Kippur*. Rather I am very stringent as regards the commandment to guard one's life."

When a student of Rabbi Zundel of Salant wrote to him asking for advice on spiritual matters, Rav Zundel started by telling him to be very careful to guard his health. Knowing that many people are not careful enough with their health, Rav Zundel wanted to emphasize the importance of this *mitzvah*. (*Tnuas Hamussar*, vol.1, p.111)

Rabbi Chayim Tzanzer was once ill on Pesach and his doctor told him that it was forbidden for him to eat *maror* because it would be dangerous to his health. At the Pesach *seder*, Rav Chayim took a large piece of *maror* and made a blessing, "Blessed are You who sanctified us with His commandments and commanded us to guard our health," and immediately returned the *maror* to the table. (*Al Hatorah*)

As a young Rabbi of Tzitovyan, Rabbi Yaakov Kamenetzky refused to officiate at the funeral of an over-zealous congregant. The man, who had been told by his doctor to eat on *Yom Kippur* for health reasons, was instructed by Rabbi Kamenetzky to follow this prescription, but fasted nonetheless, and then died. Rav Yaakov did attend the funeral and to discourage others from following this reckless behavior, announced that the family not sit *shiva*, since the man had in effect taken his own life. (Rabbi Nisson Wolpin, *The Jewish Observer*, May, 1986, p.5)

View anew each day all that you have.

כי תוליד בנים ובני בנים ונושנתם בארץ והשחתם ועשיתם פסל תמונת כל ועשיתם הרע בעיני השם אלקיך להכעיסו. (דברים ד' כ"ה)

"IF YOU BEGET CHILDREN AND GRANDCHILDREN AND BECOME OLD IN THE LAND, AND BECOME CORRUPT AND MAKE AN IDOL, THE IMAGE OF ANYTHING, AND YOU DO WHAT IS EVIL IN THE EYES OF THE ALMIGHTY, YOUR G-D, TO ANGER HIM." (*Dvorim* 4:25)

If a person merits having children and grandchildren, why does this lead to his becoming corrupt and doing evil? Shouldn't the person be grateful to the Almighty for all that He has given him? The answer lies in the word *venoshantem*, becoming old, that is, you become so accustomed to what you have that you no longer appreciate it. Taking for granted what you already have and not feeling pleasure in it prevents you from having gratitude to the Almighty for all the good that He has given you. (Heard from Rabbi Chayim Zaichyk)

There are many things that you have that you appreciated when you first got them. A person feels much joy when his first child is born. Years later, he feels great joy when his first grandchild is born. But regardless of the initial joy, a person who is not able to view what he has as if it were new loses an enormous amount of pleasure in his life. In order to have deeper gratitude for the Almighty's kindnesses develop the attitude of viewing anew all that you have. Each day look at your possessions as if you just received them that very day. Mastering this attitude will greatly enhance your life.

Internalize the awareness that all that occurs to you is from the Almighty.

וידעת היום והשבת אל לבבך כי השם הוא האלקים בשמים ממעל ועל הארץ מתחת אין עוד. (דברים ד' ל"ט)

"AND YOU SHALL KNOW THIS DAY, AND YOU SHALL TAKE THIS TO YOUR HEART, THAT THE ALMIGHTY IS G-D IN THE HEAVENS ABOVE AND UPON THE EARTH BELOW, THERE IS NO OTHER." (*Dvorim* 4:39)

The Chofetz Chayim used to stress that this verse tells us that all that happens in our lives is from the Almighty. All the profits and losses in a person's life are from the decree of the Almighty. Similarly, any pain that a person suffers, such as when someone curses or insults him, is from Heaven to atone for one's transgressions. The person doing the cursing and insulting is guilty of committing a sin, but the recipient is receiving something that is ultimately beneficial for him. A person who internalizes this attitude will have the strength and courage not to reply to the insults thrown at him. The situation is similar to someone who is washing another person with hot water to remove something that is very sticky. During the cleansing process the hot water hurts, but in the end the person becomes clean.

There are two factors here, said the Chofetz Chayim. One is having the intellectual knowledge of this principle. The other is internalizing it so that it becomes part of you and has a practical effect on your emotions. Unfortunately, many people just have the intellectual acceptance of this concept and are missing the internalization. (*Chofetz Chayim al Hatorah*, text and footnote)

The way to internalize this is to constantly repeat it to yourself. With every repetition ideas become more and more a part of your inner reality.

Rabbi Aryeh Levin was especially careful to go to homes where people sat in mourning for a departed member of the family to comfort them. He explained why this was so important, "When a misfortune or tragic event befalls a man, apart from his anguish and suffering his faith also becomes injured to some extent. When a person goes to comfort someone in mourning, not only does he give him new spirit and courage, he also returns the other's faith to its original strength." (*A Tzaddik in Our Time*, p.172)

Be willing to start a project even if others will complete it.

אז יבדיל משה שלש ערים בעבר הירדן מזרחה שמש. (דברים ד' מ"א)

"THEN MOSHE SEPARATED THREE CITIES ON THE OTHER SIDE OF THE JORDAN TO THE EAST OF THE SUN." (*Dvorim* 4:41)

The three refuge cities that Moshe set aside would not go into effect until the cities in the land of Canaan would also be set aside. Nevertheless, Moshe said, "Any *mitzvah* that I can fulfill, I will fulfill." (Rashi)

The *Kli Yokor* commented that from here we see a principle that will apply in many situations. Frequently, if a person feels that he will not be able to complete a project, he is reluctant to even start. But we see from Moshe that even though he knew that what he began would not be completed in his lifetime, he still felt it was worthwhile to accomplish as much as was possible.

Some people begin many projects but they lack the perseverance to complete them. They have much enthusiasm in the beginning but eventually lose their energy or become bored. In order to accomplish anything you need to complete what you begin. But there are others who are just the opposite. They are only willing to put in time and energy for projects that they will be able to see completed. The drawback here is that there are many worthwhile causes and projects that need much patience and the real fruits might come many years in the future. Use Moshe's behavior as a model to begin whatever you can, even though others may get the credit for completing it.

Appreciate opportunities to express gratitude.

מי יתן והיה לבבם זה להם ליראה אתי ולשמר את כל מצותי כל הימים למען ייטב להם ולבניהם לעלם. (דברים ה' כ"ו)

The Almighty said about the Israelites:

"WHO WILL GIVE THAT THE HEART THAT YOU HAVE NOW SHALL BE TO YOU TO FEAR ME AND TO OBSERVE ALL OF MY COMMANDMENTS ALL THE DAYS, IN ORDER TO DO GOOD FOR YOU AND YOUR CHILDREN FOREVER." (*Dvorim* 5:26)

The Talmud (*Avodah Zarah* 5a) states here that Moshe said to the Israelites, "You are ungrateful and the descendants of someone who is ungrateful. When the Almighty said to you, 'Who will give that the heart that you have now shall be to you (always),'" you should have said, "You give." The Talmud explains that Moshe called them ungrateful because of their complaining against the manna. They were called the descendants of someone ungrateful because of Adam's saying to the Almighty that the woman whom He gave to him caused him to eat what he should not have eaten.

Why was their failure to ask the Almighty to give them an elevated heart considered a lack of gratitude? *Tosfos* explains that they didn't want to ask Him to give them this elevated heart because they didn't want to feel grateful towards Him.

We see here two concepts related to the attribute of gratitude. First, that whenever you complain about what the Almighty has given you it shows a lack of gratitude. In our daily lives this frequently applies. Think this over carefully and see how often you complain when you should feel grateful. For example, a person might complain that he has so many things in his house that he has no place to put them. Or that his refrigerator is so full of food that he has no room to put away something else. In these instances one should be so grateful to the Almighty for what one has that the reaction should be one of joy, "Thank you Almighty for giving me so much that I now have the positive problem of where to put things." Also, be careful not to complain about other people who have helped you. For example, if someone gives you a meal and there is one item you do not like, focus on what you do like and appreciate it rather than complaining about details.

We also see from here how people will try to avoid feeling grateful. At times they would rather not receive something that could be a great benefit to them because of their unwillingness to express gratitude. At times avoiding taking from others is a virtue. But if your motivation is, "I don't want to have to be grateful to him," it manifests a lack of having gratitude. A person who appreciates opportunities to express gratitude to others does not mind continually thanking them. But the difficulty for some is that this takes humility. An arrogant person considers it a lowering of himself if he has to show that someone else is above him in some manner. He is even willing to forego something that can benefit him just because he doesn't want to have to be grateful.

Mastering the attribute of gratitude takes much thought and effort. Whenever someone helps you in some way, ask yourself what you can do to show gratitude. Take pleasure whenever you express gratitude; it is a very elevated trait.

Rabbi Nochum Zev Ziv, son of Rabbi Simcha Zissel, worked on the trait of gratitude. Gratitude is the essence of our relationship with the Almighty. Increasing gratitude towards our fellow man will enable us to internalize this trait. Someone once did Rav Nochum Zev a favor. Twenty-five years later he happened to visit that person and again thanked him for the favor. Even if someone who did him a favor also did something negative against him, he would forget the negative instance and remember only the good. (*Tnuas Hamussar*, vol.2, p.98)

Rabbi Moshe Feinstein always had fond memories of the four years he spent under Rabbi Pesach Pruskin in Shklov and Arntsislav. Sixty years later, he sent a wedding gift to Rav Pesach's granddaugher, writing, "This gift is nothing compared to the gratitude I felt to my teacher and master." (Rabbi Nosson Scherman; *The Jewish Observer*, Oct., 1986, p.12)

Rabbi Eliyahu Lopian stressed the importance of gratitude even for an inanimate object. One morning after prayers when speaking to a student, he placed his *talis* on a bench and began to fold it. Afterwards he noticed that the bench wasn't clean. Rabbi Lopian started to go outside the *Bais Midrash* to get a towel to clean the bench. The student ran to bring the towel, but Rav Eliyahu said to him, "No, no. I have to get the towel myself. Since I folded my *talis* on this bench I have an obligation of gratitude towards it." (*Lev Eliyahu*, vol.2, Intro., p.48)

Mentally visualize yourself being willing to give up your life for the Almighty.

ואהבת את השם אלקיך בכל לבבך ובכל נפשך ובכל מאדך. (דברים ו' ה')

"AND YOU SHALL LOVE THE LORD, YOUR G-D, WITH ALL YOUR HEART, AND WITH ALL YOUR SOUL, AND WITH ALL YOUR MIGHT." (*Dvorim* 6:5)

The Talmud (*Brochos* 61b) relates that when the Romans took Rabbi Akiva out to be killed it was the time of reciting the *Shma Yisroel*. The Romans tortured him by combing his skin with metal combs and he calmly accepted upon himself the yoke of the kingdom of heaven by reciting the *Shma*. His disciples asked him, "Our teacher, how can you calmly recite the *Shma* with such serenity?" He replied, "My entire life I was waiting for this moment. When the Torah tells us to love the Almighty with all our soul, it means that our love for the Almighty should be so strong that we should be willing to give up our lives for Him. I kept saying to myself that I wish to be able to fulfill this. Now that I have the opportunity, how can I not fulfill it?"

Rabbi Yeruchem Levovitz explained that a person should form the habit of mentally visualizing himself overcoming all kinds of difficulties. When you picture this in your mind in advance, you build up your ability to do this in reality later on. This is what Rabbi Akiva told his students. The reason he was able to cope with so much pain and could remain oblivious to it when he recited the *Shma* while being killed is because he had daily practice sessions. When a person keeps picturing himself giving up his life for *Kidush Hashem* (sanctification of the Almighty's name), it is as if he is actually reaching this elevated level. (*Daas Torah: Shmos*, p.195)

Continue to reflect on love of the Almighty and eventually you will experience it.

והיו הדברים האלה אשר אנכי מצוך היום על לבבך. (דברים ו' ו')

"AND THESE THINGS WHICH I COMMAND YOU THIS DAY SHALL BE ON YOUR HEART." (*Dvorim* 6:6)

Rabbi Shalom Schwadron frequently says in the name of his Rebbe, Rabbi Yehuda Leib Chasman: "Just as by *tefilin* when it says 'on your hand' it means without any obstructions, so too when the Torah says 'on your heart' it means without any obstructions. You must remove faulty character traits and emotions from your heart before you will experience love for the Almighty."

The Kotzker Rebbe commented on this verse: At times your heart might be closed and the concepts and ideas you accept intellectually do not penetrate and become part of you. Still keep them on your heart even if they do not as yet enter your heart. Once they are "on your heart," as soon as your heart opens up they will immediately fall right in. (cited in *Maayanah Shel Torah*)

There are many important Torah ideas that are crucial for a person to internalize, for only when they actually become a part of you will they actually make a difference in your life. In the previous verse the Torah states the commandment to love the Almighty. This takes much thought and reflection. You need to meditate on the infinite greatness of the Almighty and on all of the kindnesses that He does for you. But even if you do think about this there are times when it will merely remain cognitive and intellectual but will not be an emotional experience. True love is not merely saying that you love someone, but actually feeling and expressing it. Therefore even if your heart is closed, that is, you emotionally do not feel this love for the Almighty, continue to reflect on Him, His awesome power in the universe, and the myriad ways He has helped you. Be patient. Eventually your heart will open up and you will experience an inner love for the Creator and His creations.

AIKEV

Awareness of how the Almighty has already helped you will enable you to overcome worry.

כי תאמר בלבבך רבים הגוים האלה ממני איכה אוכל להורישם. לא תירא מהם זכר תזכר את אשר עשה השם אלקיך לפרעה ולכל מצרים. (דברים ז' י״ז-י״ח)

"IF YOU WILL SAY IN YOUR HEART, THESE NATIONS ARE MORE NUMEROUS THAN WE, HOW CAN I CONQUER THEM. DO NOT FEAR THEM, REMEMBER WHAT THE ALMIGHTY, YOUR G-D, DID TO PHARAOH AND ALL OF EGYPT." (*Dvorim* 7:17,18)

Bitochon eliminates worry. What is worry? You are afraid that in the future there will be a situation that you will not be able to cope with. But if you remember how the Almighty has helped you in similar situations in the past, you will find it easier to trust in Him in the present. Moshe told the Israelites that if they questioned how they would be able to defeat the nations who live in Canaan, they should recall their past experience of how the Almighty helped them in a similar situation with the Egyptians. Your heart will be free from worry when you have an awareness that the Almighty has already helped you cope with difficulties in the past. Whenever you find yourself worrying about the future, ask yourself, "In what ways has the Almighty already shown me that He can help me overcome a difficulty similar to this?"

When you have financial difficulties, remember how you worried about financial matters before and still you managed. When you are afraid you might not do well on a test, remember when you felt that way in the past and you still did well. If you fear new situations, remember other new situations you worried about and still were able to cope with satisfactorily.

Internalize the awareness that the pain you suffer is purposeful and for your benefit.

וידעת עם לבבך כי כאשר ייסר איש את בנו השם אלקיך מיסרך. (דברים ח' ה')

"AND YOU SHALL KNOW IN YOUR HEART THAT THE ALMIGHTY CHASTISES YOU JUST AS A FATHER CHASTISES HIS SON." (*Dvorim* 8:5)

Pain is subjective. The amount of suffering you feel is dependent on how you view it. A person might have injured himself and feels great pain. This is compounded if he thinks that there is a good chance that the injury is serious. But pain is lessened if someone goes to a doctor who checks him very carefully and tells him, "Although you might feel pain, nothing is broken and in a few days your pain will be entirely gone." In this situation most people feel relieved and although the pain is still there, it subjectively becomes much lighter almost immediately. Similarly, when you know that a certain pain is beneficial for you it does not really bother you too much. Some medicines are difficult to take, but when a person knows how much they will help him he is ready to take them and can cope with the discomfort much better than if he would view the matter as totally negative. Therefore the Torah tells us that whenever the Almighty causes us suffering it is for our benefit.

A kind and loving father will at times need to take a child to a doctor for stitches which can be painful. But this is entirely for the child's benefit, for his physical well-being. A young child might not understand this and could think that his father has suddenly become cruel. But an older child with more understanding realizes his father's motivation and is grateful to his father for helping him. The same parent will find times when he might have to use harsher methods than usual to discipline his child when softer approaches (which should be the norm) do not prove effective. This is also for the child's benefit and his spiritual well-being. It takes even more understanding for a child to comprehend this in the appropriate way. So, too, whenever the Almighty sends you suffering it is for your ultimate welfare. Those who have an appreciation for the kindness and mercy of the Almighty will understand this in its proper perspective. Internalizing this awareness, as this verse tells us to do, will enable you to experience suffering in a much more positive way.

Eat in order to live; live in order to do good deeds.

ואכלת ושבעת וברכת את השם אלקיך על הארץ הטבה אשר נתן לך. השמר לך פן תשכח את השם אלקיך לבלתי שמר מצותיו ומשפטיו וחקתיו אשר אנכי מצוך היום. (דברים ח' י-י"א)

"AND YOU SHALL EAT AND BE SATISFIED AND BLESS THE ALMIGHTY, YOUR G-D, ON THE GOOD LAND WHICH HE GAVE YOU. GUARD YOURSELF LEST YOU FORGET THE LORD, YOUR G-D AND DO NOT OBSERVE HIS COMMANDMENTS AND HIS LAWS AND HIS STATUTES WHICH I COMMAND YOU THIS DAY." (*Dvorim* 8:10,11)

In the blessings we make after eating a meal we mention the covenant we have with the Almighty and the Torah which He gave us. Without this it would not be fitting to bless the Almighty for food. Of what value is nourishment of the body without it giving us the strength to engage in spiritual pursuits? The reason it is worthwhile to bless the Almighty for the material benefits He has bestowed upon us is because through meeting our physical needs we are able to engage in Torah study and the fulfillment of good deeds. But if a person makes eating a high priority in itself and blesses the Almighty only for the food He has given and not for the Torah, he is likely to consider material matters very important. This will cause a person to become more and more materialistic and physically oriented and in the end he will forget the Almighty. Therefore the Torah states (verse 10) that if you will eat and are satisfied and bless the Almighty for just the land itself and not for the commandments which He gave us, then (verse 11) you must be on guard not to forget the Almighty and His commandments. (Chasam Sofer; *Toras Moshe*)

If you keep your focus just on eating or on the land alone without seeing the ultimate purpose of the food or the land, you are missing the essence of these material things. However, when you eat in order to live and live in order to do good deeds, then all that you do to sustain your body is considered a spiritual duty and the fulfillment of a *mitzvah*. Since earning money in order to eat and all the preparations necessary for food (buying it, cooking, baking, cleaning up, etc.) take up so much time and energy it is crucial for a person to develop a correct spiritual attitude towards eating.

Reflect on the entire context of the good that happens to you.

ורם לבבך ושכחת את השם אלקיך המוציאך מארץ מצרים מבית עבדים.
(דברים ח' י"ד)

"[Lest] YOUR HEART BE EXALTED, AND YOU FORGET THE ALMIGHTY, YOUR G-D, WHO TOOK YOU OUT OF THE LAND OF EGYPT FROM THE HOUSE OF SLAVERY." (*Dvorim* 8:14)

Ibn Ezra explains: Lest you forget that you were slaves who were in a very lowly state of mind, and you might forget the suffering, hunger, and thirst that you experienced in the wilderness and then the Almighty took care of your needs.

Rabbi Mordechai Gifter, Rosh Hayeshiva of Telz, commented that from here we learn a lesson about the depth of gratitude which we are required to have. It is not sufficient for a person just to be grateful for the good that he received. Rather, he should reflect on the entire context of that good. For this he must think about his entire desperate situation before he received the kindness. The more one is aware of this, the greater will be the appreciation of the benefits of the kindnesses that were bestowed on him. (*Pirke Emunah*, p.78)

This is important to remember both as regards our appreciation of what the Almighty has given us and as regards the kindnesses received from other people. One who continues to focus on this will feel greater happiness from all that he has and this will help him grow in the trait of gratitude. Whenever someone helps you, ask yourself, "What was my situation before this person helped me and in what ways have I gained because of that help?"

Difficult life-tests elevate you.

למען ענתך ולמען נסתך להיטבך באחריתך. (דברים ח' ט"ז)

"IN ORDER TO AFFLICT YOU AND IN ORDER TO TEST YOU TO DO GOOD FOR YOU IN YOUR END." (*Dvorim* 8:16)

The Chofetz Chayim commented that the affliction of the Israelites was in order to test them out to see if they would behave in an elevated manner even though they had difficulties. The Hebrew term *nasoscho*, which means test also means to be elevated. Both concepts fit together. When someone acts in an elevated manner when he has difficult life-tests, he becomes elevated. This concept applies to each individual in each generation. This is especially so when you suffer because of doing the Almighty's will. (*Chofetz Chayim al Hatorah*)

Instead of complaining when difficulties arise in your life, look for ways you can utilize those difficulties to improve your character traits and elevate yourself. When you view difficulties in this light they will be much easier to cope with.

Don't allow a feeling of righteousness to cause you to become conceited.

ואמרת בלבבך כחי ועצם ידי עשה לי את החיל הזה. (דברים ח' י"ז)

"[Lest] YOU WILL SAY IN YOUR HEART, MY POWER AND THE

STRENGTH OF MY HAND DID FOR ME ALL OF THIS SUCCESS."
(*Dvorim* 8:17)

This verse is usually quoted in reference to having an awareness of the power of the Almighty and not becoming conceited due to financial success or success with an enemy in time of war. I heard from Rabbi Shalom Schwadron in the name of the Brisker Rav, Rabbi Yitzchok Zev Soloveitchik, that this verse also applies to someone who says, "It was due to my personal spiritual merits that we were victorious." We should always realize that what the Almighty does for us is due to His kindness and compassion and we should not feel that it was our own righteousness and merits that brought success.

Joy helps you appreciate the Almighty.

והיה אם שכח תשכח את השם אלקיך. (דברים ח' י"ט)

"AND IT WILL BE IF YOU FORGET THE ALMIGHTY, YOUR G-D."
(*Dvorim* 8:19)

We find in the Midrash that the word *vehayah* refers to joy. What joy could there possibly be in forgetting the Almighty? The Kotzker Rebbe said that this verse can be understood by dividing these words differently. "If you forget to be in a state of joy," that is, you forget the *vehayah* which refers to joy, this will cause you to forget the Almighty. (*Harebbe Maikotzk*, p.96)

If someone lacks joy, he will find it difficult to appreciate the Almighty. Hence joy is one of the forty-eight tools for acquiring Torah. Lack of joy leads to many faults and difficulties. When in a state of joy, you have a greater appreciation for the Almighty and all that He has given you.

Be willing to make positive changes.

כי עם קשה ערף אתה. (דברים ט' ו')

"FOR YOU ARE A STIFF-NECKED PEOPLE." (*Dvorim* 9:6)

Sforno comments: It is impossible for there to be righteousness and straightness of heart together with the trait of being stiff-necked. Being stiff-necked refers to someone who follows the arbitrary feelings of his heart and his own subjective thinking even though a Torah scholar will show him with clear proof that his thinking is incorrect and will cause him loss or harm. That is, he will not turn to the Torah scholar, as if his neck were as hard as iron and he is physically unable to turn it this way or that. Instead of listening to reason, he continues to follow his own emotions.

Rabbi Eliyahu Eliezer Dessler summarizes this by saying: What does it mean to be stiff-necked? This is when someone sees the truth with his own eyes but is still not willing to change his negative ways. (*Michtav Maieliyahu*, vol.1, p. 63)

A person has to be willing to act according to his intellectual understanding. If a person's original way of thinking was mistaken and someone points this out to him, he should resolve to make the necessary changes. But many people find this very difficult to do. It is so much easier to continue to behave as you have done previously. It takes a strong act of will to make positive changes in one's behavior. Be flexible and open. Be willing to change anything that needs changing. Anyone having this positive trait will find that he continues to grow and improve throughout his entire life.

Keep asking yourself, "What good deeds can I do now?"

ועתה ישראל מה השם אלקיך שאל מעמך. (דברים י' י"ב)

"AND NOW ISRAEL, WHAT DOES THE LORD, YOUR G-D, ASK FROM YOU..." (*Dvorim* 10:12)

The Chofetz Chayim taught that a person should view himself as someone hired out to work for another person for a specific period of time. When such a person completes one task, he approaches the employer and asks, "What should I do next?" This should be our attitude in relationship to the Almighty. When you finish one *mitzvah* you should immediately look for opportunities to do another *mitzvah*.

This attitude can be seen in this verse. "And *now* Israel," at every present moment, ask yourself the question, "What can I do now? What does the Almighty ask of me at the present time?" (*Hachofetz Chayim*, vol.3, p.1091)

There is a great difference between enjoying what you do and failing to enjoy it. When you are involved in some job or series of tasks that you are only doing because you have to but really dislike, as soon as you complete one task you are not very anxious to start something new. You will probably procrastinate. When, however, you are involved in work that you feel great pleasure in doing, you do not consider what you are doing as work but as enjoyment. You would prefer being active in those matters rather than resting or doing anything else. When a person develops a deep sense of joy for doing *mitzvos*, he feels great pleasure and satisfaction when engaged in a *mitzvah*. When he finishes one good deed, he will immediately want to start doing another. Therefore to develop the attitude expressed by the Chofetz Chayim we need to appreciate the great value and beauty in doing good deeds. Once you feel a love for *mitzvos*, you will eagerly ask, "What good deeds can I do now?"

Develop a positive attitude towards constructive criticism.

ומלתם את ערלת לבבכם וערפכם לא תקשו עוד. (דברים י' ט"ז)

"AND YOU SHALL CIRCUMCISE THE COVERING OF YOUR HEART, AND YOU SHALL NOT CONTINUE TO BE STIFF-NECKED." (*Dvorim* 10:16)

Rabbi Simcha Zissel of Kelm cites the SMAK (9) that this verse contains a commandment to love words of correction and to love those who try to correct you. The latter half of this verse contains a prohibition against failing to listen to those who try to correct you. A person who does not want to change will resent those who try to correct him. Such a person is far from improving himself. A person pays a doctor for trying to heal him from illness and is very grateful to the doctor. This should be your attitude towards people who try to help you improve spiritually. Remove any traces of resentment towards those who rebuke you. When you have a true desire for self-improvement, you will feel love towards those who give you suggestions on ways you can improve. (*Chochmah Umussar*, vol.1, p.34)

Many people are afraid to try to correct others because they fear the resentment they assume others will feel towards them for pointing out their faults. But if people will see that whenever someone tries to correct you not only are you free from resentment, but you actually feel love towards him, they will be happy to give you constructive criticism. By developing a positive attitude towards criticism not only will you save yourself much pain, but you will be able to improve in many ways. Different people focus on different areas of improvement. By getting a lot of feedback about your behavior from others you will become aware of many things about yourself that otherwise you would not have been aware of. This will help you greatly in your quest for spiritual growth.

Think of times in the past when people criticized you and you had a negative attitude towards them. Think now of how you benefited or can possibly benefit now from that criticism. Realizing this, feel positive about that criticism and use this as a tool to feel positive in the future.

In Baranovitch, when the *mashgiach*, Rabbi Yisroel Yaakov Lubchanski, would deliver a lecture on ethics, Rabbi Elchonon Wasserman, head of the yeshiva, who was a great scholar and *tzadik*, would join the listeners, choosing a seat near the rear entrance in the middle of the second bench like one of the younger students. (Rabbi Chaim Shapiro; *The Jewish Observer*, Oct. 1973)

True joy is the joy of doing good deeds.

והיה אם שמע תשמעו אל מצותי אשר אנכי מצוה אתכם היום. (דברים
י״א י״ג)

"AND IT SHALL BE IF YOU HEARKEN TO MY COMMANDMENTS
WHICH I COMMAND YOU THIS DAY..." (*Dvorim* 11:13)

This is a section of the Torah that is recited daily in the *Shma Yisroel*. The Torah states that there will be a reward for observing the Almighty's commandments. On the first Hebrew word of this verse, *vehayah*, the *Ohr Hachayim* comments: *Vehayah* denotes joy. There is a condition in this verse that the commandments should be fulfilled with joy. True joy comes only when a person does good deeds. But if a person has high feelings without true meaning, it is only a temporary state that will not last.

There are many attitudes a person can have towards doing good deeds. One is guilt for not doing what is right. Another is fear of punishment. But even though in verses 16 and 17 the Torah warns of retribution for doing wrong, the attitude that comes first should be joy for doing good. Most people eat because they enjoy eating. If a person does not eat for a number of days, his life is in danger. But very few people sit down to a delicious meal and say to themselves, "I'd better eat or else I'll die." If a person has no appetite whatsoever he has to force himself to eat, but the vast majority of people focus on the pleasure or at least pleasantness of eating. Similarly with *mitzvos*. Keep your focus on the joy of spiritual fulfillment. If someone has no appetite for doing good, he needs to find other motivations. But a person who is spiritually healthy will experience great pleasure in doing good.

The Chazon Ish wrote a letter to someone who was financially well-off but whose brother was suffering from poverty and asked him to send money to his brother. He emphasized joy in giving charity, "If you do decide to help him in his hour of need, you should do so with joy, just as one has when he builds a *Sukah*, listens to the *shofar*, or fulfills any other *mitzvah*. An essential aspect of the *mitzvah* is the joy that we have merited to fulfill it." (*Kovetz Igros* 2:93; *P'air Hador*, vol.3, p.15)

Have compassion for all living things.

Focus on satisfaction, not desire.

ונתתי עשב בשדך לבהמתך ואכלת ושבעת. (דברים י"א ט"ו)

"AND I WILL GIVE GRASS IN THE FIELD FOR YOUR ANIMALS AND YOU WILL EAT AND BE SATISFIED." (*Dvorim* 11:15)

The Talmud (*Brochos* 40a) states on this verse that a person is obligated to feed his animals in the morning before he himself eats.

This is to teach us compassion for all living creatures. Even when you are hungry, your first thoughts should be of helping those who are unable to help themselves. A person who owns an animal will have this daily lesson for gaining more sensitivity to the needs of others.

On this verse, the Brisker Rav, Rabbi Yitzchok Zev Soloveitchik, noted that the blessing for animals is that they should have a large quantity of food, much grass in the field. But for people the blessing is to feel satisfied when they eat.

Eating excessively can be hazardous to both one's physical and spiritual well-being. Keep your focus on satisfaction and away from desire.

Bitochon gives a person peace and serenity and allows him to study Torah.

ולדבקה בו. (דברים י"א כ"ב)

"AND TO CLEAVE TO THE ALMIGHTY." (*Dvorim* 11:22)

Rabbi Meir Simcha Hacohen commented on this verse that although we find the concept of *bitochon*, trust in the Almighty, hinted at in the Torah, we do not find an explicit command, "Have trust in the Almighty." Therefore this verse is the commandment to have *bitochon*. One of the best examples of trust and reliance on someone else is that of a king's son who relies on his father. His father loves him and, being a king, has the ability to supply him with all his needs. This is our relationship with the Almighty. He is our king and father. Cleaving to the Almighty means living with this awareness. The immediate benefit to a person who internalizes this attribute is an inner feeling of peace and serenity. The spiritual benefit is the willingness to devote oneself to Torah study and to cleave to Torah scholars. A person who lacks *bitochon* is afraid to allow his children to study Torah because he is concerned about how they will manage financially. When a person has *bitochon*, however, he is free from worries and wants his sons to study Torah and his daughters to marry Torah scholars. (*Meshech Chochmah*)

At times the Brisker Rav, Rabbi Yitzchok Zev Soloveitchik, would have difficulties in obtaining enough money to give his married students for their monthly stipend. Someone commented to him that if he would be able to have a few months' money available ahead of time he wouldn't have to worry. The Brisker Rav replied, "Even if someone would offer me a gigantic sum of money to keep in a bank account in order to pay the students, I would not want it. This way each month I fulfill the *mitzvah* of *bitochon*. I would not want to forego this *mitzvah* for any amount of money in the world."

REAIH

When listening to a class or lecture take it as seriously as you would if the speaker was speaking to you personally.

ראה אנכי נתן לפניכם היום ברכה וקללה. את הברכה אשר תשמעו אל מצות השם אלקיכם אשר אנכי מצוה אתכם היום. והקללה אם לא תשמעו אל מצות השם אלקיכם. (דברים י"א כ"ו-כ"ח)

"SEE I AM PLACING BEFORE YOU THIS DAY A BLESSING AND A CURSE. THE BLESSING IF YOU WILL LISTEN TO THE COMMANDMENTS OF THE ALMIGHTY WHICH I AM COMMANDING YOU THIS DAY. AND THE CURSE IF YOU DO NOT LISTEN TO THE ALMIGHTY'S COMMANDMENTS." (*Dvorim* 11:26-28)

On the first word of this verse, *Reaih*, Ibn Ezra comments: "He (Moshe) is talking to each one individually."

Although Moshe was speaking to the entire Jewish people, he started off in the singular to tell everyone that they should listen to what he had to say as if he were speaking to him alone. When someone is delivering a lecture or giving a class, it is easy to think, "He is speaking to everyone else here. I don't have to take what he says seriously since he is not really directing his words to me." But this is an error. The way to grow from lectures and classes is to view the words of the speaker as if they were directed only to you. Try it out. The next time you are in an audience listening to inspiring words tell yourself, "The speaker has me in mind. Let me see how I can utilize what he says for self-improvement."

A friend of mine was visiting relatives in a certain city far away from his home. He wanted to speak to the congregation of the local synagogue about Jewish education. But he was afraid that what he wanted to say was quite sharp and the listeners might be offended. When he shared his apprehensions with the Rabbi of the synagogue, he was told, "Don't worry. With my congregation you can say anything you want. They are *Yenemites*."

"I've heard of Yemenites, but what do you mean by *Yenemites*?" asked my friend.

"I mean that regardless of what you will say everyone will assume that you are referring to someone else. They will each think that you are talking to *yenem* (which is Yiddish for 'the other one')," explained the Rabbi.

Sure enough, after my friend delivered a powerful lecture, someone came over to him and said, "That was really wonderful the way you spoke. So and so really needed to hear what you had to say." So certain was he that the lecture was directed to others, that he failed to relate the message to himself, which he personally had a strong need to hear.

There is no middle way, only a blessing or a curse.

Sforno comments on these verses (11:26-8) that there is no middle way. If a person follows the Torah, his life will be a blessed life. If a person fails to live by the commandments, he will live a cursed life.

At first glance, this might seem to be an extreme statement. But just a little thought will show that this is so. Life is either purposeful and meaningful or not. A life of meaning is a blessed life. A life without meaning is a life devoid of satisfaction. How then can there be a middle way? Living with an awareness of the Almighty gives one's life a context that makes everything one does a step towards one's blissful eternal home. Living without this awareness makes each day another day closer to oblivion.

How then can people live meaningless lives, as many people seem to be living? The answer is that they are sleepwalkers. They are in a semi-drugged state of unawareness. They live each day without thinking of their purpose in this world. If they do wake up from their hypnotic state to ask themselves about the meaning of their lives, they have two choices. They will either look at life as meaningless. All that they are involved in will not make any real difference when life is over. This is the greatest curse that could possibly befall anyone. On the other hand, if they become aware of the Creator and decide to live a life of fulfilling His will, they will experience the greatest of blessings in this world. Each day will be an exciting adventure full of the joy of doing the Creator's will. Truly then there is no middle way: only a curse or a blessing. The choice is yours to make: Choose life!

Appreciate the joy inherent in Torah.

את הברכה אשר תשמעו אל מצות השם אלקיכם. (דברים י"א כ"ז)

"THE BLESSING IF YOU LISTEN TO THE COMMANDMENTS OF THE ALMIGHTY." (*Dvorim* 11:27)

The *Ohr Hachayim* writes: "Besides any other blessing, just listening to the Almighty's Torah is an amazing pleasure and gives one the energy of life (*mechaya hanefesh*). When someone actually experiences the wonderful taste of Torah, he will feel that he has a debt of gratitude to the Giver of such a wonderful present. Rather than demanding a reward for what he does, he will realize that it is he who owes the Almighty."

Fortunate is the person who reaches the level expressed by the *Ohr Hachayim*. The life of such a person is one of joy and ecstasy. Even if someone is not totally on this level, just contemplating it is very beneficial.

Joy is a by-product of love for the Almighty.

ושמחתם לפני השם אלקיכם. (דברים י"ב י"ב)

"AND YOU SHALL REJOICE BEFORE THE ALMIGHTY." (*Dvorim* 12:12)

Sforno (see this verse and verse 7) comments: Serve the Almighty with joy as is befitting everyone who serves Him from love.

When you feel love for someone, you are happy to do any action that will be a manifestation of your love. Joy is a by-product of love for the Almighty. Although there is not an explicit commandment in the Torah to have joy on a regular day, included in the constant commandment of experiencing love for the Almighty is the concept of feeling joy whenever you focus on your love for the Almighty.

Rabbi Nochum of Horadna was always very joyous on *Simchas Torah*. During his last *Simchas Torah* he jumped on a table and said, "Nochumka, if you were no longer alive and the Almighty came to you and said, 'Nochumka, arise from your grave and rejoice on *Simchas Torah*,' think of the great joy you would experience. You would dance with much ecstasy and elation. Nu, so what if you are still alive, you can still experience that same joy." And with this he felt even greater joy and enthusiasm. (*Chayai Hamussar*, vol.2, p.200)

No matter how far away you are from the Almighty you can always come close when you make an effort.

אחרי השם אלקיכם תלכו ואתו תיראו ואת מצותיו תשמרו ובקלו תשמעו
ואתו תעבדו ובו תדבקון. (דברים י"ג ה')

"AFTER THE ALMIGHTY, YOUR G-D, SHALL YOU WALK, AND HIM SHALL YOU FEAR, AND HIS COMMANDMENTS YOU SHALL OBSERVE AND TO HIS VOICE SHALL YOU HEARKEN, AND HIM SHALL YOU SERVE AND TO HIM SHALL YOU CLEAVE." (*Dvorim* 13:5)

The Chofetz Chayim asked: The first Hebrew word in this verse is *acharai*, which denotes a far distance (see Rashi to 11:30). Since this verse tells us to follow the Almighty why didn't the Torah use a term denoting closeness since we should be as close as possible to Him?

This teaches us, said the Chofetz Chayim, that regardless of how far a person feels he is from the Almighty, he should never give up hope. With all of his power he should strive to come closer to the Almighty. Therefore the Torah uses a term which denotes distance. Even those who are presently far from the Almighty should seek Him and will find Him. Never allow any faults or transgressions to prevent you from coming closer to the Almighty. (*Hachofetz Chayim*, vol.3, p.1160)

When a person feels discouraged, his belief that he can no longer improve becomes a self-fulfilling prophecy and the truth is that he will not improve. But as soon as you believe that you can improve in any area you will immediately find the strength to make improvements. If you lack the knowledge of what to do to improve, you will find people you can consult. But this takes motivation and you will only feel motivated if you believe that there is hope for the future. Remember what the Chofetz Chayim said about never despairing and keep your focus on what you can do in the present to become closer to the Almighty.

Rabbi Chayim of Tzanz once said to an evildoer, "Don't think that because you give in to your evil inclination in some areas you therefore must be evil in all areas. Rather, in whatever ways you can, do good and overcome evil." (*Maigdolai Hachasidus: Hoadmor Maitzanz*)

Rabbi Levi Yitzchok of Berditchev once approached a wicked person who did much wrong in his life and said, "I am envious of you. If you will repent and return to the Almighty with love and sincerity, all of your blemishes will be transformed into a great shining light. I envy the brilliance of that light." (*ibid.*, p.74)

Give emotional support to those who need it.

כי יהיה בך אביון מאחד אחיך באחד שעריך בארצך אשר השם אלקיך נתן לך לא תאמץ את לבבך ולא תקפץ את ידך מאחיך האביון. (דברים ט"ו ז')

"IF THERE BE AMONG YOU A NEEDY MAN, ONE OF YOUR BRETHREN WITHIN ANY OF YOUR GATES, IN YOUR LAND WHICH THE ALMIGHTY, YOUR G-D, GIVES YOU, YOU SHALL NOT HARDEN YOUR HEART NOR SHUT YOUR HAND AGAINST YOUR NEEDY BROTHER." (*Dvorim* 15:7)

Ibn Ezra explains the words, "you shall not harden your heart" that you shall not refrain from speaking kind words to his heart.

When a person is poor, he suffers more than just financial deprivation. He can easily suffer much emotional pain. Many times he might become totally discouraged and broken. Therefore we have an obligation to open our hearts to such a person and to talk to him in a compassionate and empathetic manner. We must go out of our way to give him words of encouragement. Just giving the person money without trying to help him emotionally is only part of the job. It is a sign of apathy and callousness not to try to cheer up a person who needs emotional support. Moreover, just as Rashi says in verse 8 that we are obligated to help someone financially even many times if the person remains in need, so too we should keep on giving emotional support to those who need it even if we have to do so many times.

Rabbi Dovid Feinstein, oldest son of Rabbi Moshe Feinstein, said, "My father never wasted a minute. But if a poor or troubled person, or even a *nudnik*, took an hour to pour out his heart, my father could spare an hour." (Rabbi Nosson Scherman, *The Jewish Observer*, Oct. 1986, p.18)

Once Rabbi Moshe Feinstein and a student accompanying him were rushing to an important meeting; they were already quite late. A poor elderly Jew stopped them for a donation, and then started talking about his problems. The Rosh Hayeshiva gave him several dollars and then stood listening to him as if he had all the time in the world. The student wondered if perhaps the Rosh Hayeshiva had concluded that they were too late for the meeting.

Finally the poor man finished and the Rosh Hayeshiva started to walk even more quickly than before. The student asked him, "Why did the Rosh Hayeshiva stand and listen? Couldn't he have just given the money and gone on, since we're in such a rush?"

The Rosh Hayeshiva answered that listening to someone unburden his heart is worth more to the person than the money. (Rabbi Nathan Lomner, *ibid.*, p.33)

Treat a poor person you are helping with the respect shown to an essrog.

כי פתח תפתח את ידך לו והעבט תעביטנו די מחסרו אשר יחסר לו. (דברים ט"ו ח')

"YOU SHALL SURELY OPEN YOUR HAND UNTO HIM AND SHALL SURELY LEND HIM SUFFICIENT FOR HIS NEED WHICH HE LACKS." (*Dvorim* 15:8)

Rabbi Yosef Dov Soloveitchik, author of *Bais Halevi*, wrote that when you give money or gifts to a poor person, you are fulfilling the commandment of giving charity besides the other Torah commandments which are fulfilled by your kind act (such as "Loving your fellow man"). Therefore at the time of your giving him the money he is similar to an *essrog* that one takes to fulfill the commandment on the holiday of Sukos. Even though after you fulfill the *mitzvah* with the *essrog* it no longer has the same sanctity as it did when you fulfilled the commandment with it, nevertheless while you are fulfilling the commandment, it has sanctity and it is forbidden to treat it disrespectfully. So too with the poor person, when you are giving him charity he is the object of your *mitzvah* and it is forbidden to do anything that would imply disrespect towards him. (*Bais Halevi, Parshas Trumah*)

The more difficulties a poor person has the more likely he is to be bitter and sometimes even obnoxious. Regardless of his way of talking to you, make every effort to behave in an elevated manner towards him. The more difficult it is, the greater you become. An *essrog*, which the *Bais Halevi* cites as an example, is extremely vulnerable and therefore people handle it with great care. So too, a person who has suffered is more sensitive than others and special care must be taken not to hurt his feelings.

The wife of Reb Shraga Frank once came home and was shocked to find that someone had broken into the closet where they kept their money. "What happened?" she asked her husband. Reb Shraga Frank, who was the father-in-law of Rabbi Isser Zalman Meltzer and Rabbi Moshe Mordechai Epstein, explained, "Someone came a short while ago to borrow some money. I searched for the key to the closet, but I couldn't find it. I understood that either you took the key with you or you put it in some unusual place."

"I thought to myself, 'If I tell this person to return in two hours when I'll have the key, he'll probably think that I am just making an excuse because I don't want to lend him the money, and he won't come back for the loan. Should I tell him that he should wait until my wife returns? I don't know when she'll return. Waiting without knowing how long can be very uncomfortable.'

"Because of these thoughts, I decided to take a metal tool and break open the door of the closet. It was worthwhile to break the door in order to save another person from discomfort, even if for only a few minutes."(*Bederech Aitz Hachayim*, vol.1, p.73)

Feel joy when you give generously to those in need.

ושמחת לפני השם אלקיך אתה ובנך ובתך ועבדך ואמתך והלוי אשר בשעריך והגר והיתום והאלמנה אשר בקרבך במקום אשר יבחר השם אלקיך לשכן שמו שם. וזכרת כי עבד היית במצרים ושמרת ועשית את החקים האלה. (דברים ט״ז י״א-י״ב)

"AND YOU SHALL REJOICE BEFORE THE ALMIGHTY, YOUR G-D, YOU AND YOUR SON AND YOUR DAUGHTER, AND YOUR MANSERVANT AND YOUR MAIDSERVANT AND THE LEVITE WHO IS IN YOUR GATES, AND THE CONVERT AND THE ORPHAN AND THE WIDOW WHO IS IN YOUR MIDST, AT THE PLACE WHICH THE LORD YOUR G-D WILL CHOOSE TO HAVE HIS PRESENCE DWELL THERE.

AND YOU SHALL REMEMBER THAT YOU WERE A SLAVE IN EGYPT, AND YOU SHALL OBSERVE AND DO THESE STATUTES." (*Dvorim* 16:11,12)

The Ksav Sofer explains the continuity of these two verses in the following manner: There are some people who might find it hard to give financial assistance to a convert, orphan, and widow because they are not satisfied with what they themselves have. They always seek to acquire more money for themselves, so how can they give what they have to others? All the more so on the holidays it will be even harder for them to give to others since it is forbidden to work on the holidays and they do not have any new income. Even if such a person does give to the poor as he is really obligated to do, he will not feel joy when he gives charity. Therefore the Torah tells this person to remember his previous situation when he was a slave in Egypt; doing forced labor the entire day and subsisting on just the barest minimum of food. When a person remembers this and realizes how much better off he is now, he will feel happy with what he has and in his present joyous state will readily give generously to those in need. By keeping in mind how wonderful it is to have freedom, you will easily be able to fulfill all of these statutes with great feelings of joy. (*Ksav Sofer al Hatorah*)

The way we react to our present situation is always dependent on how we view it, and how we view a situation is dependent on what factors we take into account in the entire context of things. When a person feels that he is missing things, it is because he wishes that he would have more than he does. But if a person was previously in a much worse situation and now he has more than he did before, he will appreciate what he has. This enables him to experience greater happiness in his own life and also enables him to share some of his good fortune with those less fortunate.

There is a very well-known story that illustrates this point. In a shtetl in Europe a poor man with a small house and large family came to his Rabbi to complain about how crowded he always felt. The Rabbi asked him if he owned any animals. He had a small farm with some chickens, a dog, a cat, and a couple of cows. The Rabbi told him to take the chickens into his house. While he did not understand how this could possibly help him with his problem, he nevertheless listened to his Rabbi and took his chickens inside the house.

The next day he came to the Rabbi and complained that the situation was even worse. The Rabbi then told him to take the dog and cat inside his house. He again listened to the Rabbi and brought them inside. By the next day he felt even more crowded, the noise was awful, the animals kept fighting with each other and there was hardly any room for the people. He ran to his Rabbi and complained bitterly that he found his living conditions unbearable. To his surprise the Rabbi told him to bring in one of the cows. Although he was flabbergasted at this advice, he still listened to the Rabbi and brought in the cow. The next day he came as early as he could to the Rabbi and said that now he could not go on, the situation was so crowded, so noisy, and so smelly that it was literally impossible to live in his house.

The Rabbi then said to him, "Go home now and take out the animals." After removing the animals from his house, he so appreciated all the room he had plus the peace and quiet of just a group of lively children that he never again complained about his living conditions.

An American lawyer who studied in Yeshiva Aish Hatorah once told me that when he was in Kennedy airport waiting for his plane to leave for Israel, the plane was greatly delayed. Every hour or so they announced another delay. After ten hours, he was very nervous and irritated. The other people who were also planning to go on that plane were all complaining about the long delay. Then he noticed a middle-aged couple who were calmly sitting down and appeared to be very relaxed. He approached them and asked, "How is it possible to remain calm when the plane is delayed for so long?"

Their reply shook him up, "Well, in the Second World War we were in a concentration camp and so waiting a number of hours in Kennedy airport does not really bother us at all."

This vividly illustrates how our reaction towards what we do and do not have is relative. Keep in mind how your situation is better than it could be and you will live a pleasurable life.

A word of warning: when someone else complains to you, don't just say, "It could be worse." Many people resent hearing this. The first step is to empathize with the person. Try to experience some of his suffering with him. The next step is to try to show him practical ways to improve his situation. If that is not possible, then show him how he can view his present situation differently. This is a skill and takes wisdom to know what to say and what to avoid saying to any individual. Note that in the story above the Rabbi didn't just say, "It could be worse." He used a technique that would work for that specific person. Helping others out of emotional pain is a great act of kindness and the more skilled you become the more *chesed* you will be able to do.

SHOFTIM

Be a judge for your own behavior before the behavior of others.

שפטים ושטרים תתן לך. (דברים ט״ז י״ח)

"JUDGES AND POLICE YOU SHALL PLACE FOR YOURSELF." (*Dvorim* 16:18)

Rabbi Simcha Bunim of Parshischo commented: Make for yourself judges and police, that is, before you go and make judgments about other people, judge yourself first. As the Sages (*Bava Basra* 60b) have said, "First correct yourself and only then correct others." (cited in *Otzer Chayim*)

It is very easy to find fault with others. But this can easily lead to your becoming arrogant and retaining all of your faults. While we have an obligation to help others grow, keep reviewing your own behavior to see what you can improve. The purpose of police is to make certain that the laws are enforced. Similarly, when you find one of your faults don't just feel guilty about it, but take action to overcome it.

Rabbi Tzvi Michel Shapiro used to say jokingly, "If a person wants an easy way to be righteous, the solution is that he should not study *mussar*. Then he will consider himself completely righteous. But once a person starts to study *mussar* he will realize that he is far from perfect." (*Betuv Yerushalayim*, p.118)

Regardless of how wise you are if you are biased you will not be objective and will not be able to see the total truth.

כי השחד יעור עיני חכמים ויסלף דברי צדיקים. (דברים ט״ז י״ט)

The Torah prohibits a judge from taking any bribe:
"FOR BRIBERY BLINDS THE EYES OF WISE MEN." (*Dvorim* 16:19)

The Chofetz Chayim gives an analogy: If you would hear Reuven say that Shimon is wealthy, you need to know Reuven's financial situation before you can have a clear picture as to how much money Shimon has. If Reuven himself is very poor, than his considering Shimon wealthy does not mean that Shimon really has a large amount of money. But if someone who is internationally famous as one of the richest men in the world would say that someone is wealthy, we know that the person he is referring to owns a tremendous amount and has enormous financial assets. Similarly with wisdom. If Reuven says that Shimon is wise, we need to know how wise Reuven is to get a picture of Shimon's wisdom. If Rabbi Akiva Eger said that someone is wise, we have a clearer picture of the person's wisdom. All the more so, if we heard the Rambam say that someone is wise, we know that the person has much wisdom.

With the above in mind, said the Chofetz Chayim, we can gain a deeper understanding of this verse. The Almighty Himself, the Omniscient One, testifies that a person is wise. This person must have the ultimate in wisdom that is possible for a human to have. Even so, the Torah states about him that bribery will blind him. Regardless of how wise any mortal is once he is biased he will not be able to see. (*Chofetz Chayim al Hatorah*)

This refers even to a small bribe. All the more so to a large one. There is no greater bias than our desire to see ourselves in a positive light. We do not want to see any faults in ourselves, and we want to think that we are full of virtues. This bias will prevent us from taking an honest look at ourselves and objectively finding our faults and limitations. But self-improvement is the goal of our existence and because it is so important we must force ourselves to reject the bribery of our own bias. Make every effort to view yourself as if you were reviewing the life of a complete stranger about whom you are totally objective. Only when you see where and who you really are can you grow spiritually and improve your character traits.

Do not allow appearances to deceive you in spiritual matters.

לא תטע לך אשרה כל עץ אצל מזבח השם אלקיך. (דברים ט״ז כ״א)

"YOU SHALL NOT PLANT AN ASHAIRAH, ANY TREE, NEAR THE ALTAR OF THE ALMIGHTY." (*Dvorim* 16:21)

The Sages (*Sanhedrin* 7b) equate appointing an unqualified judge with an *ashairah* (a tree that was worshipped for idolatry). What is the connection? Rabbi Chayim Soloveitchik of Brisk explained: A regular idol is noticeable to all that it is an idol. Whoever sees it will easily be able to recognize that it is an idol and he must be very careful. But a tree that has been worshipped as an idol looks to the casual observer as if it is just an ordinary tree and looks harmless. But looks can be deceiving for it is really an idol and is spiritually dangerous. So too, a judge who is not qualified. From the outside he can appear very learned and even righteous. But because he is really not qualified or has certain character failings, he can be very dangerous. (cited in *Otzer Chayim*)

One needs to learn to be discerning. Even those things that appear to be harmless can be very dangerous. If someone puts poison that is colorless and odorless in some food, although the food does not appear harmful, it can inflict mortal damage. Similarly, there are many things that are detrimental to one's spiritual well-being that at first glance do not seem dangerous. When in doubt consult a reliable Torah authority.

Learn to make distinctions between different situations.

ולא תקים לך מצבה. (דברים ט"ז כ"ב)

"DO NOT ERECT A 'MATZAIVAH' [see Rashi]." (*Dvorim* 16:22)

Rabbi Tzvi Elimelech Shapiro of Dinov commented: There are people who are rigid and inflexible. They have certain habits and customs and are unwilling to deviate from them. But this is a mistake. This day is not similar to any previous day, and no two situations are exactly alike. What is the right thing to do in any situation is dependent on all the unique circumstances of that situation. This can be understood from our verse. Do not erect a way that is rigid or stubbornly unbending regardless of the situation (*matzov* meaning situation). Rather you should always take action according to the needs of that particular moment. (*cited in Otzer Chayim*)

What could be a *mitzvah* to do in one situation, could be a transgression in another situation. At times a certain act could be a *kidush Hashem*, and in other situations where some factors are a bit different, similar behavior would constitute a *chilul Hashem*. A person who does things compulsively without wisdom will make many mistakes. Only someone who has a grasp of the full panoramic view of Torah principles will have the necessary wisdom to judge what is the correct thing to do in every situation. The more Torah you learn the greater will be your ability to make distinctions between different situations.

In his eulogy on Rabbi Yitzchok Zev Soloveitchik of Brisk, Rabbi Yechezkail Abramsky said about his father, "Whoever was in the presence of Rav Chayim Brisker was not able to label his personality. People frequently type someone as being either compassionate or cruel, stingy or generous, bad-tempered or patient, etc. But Rav Chayim behaved as the Torah commands one to behave each and every second, and in every situation." (*Peninai Rabainu Yechezkail*, p.10)

The Steipler was very careful about giving advice to people. Very frequently he would say to the person who consulted him, "This is a matter that only someone who knows you very well can answer." (*Peninai Rabainu Hakehilos Yaakov*, p.123)

When in charge of the welfare of others, try to sustain your enthusiasm.

והיה כשבתו על כסא ממלכתו. (דברים י״ז י״ח)

The Torah writes about a king:
"AND IT WILL BE AS WHEN HE SITS ON HIS THRONE OF ROYALTY..." (*Dvorim* 17:18)

Rabbi Mordechai Pragamantzky of Telz, Lithuania, used to say about this that the Torah states "as when he sits on his throne" and does not say "when he sits." This is to teach us that even if a king is a ruler for a long time, he should still view himself as if he just obtained his rulership. When a person first acquires a position of leadership, he is very idealistic and has many ideas and plans that he would like to implement for the benefit of the people under his authority. But frequently after some time passes the leader becomes either bored, disillusioned, or worn out and many of his beneficial plans become lost. Therefore the Torah says about a king that he should always look at himself as if he just started sitting on his throne and this will enable him to have the same energy and enthusiasm as he originally had.

This same principle applies to anyone who is in charge of the welfare of others. Remember the enthusiasm you had when you first started out and keep trying to sustain it.

Keep a distance from arrogance for it is the father of all negative traits.

לבלתי רום לבבו מאחיו. (דברים י"ז כ')

"THAT HE SHOULD NOT RAISE HIS HEART ABOVE HIS BROTHERS."
(*Dvorim* 17:20)

Rabbi Simcha Zissel of Kelm commented on this verse which is a prohibition against a person being arrogant, "Arrogance is a reprehensible trait that is the father of all other negative traits." (*Chochmah Umussar*, vol.1, p.231)

A person who has arrogance will automatically have many other faults. He will easily become angry when others do not do as he wishes. He will not be satisfied with what he has because he arrogantly thinks he should always have more than he does. He will speak against other people because he feels above them. He will not exert himself to do favors for others because he feels that others should do things for him and he has no obligation to help them. He will seek honor and power and therefore all that he does will be motivated by selfishness. He will take advantage of other people because he feels that everyone is only in this world to serve him. He will be ungrateful for any good that others do for him because he thinks that of course others should serve him. He will not admit that he made any mistakes because that would be humiliating and he wants others to feel that he is infallible and he often believes this himself. He will not honor his parents properly because he wants them to serve him. He will boast as much as he can to build himself up in the eyes of others. He will frequently lie in order to save himself from anything that will lessen his stature in the eyes of others and in order that others should have a higher opinion of him than he really deserves. He will not ask anyone for clarification if he does not understand something for this would be belittling to him. He will frequently become involved in quarrels. He will blame others when things go wrong because he never wants to take the blame for anything himself. He will act obnoxiously towards others. He will hate any person who slights him in any way. In short, a person who is arrogant will have a multitude of faults in many areas.

Because of the negative ramifications of this trait, it is crucial to be humble. When one realizes his smallness in comparison with the entire universe and the power of the Almighty, one will have to have humility. When one realizes the vast amount of knowledge that one is missing and the mistakes that one has already made, one will have to have humility. When one realizes the frailty of the human body and how even the strongest person eventually becomes weak and dies, one will have to have humility. The only way to have arrogance then is to lack awareness of the total picture of reality. Arrogance can only come from blindness. The arrogant need only open their eyes to reality and they will lose their arrogance. Therefore Moshe who had the highest level of awareness of reality was the most humble man. Once a person gains humility he will have all the virtues that are the opposite counterparts of the faults of those who are arrogant.

Rabbi Yisroel Salanter used to say, "When I see an arrogant person, I feel such a revulsion that I almost vomit." (*Tnuas Hamussar*, vol.1, p.303)

Rabbi Levi Yitzchok of Berditchev used to say, "If it were not for the fact that the Torah mentions the concept of arrogance, I would not believe that it is possible for any human being to experience arrogance. A human being is but dust and ashes, how is it possible to be arrogant?" (*Rav Levi Yitzchok of Berditchev*, p.27)

Rabbi Akiva Eger's great learning wedded to exceeding modesty fascinated all who knew him. His loyal friend, Rabbi Yaakov of Lissa, amazed after one of his profound Talmudic discussions with him, remarked, "How can he be so modest, when I know that he knows that I know that he knows?" (*Jewish Leaders*, p.108)

Learn to distinguish between trust in the Almighty and a lack of taking responsibility.

תמים תהיה עם השם אלקיך. (דברים י"ח י"ג)

"YOU SHALL TRUST WHOLEHEARTEDLY IN THE ALMIGHTY, YOUR G-D." (*Dvorim* 18:13)

This verse enjoins us to trust in the Almighty. A question that can frequently arise is what is considered normal *hishtadlus*, that is, human efforts that we have an obligation to make and what is considered a lack of trust?

One example of an issue of this sort was raised about testing people before marriage for being carriers of Tay-Sachs disease. Some may wonder whether such testing is not contrary to the trust we are required to have in Divine Providence: why search for problems when in all probability none exist? Rabbi Moshe Feinstein clarified this point:

"Although the percentage of infants born with this disease is small and one might be apt to apply the verse: 'You shall trust wholeheartedly in the Almighty,' (which Rashi interprets as meaning that one should not delve into the future) in light of the fact that a simple test has been developed for this, one who does not make use of it is like one who shuts his eyes to what can clearly be seen... and since the birth of such a child, G-d forbid, causes great anguish... it is prudent for all who are considering marriage to undergo this test." (cited in *The Jewish Observer*, May, 1986)

Having trust in the Almighty will give a person peace of mind and serenity. But one should never use a claim of trust in the Almighty to condone laziness or rash behavior. There is a thin line between the virtue of *bitochon* and the fault of carelessness and lack of taking responsibility. Consult a Torah scholar when questions arise.

Doctors told a certain person that he needed a serious operation. But the person refused to undergo the operation and claimed that he had *bitochon*. This was told to the Steipler. His reply was, "This person does not have a mastery of the trait of *bitochon*. Rather he is just fearful." (*Peninai Rabainu Hakehilos Yaakov*, p.119)

Feel pleasure when others benefit from what you have done.

ודברו השטרים אל העם לאמר מי האיש אשר בנה בית חדש ולא חנכו ילך וישב לביתו פן ימות במלחמה ואיש אחר יחנכנו. (דברים כ' ה')

Before going to war:
"THE POLICE SHALL SPEAK TO THE NATION: WHO IS THE MAN WHO BUILT A NEW HOUSE AND HAS NOT AS YET STARTED TO LIVE IN IT, HE SHOULD GO AND RETURN TO HIS HOUSE, LEST HE DIE IN THE WAR AND ANOTHER MAN WILL LIVE IN IT." (*Dvorim* 20:5)

Rashi adds: This causes a person much emotional pain. Rabbi Yehuda Leib Chasman commented on this that the fact that in case he dies in battle he himself will not live in the house that he built is not strong enough to free him from serving in the army. What is? The fact that someone else will live in his house. Even though rationally there is no difference to him in any practical way whether or not someone else will live there, nevertheless emotionally this can cause many people great pain. Why should it bother someone more because another person will benefit from his labors when he is unable to benefit himself? Although this attitude comes from a faulty character trait, it is still the nature of people. (*Ohr Yohail*, vol.3, *Vayaira*, p.19)

This attitude is so natural and so strong that it is taken into account when the morale of the army is concerned. But it causes much resentment and pain in people's lives. "I worked so hard why should others gain when they didn't work as hard as I did?" is so easy to say to oneself. But the elevated attitude is, "Even if I don't benefit from my work, I'm glad that someone else is gaining from it." This is what a "giver" will say and think. The negative attitude causes pain, the positive attitude gives one emotional pleasure. Work on mastering the positive attitude.

KI SAITZAI

Unity helps people accomplish.

כי תצא למלחמה על איביך ונתנו השם אלקיך בידך ושבית שביו. (דברים כ"א י')

"WHEN YOU GO OUT TO WAR AGAINST YOUR ENEMIES, AND THE ALMIGHTY, YOUR G-D, WILL GIVE HIM INTO YOUR HAND." (*Dvorim* 21:10)

The Ari, *z.l.*, noted that the verse starts off in the singular ("When you go out to war" is singular in the Hebrew). "Your enemies" is plural. And then the Torah reverts to the singular ("give him"). The point here is that if you have unity and are as one when you go out against your enemies, then even though your enemies are very numerous (therefore the plural) you will be victorious as easily as if they were just one. (cited in *Biurai Hamekubalim Beniglah*)

The importance of unity for accomplishment applies not only during times of war against an enemy. It is just as necessary during times of peace. When a group of people will work on any project with a spirit of togetherness, they will accomplish much more than if they would each be doing things by themselves.

When you use your intellect, you can defeat your evil inclination.

כי תצא למלחמה על איביך ונתנו השם אלקיך בידך ושבית,שביו. (דברים כ"א י')

"WHEN YOU GO OUT TO WAR AGAINST YOUR ENEMIES, AND THE ALMIGHTY, YOUR G-D, WILL GIVE HIM INTO YOUR HAND." (*Dvorim* 21:10)

Rabbi Simcha Zissel of Kelm writes that the greatest enemy that anyone has is one's evil inclination (*yetzer hara*). He constantly wants to ambush you and capture you. He acts as if he were your close friend and loves you. But his goal is really to destroy you. How does one wage war against one's evil inclination? You must use your intellect to contradict his false arguments and to see the truth when he shows you illusory images of how you will gain by following him. Do not allow him to cause you to panic for: "when you go out to war against your enemy, the Almighty will give him into your hand." When you are resolved to overcome your evil inclination, you will be victorious. (*Chochmah Umussar*, vol.1, p.376)

When making positive changes, give yourself at least thirty days of intensive work.

ובכתה את אביה ואת אמה ירח ימים. (דברים כ"א י"ג)

If after a war one of the soldiers wants to marry someone from the other side, there is a process that is necessary.

Part of this process is:

"AND SHE SHALL CRY FOR HER FATHER AND MOTHER A MONTH OF DAYS." (*Dvorim* 21:13)

The Ramban cites the Rambam that this month of crying is to have compassion for the woman the soldier wants to marry. By crying she will find inner peace. When one is very sad, one's nerves become calmed after crying. The Ramban himself explains that this month is the amount of time necessary for her to remove the name of her idols from her mouth and heart.

Rabbi Chayim Zaitchyk commented that we see from here that to really change a trait it takes a thirty day period of intensive work. This is the principle of the month of Elul which is a time for us to focus on our behavior and traits in order to make major improvements on ourselves.

At times a person tries to work on a trait for a day or two and when he doesn't see improvement he becomes discouraged and gives up. When you want to improve any trait, give yourself thirty days of serious effort in order to see visible changes. While some people are able to make changes very quickly, even they need a significant amount of time in order to ensure that the new habits become second nature. Even if you do not see any positive changes the first week or two, if you will persevere for an entire thirty days you will begin to see the fruits of your labor.

One must differentiate between wanting and desiring.

והיה אם לא חפצת בה. (דברים כ"א י"ד)

In reference to the non-Jewish woman the soldier wanted to marry, the verse states:
"AND IT WILL BE IF YOU DID NOT WANT HER." (*Dvorim* 21:14)

The Hebrew term in this verse is in the past tense ("did not want her"). Why isn't it stated in future tense (in the beginning he wanted her and later on he didn't)? The answer is that there is a difference between the term *chaishek* which means passion and lust, and the term *chofaitz* which means wanting because of a rational decision that something is good for you. The Torah is telling us that a person who wants to marry someone only because of infatuation and a passion that is based on good looks never really wanted the person from the very beginning (therefore the past tense is used). It was just desire, not an honest love for the other person. (*Ohel Moaid*, cited in *Maayanah Shel Torah*)

Rabbi Chayim Shmuelevitz used to cite the words of Rashi on

this verse that the Torah tells us that when a person marries only because of beauty he will end up hating the other person. This, said Rav Chayim, is crucial for anyone interested in getting married to remember.

Rabbi Noach Weinberg, Rosh Hayeshiva of Aish Hatorah, frequently says: "Love is the pleasure of seeing virtue. It is based on the reality of knowing the good qualities in another person. Infatuation, however, is blind. It is when your emotions prevent you from seeing the entire picture and you mistakenly believe that the object of your infatuation is totally perfect and without any faults."

Do all you can to help others in spiritual matters.

לא תראה את חמור אחיך או שורו נפלים בדרך והתעלמת מהם הקם תקים עמו. (דברים כ"ב ד')

"YOU SHALL NOT SEE THE DONKEY OF YOUR BROTHER OR HIS OX FALLING ON THE WAY AND NOT PAY ATTENTION TO THEM. RATHER YOU SHALL LIFT THEM UP WITH HIM." (*Dvorim* 22:4)

Rabbi Simcha Zissel of Kelm wrote that the Torah prohibits us from causing any unnecessary pain to animals. This applies even to pain that is temporary, all the more so to pain that will last for a long time. We have an even greater obligation to be careful not to cause any pain to people. Take for example someone who throws mud on a path that many people need to walk on; he is causing hundreds of people to be inconvenienced. Since the positive is five hundred times as powerful as the negative, we should go out of our way to help as many people as possible. The more people we help the greater the merit. This is even so when we help people in material matters, all the more so when we help them in spiritual matters. This calculation can be a great motivating factor in helping others. (*Chochmah Umussar*, vol.1, p.135)

Learn to differentiate between altruistic kindness and being taken advantage of.

הקם תקים עמו. (דברים כ"ב ד')

"LIFT THEM UP WITH HIM." (*Dvorim* 22:4)

We are obligated to help someone whose animal has fallen with a heavy load on its back. But the Torah makes a stipulation "with him." Rashi cites the Sages that if the person who needs help tells you, "I'm going to rest right now. You have a *mitzvah* to help me, so help me all by yourself," then you are not obligated to help him.

We see from here that you need not allow someone to take advantage of you just because you want to do *chesed*. If out of laziness someone wants you to do something that he is capable of doing himself, you have a right to be assertive and say no.

But we must understand the Torah's definition of what constitutes being taken advantage of. Let us say that someone always refuses to lend you his things, but then comes over to you and requests that you lend him something, what is your obligation? Here the Torah position is very clear that you are obligated to help him and to refuse is a violation of the commandment, "Do not take revenge" (*Vayikra* 19:18). What is the difference between this and the above? The principle is that whenever a person sincerely needs your help you should help him even if he does not reciprocate by helping you in return. This holds true even if he never will. As a matter of fact, the highest level of kindness, *chesed shel emes* (kindness which is true), is when you do a kindness when you know you will receive nothing in return. If, however, someone does not really need your help because he could do it himself, but out of laziness he tries to manipulate you into doing something for him, you have a right to refuse.

Applying this principle will prevent resentment. Some people might always do what others ask them to do. But when others do not do them favors in return or are not appreciative, they feel resentment for the favors they have done. "I've been taken and used," they might say to themselves. In other situations, people ask them to go out of their way to help them and do things for them when those people could do these things themselves without too much effort. They do the favors because they tell themselves they would feel guilty if they refused. But internalizing the Torah perspective will help a person feel joy when helping others even though they do not do him favors in return and are not grateful. Since the person really needed the help, you have fulfilled an act of kindness and have gained in spiritual elevation and character improvement. But if out of laziness a person asks you to do for him what he could and should do himself, the Torah does not ask of you to allow yourself to be manipulated and you do not need to feel any guilt when you politely refuse. Note: when you have a right to refuse, you need not give a long speech and try to give excuses for your refusal. Just say, "Sorry, but I'm afraid you'll have to do it yourself." If the person offers valid reasons why he can't do it himself, then help him. If not, be confident that you have a right to refuse.

Once someone came to Rabbi Moshe Feinstein for a letter of recommendation. This in itself was hardly an uncommon occurrence, but in this case those around the Rosh Hayeshiva were incensed. The petitioner had contemptuously and publicly attacked Rav Moshe's *halachic* responsa the previous year. But when Rav Moshe agreed to supply the requested letter, they were surprised and aghast. "How could the Rosh Hayeshiva do this for such a person?"

Rav Moshe replied that a *Yom Kippur* had passed and, as is required of every Jew, he had forgiven the malefactor. Consequently, how could anyone expect him to bear a grudge for something he had already forgiven with all his heart. (Rabbi Nosson Scherman, *The Jewish Observer*, Oct. 1986, p.25)

Each person should feel joy in fulfilling his or her unique role in life.

לא יהיה כלי גבר על אשה ולא ילבש גבר שמלת אשה כי תועבת השם
אלקיך כל עשה אלה. (דברים כ"ב ה')

"A WOMAN SHALL NOT WEAR THE GARMENTS OF A MAN, AND A
MAN SHALL NOT WEAR THE DRESS OF A WOMAN. FOR IT IS AN
ABOMINATION OF THE ALMIGHTY, YOUR G-D, ALL WHO DO THESE
THINGS." (*Dvorim* 22:5)

Targum Yonoson states that the garments of a man include
tzitzis and *tefilin*. Rabbi Chayim Shmuelevitz commented on this
that we see the principle that each person has his own mission in
life. The same thing that for one person is "holy of holies," for
another person who does a similar thing, but it is not his life's task,
it is an abomination. Each person should feel joy in carrying out
his life's mission and should not try to do things that he was not
meant to do.

An example of the above is that people differ greatly in their
intellectual abilities. It is very easy for someone who lacks the
creative genius of another person, or has a poor memory, or has
difficulties understanding abstract concepts, to feel envious of
those who excel in these areas. But if the Almighty did not endow
you with these, then He did not consider them to be necessary for
your unique and individual life task. Realize that anything you do
need for it, the Almighty gives you. What you do not have and
cannot get are not needed by you. Utilize the attributes you do
have in order to fulfill your unique role in life.

A disciple of Rabbi Avraham of Sochotchov was ill and felt great
suffering because he was not able to fulfill the commandment of
putting on *tefilin*. He sent his son to consult Rav Avraham, the
author of *Avnai Nezer*. The son told Rav Avraham that his father
was crying because he could not put on *tefilin* due to his illness. The
Rebbe replied, "When I was in Kotzk, I once became so ill on the
day before *Yom Kippur* that the doctors forbade me to pray and
study that entire night. You might think that the thought of not

praying and studying would make me sad. No. I was in a state of great joy. Since this was the will of the Almighty I felt joy in carrying out His will. Similarly, you tell your father in my name that if it is the will of the Almighty that he should not be able to put on *tefilin*, he should carry out the Almighty's will with love and joy." (*Maigdolai Hachasidus: Hadmor Maisochotchov*, pp.114-5)

Do not take advantage of the good heart of others.

כי יקרא קן צפור לפניך בדרך בכל עץ או על הארץ אפרחים או ביצים והאם רבצת על האפרחים או על הביצים לא תקח האם על הבנים. (דברים כ"ב ו')

"IF YOU HAPPEN TO COME ACROSS A BIRD'S NEST ON THE ROAD OR ON ANY TREE OR ON THE GROUND, FLEDGLINGS OR EGGS, AND THE MOTHER BIRD IS SITTING ON THE FLEDGLINGS OR ON THE EGGS, DO NOT TAKE THE MOTHER WITH THE CHILDREN." (*Dvorim* 22:6)

Rabbi Yosef Chayim Zonnenfeld of Jerusalem explained this commandment: Can a person catch a bird once it is flying? Of course not. But there are mother birds who are so concerned about the welfare of their children that they stay with them and do not leave them alone when a hunter comes along. Because of this the mother falls right into the hands of the hunter. It turns out then that the hunter would want to take advantage of the mother's compassion for her children. Therefore the Torah orders a person to send away the mother. You have no right to utilize her positive trait of mercy in order to capture her. (cited in *Otzer Chayim*)

All the more so, you should not try to take advantage of another person just because he is softhearted. There are people who are very compassionate and whenever they hear that someone has a difficulty they do whatever they can to help. In monetary matters they do not like to argue or quarrel and easily give in to the demands and requests of others. Do not utilize their good-naturedness to take advantage of them in either financial matters or in taking up their time and energy by asking them to do things that you would not ask others to do.

When you are compassionate for the suffering of others your pain is growth.

שלח תשלח את האם ואת הבנים תקח לך למען ייטב לך והארכת ימים.
(דברים כ"ב ז')

"YOU SHALL SURELY SEND AWAY THE MOTHER BIRD, AND THE FLEDGLINGS TAKE FOR YOURSELF, IN ORDER THAT IT SHALL BE GOOD FOR YOU AND YOU SHALL LIVE A LONG LIFE." (*Dvorim* 22:7)

The Ksav Sofer explains the reason why the Torah promises a good and long life for fulfilling the commandment of sending away the mother bird. The Ramban explains that this *mitzvah* will implant in a person the attribute of empathy and compassion. Acting in a compassionate manner will enable you to feel empathy for all living creatures. But the Sages (*Psochim* 113b) have said that the lives of three kinds of people are not considered as really living: those with a strong degree of compassion, those who constantly become angry, and those who are finicky. When someone empathizes strongly with the pain and suffering of others, he will suffer himself whenever he hears about the suffering of others, especially when he is unable to do anything to alleviate the other person's suffering, as is frequently the case. Therefore after the Almighty commanded us to have compassion on birds in order that we should grow in this trait, He guarantees that through this we will still live a good and long life. For many years you will be able to help a large number of people and this will increase your days instead of shortening them. (*Ksav Sofer al Hatorah*)

Being compassionate causes pain. But these are growing pains. You grow as a person when you feel the pain of others. A person who is apathetic and callous towards the suffering of others might think that he is making his life eaiser. But there is a lack of depth to such a life. The more you feel for others the more elevated you become.

Even when engaged in a mitzvah be sensitive to the feelings of others.

שלח תשלח את האם. (דברים כ"ב ז')

"YOU SHALL SURELY SEND AWAY THE MOTHER BIRD." (*Dvorim* 22:7)

The Talmud (*Chulin* 141a) states that I might think this only applies if one needs the mother bird for personal use. But if one needs it for a *mitzvah*, I might think that one has a right to take it. Therefore the Torah repeats the term which denotes sending (in the Hebrew) to teach us that even if you need it for a *mitzvah*, you must send away the mother bird.

My Rebbe, Rabbi Chayim Mordechai Katz, the late Rosh Hayeshiva of Telz, used to say on this that someone might think that if he needs the bird for a *mitzvah*, he need not be concerned with feelings of compassion. That is the lesson here: even when you are engaged in fulfilling a *mitzvah*, you must be sensitive to the pain and suffering of others. Do not use your involvement in a *mitzvah* as an excuse to disturb others. For example, if you are studying Torah, do not do so in a loud voice if that would prevent others from falling asleep.

Once it was difficult to find ten people for an early *minyan* for *minchah* where the Chazon Ish prayed. By the time they had ten people it was already a quarter to one in the afternoon. Rabbi Shmuel Greineman asked his brother-in-law, the Chazon Ish, "What should I do? I told someone I would meet him at my house at one o'clock. Now that we are starting the afternoon prayers a bit later than usual, I will not be able to make it home on time for the appointment. Is it proper for me to make that person wait?"

The Chazon Ish replied, "Someone who cleaves to the trait of truth will not even have a question in this instance."

Even though the early *minyan* was losing its tenth person and had to be foregone that day, the Chazon Ish told his brother-in-law that there is no question that coming on time is a matter of truthfulness. (*P'air Hador*, vol.3, p.20)

Be careful not to cause others envy.

לא תחרש בשור ובחמר יחדו. (דברים כ"ב י')

"YOU SHALL NOT PLOW WITH AN OX AND DONKEY TOGETHER." (*Dvorim* 22:10)

Daas Zkainim explains a reason for this commandment that since an ox chews its cud and a donkey does not, the donkey will suffer the pain of envy when it sees that the ox has food in its mouth and it doesn't.

Rabbi Chayim Shmuelevitz commented: This is a great lesson in how sensitive we need to be not to cause others the pain of envy. We must be careful with the feelings of an animal, all the more so of a person. Note that the ox is not really eating any more than the donkey, the donkey only thinks this but he is mistaken.

Be very careful not to boast about your accomplishments or possessions if others might feel envious. Do not praise someone in the presence of a person who might feel envious of that person.

KI SAVO

Beware of people who try to condone their cruelty by slandering others.

וירעו אתנו המצרים ויענונו. (דברים כ״ו ו׳)

"AND THE EGYPTIANS WRONGED US AND THEY AFFLICTED US."
(*Dvorim* 26:6)

The Torah uses the Hebrew term *ohsanu* instead of *lanu*. The verse is telling us therefore that before the Egyptians afflicted our forefathers they first mounted a slander campaign against them and made them appear evil in the eyes of others. Only after they had everyone thinking that the Israelites were evil and not worthy of standard human rights could they make their decrees against them, and the rest of their people accepted this otherwise unacceptable behavior. In recent history this was the strategy of the Nazis with their propaganda vilifying us as a prelude to their actual oppression of our people. (Rabbi Mordechai Gifter; *Pirke Torah*, vol.1, p.30)

This too is the strategy of people who want to rationalize their mistreating others or their lack of helping others. They try to justify their cruelty or apathy by claiming that the other person has done much or serious wrong. Before accepting these negative reports, it is incumbent upon those hearing them to clarify if they are really true. Ask yourself, "What might be motivating this person to relate this negative material? Perhaps he is fabricating the story or greatly exaggerating what happened in order to justify himself for something he did or would like to do." Even if the negative information is true, one must ascertain if the behavior it supposedly comes to condone is proper according to Torah principles.

Be grateful for spiritual benefits before material ones.

ויבאנו אל המקום הזה ויתן לנו את הארץ הזאת ארץ זבת חלב ודבש. (דברים כ"ו ט')

"AND HE BROUGHT US TO THIS PLACE, AND HE GAVE US THIS LAND, A LAND FLOWING WITH MILK AND HONEY." (*Dvorim* 26:9)

Rashi explains that "this place" refers to the *Bais Hamikdosh*, the Temple in Jerusalem.

The question arises: why isn't the order the other way around? Since the Israelites entered the land of Israel much before they built the Temple, the land should be mentioned first.

Rabbi Naftoli Tzvi Berlin of Volozhin explained that the *Bais Hamikdosh* was a spiritual benefit and the land of Israel was a physical benefit. When we express our gratitude to the Almighty we should do so in the order of importance of the things for which we are grateful. Therefore we thank Him for our spiritual blessings before our material ones. (*Haamek Dovor*)

This too should be our order of priorities in our thinking and behavior. Our spiritual needs should be uppermost in our minds. This will have practical ramifications should there ever be a conflict between our spiritual and material wellbeing.

Gain an awareness that all that you have is a gift from the Almighty.

ועתה הנה הבאתי את ראשית פרי האדמה אשר נתתה לי השם והנחתו לפני השם אלקיך והשתחוית לפני השם אלקיך. (דברים כ"ו י')

"AND NOW I BROUGHT THE FIRST FRUIT OF THE LAND WHICH THE ALMIGHTY GAVE ME, AND YOU SHALL PLACE IT BEFORE THE ALMIGHTY, YOUR G-D, AND YOU SHALL BOW DOWN BEFORE THE ALMIGHTY, YOUR G-D." (*Dvorim* 26:10)

Rabbi Chayim Shmuelevitz noted that we do not find the idea of bowing down to the Almighty mentioned in other commandments. Why is it mentioned here in the bringing of the first fruits? The whole concept of bringing the first fruits to the *Bais Hamikdosh* was to show gratitude to the Almighty for all that He has given. It is an expression of our awareness that everything we have is a gift from the Almighty. Therefore the Torah mentions that we bow down to the Almighty, which symbolizes our total submission to His will because all that we have is from Him. This applies to our material as well as our intellectual achievements. Be grateful to the Almighty for all that you understand in Torah and any novel ideas that He has blessed you with.

The greater your awareness that all you have is a gift from the Almighty the more you will appreciate it. As many commentators point out, a small gift from a very distinguished and important dignitary is a precious possession. The greater the giver the more you treasure what you were given. When you live with the reality that all that you have is a gift from the Creator and Sustainer of the universe, you will enjoy immensely everything you have.

Rejoice with all the good the Almighty has given you.

ושמחת בכל הטוב אשר נתן לך השם אלקיך. (דברים כ"ו י"א)

"AND YOU SHALL REJOICE WITH ALL THE GOOD THAT THE ALMIGHTY HAS GIVEN YOU." (*Dvorim* 26:11)

This is a *mitzvah*. We are obligated to feel joy with what we were given by the Almighty. Why do we need a directive to rejoice since we should automatically be happy when we have good things? Man's nature is to constantly want more than he presently has. "He who has one hundred wants two hundred" (*Koheles Rabbah* 1:34). Our moments of joy are mixed with sadness over what we lack. The Torah, therefore, commands us to rejoice with what we have. We should strive to feel a joy that is complete. Lack of joy with what we have is destructive both physically and spiritually. (Rabbi Mordechai Gifter; *Pirke Torah*, vol.2, p.107; cited in *Gateway to Happiness*, p.23)

If you think that you will be happy only when you have more, you will never be happy. When you finally get what you were hoping for, you will once again focus on getting more and will feel unhappy until you acquire yet more. Since happiness is dependent on the present state of your mind, you can only be happy if your mind is focused on appreciating what you presently have and what you are presently doing. Just having things in itself will not make you happy. We find this clearly in *Pirke Avos* (4:1) that the wealthy person is only the person who experiences joy with what he has. Regardless of what you have, you are only wealthy if you have mastered the ability to appreciate what you have. For example, if someone would put a fortune in your name in a bank account in Switzerland without telling you about it and without giving the bank your address, would you be considered wealthy? Even though someplace on this planet there is a large amount of money in your name, what you own gives you no emotional pleasure since you are not able to focus on it. Similarly someone who has eyes, hands, feet, a mind to think, etc., is only considered wealthy if he allows himself to feel pleasure with what he has. Gaining this attitude is the most important thing a person can do to find happiness. If people would realize this, they would spend much more time working on internalizing this attribute than on any other things they do for pleasure. Repeat this verse over and over again: Rejoice with all the good that the Almighty has given you.

When you are deserving of blessing it will reach you even if you run away from it.

ובאו עליך כל הברכות האלה והשיגך כי תשמע בקול השם אלקיך.
(דברים כ"ח ב')

"AND IT WILL COME TO YOU ALL OF THESE BLESSINGS AND THEY WILL REACH YOU, WHEN YOU LISTEN TO THE VOICE OF THE ALMIGHTY, YOUR G-D." (*Dvorim* 28:2)

Many commentators discuss the Hebrew term *vehesigucha*, and they will reach you. What is the difficulty of the blessings reaching a person that it is necessary to mention this after the Torah has already stated "it will come to you"?

Rabbi Naftoli Tzvi Berlin explained: A person who does not study Torah with the appropriate enthusiasm and joy will experience pleasure even with small amounts of financial profit and personal success. But a person who engages in Torah study the way it should be studied with much joy and pleasure will feel so elevated that minor pleasures and profits will not affect his emotional state. Only if such a person obtains an extremely major profit or success will it have a positive emotional affect on him. Therefore the Torah states that the blessing will be so great that even when you are totally engaged in Torah study ("listening to the Almighty") you will still be able to appreciate it. (*Haamek Dovor*)

Another answer to the original question that is commonly quoted is the idea that at times a person does not realize what is truly good for him and he mistakenly runs away from the blessing. Therefore the Torah guarantees that the blessing will pursue the person and reach him even though he is trying to escape from it. Only after he receives the blessing will he become aware of what is really good for him.

This idea will save a person much suffering. When things happen that at first glance seem to be negative occurrences, you must be patient before you make a final judgment. As one event leads to another you will frequently see before your own eyes that what you originally thought would be negative is clearly positive in the end. Be aware of occasions when this already happened to you in the past and you will be able to internalize this awareness in the future.

Joy is a cornerstone of Torah observance.

תחת אשר לא עבדת את השם אלקיך בשמחה ובטוב לבב מרב כל.
(דברים כ״ח מ״ז)

"BECAUSE YOU DID NOT SERVE THE ALMIGHTY, YOUR G-D, WITH JOY AND WITH A GOOD HEART WHEN YOU HAD EVERYTHING." (*Dvorim* 28:47)

This verse tells us that the Retribution listed in this portion comes from not serving the Almighty with joy. Rabbi Simcha Zissel of Kelm asked: Isn't this an extremely severe penalty for not reaching a high level? He explained that if people give thought to what it means to fulfill the Almighty's will, they would carry it out with joy and enthusiasm. But if someone lacks joy when he does the Almighty's will, it will not last and will eventually lead to his lack of fulfilling other commandments. Therefore joy is a key attribute and is fundamental for the observance of the entire Torah. (*Chochmah Umussar*, vol.1, p.461)

To tell someone: "Either feel joy or you will be punished," is more likely to have a negative effect than a positive one. A person cannot be forced into feeling sincere joy. But the stronger your awareness of the greatness of the Almighty, the size of His universe, the length of eternity, and the benefits of observing His *mitzvos*, the greater will be your joy when you carry out the Almighty's will.

When you worry about the future, you are needlessly causing yourself mental anguish in the present.

והיו חייך תלאים לך מנגד ופחדת לילה ויומם ולא תאמין בחייך. (דברים כ״ח ס״ו)

"YOUR LIFE SHALL HANG IN DOUBT BEFORE YOU, AND YOU SHALL FEAR DAY AND NIGHT, AND YOU WILL HAVE NO ASSURANCE OF YOUR LIFE." (*Dvorim* 28:66)

The Talmud (*Menachos* 103b) explains the verse as referring to the pain and suffering of worrying about the future. "Your life shall hang in doubt before you" refers to someone who does not own land and buys a year's supply of grain each year. Though he has grain for this year, he worries about next year. The second level, "You shall fear night and day," refers to someone who buys grain once a week. He is in a worse situation, he has to find new grain every week. The most severe level, "You will have no assurance of your life," refers to someone who has to buy bread every day. He constantly has what to worry about.

Rabbi Chayim Shmuelevitz frequently cited this statement of the Sages and pointed out that a person creates his own mental torture by his own thoughts. If you have enough food for today and you appreciate what you have, you are a fortunate person and will live a happy life. But if you keep worrying about the future, you will never have peace of mind. Even if you have enough to eat for the entire year, you can easily destroy the quality of your life by keeping your mind focused on all that can go wrong next year. Regardless of what will be next year, you are causing yourself suffering right now.

Learn to have mental self-discipline. Don't dwell on what you are missing unless it can lead to constructive planning. Why cause yourself unnecessary pain and anguish when you can choose to keep your thoughts on what you do have in the present? If you are a worrier, the best thing you can do for yourself is to train yourself to be the master of your thoughts (see *Gateway to Happiness*, ch.9). Even if you never gain complete control, whatever control you do have is a great blessing.

The Chofetz Chayim used to say, "Everyone has something to worry about. It is preferable for a person to worry about spiritual matters and then he will be free from worrying about material matters." (*Chofetz Chayim al Hatorah*, p.287)

NITZOVIM

Keep a distance from negative influences.

ותראו את ש י צי יי ואת גלליהם עץ ואבן כסף וזהב אשר עמהם. (דברים כ״ט ט״ז)

"AND YOU MIGHT SEE THEIR ABOMINABLE AND REPULSIVE IDOLS, OF WOOD, STONE, OF SILVER AND GOLD WHICH ARE WITH THEM." (*Dvorim* 29:16)

The Brisker Rav, Rabbi Yitzchok Zev Soloveitchik, commented: A person might see idols and view them as abominations and feel strongly repulsed and sickened. Nevertheless, the Torah (verse 17) has to warn against being negatively influenced by them. Everything one sees makes an impression. Even though at first you feel negatively about them, eventually you might be influenced to follow them. Negative influences are powerful and must be kept at a distance. (Heard from his son, Rabbi Yosef Dov Soloveitchik, Rosh Hayeshiva of Brisk)

Do not justify wrong behavior by claiming it is your philosophy or policy.

והיה בשמעו את דברי האלה הזאת והתברך בלבבו לאמר שלום יהיה לי כי בשררות לבי אלך. (דברים כ״ט י״ח)

"AND IT WILL BE WHEN HE HEARS THE WORDS OF THIS OATH AND HE WILL BLESS HIMSELF IN HIS HEART SAYING, THERE WILL BE

PEACE UNTO ME FOR I WILL GO ACCORDING TO THE IMAGES OF
MY HEART." (*Dvorim* 29:18)

Rabbi Elchonon Wasserman used to quote his Rebbe the
Chofetz Chayim that this refers to someone who doesn't just do a
improper act because of an impulse. Rather, he makes an entire
ideology out of cruelty and the right to harm others. As we read in
verse 19 this is a most serious offense. It is not that the person just
happened to do something that was wrong. Rather he makes a
whole new set of rules for himself that are diametrically opposed to
Torah principles. (*Kovetz Maamorim*, p.85)

There are people who cause others emotional pain in various
ways and when they are rebuked, they claim, "I always do this
This is the way those people should be treated." If someone creates
for himself principles that are based on selfishness and callousness
he will not merely cause suffering just a few times. Rather he wil
repeat what he does over and over again. Since he has not lost his
temper, but premeditatedly decided to act this way, he will not
regret the harm he causes. Our behavior towards others should not
be based on our faults and negative character traits (even though
one might cover them up by claiming it is his "policy" to act this
way). Make a careful, unbiased study of the Torah to see the
elevated behavior that is our obligation. Then work on
incorporating these principles into your daily life.

When you utilize all life situations for growth, you wil experience joy.

היה כי יבאו עליך כל הדברים האלה הברכה והקללה אשר נתתי לפניך"
השבת אל לבבך. (דברים ל' א')"

"AND IT WILL BE WHEN ALL THESE THINGS COME TO YOU, THE
BLESSING AND THE CURSE WHICH I HAVE GIVEN BEFORE YOU
AND YOU SHALL TAKE IT TO YOUR HEART." (*Dvorim* 30:1)

Rabbi Yonoson Eybesheutz explained that every life situation as its unique test of our character and can either be utilized for growth or can cause a person to have new faults. When a person has blessing in his life and is financially successful, he can free his mind from things that distract his concentration during prayers and Torah study. Poverty, too, can help a person elevate himself by breaking his arrogance and conceit. This will be beneficial in his relationship with the Almighty and with his fellow man. On the other hand, wealth can cause a person to commit all kinds of wrongdoings and to remove himself from the Almighty. Poverty also can prevent a person from seeking self-improvement. Everything is dependent on how a person utilizes or misuses both the good fortune and the difficulties that the Almighty sends to test him. Therefore the Torah tells us "you shall take it to your heart." It is entirely up to you how you will respond to various life-tests. (*Tiferes Yonoson*)

A person who lives with this attitude will not be thrown by difficult life situations. He views everything that happens to him in his life as a means of perfecting his character. While everyone would wish that his life would go smoothly, such a person focuses on how to utilize whatever occurs for growth. Therefore he will be able to experience joy regardless of whether the Almighty sends him a blessing or a curse. As the *Ohr Hachayim* comments on this verse: The Torah states *vehaya*, which denotes joy, because we are supposed to thank the Almighty with joy for misfortune just as we thank Him with joy for good fortune (*Brochos* 54a). Since all occurrences are encounters with the Almighty for our ultimate benefit, joy is the proper response.

The more elevated you are the greater your awareness of your obligations.

ואתה תשוב ושמעת בקול השם. (דברים ל' ח')

"AND YOU SHALL RETURN AND HEARKEN TO THE VOICE OF THE ALMIGHTY." (*Dvorim* 30:8)

The Torah already mentioned in verse 2 that there will be a return to the Almighty, so why is it mentioned here again? Before a person does *tshuvah* and really tries to improve, he is unaware of many things he does wrong. He is far away from the Almighty and is drowning in transgressions. But after he returns to the Almighty, he is elevated and suddenly he realizes that he has done many improper things without paying attention to them. Because of his present awareness, he realizes his need to repent once more. But this time he will do so with greater depth, including many things he previously overlooked. (*Tiferes Shlomoh*)

The more elevated a person is the greater his understanding of the extent of his obligations and responsibilities. While before he might have thought that he was fulfilling all of his obligations, now he realizes that the extent of those obligations are much greater than he had originally thought. There are some people who might feel overburdened by having these new insights. But the proper attitude is to appreciate them. They will help you grow in ways you previously had not thought about.

Someone once came to the Chazon Ish's house full of complaints and spoke to him with great insolence. Although that person spoke roughly, the Chazon Ish replied with complete serenity and extreme gentleness. In a very quiet manner he made a rebuttal to the person's complaints. A Torah scholar who was standing nearby was greatly bothered by the disrespectful manner of the person. He was surprised, however, that when the person left the room, the Chazon Ish said to himself with pain and in a worried tone, "I am afraid that perhaps I didn't speak to this person in a gentle enough manner." (*P'air Hador*, vol.3, p.49)

The greater your awareness of our obligation to show respect to others, the more elevated will be your behavior.

The greater your desire to obtain Torah knowledge, the easier it will be to overcome difficulties.

לא בשמים הוא לאמר מי יעלה לנו השמימה ויקחה לנו וישמענו אתה
ונעשנה. ולא מעבר לים הוא לאמר מי יעבר לנו אל עבר הים ויקחה לנו
וישמענו אתה ונעשנה. (דברים ל' י"ב-י"ג)

"[The Torah] IS NOT IN HEAVEN, THAT YOU SHOULD SAY, WHO
SHALL GO UP FOR US TO HEAVEN AND BRING IT TO US THAT WE
MAY HEAR IT AND DO IT? NOR IS IT BEYOND THE SEA THAT YOU
SHOULD SAY, WHO SHALL GO OVER THE SEA FOR US, AND BRING IT
TO US THAT WE MAY HEAR IT AND DO IT?" (*Dvorim* 30:12,13)

The Talmud (*Airuvin* 55a) states on this verse that if the Torah
were in heaven you would still have to climb up to reach it. If the
Torah were on the other side of the ocean, you would still have to
go traveling for it.

This means that the Torah is so crucial for one's existence that
even if it were extremely difficult to acquire, you would still have to
make every possible effort to acquire it.

Once when Rabbi Zalman of Volozhin, a disciple of the Vilna
Gaon and brother of Rabbi Chayim, was studying Torah, he
needed an important Torah book that was in a place that was very
difficult to reach. An extremely heavy box was in front of the book
and it seemed to be impossible for any one person to move the box
away in order to reach the book. What did Rav Zalman do? He
walked back and forth in the house reciting the abovementioned
Talmudic statement. He repeated this statement again and again
with great love and devotion in a beautiful singing voice. He
repeated it so many times to himself that he was filled with an
overwhelming elevated spiritual desire to gain more Torah
knowledge. This gave him so much extra energy that he was able to
move the box all by himself. (*Toldos Odom*)

The more one appreciates the value of Torah study, the more one
will be able to overcome any obstacles that might prevent one from
studying Torah. What some people might feel is impossible, a
person with a burning desire to study Torah will find possible and
even easy.

A deep commitment to change immediately changes you.

כי קרוב אליך הדבר מאד בפיך ובלבבך לעשתו. (דברים ל' י"ד)

"THE MATTER IS VERY CLOSE TO YOU IN YOUR MOUTH AND HEART TO DO IT." (*Dvorim* 30:14)

Rabbi Chayim Shmuelevitz commented on this that the Torah tells us that regardless of how far away one is, if he is sincerely resolved to become a better person, he will be able to make an immediate transformation of himself. When you make a verbal commitment to the Almighty and to yourself to become a changed person, your very words put you into a different place than where you were before.

Of course, if you just say that you will change without actually improving your behavior, you have not sincerely changed. But the words you tell yourself have a major influence on your behavior. In whatever area you wish to improve, if you keep repeating over and over to yourself how you will act from now on, you will notice practical changes. Your verbal and mental suggestions are very close to you, all you need is a firm decision to make this effort. Once you have made this decision, you will be successful as long as you keep up that original resolve of yours.

There are some people, however, who keep making pledges and resolutions to make positive changes but do not actually carry out their plans. They have created a credibility gap for themselves. Since they have already said they would change and have not done so, they are likely not to really believe themselves. To overcome this, one needs action and consistency. Just as you should keep your word when you give it to someone else, so too you should keep your word to yourself.

VAYAILECH

Help people overcome their fears.

וילך משה וגו'. (דברים ל"א א')

"AND MOSHE WENT..." (*Dvorim* 31:1)

Ibn Ezra explains that before Moshe died he went to each tribe to notify them that he was about to die, but they should not be afraid because he was leaving them with Yehoshua who would be a reliable leader.

We can learn from Moshe that whenever we see that someone has fears, we should do all that we can to alleviate those fears. Moshe knew that even if they felt fear, it was based on an error. He knew that Yehoshua would be a capable and devoted leader and the people could trust him. Nevertheless, fear is a painful emotion and it is an act of kindness to help a person overcome it. Because it is so painful it is forbidden to cause someone unnecessary fear (see *Choshen Mishpot* 420:32 and *Love Your Neighbor*, p.329). Never laugh at someone because of his fears; mocking him will just cause him more emotional pain. By becoming skilled at helping others rid themselves of their fears, you will be able to fulfill more acts of kindness.

When one has attained leadership it is necessary to act from a position of strength.

ויקרא משה ליהושע ויאמר אליו לעיני כל ישראל חזק ואמץ. (דברים ל"א ז')

"AND MOSHE CALLED YEHOSHUA AND SAID TO HIM BEFORE THE EYES OF ALL ISRAEL STRENGTHEN YOURSELF AND BE POWERFUL." (*Dvorim* 31:7)

The simple meaning of the verse is that Moshe spoke to Yehoshua in public, "Before the eyes of all Israel." Rabbi Meir Simcha Hacohen wrote that this verse can also be interpreted that Moshe told Yehoshua to be strong and powerful whenever he was in the presence of the people. Yehoshua was going to take over the leadership of the Jewish people and a king is commanded in the Torah not to become arrogant. But a leader must be humble in private. As regards dealing with the people, a king has no right to forego his honor. Moshe, the paragon of humility, told his disciple and successor, Yehoshua, that he could not be submissive in his position of authority. Rather, he must be as tough as iron and as strong as a lion for the benefit of the nation. (*Meshech Chochmah*)

Humility is an awareness of one's small stature in relation to the entire universe and the infinite greatness of the Almighty. But every trait has its time and place. When in a position of authority one must ensure that one's commands will be followed. The ideal is for a person to have humility in his personal relationships with others (as Moshe did when Miriam spoke against him), but to be strong and powerful in his position of authority. This strength will be for the greater good of those who are dependent on him and this renders the trait a virtue.

Rabbi Shmuel Salanter, Rav of Yerushalayim, was noted for his extreme patience. Once when he censured a storekeeper for his improper behavior, the person insolently threatened to break all the windows in his house. Rav Shmuel calmly replied, "What do you think, I'll remain silent?" After a pause he added, "Immediately I will call someone in to put in new windows."

But even though he was very patient, when necessary he could act with great authority which always went together with his great wisdom.

Rabbi Ben-Tzion Yadler related that a certain baker owed his mother twenty *napoleons* for flour he had purchased. The fellow had a very tough demeanor and even the *Bais Din* was unable to influence him to pay the money he owed.

Upon hearing about this, Rabbi Shmuel Salanter asked him, "Why don't you pay her the thirty *napoleons* that you owe for the flour?"

"I only owe twenty," shouted the irate baker.

Rav Shmuel's strategy worked and he now heard a confession on the twenty. "I am only giving you until tomorrow at this time to bring the money," said Rav Shmuel. The man did not show up the next day; so Rav Shmuel sent him the following message: "You should know that I never start something without finishing it. If you don't bring the money right away, I will immediately send out a message to publicly announce that all of your merchandise is forbidden, and it is forbidden to include you in all religious matters." As soon as the baker heard this, he immediately appeared with the money in his hand. (*Betuv Yerushalayim*, pp.357-8)

Give children positive Torah experiences.

הקהל את העם האנשים והנשים והטף וגרך אשר בשעריך למען ישמעו ולמען ילמדו ויראו את השם אלקיכם ושמרו לעשות את כל דברי התורה הזאת. (דברים ל״א י״ב)

Every seven years the king reads the Torah in the presence of the entire nation: "GATHER TOGETHER THE NATION, THE MEN AND THE WOMEN AND THE CHILDREN, AND THE STRANGER WHO IS IN YOUR GATES, IN ORDER THAT THEY SHOULD HEAR, AND IN ORDER THAT THEY SHOULD LEARN AND THEY WILL FEAR THE ALMIGHTY, YOUR G-D, AND THEY WILL OBSERVE AND FULFILL THIS ENTIRE TORAH." (*Dvorim* 31:12)

Rashi cites the Talmud (*Chagigah* 3a) that the young children were brought along in order to bring reward to their parents. The Talmud calls this concept a precious jewel. What is so special about it? It reveals to us a major principle pertaining to the education of the very young. Young children have a tendency to make noise and can easily disturb older people who are trying to listen. Therefore one might think that it is better not to bring them. But even though they do not understand what is being said, just being there when the king reads the Torah in the presence of the entire nation will have a major influence on the child for the rest of his life. He gains an experience of how important the Torah is for the entire people. This teaches us even today to do all we can that children should learn at an early age the extreme importance of Torah. Every experience makes an impression; make certain to give your children many positive Torah experiences. (Rabbi Simcha Zissel of Kelm; *Chochmah Umussar*, vol.1, p.150)

When Rabbi Yaakov Kamenetzky once visited the kindergarten of a Torah school, he noticed that the *mezuzah* was fixed on a spot on the doorpost within reach of the children. "It's a lovely idea to let the children reach the *mezuzah*," he said, "but put the *mezuzah* where it belongs, on the upper third of the doorpost instead, and let them use a stool to reach it. Otherwise they will grow up thinking that a *mezuzah* can be put anywhere you wish. One does not raise children with untruths." (Rabbi Nisson Wolpin; *The Jewish Observer*, May, 1986)

Realizing that misfortunes are for your good decreases actual suffering.

וחרה אפי בו ביום ההוא ועזבתים והסתרתי פני מהם והיה לאכל ומצאהו רעות רבות וצרות ואמר ביום ההוא הלא על כי אין אלקי בקרבי מצאוני הרעות האלה. (דברים ל"א י"ז)

"AND I WILL BECOME ANGRY AT THEM ON THAT DAY, AND I WILL

LEAVE THEM AND I WILL HIDE MY FACE FROM THEM, AND THEY WILL BE DEVOURED, AND IT WILL FIND THEM MANY MISFORTUNES AND THEY WILL FEEL OPPRESSED. AND THEY WILL SAY ON THAT DAY, BECAUSE THE ALMIGHTY IS NOT WITH ME ALL THESE MISFORTUNES HAVE FOUND ME." (*Dvorim* 31:17)

Rabbi Eliezer Shach, Rosh Hayeshiva of Ponevez, explained: At first this verse states they will have *raos* and *tzaros*. *Raos* refers to the actual misfortunes that will befall them. *Tzaros* refers to the subjective experience of suffering and oppression that these misfortunes will cause. But this feeling comes from a lack of awareness that the misfortunes are ultimately for the person's benefit. When a person realizes that the Almighty sends him those misfortunes in order to spiritually elevate him and atone for his wrongs, he will find them much easier to cope with. At the end of this verse the people realize that the punishment they have experienced is because of their wrongs and it is for their good. Therefore the verse only uses the term *raos*, but not *tzaros*. The people will only have the suffering experience but subjectively will not feel a large amount of pain and suffering. (Introduction to *Avi Ezri* on *Nashim Vekdushah*)

The Chofetz Chayim's son once came to visit his father near the end of his life. He wrote, "He told me that his foot bothered him very much and he needed special treatment for it. I felt pain for his suffering but my father consoled me saying, 'I am very old. Nu, it is good to come to the next world already cleansed. It is so much better to suffer in this world.'" (*Michtevai Chofetz Chayim, Dugmah Maidarkai Avi*, p.13)

The Steipler, Rabbi Yaakov Yisroel Kanievsky, devoted his days to people who came to be comforted and strengthened. He would often tell them, "I envy your suffering. It is an asset that one should not sell for all the money in the world." His words constantly encouraged the depressed and the downtrodden. (*The Jewish Observer*, Nov. 1985)

When studying Torah properly you will experience much light and consolation.

ועתה כתבו לכם את השירה הזאת. (דברים ל"א י"ט)

"AND NOW WRITE FOR YOU THIS SONG." (*Dvorim* 31:19)

This verse contains the last commandment in the order of the Torah which is to write a Torah scroll. The Chofetz Chayim noted that this *mitzvah* comes right after the verse which states that the Almighty will hide His presence from the people because of their transgressions. The reason this commandment follows the previous verse is to teach us that even in times of darkness and destruction when one engages in Torah study one will find much light and consolation. (*Chofetz Chayim al Hatorah*)

The knowledge of the destruction of Telz in Lithuania was not confirmed until the winter of 1945. In the midst of Torah notes Rabbi Eliyahu Meir Bloch was writing that day, we find: "I am not able to concentrate (on this writing) as I should, for that which I feared has reached me - the terrible news of the death of... at the hands of the cursed murderers. May the Almighty avenge their blood and have mercy on his people. Should someone look at these writings let him not judge me as callous and cruel for having delved into the words of Torah after such terrible news. I feel that I could never come to peace without the toil of Torah." (Rabbi Chaim Dov Keller; *The Jewish Observer*, Sept. 1977)

Rabbi Meir Yechiel of Ostrovtzah once came to a celebration in honor of the completion of writing a Torah scroll. One of those attending approached Rav Meir Yechiel and said to him, "Give me a blessing, our Rebbe, that we should merit writing many more Torah scrolls."

"We already have enough Torah scrolls," said Rav Meir Yechiel. "The main thing we need to increase is the observance and study of the Torah." (*Rabbi Meir Yechiel Maiostrovtzah*, pp.154-5)

Have the patience to keep repeating Torah ideas to others until they understand them.

ועתה כתבו לכם את השירה הזאת ולמדה את בני ישראל שימה בפיהם.
(דברים ל"א י"ט)

"AND NOW WRITE FOR YOU THIS SONG AND TEACH IT TO THE CHILDREN OF ISRAEL, PLACE IT IN THEIR MOUTH." (*Dvorim* 31:19)

The Talmud (*Airuvin* 54) states that a teacher has an obligation to repeat a Torah lesson to his students until they understand it. As an example of this principle the Talmud cites Rabbi Praida who repeated each lesson to a certain student four hundred times until he finally comprehended it. Once in the middle of their study session someone requested that Rabbi Praida accompany him. Rabbi Praida replied that he was in the middle of teaching his student and when he finished he would go. After the standard 400 times, Rabbi Praida asked his student if he understood. When the student replied that he didn't, Rabbi Praida asked him why this time was different from other times. "Since I was afraid that you would soon leave, I couldn't concentrate well," the student said. "Don't worry," Rabbi Praida comforted him. "Even if I have to repeat the lesson another four hundred times, I will do so until you understand it."

When you have to explain something to someone, after how many times will you conclude that the person will never be able to understand? From here we see that until you repeat the lesson four hundred times you have no proof that the person will not understand if you have the patience and tenacity to keep repeating the idea over and over again. As Rabbi Chayim Shmuelevitz used to say on this, "Each repetition is another lesson in having patience and overcoming frustration."

Whenever you have to repeat a Torah thought a few times, realize that you are growing greatly by having the necessary patience.

HAAZENU

Your character traits are the key to how you will grow when you study Torah.

יערף כמטר לקחי. (דברים ל"ב ב')

"MY TEACHINGS SHOULD COME DOWN TO YOU AS RAIN." (*Dvorim* 32:2)

Rabbi Chayim Shmuelevitz used to cite the Vilna Gaon on this verse that rain helps things grow. But what grows? Only what is there from before. If someone has vegetables and fruits that are healthy and delicious, rain will help them develop. But if there are poisonous mushrooms, rain will help them grow too. Similarly, Torah study makes one grow. But it depends on one's character traits what one will become. A person who has elevated traits will become a greatly elevated person. But if a person has faulty character traits, the more Torah he studies the greater menace he will become.

An arrogant person is likely to become more arrogant when he becomes more knowledgeable. Such a person is likely to use his Torah knowledge for one-upmanship. He will try to show others that they are inferior to him. If a person is cruel, the more he knows the more pain he will try to inflict on others. When a person who is power-hungry gains more knowledge, he will feel more justified in manipulating others. A selfish person will utilize his knowledge to become even more selfish. On the other hand, a person with positive character traits will use his Torah knowledge to help as many people as he can. He will readily share his knowledge with others. The more Torah he studies the more elevated he will become. His entire behavior towards others will be a *kidush Hashem*, a sanctification of the Almighty's name.

A Rabbi told the Chazon Ish about the positive intellectual qualities of a young man whom his sister-in-law considered marrying. The Chazon Ish interrupted him with the question, "Will he also be a good husband?" (*P'air Hador*, vol.4, p.85)

A newly married yeshiva student's wife requested that he take out the garbage, but he felt that it was not fitting for someone who studies Torah to have to deal with the garbage. He approached his Rosh Hayeshiva and asked him for his opinion. "Yes it is not fitting for someone like yourself to take out the garbage," the distinguished Rosh Hayeshiva replied. The next day there was a knock on the door of the young man's house. To his surprise it was his Rosh Hayeshiva. "Could you please show me where you keep your garbage?" the Rosh Hayeshiva asked him. "I came to take it out for you."

The Almighty always does for you what is in your best interests.

הצור תמים פעלו כי כל דרכיו משפט. (דברים ל"ב ד')

"THE ROCK HIS ACTS ARE PERFECT, ALL OF HIS WAYS ARE JUST." (*Dvorim* 32:4)

The Chofetz Chayim once asked someone about how things were going for him. "It wouldn't hurt if things were a bit better," the man replied.

"How can you possibly know that it wouldn't hurt?" replied the Chofetz Chayim. "The Almighty knows better than you. He is merciful and compassionate. If He felt it would be good for you for things to be better, He definitely would have made them better. Certainly things are good for you the way they are." (*Chofetz Chayim al Hatorah*, p.284)

Things are not always the way we wish them to be, but they are always for our good. This awareness will give you an elevated feeling in your life. You have every right to try to improve your situation. But whenever you do all you can to try, and the situation is still not the way you would wish, work on internalizing the consciousness that the Almighty is doing for you what is in your best interests.

Be aware of the hand of the Almighty in history.

זכר ימות עולם בינו שנות דר ודר. (דברים ל"ב ז')

"REMEMBER THE DAYS OF YORE, UNDERSTAND THE YEARS OF EVERY GENERATION." (*Dvorim* 32:7)

My Rebbe, Rabbi Mordechai Gifter, commented: "The Torah gives us guidelines for the viewing and understanding of history from a true perspective. If one wishes to comprehend an event in history, one cannot look at it in the limited scope of the finite here and now; rather, one must understand the event as having a place in the historical continuum. A historical occurrence extends itself beyond the isolation of time and space and reaches towards the past and future to acquire true significance. But one must invariably begin with Creation and the Creator. As the Vilna Gaon explained, to understand 'the years of every generation' one must first 'remember the days of yore' - the Six Days of Creation. For in those days lies the complete plan of the development of the universe and humankind in it. This, the Vilna Gaon taught, is the only way to understand history."

"Secular sources view history in perspectives of their own, predicated on economic, social, and political principles. By contrast, the Torah directs us to view history as the unfolding of the Divine Plan. History is the metamorphosis of man through the stages of destruction and redemption, continuing towards his final redemption in the days of *Moshiach*. And all such events, the redemptions and the destructions, are perceived as fundamental testimony to the presence of the Almighty in this world, and are understood as experiential units in *hashgachah pratis*, the active force of the Hand of the Almighty." (Rabbi Mordechai Gifter; *Torah Perspectives*, pp.103-4)

Someone once visited the Chofetz Chayim at his summer residence in a small town near Radin.

"Is there anything new in the world?" the Chofetz Chayim asked him.

"There is nothing new," replied the young man.

"You are correct," the Chofetz Chayim commented. "As long as we do not hear that 'the Almighty is King,' what else is there to hear?" (*Michtevai Chofetz Chayim: Sichos Hachofetz Chayim*, part 2, p.37)

False ideologies are a test of one's virtue.

חדשים מקרב באו לא שערום אבתיכם. (דברים ל"ב י"ז)

The Torah warns us against false gods:
"NEW ONES, THAT RECENTLY CAME UP; WHOM YOUR FOREFATHERS DID NOT KNOW." (*Dvorim* 32:17)

"The process of new false ideologies," comments Rabbi Avigdor Miller, "is part of the constant test of virtue which living men must endure all their lives. But the Torah and the Torah-people are an old and established firm, which has been in business for a few thousand years and has weathered many crises and outlived many competitors. We view the opponents, physical or ideological, who rise up against us in every generation, with a calm and seasoned eye; and we know that they will go down into oblivion as did all the upstarts who preceded them." (*Rejoice O Youth*, p.25)

Be careful to use all your attributes and traits in only positive ways.

צוּר יְלָדְךָ תֶּשִׁי וַתִּשְׁכַּח קֵל מְחֹלְלֶךָ. (דברים ל״ב י״ח)

"YOU WERE UNMINDFUL OF THE ALMIGHTY WHO BEGOT YOU, AND YOU FORGOT G-D WHO BORE YOU." (*Dvorim* 32:18)

The Dubner Maggid explained this verse with the following parable: Reuven owed Shimon a large sum of money and lacked the necessary funds to repay his debt. His creditor was pestering him very much and he didn't know what to do. He therefore approached his close friend Levi and asked for advice. Levi told him that when Shimon approached him again he should act as if he were totally insane and then Shimon would have to leave him alone. Following this suggestion, he made all kinds of crazy sounds and movements when he was in the presence of Shimon and it worked well. Shimon left him alone. The next day Reuven asked Levi to lend him a sizable sum of money for a few days. A week later Levi asked Shimon to repay him but Shimon just acted crazy again. Levi was furious at him and shouted, "I'm the one who gave you the idea to use this method. It's a real *chutzpah* for you to use that against me."

The Almighty created forgetfulness as a benefit for people who have suffered in the past. If someone would always remember clearly every bit of suffering that occurred to him in his life, he would find it very difficult to cope with life. He would not enjoy the positive things in his life because of the remembrance of the pain of the past. By forgetting the misfortunes of one's life one can live a happy life even though one has suffered in the past. But forgetfulness can also be a very negative trait if one forgets the Almighty and his obligations to Him. This, said the Dubner

Maggid, is the message of our verse. The Almighty created forgetfulness (*teshi* as Rashi explains is forgetfulness). He did so for your benefit. But unfortunately you used this to forget him. (*Ohel Yaakov*)

Every trait and attribute can be used for good and can be used for bad. It is up to you to utilize all that you were given in positive ways.

If you are tempted to do something improper, think of the positive things you can do instead.

על אשר מעלתם בי בתוך בני ישראל במי מריבת קדש מדבר צן על אשר לא קדשתם אותי בתוך בני ישראל. (דברים ל"ב נ"א)

The Almighty told Moshe he would not enter the land of Israel:
"BECAUSE YOU TRESPASSED AGAINST ME IN THE MIDST OF THE CHILDREN OF ISRAEL AT THE WATERS OF MERIVOS-KADESH, IN THE WILDERNESS OF TZIN, BECAUSE YOU DID NOT SANCTIFY ME IN THE MIDST OF THE CHILDREN OF ISRAEL." (*Dvorim* 32:51)

Rabbi Meir Simcha Hacohen explains that the concept of *din* and *cheshbon* is being referred to in this verse. *Din* is the judgment for what one has done wrong. Therefore the first part of the verse mentions that Moshe trespassed against the Almighty. The second part of the verse is the *cheshbon*, that is, the calculation of what one could accomplish if one would have done what was proper. Therefore the verse states, "because you did not sanctify Me." This means that if Moshe would have done what was proper by speaking to the rock instead of hitting it, he would have had the merit of a major *kidush Hashem*. (*Meshech Chochmah*)

Before doing something that is improper, think in these terms. First, "What is the harm of the negative thing I am about to do?" Then ask yourself: "What positive things could I do in this time or with this energy?" Some people are more motivated by fear of doing something wrong, while others are more motivated when they think in terms of what they can gain by positive accomplishments. By keeping both thoughts in mind you will be doubly motivated to do good and keep away from wrong. Similarly, when you try to motivate others to refrain from doing something wrong, help them focus on both the harm of doing wrong and on how they could gain by positive accomplishments.

VEZOS HABRACHAH

Be aware of the Almighty in all of your successes.

וזאת ליהודה ויאמר שמע השם קול יהודה. (דברים ל"ג ז')

"AND THIS IS TO YEHUDAH, AND HE SAID, LISTEN ALMIGHTY TO
THE VOICE OF YEHUDAH." (*Dvorim* 33:7)

Rashi states that Moshe is referring to the prayers of the kings of
Yehudah: Dovid, Asa, Yehoshofot, and Chizkiyah.

The *Midrash* elaborates: There were four kings and each one
asked the Almighty for different things. King David asked that he
should be able to pursue his enemies and vanquish them. King Asa
said, "I don't have the ability to kill my enemies. Rather I will
pursue them and You Almighty should vanquish them." King
Yehoshofot stood up and said, "I don't have the ability to
vanquish my enemies or even to pursue them. Rather I will pray
and You Almighty should vanquish them." Chizkiyah stood up
and said, "I do not have the ability to vanquish, to pursue, or to
pray. Rather I will stay home and sleep and You Almighty should
vanquish my enemies."

What is the meaning of not being able to pursue or pray? Why
should anyone find this difficult since the Almighty will be
involved? My Rebbe, Rabbi Chayim Mordechai Katz used to
explain: Regardless of what we ourselves do to be successful in any
area, we must be aware that ultimately it is the Almighty who
causes the victory. Everything is dependent on His will, but we
must do our share. Therefore, King David said that even when he

pursues his enemies and vanquishes them he still realizes that it is the Almighty who has made the victory possible. King Asa, however, felt that he was not on King David's spiritual level. If he would finish off the job, he would feel he was the cause of the victory and therefore he asked that his pursuing his enemies should be sufficient. Since the Almighty would complete the process without any effort on his part, he would realize that it was all from the Almighty. Yehoshofot was one step below this. He felt that if he would take action and pursue his enemies, he would find it difficult to see the Almighty's Hand in the victory. Therefore he asked that he should only be required to pray. When all he would do was pray without any other action, he would see that the victory was from the Almighty. But Chizkiyah felt that even if he would pray, he would consider it his victory. Only if the Almighty would bring about the victory when he was asleep without any action on his part at all, would he be able to recognize that the entire victory was from the Almighty.

The message here is that regardless of what we do to succeed, we should always realize that everything is totally up to the Almighty.

When earning money have in mind that a percentage of your profits will go to those who study Torah.

ולזבולן אמר שמח זבולן בצאתך ויששכר באהליך. (דברים ל"ג י"ח)

"AND TO ZEVULUN HE SAID, REJOICE ZEVULUN WHEN YOU GO OUT AND YISSOCHOR IN YOUR TENT." (*Dvorim* 33:18)

This verse describes the partnership between Yissochor and Zevulun. The members of the tribe of Yissochor devoted their time to studying Torah, while the members of Zevulun were merchants who lived near the sea and were engaged in business. Rashi cites this and explains that the tribe of Zevulun was mentioned first in this verse because the Torah of Yissochor was made possible through the efforts of Zevulun.

Ohr Hachayim comments: The reason Zevulun can feel joy in his going out to do business is because Yissochor is studying Torah in his tent. Since Zevulun is enabling Yissochor to study Torah with his business ventures, it elevates all that he does to make a profit into a *mitzvah*, and when one is engaged in a *mitzvah* one should feel joy.

There is a big difference between a person who works to earn money for himself but also gives some of his money to charity, and a person who has in mind right from the start that he is working not only for himself but also for the Torah scholars and students he is planning to support. A person with the latter intention is totally involved in the fuifillment of a *mitzvah*, unlike other people who are doing things that superficially seem similar. Some people might mistakenly think that he is losing out by not keeping all of his money for himself. But the truth is that not only on the spiritual level but even on the emotional level he is much better off than those who fail to emulate his elevated example.

A resident of Bnai Brak who appeared to be a simple person passed away. The Chazon Ish, who was very old at the time, attended the funeral and walked on foot to the cemetery which was outside of the city although he usually did not do this at other funerals. He was very weak and walking such a distance was a great effort for him. When they reached the cemetery he had no energy left at all and needed to lie down on a bench. Those close to him were worried about his health. "Why did you risk your health to show respect to this particular person," they asked him.

"This person enabled a Torah scholar to study by sharing his income with him," replied the Chazon Ish. (*P'air Hador*, vol.4, pp.67-8)

Utilize all that you have to serve the Almighty.

וימת שם משה עבד השם. (דברים ל"ד ה')

"AND MOSHE THE SERVANT OF THE ALMIGHTY DIED THERE."
(*Dvorim* 34:5)

The Rambam (*Hilchos Tshuvah* 5:2) states that every person who wishes to be righteous has the ability to be as righteous as Moshe Rabainu. Rabbi Elchonon Wasserman explained that this does not mean, of course, that others can reach the elevated spiritual level of Moshe. Rather, the intent of the Rambam can be understood with the Radak's interpretation of the words "servant of the Almighty." The Radak (*Yehoshua* 1:1) explains this that just as all that a servant does is for his master, so too Moshe utilized all that he had just for the Almighty. All of his abilities and talents were devoted to serving the Almighty. Similarly, everyone else also is able to devote all that he has to serve the Almighty. (*Kovetz Maamorim*, p.48)

Rabbi Akiva Eger's will stipulated that his epitaph should contain no words of praise but the following: "Here lies Rabbi Akiva Eger, servant to the servants of the Almighty." (*Jewish Leaders*, p.113)

After the Chazon Ish passed away, Rabbi Isser Zalman Meltzer said about him, "Not everyone can become as great a Torah scholar as the Chazon Ish. But to study Torah with the same diligence as the Chazon Ish, that everyone can do." (*Marbitzai Torah Umussar*, vol.3, p.39)

Utilize any opportunity you have to learn from a Torah scholar.

ויבכו בני ישראל את משה בערבת מואב שלשים יום ויתמו ימי בכי אבל משה. ויהושע בן נון מלא רוח חכמה כי סמך משה את ידיו עליו. (דברים ל"ד ח-ט)

"AND THE CHILDREN OF ISRAEL CRIED OVER THE LOSS OF MOSHE AT ARVOS MOAV FOR THIRTY DAYS, AND THE DAYS OF THE CRYING OVER THE MOURNING OF MOSHE WERE FINISHED. AND

YEHOSHUA THE SON OF NOON WAS FULL OF A SPIRIT OF WISDOM,
FOR MOSHE HAD PLACED HIS HANDS UPON HIM." (*Dvorim* 34:8,9)

The Chasam Sofer explains these two verses together. When the
verse states that they stopped crying over the loss of Moshe, they
were still crying but over something else. Upon seeing that
Yehoshua took over the leadership of the people because he had
served Moshe, they felt deep pain. They realized that they too
could have gained high levels of wisdom as Yehoshua did if they
would not have been lazy and would have stayed as close to Moshe
as Yehoshua did. Now they were aware of the opportunity that
could have been theirs but they missed and for this they cried.
(*Toras Moshe: Chasam Sofer*)

Once an opportunity has been lost it is too late to do anything
about it. By realizing that opportunities to gain wisdom are very
precious and do not always repeat themselves, you will do
everything you can to make the best use of any chance you have to
learn from a Torah scholar.

Internalize the message of the last words of the Torah.

ולא קם נביא עוד בישראל כמשה אשר ידעו השם פנים אל פנים. לכל
האתת והמופתים אשר שלחו השם לעשות בארץ מצרים לפרעה ולכל
עבדיו ולכל ארצו. ולכל היד החזקה ולכל המורא הגדול אשר עשה משה
לעיני כל ישראל. (דברים ל"ד י'-י"ב)

The concluding words of the Torah are "before the eyes of Israel" as it is stated:
"AND THERE DID NOT RISE ANY MORE IN ISRAEL A PROPHET LIKE
MOSHE WHO KNEW THE ALMIGHTY FACE TO FACE. IN ALL THE
SIGNS AND THE WONDERS WHICH THE ALMIGHTY SENT HIM TO DO
IN THE LAND OF EGYPT TO PHARAOH AND TO ALL HIS SERVANTS
AND TO ALL HIS LAND, AND IN ALL THE MIGHTY HAND, AND IN
ALL THE GREAT FEARFUL ACTS WHICH MOSHE DID BEFORE THE
EYES OF ALL ISRAEL." (*Dvorim* 34:10,11,12)

Rabbi Avigdor Miller comments: "The fact that such an expression is put at the very end of the Torah is evidence of its extremely great importance.

"Our records state that our entire nation, numbering in the millions, witnessed with their own eyes and ears the presence of the Almighty when He gave them His law at Mount Sinai; and our writings do not record a single instance when anyone ever challenged these facts. Our records state that the plagues were openly visited upon Egypt, after being foretold they would come in a designated manner and at an appointed time, and they were experienced by the entire nation of Egypt and were witnessed by all our multitude. Our records state that all our nation witnessed the opening of the Red Sea, through which we passed and in which the Egyptians were drowned. For forty years thereafter our entire nation witnessed continually the cloud of glory by day and the pillar of fire by night, and for forty years every soul ate food which descended from the sky. These facts were not related to them by individuals but were witnessed by millions. The people were not docile, but stiffnecked; for they opposed their leaders on a number of occasions, and they accepted only what they saw. They accepted the Torah not because Moshe showed them miracles, but because they heard the voice of the Almighty speaking to them from Mount Sinai. After receiving the Torah, they spent forty years in the wilderness in close cohesion, with almost no contact with other nations, so that they consolidated their knowledge of the Torah without infiltration of foreign influence. Because they had no lands to till and no commerce, they had sufficient leisure to study the Torah with the utmost diligence. Unlike man-made religions, the Torah was not preached by individuals who afterward succeeded in persuading or coercing multitudes. From the first day, the Torah was accepted by the entire nation without exception." (*Rejoice O Youth*, pp.41-2)

Since the last portion of the Torah is read on *Simchas Torah* it is fitting to end this work with the following story: Rabbi Naftoli of Ropshitz used to relate how a simple wagon driver once bested him in an argument. "Once on the night of *Simchas Torah* I noticed a wagon driver dancing and singing with great joy and enthusiasm around the Torah scrolls in the synagogue. I knew that this person had never studied and was a totally unlearned man, therefore I was puzzled by his ecstasy. I approached him and asked, 'You haven't really studied Torah the entire year, how come you are so joyous now that they are finishing the Torah?' His reply was right to the point. 'When my brother has a *simchah* and is in a state of joy it is appropriate that I share his joy with him!'" (*Parparaos Letorah*, vol.5, p.286)

GLOSSARY

Aharon: Aaron

Ahavas Yisroel: Love for a fellow Jew

Avraham: Abraham

Bais Din: Rabbinical court

Bais Hamedrash: Study hall used for Torah study and prayer

Bamidbar: Book of Numbers

Bitochon: Trust in the Almighty

Braishis: Book of Genesis

Brocho: Blessing recited before and after eating and before performing a *mitzvah*

Chesed: Kindness in all its forms

Chilul Hashem: Desecration of Almighty's name

Chutzpah: Insolence

Davening: Prayers

Derech eretz: Proper behavior or manners

Dvar Torah: Words of Torah that are spoken

Dvorim: Book of Deuteronomy

Eretz Yisroel: Land of Israel

Essrog: Citron; one of the four species used on the holiday of *Sukos*

Gan Eden: Garden of Eden; Paradise

Gehennom: Hell; purgatory

Hakofos: Carrying the Torah scrolls around the Bimah in the synagogue on the holiday of *Simchas Torah*

Halachah: An accepted decision in law

Kashering: The process of rendering food vessels fit for use

Kashrus: The dietary laws

Kidush Hashem: Term connoting martyrdom or act of strict integrity in support of Torah principles

Kollel: Institution for higher Torah study usually comprised of married scholars

Loshon hora: Malicious gossip; a derogatory or damaging statement about someone

Lulav: One of the four species that are held on the holiday of *Sukos* to fulfill a Torah commandment

Maror: Bitter herbs eaten on Passover at the seder

Mazal: Signs of the Zodiac

Mezuzah: Parchment scroll with selected Torah verses placed in container and affixed to gates and doorposts of houses

Midrash: The name of a collection of Rabbinic interpretations of Scripture which brings out lessons by homiletics and stories

Minyan: Ten people needed to pray together

Mitzvah: Biblical or Rabbinical injunction; applied also to good or charitable deeds

Mitzvos: Plural of *mitzvah*

Moshe: Moses

Mussar: Moral and ethical teachings

Noach: Noah

Nozir: Nazarite who accepts upon himself a vow not to drink wine

Olam haboh: World-to-come

Pesach:Passover

Rav: Rabbi

Rebbe: Teacher or Chasidic Rabbi

Rivkah: Rebecca

Rosh Hashanah: The Jewish New Year, at the beginning of the month of Tishrai (either Sept. or Oct.)

Rosh Hayeshiva: Head of a yeshiva

Sanhedrin: The Rabbinical courts of 3, 23, and 71 judges

Seder: The Passover service commemorating the exodus from Egypt; also, the term for study sessions in a yeshiva

Sefer: Book, usually refers to sacred books

Shiva: The seven day mourning period

Shma Yisroel: Prayer recited daily proclaiming the oneness of the Almighty

Shmitah: The sabbatical year which occurs every seven years

Shmos: Book of Exodus

Simchah: A joyous and festive occasion

Simchas Torah: The holiday celebrating the finishing of the Torah reading in the synagogue

Siyum: The celebration of the completion of a section of Torah, either the written law or the oral law

Talis: Four-cornered prayer shawl with fringes at each corner

Tehillim: Book of Psalms

Trumah: Tithe of produce grown in Eretz Yisroel that was given to the Cohanim (Priests)

Tumah: Ritual uncleanliness

Tzaddik: Righteous person

Vayikra: Book of Leviticus

Viduy: Oral confession to the Almighty for wrongs one has committed

Yaakov: Jacob

Yerushalayim: Jerusalem

Yitzchok: Isaac

Yom Kippur: Day of Atonement

Yosef: Joseph

BIBLIOGRAPHY

A Tzadik in Our Time, Simcha Raz, Jer., trans. Rabbi E. Wengrove, Feldheim Pub., Jer., 1976

Ahavas Chesed, Rabbi Yisroel Meir Kagan (Chofetz Chayim), Warsaw, 1888

Ahavas Maishorim, Rabbi Moshe Rosenstein, New York, 1958

Aikev Anovah, Rabbi Moshe Zalman Zaturanski, Vilna, 1902

Al Hatorah, Rabbi Mordechai Cohen, Mass Pub., Jer.,1968

Alai Shur, Anonymous, B'air Yaakov, 1968

All for the Boss, Mrs. Ruchoma Shain, Feldheim Pub., Jer.-N.Y., 1984

Alshich, Rabbi Moshe Alshich, ed. Shiloh, Israel, 1970

Avi Ezri, Rabbi Eliezer Shach, Jerusalem, 1948

Bais Halevi, Rabbi Yosef Dov Halevi Soloveitchik, Warsaw, 1884

Bais Yitzchok, Rabbi Yitzchok of Vorki, Mossad Harim Levine, Jerusalem, 1975

Bastion of Faith, Comments and exposition on the Torah by Rabbi Moshe Feinstein, Rabbi Avraham Fishelis, N.Y., 1973

Bederech Aitz Hachayim, Rabbi Yadael Meltzer, Jer., 1986

Birchas Peretz, Rabbi Yaakov Yisroel Kanievsky, Bnai Brak, 1971

Biurai Hamekubalim Bemikrah, Rabbi Yishai Chasidah, Mishavim Pub., Jer., 1985

B'tuv Yerushalayim, Rabbi Ben Tzion Yadler, Netzach Pub., Bnai Brak, 1976

Chayai Hamussar, Hotzoas Chochmah Umussar, Bnai Brak, 1963

Chayai Olam, Rabbi Yaakov Yisroel Kanievsky, Bnai Brak, 1961

Chazon Ish, Emunah Ubitochon Veod, Jerusalem, 1954

Cheshbon Hanefesh, Rabbi Mendel Zarbaraz, Pub. by Histadrut Talmidai Slobodka, Lithuania, Kaidan, 1937

Chidushai Maran Rav Yitzchok Zev Soloveitchik, Jer. 1963

Chinuch, Rabbi Aharon Halevi's compilation of 613 commandments, ed. Vilna, 1912

Chizkuni, Rabbi Chizkiyahu ben Menoach, Meoz Meir, Israel

Chochmah Umussar, Rabbi Simcha Zissel Ziv, New York, Aber Press, 1957, 1964

Chochmas Hamatzfun, Rabbi Moshe Ibgui, Israel, 1974

Chofetz Chayim al Hatorah, Rabbi Shmuel Greineman, N.Y., 1943

Chovos Halvovos (Duties of the Heart), Rabbi Bachya Ibn Pekudah (11th cent. Spain); Eng. ed., Feldheim Pub., Jer., 1970

Chovas Hashmirah, Rabbi Yisroel Meir Kagan (Chofetz Chayim), Warsaw, 1920

Chut Hameshulash, Rabbi Shlomo Sofer, Mesorah Pub., Tel Aviv, 1963

Daas Chochmah Umussar, Rabbi Yeruchem Levovitz, N.Y., 1969

Daas Torah: Limudai Musray Hatorah, Rabbi Yeruchem Levovitz, pub. Jer., 1976-85

Dmuyos Hod, Rabbi Aharon Surasky, Bnai Brak, 1968

Darkai Mussar, Rabbi Yaakov Neiman, 3rd ed, Jer., 1979

Emes Maikotzk Titzmach, Rabbi M. Sheinfield, Netzach Pub., Bnai Brak, 1961

Erech Apayim, Rabbi Avraham Yellin, Jer., 1963

Eser Oros, Rabbi Yisroel Berger, Piotrkov, 1907

Eser Tzichtzachus, Rabbi Yisroel Berger, Piotrkov, 1910

Eser Zchuyos, Rabbi Azriel Chayim Zamlung, Warsaw, 1937

Even Shlaima, Rabbi Eliyahu ben Shlomo Zalman (Vilna Gaon); Eng. translation by Rabbi Chayim Dovid Ackerman and Rabbi Yaakov Singer, entitled The Vilna Gaon Views Life, Jer., 1974

Gateway to Happiness, Rabbi Zelig Pliskin, Aish Hatorah Pub., Jer., 1983

Haamek Dovor, Rabbi Naftoli Tzvi Yehudah Berlin, Vilna, 1879-1880

Hachofetz Chayim, Rabbi M. Yoshor, Netzach Pub., Tel Aviv, 1958

Hadaios Vehamidos, Ralbag, ed. by Rabbi Yechiel ben Shlomo Mahariach, Warsaw, 1865

Hagaon Hachasid Maivilna, Rabbi Betzalel Landau, Usha Pub., Jer., 1965

Haish al Hachomah, Rabbi S. Z. Sonnenfeld, Jer., 1971

Haksav Vehakabalah, Rabbi Yaakov Tzvi Mecklenburg, Frankfurt, 1880

Hamaggid Maikoznitz, Z.M. Rabinowitz, Tel Aviv, 1947

Hameoros Hagdolim, Rabbi Chayim Zaitchik, Jer., 1969

Hashlomas Hamidos, Rabbi Shlomo Finesilver, ed. Jer. 1975

Hatorah Vehamitzvah, Rabbi Meir Leob Malbim, Vilna, 1844

Hatzadik Rav Zundel, Rabbi Eliezer Rivlin, Jer., 1927

Hegyonai Mussar, Rabbi Ben-Zion Bruk, Jer., 1969

Hirsch's Commentary on the Pentateuch, trans. Rabbi Isaac Levy, Judaica Press, Gateshead, 1973

Ibn Ezra, Rabbi Avraham Ibn Ezra, (1090-1167) Spanish Biblical Commentator

Imrai Shaifer, Rabbi Shlomo Kluger, ed. Brooklyn, 1962

Jewish Leaders, Rabbi Leo Jung, Boys Town, Jer., 1964

Jewish Observer, published monthly by Agudath Israel of America, ed., Rabbi Nisson Wolpin, N.Y.

Kdushas Levi, Rabbi Levi Yitzchok of Berdichiv, Hamosad L'hafotzas Mussar Vechasidus, Jer., 1958

Kli Yokor, Rabbi Efrayim Shlomo of Lutshitz, d.1619, Biblical Commentator

Kol Tzofayich, Rabbi Chayim Zaitchik, Jer., 1976

Kovetz Igros Chazon Ish, Rabbi Avraham Yeshaya Karelitz, ed, Rabbi S. Greineman, Mesorah Pub., Bnai Brak, 1976

Kovetz Maamorim, Rabbi Elchonon Wasserman, Jer., 1963

Kovetz Sichos, Rabbi Chayim Shmuelevitz, Jerusalem, 1973

Ksav Sofer, Rabbi Avraham Shmuel Sofer, ed. Sinai, Tel Aviv, 1966

Leket Sichos Mussar, Rabbi Yitzchok Isaac Sher, Bnai Brak, 1968

Lev Eliyahu, 2 vol., Rabbi Eliyahu Lopian, (Heb. ed.) Jer., 1972-5

Madraigos Haodom, Rabbi Yosef Y. Hurwitz, N.Y., 1947

Maidmuyos Yerushalayim, Rabbi Yaakov Gelis, Jer., 1962

Maigdolai Hachasidus: Haadmor Maitzanz, Rabbi A. I. Bromberg, Jer., 1954

Maigdolai Yerushalayim, Rabbi Yaakov Gelis, Jer.,1967

Maishiv Dovor, Rabbi Naftoli Tzvi Yehudah Berlin, ed. Jer. 1968

Marah D'arah Yisroel, Rabbi Menachem Gerlitz, Jer., 1969

Marbitzai Torah Umussar, Rabbi Aharon Surasky, Israel, 1976

Maayanah Shel Torah, Rabbi Alexander Zushe Friedman, Warsaw, 1938

Mechilta, the Halachic Midrash on Exodus consisting of a collection of *Beraisos*, from the period of the Tanaim, ed. Malbim

Meshech Chochmah, Rabbi Meir Simcha Hacohen, ed. Jer., 1974

Mesilas Yeshorim, (Path of the Just), Rabbi Moshe Chayim Luzzatto, Eng. ed, Feldheim Pub., Jer.,1966

Michtav Maieliyahu, Rabbi Eliyahu Dessler, Bnai Brak, 1965

Michtevai Chofetz Chayim, Rabbi Aryeh Leib Kagan, N.Y., 1953

Midrash Rabbah, Classic Rabbinical exposition of the Torah, ed. Romm, Vilna, 1923

Midrash Tanchuma, ed. Horeb, Berlin, 1927

Mimayonos Hanetzach, Rabbi Aharon Surasky, Bnai Brak, 1974

Mishle Yaakov, Rabbi Yaakov Kranz (Dubner Maggid), Tarna, 1887

Mofes Hador, (Rabbi Yechezkail Levenstein), Rabbi Elchonon Hertzman, Jer., 1976

Mussar Hatorah, Rabbi Hillel Witkind, Jer., 1944

Nachalas Yosef, Rabbi Yosef Zev Leipowitz, Tel Aviv, 1966

Niflaos Hamaggid Maikoznitz, A. J. Kleiman, Piotrkov, 1911

Niflaos Yisroel, A. J. Kleiman, Warsaw, 1930

Nitzutzai Ohr Hamair, Rabbi Meir Shapiro, Israel, 1973

Noam Elimelech, Rabbi Elimelech of Lizensk (1717-1787)

Nofes Tzufim, Rabbi Pinchos Shapiro of Koretz, Warsaw, 1929

Ohel Yaakov, Rabbi Yaakov Kranz (Dubner Maggid), ed. Israel, 1969

Ohr Elchonon, Rabbi Aharon Surasky, Israel, 1978

Ohr Hachayim, Rabbi Chayim ben Moshe Attar, Biblical Commentator, (1669-1743)

Ohr Hamussar, Yeshivas Nevardok, Bnai Brak, 1965-6

Ohr Hatzafun, Rabbi Noson Tzvi Finkel, Jer., 1968

Ohr Yohail, Rabbi Yehuda Leib Chasman, Jer.,1960

Orach Maishorim: Shulchan Aruch L'midos, Rabbi Menachem Taryash, Megenze, 1878

Orchos Tzadikim, (The Ways of the Righteous), unkown 14th cent. author, Eng. ed, Feldheim Pub., Jer.-N.Y., 1974

Oros Maimizrach, Rabbi Aharon Sorosky, Bnei Brak, 1974

Otzer Chayim, Rabbi Chayim Yaakov Zuckerman, Tel Aviv, 1971

P'air Hador, ed. Rabbi Shlomo Cohen, Netzach Pub., Bnai Brak, 1967-75

Parparaos Letorah, Rabbi Menachem Becker, Omen Pub., Jer., 1986

Pele Yoatz, Rabbi Eliezer Papu, Kushtandia, 1824

Peninai Rabainu Hakehilos Yaakov, Rabbi Moshe Mordechai Shulsinger, Bnai Brak, 1986

Peninai Rabainu Yechezkail, Rabbi Moshe Mordechai Shulsinger, Bnai Brak

Pirke D'Reb Eliezer, ed. Eshkol, Jer., 1973

Pirke Torah, Rabbi Mordechai Gifter, Jer. 1973

Rabosainu, Rabbi Avraham Wolf, Bnai Brak, 1975

Ralbag, Rabbi Levi ben Gershon (1288-1344), French Biblical Commentator

Ramat Shmuel, Rabbi Shmuel Walkin, Jerusalem, 1982

Ramban's Commentary, Rabbi Moshe ben Nachman, (1194-1270)

Rav Boruch Ber Leibowitz, Rabbi Yitzchok Edelstein, Tel Aviv, 1957

Rav Meir Shapiro: B'mishnah b'omair ub'maas, Rabbi Ahraon Surasky, Netzach Pub., Bnai Brak, 1964-7

Rav Shimon Vetoroso, Rabbi Aharon Surasky, Netzach Pub., Bnai Brak, 1971

Rejoice O Youth, Rabbi Avigdor Miller, N.Y., 1962

Ruach Chayim, Rabbi Chayim of Volozhin, Kerem Shlomo Pub., Jer., 1967

Sforno, Rabbi Ovadiah (1475-1550), Italian Biblical Commentator

Shaar Bas Rabim, Rabbi Chayim Aryeh Leib of Yedvobna, Warsaw, 1890

Shiurai Daas, Rabbi Yosef Yehudah Leib Bloch, Pub. by Telz Yeshiva, Cleve., 1964

Shmiras Haloshon, Rabbi Yisroel Meir Kagan (Chofetz Chayim), ed. N.Y., 1960

Shnai Luchos Habris, Rabbi Yeshayahu Hurwitz, ed. Jer., 1969

Siach Sarfai Kodesh, Yoatz Kim Kodosh Rokotz, Lodz, 1929

Sing, You Righteous, Rabbi Avigdor Miller, Rugby Young Israel, N.Y., 1973

The Living Torah, Rabbi Aryeh Kaplan, Moznaim Pub., N.Y.-Jer., 1981

The Nineteen Letters, Rabbi Samson Raphael Hirsch, Feldheim Pub., Jer.-N.Y., 1969

Tnuas Hamussar, Rabbi Dov Katz, Tel Aviv, Baitan Hasefer, 1952-63

Toldos Odom, Rabbi Yechezkail Feivel, Lemberg, 1864

Torah Persepctives, Rabbi Mordechai Gifter, The Artscroll Mesorah Series, Mesorah Publications, N.Y., 1986

Toras Avraham, Rabbi Avraham Grodzinsky, Jer., 1963

Toras Moshe, Rabbi Moshe Sofer (Chasam Sofer), (1762-1839)

Yechidai Sgulah, Rabbi Isser Frankel, Tel Aviv, 1964

INDEX

Jud
RelYHO
PLI

7685

Date Due